ENGLISH NOW:
SELECTED PAPERS FROM THE 20TH IAUPE CONFERENCE IN LUND 2007

LUND STUDIES IN ENGLISH 112

Editor

Marianne Thormählen

LUND STUDIES IN ENGLISH was founded by Eilert Ekwall in 1933. Published by the Centre for Languages and Literature at Lund University, the series consists of books on the English language and on literature in English.

ENGLISH NOW

Selected Papers from the 20th
IAUPE Conference in Lund 2007

Edited by
Marianne Thormählen

LUND
UNIVERSITY

LUND STUDIES IN ENGLISH

ENGLISH NOW:
SELECTED PAPERS FROM THE 20TH IAUPE CONFERENCE IN LUND 2007

Edited by *Marianne Thormählen*

LUND STUDIES IN ENGLISH 112
ISBN 978-91-976935-0-9
ISSN 0076-1451

Publisher

Centre for Languages and Literature, Lund University
English Studies
P. O. Box 201
SE-221 00 LUND
Sweden

Printed by Wallin & Dalholm
Lund 2008

In memoriam

William Speed Hill
1935-2007

Contents

Acknowledgements

The 20th Triennial Conference of the International Association of University Professors of English (IAUPE) at which the contributions to this book were presented as papers took place in Lund from 6 to 10 August 2007, generously sponsored by Lund University, The Royal Academy of Letters, History and Antiquities, The Crafoord Foundation, The Royal Society of Letters in Lund, The Elisabeth Rausing Memorial Fund, and the City of Lund. The munificence of the first two created the financial basis for this publication, for which I, as conference organiser and editor, am profoundly grateful.

Warmest thanks, too, to those without whom there would be no book, namely the 26 contributors who kindly allowed their papers to be included in the present volume. The two plenary lecturers Professor Elizabeth Traugott and Professor Helen Vendler granted me permission to publish their papers even before the conference, thereby ensuring that there was going to be a book in the first place, and one that the other contributors would be happy to have their work appear in.

The selection of papers for publication, a process of which more is said in the Preface, was the work of the 37 Conference Chairs. Warm thanks to Beatrice Warren, Monika Fludernik, Tamar Yacobi, David Johnson, Elaine Treharne, A. C. Spearing, Ian Kirby, Carol Kaske, Lars-Håkan Svensson, Judith Scherer Herz, Paul Stanwood, Vera Nünning, Peter Sabor, Simon Haines, Stephen Prickett, Dinah Birch, Francis O'Gorman, Lawrence Buell, Andrew Hook, Robert Rehder, Thomas Vargish, Michael Bell, Christopher Innes, Gunilla Florby, Susana Onega, Herbert Grabes, Ansgar Nünning, Risto Hiltunen, Irma Taavitsainen, Jürg Schwyter, Dieter Kastovsky, Leonhard Lipka, Karin Aijmer, Andreas H. Jucker, Merja Kytö, Jan Svartvik, and William Baker. Professor Beatrice Warren's advice and support with regard to the linguistic sections extended over three years and were invaluable from first to last. I am also deeply grateful to Professor Dinah Birch for swift and effective assistance with editorial matters.

As organiser, I received help and support from so many people that I cannot list them all here. However, special mention must be made of the patient assistance and encouragement I received from my predecessor as IAUPE President, Professor Paul Stanwood, and from the Secretary-General of IAUPE, Professor Ian Kirby. My assistant Kiki Lindell was not only a ubiquitous trouble-shooter throughout the conference but provided sterling service in the preparation of this volume. Axel, Åsa, and Imke Thormählen gave countless hours of cheerful labour both before and during the conference, which was in a very real sense a family undertaking.

Acknowledgement is due to the British Academy for the support that enabled Professor Elisabeth Jay to attend and present the research project outlined on pp. 110-117 in this book.

Permissions to reproduce material in copyright have been gratefully received. The figure representing symmetric communication on p. 202 was taken from Ferdinand de Saussure, *Course in General Linguistics*, trans. Roy Harris, published by Open Court, Chicago, in 1983 (p. 11); it is reprinted by permission of Open Court Publishing Company, a division of Carus Publishing Company, Peru, IL. The example of branching XPs on p. 203 was taken from Guglielmo Cinque, *Restructuring and Functional Heads: The Cartography of Syntactic Structures*, ch. 6, p. 46, published in 2006 by the Oxford University Press, reproduced here by kind permission of Oxford University Press, Inc. The diagram on p. 206 was taken from Mirjam Fried and Jan-Ola Östman, eds, *Construction Grammar in a Cross-Language Perspective*, 2004, p. 34, and is reprinted by kind permission of John Benjamins Publishing Company, Amsterdam/Philadelphia, www.benjamins.com. In respect of the extended prose quotations on pp. 144-9, the following permissions are gratefully recorded: Excerpt from 'How to Tell a True War Story', from *The Things They Carried* by Tim O'Brien, copyright © 1990 by Tim O'Brien, reprinted by kind permission of Houghton Mifflin Company, all rights reserved. Excerpts totalling 1 ½ pages from 'The Liar' from *In the Garden of North American Martyrs* by Tobias Wolff, copyright © 1981 by Tobias Wolff, were reprinted by permission of HarperCollins Publishers. The quotations from 'Parts of Speech', *Stones for Ibarra*, by Harriet Doerr, copyright © 1978, 1981, 1981, and 1984 by Harriet Doerr, are used by kind permission of Viking Penguin, a division of Penguin Group (USA) Inc.; UK reprint rights by kind permission of Darhansoff, Verrill, Feldman Literary Agents, New York, NY. The quotations from William Gass were taken from *On Being Blue: A Philosophical Inquiry* and are reprinted by kind permission of David R. Godine, Publisher, Inc. Copyright © 1976 by William Gass. With regard to the poetry quotations on pp. 189-97, acknowledgement is due to the following: Wallace Stevens' 'Large Read Man Reading' is quoted from *The Collected Poems of Wallace Stevens*, copyright 1954 by Wallace Stevens and renewed 1982 by Holly Stevens, by permission of Alfred A. Knopf, a division of Random House, Inc. Stevens' 'Tradition' is quoted by gracious permission of the Saint Nicholas Society of New York, which commissioned it in 1945. James Merrill's 'The Thousand and Second Night' and 'Processional' are quoted from *Collected Poems* by James Merrill, edited by J. D.

Every effort has been made to secure permissions for all relevant works, and if there has been any oversight I will be happy to rectify the situation at the earliest opportunity.

Marianne Thormählen

Preface

English Now is an unusual conference volume. Its origins in an exceptionally large and wide-ranging international conference provided an opportunity to publish outstanding work by senior researchers active in a remarkably diverse and vigorous academic discipline. This formal and thematic variety is part of the *raison d'être* of this book. Two of the 26 papers presented here were plenary lectures by leading scholars in English literature and linguistics, and Helen Vendler and Elizabeth Traugott were invited to express their views on the state and future of English in any way that seemed good to them. The remaining 24 contributions were drawn from the nearly 150 papers that were presented in 19 conference sections, a programme that ranged from *Beowulf* to the niceties of present-day courtroom discourse. This vast scope is characteristic of IAUPE conferences, which last for a full week and constitute a triennial temperature-taking of English studies as a discipline, language as well as literature.* Contributors have been free to choose their own reference system and whether to use British or American spelling, as well as double or single quotation marks.

Another uncommon characteristic of the present volume is that its editor has stood back from the selection of papers (apart from the fact that the choice of plenary speakers naturally reflected Lund preferences). The 37 Conference Chairs who chose the 24 section papers had been issued with a simple directive which urged them to consult their own research values and commitments: they were asked to pick out papers which were not only excellent in themselves – the high overall quality of the 2007 IAUPE presentations was obvious to all participants – but which also imparted a sense of where English is heading. The outcome of their collective deliberations is found between the covers of *English Now*.

It should be pointed out that some of the contributions thus chosen turned out not to be available for publication in this volume, usually because they were already spoken for. In a couple of cases, selected authors were reluctant to publish

---

* It is not necessary to be a professor of English to become an IAUPE member; individual scholarly distinction is what matters. Membership is by election, but IAUPE welcomes new members, and anybody who would like to join may set the wheels in motion by contacting the Secretary-General. For instructions on how to do this, and for more information about IAUPE, see the organisation's website, www.iaupe.net.

what they felt to be work in such an early stage of progress that publication now seemed premature, however happy they had been to share it with IAUPE colleagues. The fact that so many papers presented in Lund in 2007 were exploratory and experimental testifies to the special character of an IAUPE conference: stimulated by the relaxed and creative atmosphere at these meetings, where social activities are essential and academic friendships often made for life, IAUPE members are apt to use this opportunity to air innovative ideas. That circumstance gives me occasion to say something about the reason why I was eager to bring the 2007 IAUPE to Lund.

As trust is conducive to original thought, and as senior scholars enjoying themselves among their peers are especially likely to come up with thoughts worth listening to, providing a setting for such activity was a tempting prospect. When, in 2003, I offered to arrange the 2007 meeting, my main motive was a desire to hear constructive views on the state and future of English on my home ground – the splendid new Centre for Languages and Literature at Lund University, to which English in Lund would belong as from 2006 (and which was at that point still on the drawing-board).

There were special reasons why an English-Literature academic would feel in particular need of fresh thinking just after the turn of the millennium. The late-twentieth-century phenomenon known as 'Theory' was lifting like a morning mist, lingering in patches here and there but unmistakably passing into history. Its leading exponents had to a great extent repositioned themselves as early as the 1990s. But large numbers of people, not least younger scholars who had come to believe that anyone who wants to get on in the Humanities must declare his or her 'situatedness' in relation to a particular theorist or ideological position, were left hanging, often without realising it themselves. For any senior academic aware of his or her responsibilities to graduate students and junior colleagues, the question of what sort of guidance to provide in this destabilised situation was impossible to ignore.

The evaporation of 'Theory' – which was, after all, mostly a concern for the literary branch of the subject – was not the only challenge to representatives of English in the first years of the 21st century. The issue of the identity of the subject at a time when interdisciplinary research was becoming more than a catchphrase was another question which needed to be faced. Would collaboration across disciplinary boundaries lead to the disintegration of English? In so far as the subject had anything worth calling a core, would the definition and maintenance of that core be a worthwhile occupation, or would such efforts merely delay desirable reorientations? Had the time come to sever the traditional institutional link between the English language and English literature, allowing the former to merge with general linguistics and the latter to undergo a process of fragmentation, some bits of it drifting off to the cultural-studies domain while others formed part of a comparative-literature complex?

Over the last few years, falling student numbers and shrinking resources in the arts have lent a grim urgency to these questions. Anxiety about the erosion of the very basis of daily activities has blocked attempts to devise long-term self-help strategies and weakened the resolve of beleaguered senior academics. Any pleas for more money are sure to fall on deaf ears unless decision-makers accountable to taxpayers – and colleagues in other faculties, who are also feeling the pinch and competing for the same funds – can be persuaded of the value of what the Humanities are doing. It is hard to be persuasive if one does not have a clear idea of the virtues of one's cause, or even of what that cause is. Even so, it was and is clear that any decisive turn for the better must be set in motion from within.

It might seem over-optimistic to have expected a single meeting of senior scholars from all over the world to provide the kind of galvanising guidance I just referred to – but the 20th IAUPE conference did precisely that. For all its variety with regard to topics, approaches, and findings, an undertow soon manifested itself and became more and more noticeable as the days went by. The most adequate designation for it that I can find is 'the rehumanisation of English'. Editing the contributions to this book, I found evidence of it in every single paper that the Chairs had – independently of one another – selected as saying something significant about developments in our subject.

Elaine Treharne's challenge to the dominance of a single author to the detriment of others is touched with the modern scholar's human irritation with the likewise human ambitions of a man dead over a thousand years. The illumination offered by Ian Kirby's explications of knotty passages in medieval texts to a great extent derives from an understanding of timeless human behaviour. Rosamund Allen's invitation to reconsider a conventional prejudice against a once much-appreciated poet is partly inspired by human curiosity as to what caused that appreciation in our forebears and how it came to be replaced by condescension. When William Blissett found that the modern poets who admitted to reading and enjoying Spenser tended to be non-academics, he put his finger on aspects of human activity in the academy which we would do well to ponder. Mapping the involvement of Marvell and Milton in 17th-century international politics, Nicholas von Maltzahn indicates ways in which these two men's personal experiences fed into the development of political ideologies that very much concern present-day humanity. Paul Giles shows that the evolution of an 'Augustan American' consciousness in seventeenth- and eighteenth-century America engaged hitherto neglected personal motives in a complex interplay of colony and empire. Simon Haines's analysis of Kantian spontaneity of the understanding in relation to Romantic spontaneity of affection brings human desires and capabilities together in a way that resolves some of the most stubborn problems in reading and teaching Wordsworth and Coleridge. When Birgitta Berglund encourages us to read Austen with attention to the effects of childbirth and childlessness, she creates a human context which enriches any subsequent reading of these ostensibly so familiar texts. Lawrence Buell explains why the dream of writing the 'Great American Novel', though mutated (and questioned) over the years, retains its fascination for writers and stimulates the ambition of readers and critics to establish the criteria for that elusive phenomenon. Dinah Birch demonstrates the extent to which Charlotte Brontë and Matthew Arnold were – in very different, and very human, ways – products of the most pressing social issue of their time, that of the education of the people. Meeting the Thackerays and the Brownings, among others, in the Parisian milieus drawn by Elisabeth Jay reminds us that nineteenth-century British intellectuals were as likely to run into one another in the French capital as in London. Susan McCabe reveals the importance to modernism of a woman whose efforts to help struggling human beings have been overlooked and/or disparaged partly because of reluctance on the part of modern scholars to celebrate a person who (like the original Good Samaritan, as pointed out by Margaret Thatcher) had money.

After these contributions where a historical element operates, albeit in highly diverse ways, come six papers which engage with the way we live (and write, and teach) now. Challenging the widespread notion that the origins of 'magical realism' are essentially Latin American, Michael Bell shows that this phenomenon is rooted in a universal desire to experience the marvellous and have the imagination fired by its operations in seemingly everyday settings. A different kind of contemporary myth-making features in Donald Anderson's explorations of how human beings narrate factual untruths in order to convey dimensions of themselves, and the worlds they inhabit, which are of overriding importance to them and hence 'true' on an imaginative level. Jürgen Schlaeger suggests that the predominance of narrativity, both as a literary mode and as a way of comprehending the human predicament, is gradually being replaced by a non-chronological, spatialised understanding of the self and its concerns. Ihab Hassan's scrutiny of the 'Australianness' of Australian literature resists the diminishing implications of defining artefacts as the property of any one geographically defined sphere, reminding us that 'identities dissolve where human beings attain their fullest destiny'. Hassan's ensuing paper on ways in which literary theory may reinvent itself in the 21ˢᵗ century marshals a set of deftly positioned possibilities while drawing attention to the spiritual dimensions of any engagement with the arts. The literary section of the book is concluded by Helen Vendler's plenary lecture, which forms a powerful plea for the reinstatement of poetry in the academic curriculum. Her main argument is that future generations of poets will not be able to find their own voices without having encountered the voices of their predecessors, and that the academy is neglecting its responsibility to ensure that these encounters can take place. In addition, the dominance of prose in the teaching of English literature today endangers the survival of another essential category, that of poetry readers.

The linguistic section of *English Now* occupies a smaller proportion of the volume than the literary papers. That is the natural result of the fact that more IAUPE members belong to the literary field than to that of the English language; hence the number of linguistic sections is usually lower at conferences. In Lund, though – as befits the home university of that legendary scholar, and founder of Lundian English studies, Eilert Ekwall, and his distinguished successors – special efforts were made to ensure that the English language occupied as prominent a position as possible. The presence of Elizabeth Closs Traugott made a significant contribution to the success of those efforts. Traugott's plenary lecture introduces the linguistically orientated part of the book, beginning with a survey of twentieth-century linguistics comprehensible even to lay readers and proceeding to a careful outline of the changes currently taking place in the discipline. In those changes, the emphasis is on context, pragmatics, human interaction, and empirical evidence drawn from an ever-wider variety of sources. The ensuing linguistic papers adhere to the general picture presented by Traugott. Minoji Akimoto's study of the historical power struggles between individual words is conducted with an eye to what human beings may have felt to be the most effective way of communicating their wishes to others. Andrea Sand shows how varieties of English around the world are influenced by vernaculars spoken in the relevant country or region, looking at both similarities and differences and at written as well as spoken human communication. Nobody who has read Yoshihiko Ikegami's study of subjective and objective construal will ever forget the difference between the two, or the examples chosen by Ikegami to help his reader grasp the distinction between the ways in which the Japanese and the European subject positions himself/herself in relation to an ongoing action. Likewise, Dieter Kastovsky and Barbara Kryk-Kastovsky's investigation of legal terminology in the context of lexical semantics and pragmatics makes its points with the aid of a peculiarly memorable example, Bill Clinton's all-too-human 'zippergate' equivocation. The empirical material on which Anita Fetzer draws in her study of cognitive verbs in discourse is similarly arresting, leaving the reader with a very clear sense of what a parenthetical 'I think', or 'I believe', says about the person who utters it, depending on its immediate context and placing in the sentence.

English Now ends with two contributions that do not belong either within the literary or the linguistic field. Aleksander Szwedek proposes a theory of metaphor which is in part founded on the very first principles of human behaviour, going back to the stage in the life of a foetus when the fundamental sense of touch is programmed into the neural system. Finally, Alexis Weedon analyses cross-media production between the two World Wars, mapping the effects of film adaptations of popular novels on the desire – manifested in fluctuating sales – to own the adapted books and looking at the impact of rights management in that context.

For all the multifariousness of the contributions to this volume, all the authors are concerned with the diverse ways in which real people use the English language. There are no glass-bead games here: English is seen to be the chief medium by which the human beings who speak, write, and understand it – in all corners of the globe – interact, for whatever purpose and to whatever effect, deliberately or unconsciously. To be able to spend a lifetime studying its infinite variety is to be privileged beyond expression.

That was the outcome of the 20th IAUPE conference at Lund, a shot in the arm from which all the contributors felt the benefit. We can have every confidence in affirming the value of our composite subject, recognising the potentials of interdisciplinary work but also realising that the stronger our core competence, the more we will be able to bring to collaboration with academics in other disciplines. English in the global academy is in fine fettle and should be in good heart. We who represent it can do so in the conviction that the young people whose fires were lit by English and whom we attempt to enrol in its service will find that service enduringly stimulating and rewarding.

Lund, in May 2008
Marianne Thormählen

Elaine Treharne

The Canonisation of Ælfric

Substantial research on Ælfric in the last few decades by Mary Clayton, Peter Clemoes, Malcolm Godden, Joyce Hill, Gordon Whatley, Jonathan Wilcox and many other scholars has assisted greatly in our understanding of this prolific Anglo-Saxon homilist.[1] In the last three decades, research has focused on identifying and editing Ælfric's complete oeuvre, on describing and analysing his sources, and on interpreting his role within the European traditions of religious and educational prose production. Recently, his homilies and saints' lives, in particular, have been scrutinized for their social and cultural significance, informed by contemporary theoretical approaches.[2] Other strands of research have focused

---

[1] See, for example, Mary Clayton, 'Ælfric's Esther: a *Speculum Reginae?*', in *Text and Gloss: Studies in Insular Learning and Literature Presented to Joseph Donovan Pheifer*, ed. Helen Conrad O'Brian, Anne Marie D'Arcy, and John Scattergood (Dublin and Portland, OR: Four Courts Press, 1999), pp. 89-101; P. Clemoes, ed., *Ælfric's Catholic Homilies: The First Series: Text*, EETS s. s. 17 (London: OUP, 1997); M. Godden, ed., *Ælfric's Catholic Homilies: The Second Series Text*, EETS s.s. 5 (London: OUP, 1979); M. Godden, *Ælfric's Catholic Homilies: Introduction, Commentary and Glossary*, EETS s.s. 18 (Oxford: Oxford University Press, 2000); Joyce Hill, 'Ælfric and Wulfstan: Two Views of the Millennium', in *Essays on Anglo-Saxon and Related Themes in Memory of Lynne Grundy*, ed. Jane Roberts and Janet Nelson, King's College London Medieval Studies 17 (London: Centre for Late Antique and Medieval Studies, King's College, University of London, 2000), pp. 213-35; Joyce Hill, 'Ælfric's Authorities', in *Early Medieval English Texts and Interpretations: Studies Presented to Donald G. Scragg*, ed. Elaine Treharne and Susan Rosser, Medieval and Renaissance Texts and Studies 252 (Tempe, AZ: Arizona Center for Medieval and Renaissance Studies, 2002), pp. 51-65; Hugh Magennis, 'Warrior Saints, Warfare, and the Hagiography of Ælfric of Eynsham', *Traditio* 56 (2001): 27-51; Gordon E. Whatley, E. '*Pearls before Swine*: Ælfric, Vernacular Hagiography, and the Lay Reader', in *Via Crucis: Essays on Early Medieval Sources and Ideas in Memory of J. E. Cross*, ed. Thomas N. Hall, with assistance from Thomas D. Hill and Charles D. Wright, Medieval European Studies 1 (Morgantown, WV: West Virginia University Press, 2002), pp. 158-84; Jonathan Wilcox, ed., *Ælfric's Prefaces*, Durham Medieval Texts 9 (Durham: University of Durham Department of English, 1994). See also Aaron J. Kleist, 'An Annotated Bibliography of Ælfrician Studies: 1983-1996', in *Old English Prose: Basic Readings*, ed. Paul E. Szarmach, with the assistance of Deborah A. Oosterhouse, Basic Readings in Anglo-Saxon England 5 (New York: Garland, 2000), pp. 503-52; Aaron J. Kleist, 'Ælfric's Corpus: A Conspectus', *Florilegium* 18.2 (2001): 113-64.

[2] See, for example, Clare A. Lees, *Tradition and Belief: Religious Writing in Late Anglo-Saxon England*, Medieval Cultures 19 (Minneapolis: University of Minnesota Press, 1999); Stacy S. Klein, 'Beauty and the Banquet: Queenship and Social Reform in Ælfric's *Esther*', JEGP 103 (2004): 77-105; Andrea Rossi-Reder, 'Embodying Christ, Embodying Nation: Ælfric's Accounts of Saints Agatha and Lucy', in *Sex and Sexuality in Anglo-Saxon England: Essays in Memory of Daniel Gillmore Calder*, ed. Carol Braun Pasternack and Lisa M. C. Weston, Medieval and Renaissance Texts and Studies 277 (Tempe, AZ: Arizona Center for Medieval and Renaissance Studies, 2004), pp. 183-202; Robert K. Upchurch, 'For Pastoral Care and Political Gain: Ælfric of Eynsham's Preaching on Marital Celibacy', *Traditio* 59 (2004): 39-78.

on the role of translation in the transmission of texts and the status of English as a language of authority.[3]

The considerable bibliography on Ælfric demonstrates the sustained scholarly interest in this writer and the dominance that he has come to achieve in Old English prose studies. Part of the reason for this may be that Ælfric literally speaks to us in his *Prefaces*, his *Grammar*, and his authoritative statements to his monks and other audience members.[4] This self-reflexive positioning demands response, and with the exception of King Alfred, Ælfric is arguably the most accessible or visible author from this early period. Thus, the relationship we can potentially have with him is personal; it appears we can know Ælfric more than any other late Old English writer.

Among Ælfric's concerns in writing his homilies and saints' lives, as well as other works in his corpus, such as the *Hexateuch*, is the major impetus of providing for monastic and secular religious audiences the means by which they could safely better their spiritual lives. This safety is reinforced by the enumerations of his employed patristic heritage, a noble and authoritative lineage into which Ælfric aligns himself: the inheritor of *auctoritas*, often mediated through the Carolingian homiliaries about which Joyce Hill has so eruditely written.[5] This insistence on orthodoxy—as relatively unformulated as it was in this period—and the careful sifting of exemplary texts is one of the main aspects marking out Ælfric as more self-conscious, more aware of his responsibility as a teacher and author, than many of his predecessors and most of his successors in the earlier medieval period.[6]

In what follows, I shall concentrate on Ælfric's *Prefaces*, edited and very thoroughly commented upon by Jonathan Wilcox in his 1994 volume, and subsequently examined by Godden in his Commentary on the two series of *Catholic*

---

[3] Richard Marsden, 'Ælfric as Translator: the Old English Prose *Genesis*', *Anglia* 109 (1991): 319-58; Richard Marsden, *The Text of the Old Testament in Anglo-Saxon England*, Cambridge Studies in Anglo-Saxon England 15 (Cambridge and New York: Cambridge University Press, 1995); Robert Stanton, *The Culture of Translation in Anglo-Saxon England* (Cambridge: D. S. Brewer, 2002); Elaine Treharne, 'The Politics of Early English', The Toller Lecture 2005, forthcoming in *The Bulletin of the John Rylands University Library of Manchester*, 2008.

[4] See Wilcox, Ælfric's Prefaces, 'Introduction'; see also Melinda J. Menzer, 'The Preface as Admonition: Ælfric's Preface to Genesis', in *The Old English Hexateuch: Aspects and Approaches*, ed. Rebecca Barnhouse and Benjamin C. Withers, Publications of the Rawlinson Center 2 (Kalamazoo, MI: Medieval Institute Publications, Western Michigan University, 2000), pp. 15-39.

[5] Joyce Hill, 'Translating the Tradition: Manuscripts, Models and Methodologies in the Composition of Ælfric's Catholic Homilies' [revised text of the 1996 Toller Lecture, originally published in 1997], in *Textual and Material Culture in Anglo-Saxon England: Thomas Northcote Toller and the Toller Memorial Lectures*, ed. Donald Scragg (Cambridge: D.S. Brewer, 2003), pp. 241-59; and Joyce Hill, 'Authority and Intertextuality in the Works of Ælfric', *Proceedings of the British Academy*, 131 (2005), 157-81 [The Sir Israel Gollancz Memorial Lecture for 2004].

[6] For the complex issue of orthodoxy in the late Anglo-Saxon period, see the excellent essays in *Apocryphal Texts and Traditions in Anglo-Saxon England*, ed. Donald G. Scragg and Kathryn Powell (Woodbridge: Boydell and Brewer, 2003).

Homilies.[7] I shall look at these texts in the light of a few other, earlier and contemporary *Prefaces* to argue that Ælfric's own declared position of 'authority' has often caused scholars to take him at his word to the detriment of the tradition in which he worked. Placing Ælfric on a pedestal of his own creation has also led inadvertently to the subordination of other homiletic writers and works from the period to a very serious extent, and created a neglect of a large proportion of the religious prose corpus that will take years of sustained research to redress. My conclusion is thus (and somewhat heretically) that while Ælfric did not achieve the recognition of saintly status which he may have implicitly desired for himself in his own milieu, and which may have been reflected in the beatification of Ælfric's *magister* Æthelwold of Winchester, modern scholarship has nevertheless conferred upon Ælfric the privilege of canonisation (from his canonical status, to the idea that he could do and think no wrong) that he failed to achieve in late Anglo-Saxon England.

Ælfric's Reputation

Modern scholarship has received Ælfric as:

> one of the most learned scholars of Anglo-Saxon England and a prolific and elegant writer of vernacular prose whose works were widely read in his own time and later played an important part in Reformation controversy…As a scholar, Ælfric was the leading product of the tenth-century monastic reform, reflecting that movement's characteristic concerns with learning and monastic ideals and also its close relations with the leading laity.[8]

Here is another present-day appraisal:

> Obviously a careful and scrupulous teacher, Ælfric seems to have seen as his main task the provision not just of learning but of correct learning—true doctrine. His decision to compose the first series of *Catholic Homilies* was, he claims, taken because he saw and heard much heresy in many English books, which ignorant men through their ignorance held to be great wisdom. This concern for the ignorant led him also to place some restrictions on the use of the vernacular…In his homilies and sermons Ælfric is likewise both selective and critical, drawing on a wide range of Latin texts…[9]

---

7   Wilcox, *Ælfric's Prefaces*; Godden, *Ælfric's Catholic Homilies: Introduction, Commentary and Glossary*.
8   Godden, s.v. 'Ælfric', in Michael Lapidge et al., eds, *The Blackwell Encyclopaedia of Anglo-Saxon England* (Oxford: Blackwell, 1999), pp. 8-9.
9   Janet Bately, 'The Nature of Old English Prose', in Malcolm Godden and Michael Lapidge, eds, *The Cambridge Companion to Old English Literature* (Cambridge: Cambridge University Press, 1992), pp. 78-9.

The diction employed by modern commentators in describing Ælfric is often wholly laudatory: 'selective', 'critical', 'true', 'orthodox', 'learned', 'prolific', 'influential' as well as 'self-aware', 'self-conscious' and 'extremely concerned with… integrity'.[10] All these are aspects of writing and scholarship that are highly privileged in intellectual endeavour, and have been so since the Romantic period. These reflections on Ælfric's writing, especially when made by senior scholars, simultaneously reflect and produce his pre-eminent status: he exemplifies all the creative criteria that we adjudge excellent. Therefore, while his chosen form of composition—homiletic and hagiographic prose, for example—is not in itself a common pastime for modern scholars, or indeed a prized form of creative writing in contemporary society, Ælfric's methodology and motivation still make him one of us: a scrupulous, discerning, intelligent and, rather anachronistically, original scholar. However, one might argue,[11] the result of privileging these particular characteristics is that not only do we heighten the status of Ælfric, but we also explicitly derogate other authors and works that do not match up to the criteria he evinces. These are principally the other homiletic writings of the period, particularly those of anonymous origin, and the entire corpus of material that is derived from more 'original' sources.[12] Moreover, until recently Ælfric's work, with its status as gospel, has been scoured for what it can yield about late-tenth- and early-eleventh-century reformist ideals or social mores, with only a nod to his singularity. The work of Hill and others has begun to demonstrate that Ælfric is, in fact, at the 'extreme' end of reformist opinion, and thus rather more idiosyncratic in his views than we have assumed to date.[13] It is clear that we now need to reappraise the use of Ælfric as a representative guide to his own contemporary world.

What is it, then, precisely, that Ælfric achieves or sets out to achieve through the self-conscious personalisation of his work? This is well summarised by Joyce Hill:

> [I]t has to be admitted that Ælfric's reformist position, for all the humanity of his writings, was more extreme than that of others, even including, in some respects, his revered teacher Æthelwold. No other writer begged for his work to be kept apart from

---

[10] The latter attribute, 'extremely concerned with the integrity of the copying and distribution of his works', is from Wilcox, p. 70.

[11] As Clare Lees does, in fact, in *Tradition and Belief*, among other publications.

[12] Again, a point made by Lees in *Tradition and Belief*. See also Elaine Treharne, 'Periodization and Categorization: The Silence of (the) English in the Twelfth Century', in Rita Copeland, Wendy Scase and David Wallace, eds, *New Medieval Literatures* 8 (Brepols, 2007), 248-75.

[13] See note 5 above. See also Elaine Treharne, 'The Political Implications of the Life of St Swithun', in E. M. Tyler and Ros Balzaretti, eds, *Narrative and History in the Early Medieval West*, Studies in the Early Middle Ages 16 (Turnhout: Brepols, 2006), pp. 167-8.

that of others, made such insistent pleas for correct copying, or deployed such a range of devices for establishing his orthodoxy and identifying the authority of the tradition within which he worked. He was also clearer than anyone else in stating the limits of what he would and would not do (although he sometimes allowed himself to be persuaded otherwise), and the line that he took was often an independent one.[14]

Most of what Ælfric set out to achieve, as summarised here, is relatively well known; but also well known is the sequence of eleventh- and twelfth-century manuscripts manifestly demonstrating that he was not entirely successful in his aims. This very familiar fact should alert us to the unrealistic expectations that Ælfric had for his own work, unrealistic expectations that are underpinned by his over-reliance on his own authority: it seems he overestimated the value of his opinion or his authority in a period where, for most, pragmatism and practicality took precedence over particularity.

Ælfric and the Preface

In many ways, then, Ælfric was not a typical product of the Benedictine Reform, especially in his sense of the requirement for a very strict adherence to specific monastic guidelines, and in his own views on women, celibacy, dreams, and many other topics.[15] He was not typical of the majority of vernacular authors in general in this period, who usually did not lay claim to their own work, its authenticity, and its reliability; in this sense, he has more in common with his peers who produced Latin texts. The high status accorded Ælfric's work parallels the high status of the positions of his contemporaries, who are known authors of many texts (but who often cannot be ascribed with certainty to everything that is attributed to them). As Bately says, making Ælfric's elite positioning clear:

> Much of the surviving Old English prose corpus is anonymous, and some of it is strictly utilitarian, but the status which it achieved is indicated by the fact that its authors included a king (Alfred), an archbishop (Wulfstan), two bishops (Werferth and Æthelwold) and an abbot (Ælfric).[16]

---

[14] Joyce Hill, 'The Benedictine Reform and Beyond', in *A Companion to Anglo-Saxon Literature*, ed. Phillip Pulsiano and Elaine Treharne (Oxford: Blackwells, 2001), pp. 151-69, at p. 162; Catherine Cubitt, 'The Tenth-Century Benedictine Reform in England', *Early Medieval Europe* 6 (1997): 77-94.

[15] See, for example, Robert K. Upchurch, 'For Pastoral Care and Political Gain: Ælfric of Eynsham's Preaching on Marital Celibacy', *Traditio* 59 (2004): 39-78; Catherine Cubitt, 'Virginity and Misogyny in Tenth- and Eleventh-Century England', *Gender and History* 12 (2000): 1-32; Elaine Treharne, 'The Invisible Woman: Ælfric and his Subject Female', in *Leeds Studies in English* 37 (2006), ed. Mary Swan, *Essays for Joyce Hill on her Sixtieth Birthday* (Leeds, 2006), pp. 191-208.

[16] Bately, 'The Nature of Old English Prose', p. 71.

Here it is not so much the emphasis on named authors of privileged position that is notable, but the pushing aside of Old English material that cannot be attributed. Bately's linking of Ælfric to Alfred and Æthelwold also provides an appropriate context for analysis, as these writers are among the few in English at this time to use the *Preface* in order to explicate their motives, methods, and means for the reader. It is worthwhile comparing Ælfric's *Prefaces* with others' declarations of intent, though not with Alfred's, which has already been the subject of considerable scholarly attention.[17] Rather, a comparison can be made between Ælfric and Byrhtferth of Ramsey, both contemporary monks who wrote English for the understanding of the *illiterati*. In Byrhtferth's case, he passed his scholarly information to the priests who taught the clerks. In his comments about the motivation behind the composition of his *Enchiridion*, Byrhtferth of Ramsey discusses, in Latin, why he composed this work:

> Through God's mercy we found all these things in wondrous measure at Ramsey. And therefore I shall not pass over this in silence: that is, it is appropriate to reveal various things to the ignorant and not to fall silent because of the learning of wise men, but to explain to the ignorant and to set out in writing what these holy names signify. We have touched on the deep sea of this work through the precious words of the fathers, that is, the mystery of allegorical meaning. In this trivial work, it is fitting that I, who am trivial in respect of my accomplishments, should now work towards a weightier result in that matter which I undertook with a hasty pen, the Lord operating through me.[18]

In the introductory stages of his work, Byrhtferth insistently begins his explanations in Latin, then switches to English to 'speak of this a little'.[19] Within the English, Byrhtferth self-consciously and deliberately addresses the 'reverend clerk', urging the recipient to pay close attention as a 'geornfulla scoliere' ('eager pupil') and an 'arwurða leorningcniht' ('reverend disciple'). Later he admits to finding the Latin *computus* difficult to translate into the vernacular:

> These things are difficult to say in English, but with Christ's help we shall reveal them as well as we can, and lay the pearls before those who wish to pay heed to these things.[20]

---

[17]   See Nicole Guenther Discenza, *The King's English: Strategies of Translation in the Old English Boethius* (Binghamton: SUNY Press, 2006) and 'The Persuasive Power of Alfredian Prose', in David Johnson and Elaine Treharne, eds, *Readings in Medieval Texts: Interpreting Old and Middle English Literature* (Oxford: Oxford University Press, 2004).

[18]   Peter Baker and Michael Lapidge, eds, *Byrhtferth's Enchiridion*, EETS (Oxford: Oxford University Press, 199), pp. 16-17.

[19]   *Enchiridion*, p. 33.

[20]   *Enchiridion*, p. 67.

While dealing with complex scientific matter—calculations of months and days, epacts, and the like—Byrhtferth is aware of the potential inadequacy of the vernacular in coping with the specialised vocabulary. On occasion he needs to mix Latin with English to expound his meaning. Christ clearly assists him, though, inasmuch as he is perfectly able to adapt his Latin sources for explanation in English. He is conscious of the 'rusticity' and 'laziness' of his audience, occasionally labelling his audience as such: 'O rustic priest, I suppose you do not know what an atom is, but I will inform you about this word'.[21] His direct addresses, of course, draw the reader in, but also inform us about his perception of English: that it is necessary to use it as a functional tool for the unlearned who must have computistical material at their disposal. His underplaying of the significance of the vernacular is belied by his writing in it at all, and he employs the topoi of classical interruption and inspiration, firstly to show his erudition and secondly to beseech assistance in the writing of English:

> I command to depart from me the mermaids who are called Sirens, and also the Castilian nymphs…And I trust that the sublime Cherub will be present and with his golden tongs bring to my tongue sparks of the embers from the supreme altar, and touch the nerves of my dumb mouth so that I may therefore *argute arguto meditamine fari*, that is, so that I may with wise deliberations wisely translate this cycle into English.[22]

This kind of affected modesty trope has more to do with the Latin classical and patristic tradition than with anything in English; here, it is derived from Isaiah via Aldhelm. In other classical writers, such as Arator and Prudentius, we see similar pleas for the gift of eloquence. In Prudentius's *Peristephanon*, Book X, the author begins with a call for inspiration from his saintly intercessor, Romanus, a deacon martyred at Antioch in 303. He requests his own miracle of divine intervention to permit meaningful utterance from silence and compares this to the miracle of Romanus, who had his tongue cut out by his persecutors but was nevertheless able to speak:

> Romanus, stout defender of the divine Christ, grant thy favour and stir up the tongue within my speechless mouth, bountifully bestow graceful song on the mutest of men and enable me to sing the wonders of thy glory; for thou knowest, thyself too, that the dumb can speak. The cruel torturer tore out from thee the tongue that played on palate and throat, and yet did not impose silence on the lips wherewith thou wert confessing God. The voice that bears witness to the truth cannot be annihilated, even

---

[21] *Enchridion*, p. 111.
[22] *Enchiridion*, p. 135.

if its passage be cut away and it can only gasp. So my speech sticks and stammers with feeble tongue and labours in inharmonious measures; but if thou sprinkle my heart with the dew from on high and flood my breast with the milk of the spirit, my hoarse voice will unloose the sounds which are now obstructed.[23]

This form of grandiloquence encapsulated within a treatment of the modesty topos, elevated even by its own high-flown rhetorical norm, effectively illustrates the authorial conceit of the voice of the subject of biography beneficially influencing his very own graceful writing at the hands of the biographer. The explicit connection between writer and miraculous powers or divine intervention is made very apparent by the success of the biography itself. Indeed, Byrhtferth's use of the call to his muse to unloosen his tongue shows the persistent usefulness of this topos into late Anglo-Saxon England, both in Latin and in vernacular religious discourse. However, it is nowhere seen in Ælfric's more personal statements, and he—quite deliberately, it seems—sets himself apart from this overt claim of divine or saintly favour through intercession. His modesty tropes are of quite a different, and within an Anglo-Saxon context more unusual, kind:

> I, Ælfric, monk and mass-priest, even though more insignificant than is fitting for such an order, was sent in the days of King Æthelred from Bishop Ælfeage, Æthelwold's successor, to a certain monastery, which is called Cerne, by the request of Æthelmær the thane, whose parentage and goodness are known everywhere. Then it came into my mind, I believe through a gift of God, that I should translate this book from the language of Latin into English speech, not through the confidence of great learning, but because I saw and heard much heresy in many English books, which unlearned people through their simplicity esteemed as great wisdom.[24]

> I know very well that in this land there are many more learned men than I am, but God reveals his miracles through those that he desires. Likewise, the almighty Creator performs his work through his chosen, not because he has need of our help at all, but

---

[23] *Crowns of Martyrdom*, X, trans. H. J. Thomson, Loeb Classical Library 398 (Cambridge, MA: Harvard University Press, 1953), pp. 229-30; *Patrologia Latina* 60, 444 ff. See R. Levine, 'Prudentius' Romanus: the rhetorician as hero, martyr, satirist, and saint', *Rhetorica* 9, 1 (1991): 5-38, for a discussion of this saint's depiction.

[24] *Ælfric's Prefaces*, p. 108, for the Old English, and Elaine Treharne, *Old and Middle English: An Anthology* (Oxford: Blackwell, 2003): 'Ic, Ælfric, munuc and mæssepreost, swa ðeah waccre þonne swilcum hadum gebyrige, wearð asend on Æþelredes dæge cyninges fram Ælfeage biscope, Aðelwoldes æftergengan, to sumum mynstre, ðe is Cernel gehaten, þurh Æðelmæres bene ðæs þegenes, his gebyrd and goodnys sind gehwær cuðe. Þa bearn me on mode, Ic truwige ðurh Godes gife, þæt Ic ðas boc of Ledenum gereorde to Engliscre spræce awende, na þurh gebylde micelre lare, ac for ðan ðe Ic geseah and gehyrde mycel gedwyld on manegum Engliscum bocum, ðe ungelærede menn ðurh heora bilewitnysse to micclum wisdome tealdon.'

so that we earn that eternal life through performing his work. Paul the apostle said: 'We are God's helpers', and even so, we do not do anything for God without God's help.[25]

In these excerpts from the Old English *Preface* to the *Catholic Homilies* I, Ælfric affects humility through prolepsis, as one who is compelled to write not through the confidence or, possibly, arrogance acquired through scholarship, but rather as the much-required corrective to the proliferation of error. This somewhat paradoxical stance (how could he know what was error if he was not confident about his scholarship and his theological rigour?) is consolidated and enhanced by his declaration that despite being less learned than others, Ælfric himself has been chosen to reveal God's miracles: he is chosen to be the recipient of 'Godes gife'. One cannot refute the incontrovertible authority that divine patronage bestows on Ælfric. Thus his modesty topos must be qualified by the confidence he has in being selected by God to do his work. If one wished to be contentious, it could be surmised that Ælfric is, in essence, announcing his own election through his God-given gift of authorship, and declaring, in the fulfilment of God's wish for him, his own knowledge of personal salvation.

In the Latin *Preface* to *Catholic Homilies* I, Ælfric, as suggested by Jon Wilcox, is addressing a quite different, clearly Latinate audience—specifically in the first instance the Archbishop to whom he dedicates the work. Ælfric makes an interesting remark to Sigeric, his dedicatee:

> I, Ælfric, a student of the benevolent and venerable prelate, Æthelwold, send a greeting in the Lord to the Archbishop Sigeric. Even if rashly or presumptuously (*temere vel presumptuose*), we have, nevertheless, translated this book from Latin works, namely from Holy Scripture, into the language to which we are accustomed for the edification of the simple, who know only this language…[26]

These curious adverbs—'rashly' and 'presumptuously'—beg the question of Ælfric's confidence in the positive reception of his work at this highest level. He clearly forecasts potential criticism of his work, perhaps because the homilies were not requested, perhaps because of the apparent self-promotion of such an activity. Anticipating this criticism is shrewd, since it can be refuted before it has

---

[25] Treharne, *Anthology*: 'Forwel fela Ic wat on ðisum earde gelæredran þonne Ic sy, ac God geswutelað his wundra ðurh ðone ðe he wile: swa swa ælmihtig Wyrhta, he wyrcð his weorc þurh his gecorenan, na swylce he behofige ures fultumes, ac þæt we geearnion þæt ece lif þurh his weorces fremminge. Paulus se apostol cwæð: "We sind Godes gefylstan", and swa ðeah, ne do we nan ðing to Gode buton Godes fultume.'

[26] *Ælfric's Prefaces*, p. 127, Latin at p. 107.

even been voiced: Ælfric's explication of his didactic aims, his desire for orthodoxy, the naming of his sources, and his philanthropic motives are all evinced within lines of his acknowledgment of his ostensible presumption, offsetting it completely in a clever rhetorical exchange. This seeming foresight of potential criticism, which one might imagine derives from a lack of confidence, is also apparent in the Latin *Preface* to the Second Series of *Catholic Homilies*:

> Ælfric, the humble servant of Christ, wishes perpetual well-being in the Lord to the honourable and beloved Archbishop Sigeric. I confess to your benignity, venerable lord, that I am utterly unworthy and, as it were, full of fear because I have presumed to address you with holy homilies, namely through the little book which we have recently directed to your authority. But because you have too much praised our zeal, graciously receiving that translation, we have hastened to translate the following book just as the grace of Almighty God dictated it to us, not with garrulous verbosity nor in unfamiliar diction but in the clear and unambiguous words of this people's language, desiring rather to profit the listeners through straightforward expression than to be praised for the composition of an artificial style, which our simplicity has by no means mastered.[27]

Rhetorically, this is a dense and strangely shifting sequence of perspectives, moving swiftly among objective description, prophecy, apology, defensiveness, flattery, confidence, and false modesty. Through a series of carefully constructed clauses, Ælfric, expressing humility, subordination through confession and unworthiness, and fear of presumption illustrates his impressive command of Christian virtues and counters, through anticipation, any claims of pride or overconfidence. Simultaneously, and rather ironically, it is his clear desire for approval and praise that leads to his elaborate justification of English, the 'simple style', rather than the artifice of a more hermeneutic style. Reading this Preface, a masterclass in convincing rhetoric, it is impossible not to approve of Ælfric and his mission. It is notable, though, that the extravagance of this lengthy *apologia* in the Latin *Prefaces* is not matched by anything as elaborate in the vernacular *Preface*. In other words, his clear unease with using his native language does not appear in the English adaptations of his sources; it is not made explicit for the potential readership, presumably because it might seem to derogate the prestige and function of English. Still, Ælfric happily divulges his concern about the perceived inferiority of his medium to his superior in the Latin form that would be beyond the understanding of his actual audience. And just in case anyone was in any doubt about Ælfric's false modesty, he allows that:

---

[27] *Ælfric's Prefaces*, p. 128, Latin at p. 111.

> The censure of the envious will in no way move us if this work is not displeasing to your benignity.[28]

Now this doubt about the fitness of English to meet its purpose in the eyes of others does not altogether tally with Ælfric's self-declared God-given support (twice given) in his enterprise. His concern about the reaction of others—who might, he believes, be envious of his achievement—is not echoed by writers such as Wulfstan or Byrhtferth; it suggests a writer who is eager to be thought well of and to please, and who is not entirely altruistic in his undertaking. Joyce Hill proposes that Ælfric's comments in his *Prefaces* and prayers do not stem from 'intellectual arrogance but a self-conscious and in many respects polemical commitment to a particular tradition within reformed monasticism, coupled with a corresponding desire to avoid—and in fact to replace—what in his view were the unreliable vernacular homilies of the kind which survive now in collections such as those of the Blickling and Vercelli manuscripts'.[29] Even so, there may be room for a more cynical and suspicious response, particularly in the context of contemporary vernacular writings. Ælfric's peers—Æthelweard, Wulfstan, Byrhtferth, those who are named and all the anonymous writers not named—simply do not show the same level of self-authorisation, the same sureness that they are chosen to write on behalf of God, and the same concern for the maintenance of reputation that Ælfric does. One might wonder whether or not their unselfconscious writing is more a product of a genuine altruism than Ælfric's self-seeking and self-righteous mode of expression.

The distinctions that can be drawn between Ælfric and his contemporaries throw up very important questions about the 'extreme' role that Ælfric takes up as a second-generation product of the so-called Benedictine Reform. A subsequent issue arising from this is just how much weight we should attribute to Ælfric's self-declared position as the mouthpiece of divine orthodoxy; how much we should propagate and repeat his oft-repeated derogation of other materials circulating in the vernacular in the late tenth century; and, more importantly, how much we should let his utterances influence our readings of, and our approach to, non-Ælfrician homilies, particularly those of anonymous origin.

It seems clear that one could choose to read Ælfric's words as indicating that he believes himself to be one of God's chosen authorities, an oracle of late Anglo-Saxon morals and Christian tenets. In the Old English *Prefaces*, he is quite comfortable with saying as much in a more than indirect way; one could argue,

---

[28] *Ælfric's Prefaces*, p. 129, Latin at p. 112.
[29] Hill, 'Benedictine Reform and Beyond', p. 158.

ELAINE TREHARNE

perhaps, that he declares vatic status for himself.[30] Casting himself in the traditional role of the *vates*, he claims to be revealing the divinely inspired truth. This self-declaration of a prophetic role is, of course, potentially questionable from a theological perspective; but the significant change between his vatic expression in the Old English *Preface* and that in the Latin (for he still claims prophetic standing in the latter) is that in the Latin, he is 'dictating' from God, in a parallel world to that of John on Patmos, hearing and writing the words of God. As an instrument of divine revelation quashing the heresy prevalent in contemporary written works, he is on safe ground, standing in a line with his very worthy evangelical ancestors. For his superiors, including the Archbishop of Canterbury, and for his Latinate audience, he practises *sermo humilis*: the plain style in the fashion of Jerome; for the less-informed audience, he claims his Pauline inheritance of Christ-appointed truth-speaker.

So, where he can promote his role as sanctioned cipher of God's word, he does so, to those who are not likely to challenge his self-appointed role of censor and dispenser, evangelist, and law-provider. It might be added here that there seems to be an inherent preservation of the distinction in the early Church between those who attended to the flock and those who prophesied: the bishops as opposed to the prophets and teachers. This might go some way towards explaining his Pastoral Letters to Wulfsige and Wulfstan;[31] he is the late Anglo-Saxon church's seer, though his reputation did not outlive him and his efforts to counter what he perceived to be 'heresy' or 'dark fallacy' did not succeed. Both the Vercelli Book of homilies and the Blickling Homilies survived the period, together with

---

[30] Rather like Jerome, one of Ælfric's own sources, in his Preface to the Life of Hilarion: '1. Before I begin to write the life of the blessed Hilarion I invoke the aid of the Holy Spirit who dwelt in him, that He who bestowed upon the saint his virtues may grant me such power of speech to relate them that my words may be adequate to his deeds. For the virtue of those who have done great deeds is esteemed in proportion to the ability with which it has been praised by men of genius. Alexander the Great of Macedon who is spoken of by Daniel as the ram, or the panther, or the he-goat, on reaching the grave of Achilles exclaimed "Happy Youth! to have the privilege of a great herald of your worth," meaning, of course, Homer. I, however, have to tell the story of the life and conversation of a man so renowned that even Homer were he here would either envy me the theme or prove unequal to it. It is true that that holy man Epiphanius, bishop of Salamis in Cyprus, who had much intercourse with Hilarion, set forth his praises in a short but widely circulated letter. Yet it is one thing to praise the dead in general terms, another to relate their characteristic virtues. And so we in taking up the work begun by him do him service rather than wrong: we despise the abuse of some who as they once disparaged my hero Paulus, will now perhaps disparage Hilarion; the former they censured for his solitary life; they may find fault with the latter for his intercourse with the world; the one was always out of sight, therefore they think he had no existence; the other was seen by many, therefore he is deemed of no account. It is just what their ancestors the Pharisees did of old! They were not pleased with John fasting in the desert, nor with our Lord and Saviour in the busy throng, eating and drinking. But I will put my hand to the work on which I have resolved, and go on my way closing my ears to the barking of Scylla's hounds.'

[31] See, most recently, Joyce Hill, 'Authorial adaptation: Ælfric, Wulfstan and the Pastoral Letters', in *Text and Language in Medieval English Prose: A Festschrift for Tadeo Kubouchi*, ed. by Akio Oizumi, Jacek Fisiak and John Scahill (Frankfurt: Peter Lang, 2005), pp. 63-75.

numerous individual texts that share the textual tradition of these two manu-scripts.[32] We do not know, of course, whether or not these codices constitute the 'heresy' to which Ælfric refers, but modern scholarship has assumed this to be the case.[33] The longevity of homilies not attributable to Ælfric, or even likely to be condoned by him, suggests that his own sense of authority was not widely shared within the monastic and secular institutions responsible for copying vernacular texts in the period 990-1220.

To my mind, the diction that he employs, the certainty of this assigned role for himself, is all rather reminiscent of the hagiography he went on to write. And here, I would suggest—heretically and contentiously, naturally—that we might imagine that Ælfric deliberately casts himself into the role of the confessor saint, maybe hoping for local canonisation, similar to that of his *magister* Æthelwold, a canonisation authenticated and promoted by Ælfric's hagiography of the Win-chester bishop. Ælfric failed in his own imagined sanctity, of course. But the modern canonisation of this abbot has left us with the consequences of his self-determination: that other texts, those we imagine are declared heretical by this late Anglo-Saxon prophet, are non-canonical even to the point where they are exiled in mainstream Old English scholarship today. Moreover, if Ælfric failed to gain the authority and respect he felt to be essential for his mission in his own day, it is clear that modern scholarship has ironically assigned to him this very prestige and privilege: unfortunately, though, this has been much to the neglect of many excellent contemporary texts and authors.

---

[32] On the homiletic tradition in this period, see the essays in Aaron Kleist, ed., *The Old English Homily: Precedent, Practice and Appropriation*, Studies in the Early Middle Ages 17 (Turnhout: Brepols, 2007).

[33] See, for example, Wilcox's *Ælfric's Prefaces*, p. 22: 'The two series of *Catholic Homilies* are Ælfric's first known works. The Carolingian homiliaries…provide grander-scale Latin models, and the Blickling and Vercelli homilies demonstrate the pre-existence of some Old English homily collections. Nevertheless, Ælfric's two series of *Catholic Homilies* are innovative in scope and achievement as the first surviving example of an extended homiliary in a vernacular language'.

2

Ian Kirby

Gradual Revelation as Narrative Strategy in Medieval Literature

Gradual revelation is a not uncommon narrative device in both Old and Middle English literature. It is relatively frequent in the former, more occasional in the latter. It is superficial in some works, fundamental in others. In its simplest form, as in *Beowulf,* it includes the identification of the hero: though he is first mentioned at lines 194-198 as thane of Hygelac, noble among the Geats, and the strongest man of his time, he is not actually named until line 343. Similarly, the terrifying approach of Grendel to Heorot is accentuated by his being gradually introduced: we visualise him first as dark shadow (703), then as monstrous figure from whose eyes gleams an ugly light, like fire (726-7). In *The Dream of the Rood,* the cross is first a tree, then a beacon or symbol, then a gallows; confirmation of its identity comes only at line 25, where it is called the tree of the Saviour. In *Andreas,* we are introduced to twelve glorious heroes, thanes of their lord, whose glory did not fade in battle; but any misapprehension we might have is quickly corrected by the identification of their lord as the high king of heaven.

More sophisticated use of gradual revelation is found in the Riddles of the Exeter Book, where the hearer or reader is invited to identify the subject of the riddle on the basis of the information given. Some, like Riddle 16 ('anchor'), are readily solved, others are all but incomprehensible, at any rate to us; yet others, like Riddle 25 (which is interpretable as 'onion' or 'penis'), are deliberately ambiguous. But the elucidation of each riddle calls for close attention to each and every detail; and these details are often so elusive that modern scholars frequently differ as to the correct interpretation in individual cases.

One riddle which has almost as many interpretations as interpreters is number 60. In Volume II of his *Exeter Anthology of Old English Poetry,* Bernard Muir listed those interpretations offered so far: rune staff, reed pen, reed flute, letter beam cut from the stump of an old jetty, kelp weed, cross, and spirit/revenant! In an article published in *Notes and Queries* in September 2001, I hope to have demonstrated that there is an eighth meaning that is more likely than any of these. The narrator tells us that the object in question was by the sand, close to the sea wall, in a place where few would see it, and lapped (or covered) by the tide every day. It did not expect ever to exchange words over the mead, mouthless as it was; yet it is remarkable that a weapon's point and a warrior's thoughts could convey a message from one person to another in a way that a third person could not understand.

In my view, taking into account all the information contained in the poem, what is referred to by the narrator is an inscription, probably runic, on a rock situated between low and high tide which may possibly have functioned as a way marker or warning indicator for a mariner who could understand its coded message. Such inscriptions are not common, but two such have come to light in the British Isles in recent years, both runic and close to the sea: one near Dunbeath, in north-east Scotland, the other in Orkney. And as it happens, an inscription which almost exactly fits my reading of Riddle 60 is to be found in Narragansett Bay, Rhode Island State, though it is currently uncertain whether this inscription is ancient or modern. My provisional report on this American inscription will be found in *Beowulf and Beyond,* the recently-published collection of papers given at the IAUPE medieval symposia at Bamberg and Vancouver.

The point I want to make on this occasion, however, is that the gradual revelation which is fundamental to the riddles is a very important feature of other poems in the Exeter Book. In the fragmentary text known as *The Ruin,* we have a simple use of this narrative strategy: the author gradually reveals details of the ruined city, probably Bath, as it appeared to his admiring eyes. More complex and allusive is the approach in *Deor.* The narrator refers to certain of the great stories of Germanic tradition, showing how their protagonists underwent and survived great suffering; but the reason for these references is revealed only in the final strophe, when the poet likens his own situation to theirs. Most allusive of all is *Wulf and Eadwacer:* its riddling approach has baffled generations of scholars, and no one interpretation of it has as yet gained general acceptance.

However, it is in certain of the other, longer poems in the Exeter Book that gradual revelation is used as a fundamental strategy. This is true *inter alia* of *The Seafarer.*

The first part of this poem, to line 66a, places us, in turn, in two very different time-and-space contexts. The narrator first takes us into the past, gradually revealing details of a specific series of hardships he has undergone. It is a winter setting: he is on a ship which would appear to be making a coastal voyage, he is a member of the crew, and one of his duties is to take the night-watch and to ensure that the ship does not strike the rocks. It is bitter cold, and he is sick at heart, and hungry; he is exiled from his kinsmen and comitatus, though he has sea-birds for company, as well as the ice which weighs down the ship and perhaps threatens its, and his, existence.[1] The narrator's memories of this and comparable experiences are negative: the comforts of the land, the laughter of men, the mead-drinking, all are positively recalled by one who is weary of the sea. Then, at line 33b, there is an abrupt transition to the present and, as we learn only at line 48, from winter to spring. Now, the voyage envisaged is not a coastal one, but a long-distance one across the high seas, normally undertaken in spring or early summer; the feelings the narrator has about it are mixed, echoing the voice of the cuckoo, since any voyage has its concomitant dangers. But optimism triumphs over pessimism: the rebirth of nature after the cold of winter, and the attractions of journey's end, persuade the narrator to leave the sterile and transitory comforts of life on land, now viewed negatively, for the sea voyage to a distant foreign land.

So far, in my view, the poem holds together as a work in which the narrator gradually reveals why the negative experiences of past winter voyaging do not now deter him from undertaking a voyage across the high seas in springtime. But what is his destination? In more recent years, scholars have opined that it is not an earthly but a spiritual one: that he is engaged on a pilgrimage, and that the foreign land of line 38 is in fact Santiago di Compostela, Rome, Jerusalem, or even the narrator's heavenly home. And this is an attractive argument in terms of my theme; for as elsewhere in medieval literature there is an element of contradiction in the earlier part of the poem. We cannot immediately understand why the narrator should look forward to the voyage, in view of his past experiences; only when the time of year is mentioned does this become clear. Similarly, it may be argued, it is only when the spiritual nature of his destination is revealed at line 65 that his change of mind about life on land can be fully understood.

The Wife's Lament and *The Husband's Message* are two other poems in the Exeter Book whose interpretation also depends, I consider, on the recognition that their author makes use of the strategy of gradual revelation to build up his story, detail by detail. *The Wife's Lament* begins with the statement that in her sadness she has made this song about herself and her present situation, recalling the journeys into exile that have caused her torment. The first cause of her sorrow was the departure of her lord, who had left his people to go overseas, leaving her a friendless exile with no knowledge of his whereabouts. His relatives had determined to keep them apart. Her lord had commanded her to make his land her own, though she had no friends in it; and she recalls the ambivalence of his behaviour, cheerful of expression but meditating some deadly act. They had vowed that only death would separate them; but this is now at an end, and she has to endure the

---

[1] I consider it probable that more than a half-line is missing after *winemægum bidroren* (16a); after all, it seems more appropriate that the ship rather than the speaker should be said to be hung with icicles, and one of the main winter tasks of Icelandic fishermen (for example) was and is to chop off ice as it forms on the ship to prevent it sinking under the weight.

results of her loved one's feud. She had been obliged to live alone in a remote and cheerless place, and there she reflects on her own discomfort and loneliness, and the probable similarity of her loved one's situation.

Many attempts to interpret this poem have been made, but I would suggest that there is an account of the circumstances which fits the evidence the author gives us. We need to note the similarity with the Riddles, as the poet gradually reveals to us the woman's situation and feelings; and we need also to note the position of emphasis in the text of key words, notably *wræcsiðas* (lines 5 and 38) and *fæhðu* in line 26.

The wife is a lady of rank, married to the lord she speaks of throughout the poem. She has come from another land, probably as a peaceweaver, to live among her husband's people; in consequence, she is already in a situation of exile from her own nation. But her husband has become involved in a feud; he has committed a violent act in pursuit of this feud, no doubt a killing, and has had to leave his country in consequence. She has been left behind; and to ensure her safety her husband's relatives have hidden her away in a remote place, possibly after an attempt on her part to rejoin her husband (which could have put his life, and perhaps hers, in danger). She is therefore doubly an exile: from her own native country, and now from her husband's hall. Her husband, too, is an exile – from his own land, and from her; and she can, and does, feel for him as well as for herself, as she imagines him isolated in a desolate winter landscape, remembering happier places.

Certain points in this interpretation will be thought to need defence. First: the view that she has been married to her lord as a peaceweaver takes its roots in the plural form of *wræcsiðas* (she has had to go on an exile journey more than once) and her friendlessness in her husband's country, as indicated in lines 10 and 16-17. Second: I see no reason to regard the action of the relatives as indicated in lines 11-14 as the hostile act most critics think it to be; rather, the relatives are acting to protect the lives of husband and wife, whose separation is thus the outcome of a necessary action on their part, not deliberate malice.[2] Third: though she is miserable, even angry (line 32), as a result of his departure, her mood changes as she recognises that he is likely to be as sorrowful as she is as a result of their separation. Finally, this kind of situation, though less usual in Old English literature, is very familiar to those who have immersed themselves in Old Norse literature: outlawry for killing was the punishment of Eric the Red in the saga that bears his name, and of Gunnar Hámundarson in *Njáls saga* (though Gunnar finally refused to leave his home at Hliðarendi), to cite just two of the better-known instances.

---

[2]   This is supported by the indicative, not subjunctive, mood of *lifdon* in line 14.

If my reading of the poem is correct, it has a significant bearing on one of the oldest points of contention in the critical literature on Old English elegiac verse: the relationship between *The Wife's Lament* and *The Husband's Message*.

Three people are involved in *The Husband's Message*: the speaker, the speaker's lord, and the person addressed, a lady of rank as we learn from lines 14 and 47 (*sinchroden, þeodnes dohtor*). The speaker has often undertaken voyages across the high seas at the behest of his lord; on this occasion, he has come to assure the lady of his lord's devotion to her, to remind her of the promises they made to each other when they lived and loved together in one land, one mead-hall (lines 15-19). A feud had driven the lord away from his own people, and he had had to sail away from his own land secretly and in a hurry (line 40): but he has now made a new and equally prosperous life for himself in another land to the south (line 27), and his happiness will be complete there if she joins him. He therefore invites her to take ship, as soon as the first cuckoo is heard, and to allow no one to prevent her from rejoining him. As evidence of the reliability of this message, the speaker has brought with him a wooden stick on which the lord himself has carved five runes.

Two often-posed questions arise from this: what is the message conveyed by the runes; and is there a relationship between the poem and *The Wife's Lament*?

Many scholars have attempted to solve the problem of the runes, and such solutions have usually supposed either that they make up a single word, or that they should be read in terms of the names of the runes (thus, the first two, **s** and **r**, should be read together as *sigel-rad*, indicating "sun-path", or heaven). Both ideas are valid, of course, in principle: but I should like to suggest a third possibility. In this age of computer passwords and bank-card PIN-codes, we may do well to remember that in Riddle 60, which immediately precedes *The Husband's Message* in the Exeter Book, it is implied that one of the great advantages of runes is that they can convey secret messages between two people. Is it not then possible that the sender has agreed a coded message in runes with the receiver, which in the circumstances of their parting will validate the authenticity of the message? The first two runes together,[3] and the other three in that order, do not then need to be more than a random choice agreed between the couple, and entrusted to a reliable messenger so as to reassure the lady that she is not falling into a trap.

As to the question of a relationship between *The Wife's Lament* and *The Husband's Message*, it seems to me that recent scholarship is unduly critical of this possibility. My own reading of the poems gives us an almost identical situation: the lord forced to leave his wife and homeland because of a feud, but now in a

---

[3] This is very reminiscent of the Germanic use of bind-runes, a practice found occasionally in England; see R. I. Page, *An Introduction to English Runes*, p. 48.

position to invite her to his new hearth and home in a land alien, but welcoming, to them both. In the introduction to his edition Roy Leslie wrote: "There is nothing in the plot of *The Wife's Lament* ... that is incompatible with the situation in *The Husband's Message,* but it has not been conclusively shown that they must be parts of the same story". True: but in view of what I have said, I am inclined to think that the onus is rather on those who doubt it to prove their case, for such arguments as have appeared to date do not seem very convincing.

By contrast with Old English literature, gradual revelation as narrative strategy is relatively infrequent in Middle English literature. Chaucer uses it on occasion: in his earliest long poem, *The Book of the Duchess,* he gives us first the sad classical tale of a queen, Alcione, whose husband Ceyx is drowned, then his own dream conversation with a knight dressed entirely in black. But the overall purpose of the tale is not revealed until the final lines of the poem, when we also realise the significance of the name of the lady whose death he is mourning. In *The Canterbury Tales,* Chaucer introduces us to the Host of the Tabard Inn towards the end of the General Prologue, but we have to wait until the Cook's Prologue to learn that his name is Herry Bailly, and until the Prologue to the Monk's Tale for detailed information about his marital situation. And in general Chaucer uses the tales and their prologues to build up the overall picture of the pilgrims. Some of these developments add little to the impression we have of the pilgrims from the General Prologue, while others give us much or even most of what we know of them; witness the Wife of Bath, whose portrait in the general prologue is substantially developed in the prologue to her tale, the Nun's Priest and the Second Nun, who are nobodies in the general prologue, and indeed Chaucer himself. And Chaucer introduces a further colourful character in the course of the pilgrimage, the Canon's Yeoman.

More substantial is the use of gradual revelation by the unidentified author of *The Owl and the Nightingale.* What seems at the beginning to be a relatively simple tale of a quarrel between two birds has by the end developed into a highly complex representation whose exact significance has defied interpretation. Or rather, has defied a single interpretation which commands general assent. Over the decades argument has raged about the significance of the information the author gives us, and we are still far from agreement about such matters as the identification of the birds and their relationship with the human world, the implication of indications by the author that the birds are female, the identity of Nicholas of Guildford and the reason for the choice of him as arbiter, and so on. The final solution to the numerous riddles the author sets before us seems as far off as ever. And this, of course, is one of the principal attractions of this work.

Much of Middle English literature is essentially religious, and the use of gradual revelation is correspondingly limited. This is true *inter alia* of the medieval cycle plays, for the obvious reason that the subject-matter of these is essentially well-known Bible stories which admit of little if any modification. Although the author of the Towneley play of Noah's flood is able to build up the audience's uncertainty as to whether Noah's wife will accompany him into the ark, and suspense reaches agonising levels in the Brome play of Abraham and Isaac, the outcome can never be in doubt. However, a few medieval plays do make significant use of gradual revelation, and of these the best are the Towneley shepherds' plays. Thus, in the Second Shepherds' play the English setting and entirely secular main plot, with its hilarious treatment of Mak and Gill and the sheep-stealing, divert our attention from the identification of the shepherds as those of the Nativity, and it is only with the appearance of the angel at the end of the play that this connection is made.

The Middle English works which most substantially exemplify the use of gradual revelation as narrative strategy are those of the author (or conceivably authors) of *Sir Gawain and the Green Knight* and *Pearl*. In the former this has been identified and commented on by many critics; in regard to the latter, a recent publication sets out to identify a further twist to the presentation.

The essential aspect of gradual revelation in *Sir Gawain and the Green Knight* relates, of course, to the Green Knight himself. When he rides into Arthur's hall, it is his size and general appearance which are first described, and only at the end of the stanza are we told that he is *oueral enker-grene*. His aggressive behaviour at Arthur's court contrasts sharply with his courteous welcome to Gawain in his other persona as Lord of Hautdesert, and the final revelation, made almost offhand at line 2347, is thus as much of a surprise to the first-time reader as it is to Gawain. Similarly surprising is the revelation that the old and highly respected lady of Hautdesert is in fact the malignant Morgan le Fay, Gawain's aunt, and that she is the motivating force of the Green Knight's challenge and Gawain's quest, which turns out to be the exact reverse of the norm: for it seems that Gawain's successful fulfilment of the quest will lead to his death, while failure will entail dishonour.

More sophisticated is the poet's practice in *Pearl*: not only is his revelation of the identity of the Pearl-maiden gradual, but he deliberately contradicts the expectations of his hearers. We are allowed to assume that Pearl is a precious stone, that the herb garden is a herb garden, that the dream landscape is to be equated with the 'love garden', that the river is, albeit studded with precious stones, merely a river, and so on, only to have these and many of our other assumptions contradicted as the poem progresses. And one of the revelations of the poem, I consider, remained unperceived until one of my doctoral students, Jean-Paul Freidl, noticed it a few years ago.

One of the ongoing arguments about *Pearl* relates to the question whether the protagonist is a human being or not. The evidence of the poem has been generally, though not universally, taken to indicate that the Pearl-maiden was a child who was the narrator's daughter, probably named Margaret, who died before her second birthday. But one aspect of this which has not received much attention from those who accept the interpretation is why, in an age when families were large and many children did not reach their fifth birthday, the father's grief should be so inordinate. We think we can explain this. In our opinion, there is ample evidence in the poem to justify the view that the child died in one of the outbreaks of the Black Death.

A full account of the evidence can be read in our article published in *Neuphilologische Mitteilungen* 4 CIII 2002. To summarise a part of this: the concatenation element of the first stanza of the poem, 'without a spot', which apparently emphasises the perfection of the precious stone, is echoed in line 782, when the Pearl-maiden says of herself that she is without a *blot*. The poem makes very frequent use of other words which also indicate the black spots, or buboes, characteristic of the plague: *gall, mascle, mot, teche*, and *wem* are some of them. When the narrator describes his first sight of her on the other side of the river, he notes in particular the pure whiteness of her face, implying as it does that the last time he had seen her on earth it was not as it now is. On many occasions in the poem, the poet emphasises the pure, unsullied beauty of the heavenly sphere. Above all, in line 945 of the poem the Lamb of God is specifically described as being without black spots. We can thus conclude that the poet of *Pearl*, like some other medieval writers, has made very substantial use of the strategy of gradual revelation, and that a recognition of this is fundamental to our understanding of his and their works.

References (in the order of occurrence in the text):

Anglo-Saxon Poetry, translated and edited by S. A. J. Bradley, London 1982

Anglo-Saxon Poetic Records vol. 3: The Exeter Book, eds. G. P. Krapp and E. v. K. Dobbie, New York and London 1936

The Exeter Anthology of Old English Poetry, vol. 2, ed. B. J. Muir, Exeter 1994, 648

'The Exeter Book, *Riddle* 60', in *Notes and Queries New Series* vol. 48, September 2001, 219-220 (Ian Kirby)

'The Narragansett runic inscription, Rhode Island', in *Beowulf and Beyond*, eds. H. Sauer and R. Bauer, Frankfurt 2007, 89-98 (Ian Kirby)

Eirik the Red and other Icelandic sagas, selected and translated by Gwyn Jones, Oxford 1961, 128

Njáls saga, translated by Magnus Magnusson and Hermann Palsson, Harmondsworth 1960, 165

An Introduction to English Runes, R. I. Page, 2nd ed., Woodbridge 1999, 48

Three Old English Elegies, R. F. Leslie, Manchester 1961, 18

The Riverside Chaucer, 3rd edition, ed. L. D. Benson, Boston 1987

The Owl and the Nightingale, Text and Translation, ed. N. Cartlidge, Exeter 2001

English Mystery Plays, ed. P. Happé, Harmondsworth 1975

The Poems of the Pearl Manuscript, eds. M. Andrew and R. Waldron, London 1978

'The Life, Death and Life of the Pearl-Maiden', in *Neuphilologische Mitteilungen* 4 CIII 2002, Helsinki 2003, 395-398 (Ian Kirby and Jean-Paul Freidl)

3

Rosamund Allen

Could Lydgate write in true metre after all?

Introduction

This is an interim report on a project to examine the prosody of seven texts from 1300 to 1450 by collating around one thousand lines from a number of manuscript witnesses.[1] An extract from Book III of Lydgate's *Troy Book*, the middle of this five-book text, forms part of this project.[2] The extract covers the verbal encounter between Achilles and Hector, so as to admit speech as well as third-person narrative, and the parting of Troilus and Criseyde, to allow for emotive interaction to offset the martial combat. The following presents the interim results from this survey of 1,226 lines of *Troy Book*.

Lydgate was chosen for the project because, from having had the status of Chaucer's equal, he went through a catastrophic decline in reputation in the early nineteenth century – a decline from which, despite recent attempts to re-evaluate his poetry,[3] his metre still seems to suffer, disparaging comments on it ranging from superior sniffs of disapproval to hoots of derisory laughter. An article by Emerson Brown published in 2000 is entitled 'The Joy of Chaucer's Lydgate Lines', but no

---

[1] This is a collaborative project with Dr Judith Jefferson, University of Bristol. The other texts in the survey are: *The Pricke of Conscience* (Book VI); Mirk, *Instructions for Parish Priests*; Chaucer: *Knight's Tale* and *Book of the Duchess*; Hoccleve: *The Series, Letter of Cupid; Palladius on Husbandry*. Dr Jefferson has published the results of her work on Hoccleve as 'The Hoccleve Holographs and Hoccleve's Metrical Practice' in *Medieval English Measures: Studies in Metre and Versification*, ed. Ruth Kennedy (Parergon Special Issue (NS 18:1), July 2002), 203-26.

[2] The eleven manuscripts (from a total of 23 and three fragments) of Lydgate's *Troy Book* used in the survey are: London, British Library MS Cotton Augustus A.iv (Ag); London, British Library MS Arundel 99 (Ar 99); Oxford, Bodleian Library MS Digby 232 (D2); Manchester, John Rylands Library MS Eng 1 (Jr); Oxford, Bodleian Library MS Rawlinson C. 446 (R2); London, British Library MS Royal 18.D.ii (Ro1); Cambridge, Trinity College MS O.5.2 (Tr); Oxford, Bodleian Library MS Digby 230 (D1); London, British Library MS Royal 18. D. vi (Ro2); Oxford, Bodleian Library MS Rawlinson poet. 144 (R1); Cambridge University Library MS Kk.v.30 (Kk). Bergen's copy text was Ag.

[3] For example, Larry D. Scanlon and James Simpson, eds, *John Lydgate: Poetry, Culture, and Lancastrian England* (Notre Dame, IN: University of Notre Dame Press, 2006), designed to recover Lydgate from critical neglect and disdain and "take Lydgate seriously as a major poet" (6), while justifying his "uneasy syntax" and rhetoric, does not tackle his allegedly poor metrical performance.

one seems to find Lydgate's Lydgate lines at all funny.[4] Brown himself says, 'for many of his lines it is probably wishful thinking to posit any coherent verse pattern at all, much less a felicitous one'.[5] Derek Pearsall foretells humiliation for all who would attempt to claim excellence for Lydgate's metre: 'if anyone tried, they would only have to quote a few lines and the argument would be flat on its face in the mud'.[6]

In his introduction to the 1998 TEAMS edition of *Troy Book*, Robert E. Edwards makes the wry observation on Lydgate's verse that 'the metrical features that Chaucer used occasionally and even then with a rhythmic purpose in mind become frequent and systematic ... characteristic are the headless line ... with the first [offbeat] syllable missing, and the so-called "Lydgate line" or "broken-backed line" in which the unaccented syllable is missing after the caesura"', citing the example of *Troy Book* I, 224: 'That his entent // can no man bewreye'.[7] (13) Josef Schick termed these types D and C.[8] Together with trochaic inversion in the first foot (Schick type E) and elsewhere in the first half line, especially at the caesura (Schick type B), these are held to be the hallmark of Lydgate's prosodic ineptitude because of the frequency and irrelevance of their occurrence. For Chaucer such uncommon features are often deliberate indices of meaning. For example, drawing the reader in at the start of a text: 'Whan that April with his shoures sote' (*Canterbury Tales*, General Prologue, 1: headless); 'Hath in the ram his half cours yronne' (General Prologue, 8: held to be broken-backed, with trochaic inversion). However, Derek Pearsall has recently reminded us of the Middle English grammar we learned as undergraduates and pointed out that a weak adjectival ending follows a possessive adjective, so that the reading in General Prologue 8 should therefore be 'Hath in the Ram his **halve** cours yronne'.[9] Line 3271 of the *Miller's Tale*, 'Now sire and eft

---

4   In Alan T. Gaylord, ed., *Essays on The Art of Chaucer's Verse* (London and New York: Routledge, 2001), pp. 267-279.

5   *Ibid.*, p. 268.

6   Review of James Simpson, Oxford Literary History, vol. 2: 1350-1547, *Reform and Cultural Revolution* (Oxford: Oxford University Press, 2002) in *Journal of Medieval and Early Modern Studies*, 35 (2005), 31. The failings Pearsall notes in Lydgate's verse are: halting versification, turgid syntax, repetitiveness, long-windedness and verbosity. This essay may well prove Pearsall right, but an attempt at vindication for Lydgate's metre is timely.

7   Robert R. Edwards, ed., *John Lydgate: "Troy Book": Selections*. TEAMS Middle English Texts Series (Kalamazoo, MI: Medieval Institute Publications, 1998), p. 13. Yet Edwards admits that, following Bergen's edition, he has frequently added –e 'to regularize the meter of Lydgate's verse' (p. 341). Such emendation should surely be subject to rigorous assessment of grammatical function.

8   Josef Schick, ed., *Lydgate's Temple of Glas*, Early English Text Society, e.s. 60 (London: Kegan Paul, 1891). The five types of Lydgatian metre (including the regular five iambics, which Schick terms A) are also listed in Walter Schirmer, *John Lydgate: A Study in the Culture of the XVth Century*. Translated by Ann E. Keep (London: Methuen, 1961), pp. 71-2; Schirmer calls Lydgate's verse technique 'peculiarly heavy, almost ponderous' (p. 72).

9   Derek Pearsall, 'The Weak Declension of the Adjective and its Importance in Chaucerian Metre', in Geoffrey Lester, ed., *Chaucer in Perspective: Middle English Essays in Honour of Norman Blake* (Sheffield: Sheffield Academic Press, 1999), pp.178-93. I am most grateful to Professor Pearsall for drawing my attention to this article.

sire / so bifel the cas', with trochaic inversion (and epic caesura), justifies its metrical shape as a dramatic call for attention. All three of these lines, however, give a trochaic rather than iambic beat to the line, and line 1 could, as Brown suggests, be heard as a four-beat line, as can the following line:

/   /   /   /

'The droght of March hath perced to the roote' (Gen. Prol. 2). All these types occur in Lydgate, who knew the General Prologue fairly well – though not well enough to avoid conflating three of the pilgrims.[10] But it has been assumed that Lydgate himself uses these metrical equivalents of the marginal pointing finger as a merely virtuoso effect.

However, even Derek Pearsall, in his much acclaimed 1970 book *John Lydgate*, raises the faint cheer that 'few lines are totally unscannable',[11] and implies that Lydgate uses final –*e* in much the same way as Chaucer, especially in his earlier work.[12] As *Troy Book*, composed between 1412 and 1420, is just such an early work, it seems an appropriate choice of text for examining the distribution of Lydgate's final –*e* in metrical positions in terms of the evidence for its survival in manuscript tradition, and the effect that scribal incomprehension about final –*e* and about Lydgate's other metrical practices – where these are discoverable, of course –, would have on our perception of 'true Lydgate'. I wanted to test why a poet now so unreservedly demoted to second rate could have been popular for over three centuries: there are 23 manuscripts of *Troy Book*, a vast enterprise for a copyist with its 30,000 lines. Can there be an explanation for Lydgate's poor reputation as metrist? Might it be that the denigrations of his scansion are based on editions which used metrically inaccurate base texts? At least the exploration would highlight how scribes did respond to the then revered Lydgate: were they respectful or typically careless?

There is of course a word of caution here. It is now generally accepted that Chaucer played cheerily with the metre where it suited him, that the often 'irregular' lines in Hengwrt are authorial and scribes tidied to produce a smoother rhythm in Ellesmere and Harley 7334 (Ha4). I am more sceptical, as most scribes seem to be rather more cloth-eared than super metrists, but let us assume that this hypothesis is right. Can there then be any point in comparing eleven manuscripts of Lydgate's *Troy Book* in the hope of discovering whether the infamous 'Lydgate metres' of Bergen's printed edition of *Troy Book* have regular metrical equivalents hidden among the variants of the other ten manuscripts?[13] In my view such a collation of readings

---

[10] Lydgate apparently conflates the Pardoner, Summoner and Reeve, or the Reeve's Tale Miller, though the apparent inaccuracy may be intentional (see Derek Pearsall, 'Lydgate as Innovator', *Modern Language Quarterly*, 53 (1992), 5-22).

[11] *John Lydgate* (London: Routledge and Kegan Paul, 1970), p. 62.

[12] *Ibid.*, p. 61.

[13] Henry Bergen, ed., *Lydgate's Troy Book*, EETS ES 97, 103, 106, 126 (London and Oxford, 1906-35).

does have point. In 1412 to 1420, when Lydgate wrote the five books of *Troy Book*, final *–e* (schwa) had dropped out of colloquial speech – as it was probably already doing while Chaucer was writing. If, as we are assured, Lydgate did use final *–e* in a Chaucerian way where metrically needed, then if it appears in scribal copies of his work, it is likely to be original. It will be unfamiliar to scribes from their own usage, unless they are habitual copyists of Chaucer. If one manuscript presents a final *–e* which supports a regular off-beat/beat pattern consistent with what came to be called pentameter, then it is probably, though I admit not inevitably, Lydgate's own. Conversely, where the metre halts, why may this not be scribal rather than authorial, especially if other manuscripts offer a superior metrical shape to the line? Pearsall himself says that many lines can be rectified by 'minor emendation', and this collation often provides supporting evidence for such emendation.

The issue boils down to the reasons why editors choose a base manuscript for their edition. This is usually because it is the most complete version (as in the case of Cotton Caligula A iv for *Troy Book*) or is in the right dialect – many of the earliest manuscripts of *Troy Book* form a 'Suffolk group' corresponding to Lydgate's birthplace in the Suffolk village of Lydgate and his intermittent membership of the Bury St Edmunds Benedictine house. Very rarely are base texts chosen because they have the best readings throughout, and never because they are metrically soundest: these two features usually only emerge once the editing process is completed anyway. In fact, editors choosing a manuscript on the basis of date may be wrong: Bergen's notes to *Troy Book* identify Cotton Augustus A iv as the earliest witness, dated to 1420-30;[14] Kathleen Scott has now dated it to 1430-40,[15] and not much earlier than Tony Edwards' dating of Arundel 99 as mid 15th century, ascribed to a 'Lydgate scribe'.[16] Bergen traces Arundel 99 to Suffolk, and he surmises that the scribe was associated with Lydgate's monastery at Bury.[17] Bergen also concludes that Cotton Augustus A iv, Bodleian Digby 232 and Rawlinson 446 (with Bristol Reference Library, MS 8) may all have been produced for Bury St Edmunds;[18] the same scribe wrote Digby 230 and Rawlinson C. 446.[19] These seven manuscripts

---

[14] *Lydgate's Troy Book*, EETS ES 126, pp. 1-4: 'perhaps quite early in the decade', 1, fn.1; 'not only one of the oldest and best manuscripts of the *Troy Book*, but the most complete that has come down to us' (p. 4).

[15] Kathleen L. Scott, *Later Gothic Manuscripts*: 1390-1490, 2 vols (London: Harvey Miller, 1996). Cited in R. R. Edwards, ed., *Troy Book: Selections*, p. 15.

[16] A.S.G. Edwards, 'Lydgate Manuscripts: Some Directions for Future Research', in *Manuscripts and Readers in Fifteenth-Century England: the Literary Implications of Manuscript Study*, ed. Derek Pearsall (Cambridge: D.S. Brewer, 1981), pp. 17-19.

[17] *Lydgate's Troy Book*, vol. 4, EETS ES 126, p. 87.

[18] *Ibid.*

[19] A.I. Doyle and M.B. Parkes, 'The Production of Copies of the *Canterbury Tales* and the *Confessio Amantis* in the Fifteenth Century', in M.B. Parkes and Andrew Watson, eds, *Medieval Scribes, Manuscripts and Libraries: Essays Presented to N.R. Ker* (London: Scolar Press, 1978), pp. 163-210, at p. 201 n. 100 and p. 210 n. 128; cited in R.R. Edwards, *Troy Book: Selections*, p. 15.

(plus the Bristol MS) form the 'Suffolk group', and while they are far from identical in spelling and grammar, they provide the soundest evidence for the *Troy Book* metrical patterns. Frequently, though of course not always, Arundel 99 actually metres better than Cotton Augustus A iv, Bergen's base manuscript.

Before I present the results of the survey of the 1,226 lines of *Troy Book* Bk 3, I want to explain the rationale for identifying a reading as probably superior to other variants and how that reading may reveal Lydgate's typical prosodic practice.

To identify a reading as original simply because it 'sounds right' is clearly to argue in a circle. To reason that the line presenting what the modern reader thinks is the best metre must therefore be original, and therefore Lydgate's, is not editing. Such reasoning assumes first that metre is always as regular as a metronome, and secondly that Lydgate was a good metrist, which begs the question.

2. Identifying the 'right' reading

It is essential to apply a full editorial method to all variants. This involves: identifying the harder reading with non-prose word order, unusual words or constructions; recognising the more explicit meaning which dilutes sense; isolating the more emphatic reading which overstates; and rejecting the reading which mistakes the grammatical construction or the contextual sense. Always assuming, of course, that Lydgate did write sense grammatically, which some doubt. It is actually impossible to edit a poor or unpredictable writer. But, wishfully thinking again, I am going to assume that there was at least some reason for Lydgate's popularity and that, some of the time anyway, he could write.

Once harder, less explicit or more emphatic readings are identified, the shape of Lydgate's preferred dialectal forms and ways of stressing words begins to emerge; thus his prosodic habits become evident, and can be applied elsewhere – by conjectural emendation if no witness for a specific line seems to present what looks from elsewhere like Lydgate's habitual usage. The devices he uses to secure metricality are similar to Chaucer's, in fact: *for to, gan,* promotion of particles, and especially prepositions, to carry a beat. With Lydgate's own habits becoming at least clearer, the scribal re-writings stand out as a distinct metrical system, reliant mainly on syllable count, but often without the realisation that stress-syllabic verse also has a pattern of off-beat/beat (or, with Lydgate, the other way round).

Finally, then, it is possible to make a rough count of the numbers of trochaic inversions, headless and broken-backed lines in this mid-section of *Troy Book* which really do seem to be Lydgatian. I will then conclude by suggesting what seems to be 'true Lydgate' and why he is not brilliant but rather better than his reputation.

3. The evidence

The following are some instances of scribes re-writing lines or re-wording or spelling parts of lines.[20]

Scribes rewrite in prose order:
3758 Til monthes iij ben comen & gon (Ro2); Til þre monþes come be and goon (rest).
Read: *Till monthes three ycome ben and goon.

Scribes use a different dialectal form from Lydgate's preferred form:
3466 Agein his shot miȝt pleinli endure (Ro2)
Read: (with Kk) Ageyn(e)s his shote pleynly myght endure

Scribes supply a more explicit reading:
4192 Yt walde me fule longe tyme occupye (Ro1)
Read (with rest): ful longe occupie.

Scribes stress words differently from Lydgate's own practice:
4221 Til fortune gan vpon him froune (rest: stress on first syllable of *fortune*)
Read (with Ro2): Til that fortune gan vpon him froune (stress on second syllable)

Scribes supply a more emphatic reading:
4318 But it is foly for to byen to dere (Ag)
Read (with Ar99): But it is folye for to beyen deere
3325 ful worþi (rest)
Read: worthi of renoun (Ro2)

But the identification of scribal re-working is never entirely secure, as the following examples indicate; readers are invited to supply their own resolutions of the following cases:

Scribes re-order to give prose word order?
4328 At spectacles in Citees and tounes
? Read: At spectacles in Citees and in towuns (Ar99)

---

[20] To make the nature of the wrong reading clear, I have included with identification of the right reading a conjecture of the possible original where no witness presents it; this actually occurs at a later stage in the evaluation.

3522   In ful purpos ech othir to confounde (Ro2);
          In purpos fully eche oþer to confounde (rest)
? Read * In purpos ful ech othir to confounde

Are scribes acting as censors here?
4344 Which deliteth to speke on-curteisly (Ro2)
? Read: þat haþ delyt to speke cursidly (rest)

Stressing of proper name causes scribes problems:
3566 And Aurora well bygan adowe (Kk)
the rest have: And aurora newe gan adewe (rest)
Auro**ra** or Au**ro**ra ?
Both must be headless, but the second (modern) version contradicts Lydgate's usual practice of stressing the first and final syllable in trisyllabic proper names.

What they all get right!:
3688 (padding) þe story seith certeyn (all!)

4. Identifying Lydgate's original readings

As scribal readings begin to be distinguishable from what Lydgate must have written, it becomes possible to pinpoint his preferred linguistic forms and metrical habits, and to assess how far scribes were aware of these. This is not an evaluation of *what* is said (lexical meaning) but of *how* it is said (metrical shape), and therefore two scribes who write *oþre kinge* and *oþir kinges* respectively (3701) have produced identical scansion. I classified lines as follows: (1) if all MSS agree in similar unstress/stress/unstress/stress alternation they are all metrically identical, whatever the lexical content of the line, and I classified these instances of agreement as **A1**. Similarly, absence of final –*e* where it would elide anyway, that is, a final –*e* followed by a vowel or *h-*, is equivalent to a form without –*e*. In fact, several manuscripts omit –*e* where it is elided or subject to apocope, while recording functional final –*e*.[21]

    (2) Where one or more, but not all, manuscripts present a superior reading compared with others, I have classified that line as **A2**. Once Lydgate's metrical preference has been established, further instances of superior, probably correct, readings can be classed as A2. (3) Lines which seem to present no metrical pattern that accords with Lydgate's apparent usual practice are deemed to have failed

---

[21] Lydgate regularly practises elision, even across the caesura, though *to* and *be* (vb and prep) do not elide.

(**F**). However, where a 'minor emendation' not presented by any variant in my eleven manuscripts would restore Lydgate's habitual metre, this is designated **R**, repairable. This last is, of course, a case of conjectural emendation. As such it is controversial, especially as this is emendation *metri causa*, but in accordance with Lydgate's practice, not the editor's own preference.

In these 1,226 lines, there are 235 lines where all eleven manuscripts agree in presenting what seems to be a metrical line (A1). In 660 lines, not all but at least one (occasionally more) manuscript presents such a metrical reading; eighty-six of these apparently metrical readings occur in MS Ar 99 but not in Bergen's base MS, Ag. Two hundred and twenty-six lines seem to fail altogether to match Lydgate's usual practice. But a 'minor' adjustment (for example: supplying a final *–e*; re-ordering the words in the line; or re-spelling to adopt Lydgate's habitual forms) would remedy 122 of these 226 'failed' lines. I presume, therefore, that these 226 lines contain scribal errors. 'Broken-backed' lines occur 118 times; of these, 108 seem to be original.

5. Lydgate's original usage

The accumulated evidence for Lydgate's idiolect includes the following: *love* is usually a monosyllable (as in Chaucer); *han* is the usual form of 'have'; the *-ing* inflexion may often be stressed, as may the final syllable in adjectives ending in *–y*; *hors* and perhaps *force* seem to be disyllabic; *vpon* and *without* are often stressed on the first syllable (as perhaps are *vnto/into*); *ageynes* is nearly always trisyllabic; *many a* will usually elide, as will *fully a*; *evri* is usually/always a disyllable (as in Chaucer); *for to* is stressed on the first element; *sleen* (ppl) is disyllabic as are, apparently, other monosyllables with long vowel; *becaus(e)* is a disyllable; some verb plural forms end in *–en* for metrical convenience, and *hemselven* serves the same purpose. Most significantly, since the word occurs often, 'through' is a monosyllable, represented in several MSS as *throgh, thorgh or thurgh*, though both Ag and Ar99 have *thorough* and spoil the metre.

In addition to recognising these lexical choices Lydgate makes from alternative available forms, it is possible to identify some of Lydgate's metrical habits. Form words are very frequently stressed and thus promoted to carry the beat, and this includes demonstrative adjectives (*that, this*), conjunctions (e.g. *til*) and personal pronouns in all cases; it also includes, and very regularly, prepositions and the copula *and*. The most regular stressing of Classical personal names is on the final syllable in disyllables, on the first and last in trisyllables, and second and last in 4-syllabled names: Hect**or**, **Ach**ill**es**, Phe**bus**, Cal**chas** (not as in Chaucer), **U**-lix**es**, **Pri**am**us**, **An**then**or**, **Pat**ro**clus** and A**ga**me**noun**, though Thoas seems to take stress on either vowel. Once these building-blocks forming the metre have been isolated, a pattern seems to emerge whereby the second line in a couplet with run-on from the first line often begins as headless or with trochaic inversion.

These identifications of Lydgate's linguistic and metrical preferences can often be used to resolve cases where no manuscript seems to have the right form, the 'repairable' or 'remediable' classification in otherwise 'failed' lines.

For example, line 3663 presents the following variation:

Ag Miȝt haue leiser hemsilfe to recure (also Jr, R2)
Kk Myght haue leysere (elision) **hem selven** to recure
Tr (also R1) Might haue leyser hemself to recure
Corrected, the line should read:
*Might *han* leis*er* hem*seluen* *to* recure

One point which becomes clear is that a 'bad' manuscript, such as Kk and the highly inventive Ro2, may quite often carry a right reading, lacking the kinds of additions or respellings the above discussion has identified as typical scribal behaviour: you weigh readings, not manuscripts.

6. Conclusion

What can we say finally about Lydgate as a poet? Of course he wrote fast and often carelessly, and he had inherent faults. The worst of these, I think, is that he nearly always places a phrase division (i.e. caesura) after the third, fifth or seventh position rather than the usual (and Chaucerian) fourth, sixth or eighth; in a headless or broken-backed line, with only 9 positions (syllables), this inevitably gives a trochaic rather than iambic line:

e.g. 3935 *þat ȝe grekis / ga*dred *he*re in *on*
All manuscripts have a headless line here.

This trochaic effect is compounded by the fact that Lydgate also almost invariably has the 'foot pattern' crossing this phrase break, so that the offbeat comprising the start of the third or fourth 'foot' ends one phrase. The beat in sixth or eighth position then begins the new phrase, also contributing to the trochaic feel of the lines:

And þer in / *made non* excep*cio*un

There is one line where the broken-backed effect is justified – a sudden death:

3506 þat *he* fil *ded* // *gruf* vn*to* the *grou*nde.

But ultimately Lydgate's failure is in poetics rather than in prosody. His lines have little poetic density. In Chaucer's verse, it is usual to have four lexical words per line:

General Prologue 17   The *holy* blis*ful* mar*tir* / *for* to *se*ke
Knight's Tale   2773 All*as* the *deeth*, all*as* myn *E*me*ly*e...
                   2775 All*as* myn *her*tes *queen*e / all*as* my *wyf*
                   2776 Myn *her*tes *la*dy / *end*ere *of* my *lyf*.

But in Lydgate's poetry the average seems to be three, or even two, lexical words in the line; and in one horrendous instance in this analysis, one line appears to be entirely composed of form words:

3994 Of *al* þat *eu*ere *þat* I *seid*e ȝ̣ou *her*e
(Ag is so confused by this that he leaves out 'I').

This preponderance of form words means that words not normally stressed are promoted to carry the beat:

3993 So *þat* °e *shal* of *no* þing *be* in *we*re
There are three/four promotions here and only one lexical word.

3827 Of *me* all*as* // *and* of *pa*t*ro*clus

The broken-backed line further deteriorates because the third foot lacks an initial off-beat and then provides the beat itself by promoting the copula.

Ultimately, then, Lydgate did not pack his lines with meaning, and yes, he does seem 'voluminous' in consequence. But I think his ear was good enough. As can be seen, even in the fourteen lines which I attempt to metre in the Appendix, seven emendations have been made to secure metre. Yet each of these emendations follows what, from its frequency elsewhere in the extract from *Troy Book* selected for analysis, seems to be Lydgate's favoured style. Full critical editing of Lydgate's works is essential.[22] A full concordance would be needed of his preferred dialectal and grammatical preferences for each text, obtained from readings where there is no uncertainty about sense or grammatical form, and where manuscripts are either in agreement or direction of variation is undisputed. This would supply evidence for correction of scribal interferences, and might secure a far more favourable view of Lydgate's metrical practice. It will be a mighty task!

---

[22] Also urged by Pearsall in 'Weak declension', p. 190.

Appendix

If the best way to assess verse is to read it, let us try scanning a few lines (here Troilus has just learned of Criseyde's imminent departure):

```
        /  x   /   x  / x   X   x / x
4093 Whan he knewh þe partyng of Cryseyde
        x  /   x  / (x) X  x  /  () x  / x
     Almost for woo  and for peyne he deyde
     x    / x  / x   /  x / x   /
     And fully wyste she departe shal
     X  x  / () x  /  x   /  x /
     By sentence and Iugement fynal
     x X  x  / x  / () x  /  x /
     Of his fader y[3]ove in parlement
      x   /   x   /() x   /   x / x  /
     For which with woѳ and torment al to-rent
        x / x  /   x X x   / () x / x
     He was in poynt[e] to ha[n] falle in Rage
        x  / x   /    () x /x /  x /  x
4100 þat no man myghte apese nor aswage
        x / x  /    x  X x  /   x  / x
     The hydde peyns which in his breest gan dare
      x  /() x /  x   /x() /  x  / x
     For like a man in Furye he gan fare    [?gan he]
     x   /   x  / x /  x    /   x  / x
     And swych[e] sorwe day and nyght to make
      x  /   x  /   x /  x   X x  / x
     In compleynyng oonly for hir[e] sake ²³
        X  /  x / x   X  x   / () x /
     For whan he sa[we] that she shulde away
        x / x () /  x  /   x X x  /
     He levere hadde pleynly for to dey
```

Key: x : offbeat; / : beat; X : promoted syllable; (): elided syllable;
Deleted forms: these signal error followed by emendation.

---

²³ Or: X x   / x   / x X x / x
      In compleynyng oonly for hir sake
   The former is the more grammatical (with oblique form of possessive after preposition) where stress
   on the present participial ending and on the suffix of *oonly* is a type which often occurs in Lydgate; the
   alternative is metrical, but (as also frequently in Lydgate) has two promoted syllables on prepositions.
   Sense would demand emphasis and thus metrical stress on 'her', as in the first option.

And no, the verse is not 'excellent': you cannot read Lydgate aloud confidently; but for all that, Pearsall's more recent view that Lydgate cannot 'have misunderstood everything that Hoccleve understood perfectly' does indeed point the way to a reinterpretation of Lydgate's verse.[24]

---

[24] 'Weak declension', p. 189.

4

William Blissett

"Who Knows Not Colin Clout?" Spenser and the Poets of the Mid-Twentieth Century

Thomas Carlyle to Jane Welsh Carlyle, 12 April 1841: Monckton Milnes "answered me the other day when I asked, If he liked Spenser's Faery Queen? *'Is it as a* public *question that you ask me, or as a private confidential one?' Nobody could answer better."*

Randall Jarrell, Poetry and the Age, *New York, Knopf 1953, 171: "Your readers will have to infer that taste mainly from the more unusual inclusions and omissions of your anthology. (You may leave out James Whitcombe Riley because you are afraid of being laughed at, but if you leave out Spenser you mean business.)"*

"The Poets' Poet": Charles Lamb's phrase for Edmund Spenser is widely known, often kidnapped, sometimes mangled. There is no doubt that Lamb was right on the simplest and most downright plane. Spenser was also called "the Prince of Poets in his Day" and is one of the earliest of the poets buried in Westminster Abbey. The young John Milton fell under the spell of his

> Forests and enchantments drear
> Where more is meant than meets the ear,

and in the controversies of middle life praised "our sage and serious poet Spenser whom I dare be known to think a better teacher than Scotus or Aquinas." "Milton acknowledged to me that Spenser was his original," said Dryden of the poet in old age. Alexander Pope for a lark wrote some Spenserian stanzas descriptive of a London slum and on another occasion read aloud some passages from *The Faerie Queene* to an old lady: "you have shown me a gallery of pictures," she observed. That was in the heyday of the heroic couplet, the metre of broad daylight and full waking consciousness. The eighteenth century was to see the revival of many other verse forms including the Spenserian stanza, with or without Spenser's diction and spelling, with or without the sort of action they called "derring-do." In their different ways, three poets of this time in the Spenserian stanza hold a small but secure place in the wider canon – James Thomson's deliquescent *Castle of Indolence*, William Shenstone's delightful *Schoolmistress*, and *The Minstrel* of James Beattie, a forerunner who decreased as Wordsworth increased.

By a process of metabolism Spenser became part of the substance of Wordsworth and the other Romantics; it would require an extensive study to describe and assess this process. Two lines from *The Prelude*, in tribute from one Cambridge man to another, cannot be left uncited:

> Sweet Spenser, moving through his clouded heaven
> With the moon's beauty and the moon's soft pace.

The lines represent the polar opposite to Milton's "sage and serious poet." Together, the two span the gamut from strength to sweetness, from solar to lunar, from explicit to implicit, from yang to yin.

Hawthorne and Melville, Ruskin, the Pre-Raphaelites in painting and poetry: all are "worthy to be filed" on the Spenserian beadroll, but it is Yeats who stands as the last embodiment of the unbroken Spenserian tradition – before he became one of the first voices of a Modernism that seemed to have no connection with the likes of Spenser. In October of 1902, Walter de la Mare was a young man of 29, Wallace Stevens was 22, Ezra Pound and William Carlos Williams in their late teens, Marianne Moore 15, T. S. Eliot 14. It was then that W. B. Yeats brought out his selection of Spenser in the "Golden Poets" series, with an extended introduction, the essay that takes its place in collections of his prose. The book is a pleasure to handle, with a frontispiece and vignette title by A. S. Hartrick (soon to be David Jones's teacher at Camberwell Art School) and coloured illustrations by Jessie M. King – eight of them, the last melodious gasp of Pre-Raphaelitism, showing the delicacy of Aubrey Beardsley without his indelicacy. Yeats by 1902 was a well-known poet on both sides of the Atlantic, very much a stanzaic and often a narrative poet, in his own way a creator of a land of faerie, though no allegorist. Space does not permit a discussion of either his selection or his comments. What I must do is to quote a great sentence he had published two years earlier, in an essay about "The Symbolism of Poetry." Spenser's name does not appear in the essay; nevertheless, in teaching Spenser, I would dictate this sentence, to make sure it went (at least) into the students' notebooks:

> The purpose of rhythm … is to prolong the moment of contemplation, the moment
> when we are both asleep and awake, which is the one moment of creation, by hushing

us with an alluring monotony, while it holds us waking by variety, to keep us in that state of perhaps real trance, in which the mind, liberated from the pressure of the will, is unfolded in symbols. (*Essays and Introductions*, 159)

I regard this, along with Milton's great phrase and Wordsworth's, as a third apex in an easy and ample enclosure of the poet for our closer acquaintance.

II

As a member of the Department of English in the University of Saskatchewan in the 1950s, I was generously assigned, in alternate years, senior courses in Renaissance Non-Dramatic Literature and in Modern Poetry. The combination of interests made acute the question, Why was Donne then everywhere and Spenser (apparently) nowhere? From this particular question arose my great enquiry, a flotilla of letters which, late in 1954, I sent to all or most of the living poets represented in the *Faber Book of Modern Verse* and its sequel, the *Faber Book of Twentieth-Century Verse*. This was the model, varied from time to time to suit the recipient:

> As you know, Edmund Spenser has long been spoken of as "the poets' poet" because of the esteem in which he has been held by poets of successive literary generations from Milton to Yeats. Since the appearance half a century ago of Yeats's selection, however, Spenser seems more and more to have dropped from notice. I wonder if the old title is still applicable. There is one way to find out, and so I have been writing to some contemporary poets in Canada, Britain, and the United States to ask if they still read and admire Spenser and if they regard the Spenserian tradition as a living one. I would be pleased if you could find time to let me know your thoughts on the subject.

Dylan Thomas had just died. The poets known as the Movement and the Beat were not yet on the scene. In addition to the Faber poets, I reached out to a number of Canadians, and reached back to eminent older figures like Masefield and de la Mare, and included one newcomer whose major poem, *The Anathemata*, I had reviewed, David Jones.

That was probably the last decade in which such an enquiry could be made. Now one would need funding and a staff and letterhead and referees and accounting and computer time and a hubbub of publicity. I sent out almost a hundred letters and received more than forty replies. These replies are, for the most part, not deeply pondered, not meticulously expressed, but they do form a sample of poet readers and non-readers of Spenser. It is well at the outset to keep two things in mind. The first is that any genuine impression of Spenser is bound to be a big impression: *The Shepheardes Calender* is a book-length collection of poems in a wide and adventurous range of verse forms and metres; the *Four Hymns* are more like four cantatas; the *Amoretti* are a full sequence of sonnets; *Prothalamion* and *Epithalamion* are lyrics of great amplitude; and *The Faerie Queene* is the longest poem in the canon. On the other hand, it is well to remember how much of the life of even the most ardent Spenserian (poet or professor or private reader) is *not* spent in reading Spenser, let alone writing about him or in imitation of him.

There must have been many plausible reasons for not replying at all, simple disinclination being the first and strongest. With a few, a desire to say something in one's own time and terms may have been decisive. Such may well have been the case with Auden, of whom it is said that he tried every existing verse-form, though I have found no Spenserian stanza. It is very likely to be the case with William Empson, who was to give a Third Programme talk on Spenser, and with Louis MacNeice, who was to devote one of his Clark Lectures to Spenser and Bunyan. As for T. S. Eliot, then the king of the wood, I decided to include in my survey a letter of considerable length, unsigned, unposted; if asked to testify under oath that I had not written it myself, I would be compelled to equivocate.

Perhaps outweighing, certainly outvoting, the absentees were the poets who replied. Trying to assess the liveliness of a poetic tradition is like trying to assess the efficacy of prayer, but I will make the attempt. What would be proof of a strong conscious Spenserian influence, or evidence at least of a taste for Spenser? Some presence or combination of these elements: a recognition of the magnitude of Spenser's achievement, his mastery of rhyme and stanza and delight in that mastery, his continued allegory and dark conceit, his moral and patriotic motives, his creation, in diction and idiom, in small effect and large, of an imaginary "land of faerie."

In this context of expectation, here in general summary is what I think the letters show. (1) Spenser was well above the horizon for many poets, modern as well as traditional, at a time when he seemed to be at the nadir. (2) He was more read and admired by poets unconnected with universities than by academic poets. (3) The Spenser that was read and admired was "sweet Spenser," not "our sage and serious poet." (4) Most were not influenced to the point of imitation by the most characteristic qualities of Spenser – his allegory or his extended regular verse form. (5) Many of the letters are highly characteristic of the writer and so have a literary value of interest beyond the immediate question.

These replies posed for me an initial problem: shall I wait for the other half? I did wait a long time as the last letters trickled in. Another, related question: shall I acknowledge each one of them promptly? This I ducked, to my lasting shame. All the time I planned the Grand Response that would prove my seriousness and my gratitude. I resolved to read the complete poems, the complete works including letters, the full biographical and critical record, of each poet. Backbreaking!

My back broke. I did it for perhaps a dozen, and then I was caught up in the whirl of other interests, other demands. That project went under. Twenty-five years later I thought to revive it and wrote to survivors and literary executors for permission to quote. That was twenty-five years ago, the silver jubilee, and here I am at the golden.

On this occasion I should like to discuss three respondents: Walter de la Mare from the older generation and, from the poets then in their prime, Robert Penn Warren and Marianne Moore.

III

In November, 1954, the Poet Laureate, John Masefield, wrote: "You ask, 'if I still read and admire Spenser, & think his tradition still a living one?' Yes, I do." At seventy-six he writes like a man of twenty-six who knows his own mind and wields a calligraphy pen with good black ink. In the same month Walter de la Mare, eighty-one and in the last year of his life, wrote thus:

> I think what you say about Edmund Spenser and the present coolness towards him is only temporary – unless humanity is actually going to lose one of its rarest blessings, and *that* would be with its own connivance. You may perhaps have seen an anthology I did years and years ago called *Come Hither*. Unless my memory is as bad as I think it is there's a note about him in it.
>
> And what a strangely solid creature there is on the other side of his incessant honeyed verse. He absolutely insisted on having music wherever he went, and what a time he would have had among the publishers at the present moment. It is this beastly money problem that is putting the worst possible mould on books nowadays.
>
> You will excuse this rather brief reply to your letter I know, but my health is not too good lately, and I have to keep correspondence down to a minimum.
>
> > With all good wishes
> > > Yours sincerely
> > > Walter de la Mare

I am struck by the sentence, "and what a strangely solid creature there is on the other side of his incessant honeyed verse." To call Spenser a "creature," rather than a figure or a person, is to emphasize "strangely" and to empty "solid" of any humdrum heaviness; the addition of "incessant," with its activity of bees and suggestion of their constructive power, prevents "honeyed" from being cloying; and "on the other side" claims Spenser as kin to de la Mare, whose whole art as poet, story-teller and anthologist has been to approach and explore the "other side" in dream, nightmare, vision, his own land of faerie.

Robert Penn Warren wrote me two short friendly letters, thirty years apart. The first, dated 17 December 1954: "Sad to say, I don't take much satisfaction in Spenser. I taught a graduate course involving him, and that may have soured me." The second, dated 4 July 1984: "Sure, you may quote my old comment and my new PS. By the way I gave up teaching Spenser more than forty years ago. All good luck with your book – in which I know I'll be a minority."

Not such a small minority: his friend Allen Tate is with him, and Archibald MacLeish, Richard Eberhart, and others of what may be called the anti-Spenserian generation of poets, largely academic and, within the academy, associated with Modernism (in the dated sense) and the New Criticism (in a sense even more dated). I single him out for that reason and for a second reason, more surprising – that the influence of Spenser is strongly marked in two of his novels.

Appearing first in 1938, with a major revision and expansion in 1952 and so very much current at the time of my enquiry, was a college anthology, *Understanding Poetry*, a teaching anthology with an ingenious apparatus designed to educate the teacher as well as the student, the whole being put together by Cleanth Brooks and Robert Penn Warren. It was something of a manifesto, designed to break the power in departments of English of those whose real interest was in philology, philosophy, sociology or history (or uncritical "appreciation") rather than literature itself, "the poem on the page". Even now, with its long ascendancy gone and its immense influence absorbed, the book remains lively and tendentious. Its clear bias is against the long poem: it is for stone poems not stem poems, gem poems not tree poems, in favour of poems that demand or at least permit close analysis. True, it is on its guard against reducing poems to atomic images ("I'll lug the guts into the neighbour room") and strongly insists on the "organic" nature of the poem, but it clearly prefers the smaller organisms. Of its seven hundred pages, five are given to Spenser, the obligatory *Prothalamion*, with no commentary, no mind-stretching questions.

Spenser is scanted in the anthology, the meagrest representation of any poet of the first rank. It is strange, therefore, that in some early versions of Warren's *All the King's Men* the Huey Long figure, Willie Strong and finally Willie Stark, should have been named Willie Talos, an unmistakeable allusion to the man of metal in the fifth book of *The Faerie Queene*. Not only that: facing the opening page of *World Enough and Time*, there are three stanzas from the proem to the same book, the Legend of Artegall or of Justice. These facts slipped Warren's memory in his candid letters to me. Here I risk a conjecture.

Warren belongs to the first generation in which a man of letters would normally earn his living through a university appointment. Early, as a graduate student specializing in "sixteenth-century non-dramatic poetry," and later as a conductor of seminars, he would need for academic reasons to handle Spenser.

A graduate seminar on Spenser; four students; they read Book I together; each of the students chooses another book to present to the class; the least attractive book is left to the instructor to prepare. He fights it, every canto, every stanza, and vows never again, but it has scarred him with its recalcitrance, its fury, its cussedness – those very qualities he needed to evoke, at least twice, in his fiction. To use a favourite word of Brooks and Warren, it is "ironic."

The grim figure of Talus lodges in his memory, even the fact that the original Talos was a bronze monster given by Hephaestos to Minos to guard the shores of Crete. In Spenser, Artegall is the chivalric champion and embodiment of the virtue of justice, and Talus is his groom, an iron man armed with a flail, in the allegory quite clearly and consistently a figure of Law Enforcement, civil and military. His actions, always in execution of law, are simple, rigorous, forceful, severe – so severe that he needs to be reined in from time to time. Any Spenserian can see how inapplicable the name of Talus, or Talos, is to such an unprincipled opportunist, such an inspired scamp, so human and erring a figure as Willie Stark. The Talus notion was untenable from the outset, and yet it remained almost until the end – and seems to have troubled none of Warren's critics. How could so careful and critical a handler of texts have slipped up? Simply by not going back: the fifth book of *The Faerie Queene* must have made a strong initial impression of the welter of violent and fraudulent politics under the eyes of Justice, but not strong enough to recall the figure of the rigid, single-issue, law-and-order sheriff. In contrast, the three stanzas on justice prefixed to *World Enough and Time* point to no particular character or incident in Spenser's poem but prepare the reader for a serious probing of justice and the conduct of life in a turbulent and obdurate world.

IV

Had we but world enough and time, we might look at five non-academic American poets who responded positively to Spenser – Ezra Pound, Wallace Stevens, E. E. Cummings, William Carlos Williams, and Marianne Moore. The strictures of this paper narrow it down to one.

Randall Jarrell playfully referred to some of Marianne Moore's poems as "postcards to the nicer animals." Here is her postcard to me:

> Dear Mr Blissett,
>   I could never tire of Spenser, read
> him with zest, hope, and somehow suspect,
> that that is how you feel.

Incidental references to Spenser are to be found scattered in her prose writings; no reference at all in the five hundred pages of her *Selected Letters*, surprising until we read in the introduction how small a selection this is, chosen mainly, and rightly, for its biographical interest. And then there is the poem "Spenser's Ireland." It was first published in *Furioso*, Summer 1941, and has appeared in many anthologies as well as her own collections, and so it is very much a favourite poem. "The greenest place I've never seen" is on its way to becoming as memorable as "imaginary gardens with real toads in them." The poet herself in her meticulous way supplies a note to some phrases and notions – to an illustrated article on Ireland by Donn Byre in the *National Geographic*, to a lecture she heard by the Irish-American poet Padraic Colum, to *Happy Memories* by Denis O'Sullivan, and to two novels by Maria Edgeworth. All have "gusto" or "zest", that combination of appetite and good taste and quiet enthusiasm that Moore prized, and all put one in an Irish mood.

To that short list must be added Spenser's *View of the Present State of Ireland*. It affords the quirky sort of information she pounces on – about the Irish loose cloak under which weapons could be concealed – but displays no zest. Spenser's *View* is a useful account of the difficulties faced by the occupying power in its attempts to bring peace, order, and good government to a savage people – *salvage* in the older sense of a people of the *silva*, woods, hedges, wilds. There is nothing in it that may be called greenery or kindness, such as belong to the world of the *Epithalamion*, that grandly achieved happy poem set in greenest, kindest Ireland.

Moore's poem "Spenser's Ireland" begins with a sort of Irish bull, the famous line about Ireland's unseen greenness being preceded by the statement that Spenser's Ireland remains unaltered, "a place as kind as it is green". Poems are not affidavits, however: never having seen it, Moore cannot really vouch for its greenness, or its kindness; and at the end, after many hindrances, she writes: "The Irish say your trouble is their / trouble and your / joy their joy? I wish / I could believe it. I'm dissatisfied, I'm Irish."

Underlying the poem, deeply present even if Spenser's name had not been its title, is a stanzaic form analogous to Spenser's and a rhythm comparable to his. It is in six stanzas, of eleven lines each, most of the respective lines matching in syllabic count their five siblings. As in Spenser, the last line of each stanza is the longest.

Another consideration: English is an emphatic, stressed, explosive language. Of its great poets, Spenser (having got *The Shepheardes Calender* and *Mother Hubberds Tale* out of his system) gives the smoothest ride. While the Spenserian stanza is capable of an astonishing range of effects, Wordsworth was right about its salient virtue of sound and movement – "the moon's beauty and the moon's soft pace."

Several modern poets have worked independently to reduce the insistent regular beat or thump of the pentameter, "Penty" in Ezra Pound's sassy term. Two pioneers, Hopkins explored the direction of more stress and Bridges that of less. Eliot, under strong French influence, began his career by achieving a level English alexandrine with the "patient etherized" line (and its predecessor) from "The Love Song of J. Alfred Prufrock," ending it with another, "Both intimate and unidentifiable." What may well have attracted Eliot to Moore early on, and led him to publish her *Selected Poems* (1935) with his introduction, was her mastery of the light touch. She combines compression, that "first grace of style," with delicacy, "soft pace."

In delivering this paper in Lund, I closed by reading out Moore's poem as well as I could, believing as I do that to be the best way to support one's observations. I would urge any interested reader to follow the same procedure and read some Moore and Spenser aloud. At approximately half an hour a day, the whole of *The Faerie Queene* can be delivered orally in seventy-four days.

5

Nicholas von Maltzahn

Liberalism or Apocalypse?
John Milton and Andrew Marvell

John Milton and Andrew Marvell have long been claimed for the tradition of liberalism. But their contrasting examples should enlarge our conception of the seventeenth-century English prelude to the liberal tradition, however much their intersecting careers and personal association have led commentators to collapse important religious and political distinctions between them. Elsewhere I have explored some telling differences in their views on toleration and the English church.[1] The present argument turns on their differing responses to the shift from confessional to interest politics, the latter being the emerging idiom of international relations after the Treaties of Westphalia (1648) and one that left an important legacy to later liberalism. Revealing of their differences are Milton and Marvell's services to the state in the 1650s, not least in Baltic affairs during the long contest as to whether Sweden or Denmark might control the Sound (the Öresund) that runs between them. That contest came to a head with the Danish declaration of war against Sweden in June 1657; two months later, Marvell formally joined Milton in secretarial service to Oliver Cromwell's Protectorate.

At issue for the English in the 1650s were conflicting world-views, between an older vision of politics based on confessional concerns—Protestant against Roman Catholic—and a newer one based on economic interest. In sum, Milton favoured a religious perspective on geopolitics, which we may style his universalism. This is the apocalypse of my title, in which international relations are seen as contributing to an unveiling of final Truth. Marvell favoured a more secular perspective, which we may style his particularism or relativism. This is the liberalism of my title, in which allowance is made for difference of national characters and purposes, for the rule of contingency, and for the coexistence of contending truths.

---

[1] 'Milton, Marvell and Toleration', in *Milton and Toleration*, ed. Sharon Achinstein and Elizabeth Sauer (Oxford: Oxford University Press, 2007), pp. 86-104; 'Ruining the Sacred Truths? Marvell's Milton and Cultural Memory', in *Writing and Religion in England, 1558-1689*, ed. Roger Sell and Anthony Johnson (London: Ashgate, 2008).

Milton and Marvell are thus on different sides of that great watershed in early modern international relations, the Treaties of Westphalia, which in 1648 at last brought the Thirty Years War to an end and introduced what was thought of as something like a New World Order. Milton holds to an older conception of the international Protestant brotherhood, in keeping with his youthful preoccupation with Protestant fortunes in the Thirty Years War.[2] Marvell, by contrast, becomes a proponent of what may be called 'modern reason', notably in the assessment of international politics in his late prose work, *An Account of the Growth of Popery and Arbitrary Government*, and also in his other pamphlets challenging High Church pretensions in the 1670s.

It is not only the meeting of the 2007 IAUPE conference in Lund that invites attention to Milton and Marvell's relation to the Öresund. The Danish-Swedish conflict was a major episode in that astonishing emergence of Sweden as a world power in the seventeenth century, a power that developed as quickly as it then ended. In the east, Riga had been taken only in 1621; it was lost in 1710. By the death of Karl XII in 1718, the wild career of that king and more generally of the Swedish empire might exemplify the vanity of human wishes, as when Samuel Johnson in his poem of that title recalls of the 'Swedish Charles': 'He left the Name, at which the World grew pale, / To point a Moral, or adorn a Tale.'[3] Milton and Marvell's involvement with this geopolitical convulsion followed from their careers as state servants. Their service will first find description here, with a view to then comparing their divergent responses to the changing politics of the Cromwellian Protectorate. In the 1650s, the conflict between Lutheran Sweden and Lutheran Denmark challenged the confessional basis of English foreign policy. Where Milton remained a useful mouthpiece for apocalyptic rhetoric, Marvell came to enjoy a suppler role as an interest politician. By way of conclusion, this comparison of their politics invites consideration also of these poets' contrasting fortunes in later literary history, which revealingly reflect their differing positions. Milton's apocalypticism lent itself to appropriation by the later esteem for the Sublime, his older religious politics inviting aestheticization in a way that Marvell's newer politics did not.

I

Andrew Marvell spent Christmas week, 1664, not far from Lund. He had just

---

[2] This finds fuller description in Nicholas von Maltzahn, 'Blank Verse and the Nation: Milton and his Imitators,' in *Early Modern Nationalism and Milton's England*, ed. Paul Stevens and David Loewenstein (Toronto: University of Toronto Press, 2008).

[3] Samuel Johnson, *Poems*, ed. David Nichol Smith and Edward L. McAdam (Oxford: Oxford University Press, 1974), 'Vanity of Human Wishes', lines 221-2.

sailed up the Sound to Helsingør, and was at anchor there along the Danish coast. His ship was awaiting a change in the weather to allow it around the cape at Elsinore, so that it might sail away northwest, back across the North Sea to London. Marvell was nearing the end of eighteen months of travels, chiefly to Russia and then to Sweden and Denmark, as secretary to a grand English embassy to those nations led by the Earl of Carlisle.[4] In Russia, Marvell's services as a humanist secretary had proved a liability. For in Moscow the Renaissance never arrived. The result had been that Marvell's Latin contributions in negotiation only invited the Russians' mischief, as they ferreted for breaches of protocol with which to frustrate the English mission. But then, after the rigours of Moscow, how pleasant at last to reach Swedish territory late in the summer of 1664. Already in Riga the welcome was agreeably warm. In Stockholm, the English found that French manners mingled pleasingly with Lutheran piety.[5] Thereafter in Copenhagen the hospitality was also lavish, with the first three days spent in entertainments that one participant recalled as 'Bacchanalian'.[6] Moreover, in Stockholm and in Copenhagen Marvell's courtly Latin and French served much better, even if, at both these courts, the diplomacy remained somewhat ceremonial with nothing much to conclude.

How did Marvell now amuse himself at anchor in Elsinore? Did he play with the tame bears aboard the ship, a pair brought back from Russia, one playful as a spaniel (we are told) and the other eager to 'suck peoples fingers'? Did he ponder Hamlet's case as he looked across to the battlements of the Kronborg? Did he guess already that this was the end of his own career as a state servant?

Six years before, Marvell had already been immersed in Baltic business, late in the Protectorate. He had in revolutionary times long sought service to the House of Cromwell. In 1657 he won his way into the secretariat for foreign languages. There he worked for the skilful secretary of state John Thurloe, this in harness with the blind Milton. Marvell was now, as a royalist report had recently termed him, a 'notable English Italo-Machavillian.'[7] And he needed to be Machiavellian in his new employment. New lessons were being learnt in international politics.

For this was just the point when interest politics found freer expression in English foreign policy with the unravelling of Cromwellian confessional objectives.

[4] This and related details are chronicled in my *Andrew Marvell Chronology* (Basingstoke: Palgrave, 2005), pp. 74-88.
[5] For how expensive and sophisticated a city Stockholm now quickly became, see Michael Roberts, *The Swedish Imperial Experience, 1560-1718* (Cambridge: Cambridge University Press, 1979), p. 138.
[6] Guy Miège, *A Relation Of Three Embassies From his Sacred Majestie Charles II to the Great Duke of Muscovie, The King of Sweden, and The King of Denmark* (London, 1669), pp. 382-3.
[7] Letter from James Scudamore (Saumur) to Sir Richard Browne (Paris), 15 August 1656 (British Library, Add. MS 15858, fo. 135, Elsie Duncan-Jones, 'Marvell in 1656', *Times Literary Supplement*, 2 Dec. 1949, 791).

The almost Elizabethan foreign policy that had so dominated proceedings earlier in the 1650s—hostile to Spain, dangerously indulgent of France—now gave way to a bracing *Realpolitik*. During Marvell's employment, the old confessional war with Spain and some dubious compromises with France were superseded by the contest between Lutheran Sweden and Lutheran Denmark, especially over Baltic trade. This struggle brought into focus 'the conflict between an older vision of politics based on universalist concerns and one based on economic interest.'[8]

Marvell's education in these points shows in his state service in the late Protectorate. Take, for example, the longest single manuscript we have in his distinctive hand. This is his translation early in 1658 of a Swedish tract which explains how what might seem an intra-confessional contest between Lutheran Sweden and Lutheran Denmark was in fact still an inter-confessional one. Probably based on a Latin document presented by the Swedish envoy to England, Johann Friderich von Friesendorff, this forty-page text is revealingly entitled 'The Justice of the Swedish Cause and the danger of the Protestant Cause involved therein'.[9] It repeatedly speaks to vying interests as determining international relations: 'the interest of the House of Austria' here jostles with those of Sweden, Poland, Denmark, Holland, and England, with the Swede at another point cautioning those who would 'so labour most earnestly against their own interest'.[10] On this basis, the tract asks Cromwell to act on the common Anglo-Swedish interest, and to join his navy with that of Sweden to overcome those of Holland and Spain. The Dutch had, with Danish support, long dominated the Baltic trade. Moreover, with the Danish-Swedish conflict of the 1650s the English had lost access to the Baltic, which had been valuable for many reasons but especially for strategic naval supplies unavailable elsewhere—think of Satan's spear in *Paradise Lost*, which Milton compares to 'the tallest Pine / Hewn on Norwegian hills, to be the Mast / Of some great Ammiral' (*PL*, 1:292-4). Though it hurts the metre, this might as well read 'Swedish hills', for that is what Milton had in view: in parliamentary debate in February 1658/9, just when Milton may well have been working on Book One of *Paradise Lost*, lasting concerns were again raised about the potential 'ruin of our shipping; hemp, pitch, tar, cordage and mast, coming all from thence'.[11]

---

[8] Steven Pincus, 'From holy cause to economic interest: the study of population and the invention of the state,' *A Nation Transformed: England after the Restoration*, ed. Steven Pincus and Alan Houston (Cambridge: Cambridge University Press, 2001), pp. 283-4.

[9] British Library, Add. MS 4459, fos. 175-196v, much of which is published in *Prose Works of Andrew Marvell*, ed. Annabel Patterson, Martin Dzelzainis, Nicholas von Maltzahn, Neil Keeble, 2 vols (New Haven: Yale University Press, 2003), vol. 1, pp. 441-9. First noted by Hilton Kelliher, 'Some Notes on Andrew Marvell,' *British Library Journal*, 4 (1978), 130-3.

[10] British Library, Add. MS 4459, fos. 176v, 179v, 188r.

[11] *Diary of Thomas Burton*, ed. J.T. Rutt, 4 vols (London), vol. 3, pp. 376-84 [esp. 380], 460: 21 February (Thurloe) and 24 February 1658/9 (Lenthall).

The Swedish Friesendorff pictures his nation's struggle with Denmark as a continuation of the Thirty Years War. Hence his relation of the Swedish national cause to the Protestant international one, of the particular to the universal. He thought he knew his audience. So to construe the Danish alliance with the Dutch as just a manifestation of Spanish power spoke to lasting Cromwellian concerns. And that this was a Cromwellian rather than any republican concern appeared in later debate. Henry Neville, for example, trenchantly observed of the dispute: 'I can see nothing [in it] of religion or Protestant religion. There are Calvinists and Lutherans on both sides. Brandenburgh, Holland, Denmark, are all Protestants; and as good, if not better than the Swede; and therefore I cannot see how the Protestant religion is particularly concerned in this.'[12] Indeed, the idea that either Dane or Dutchman was Spanish in his allegiance may surprise us. But the English of that date were accustomed to think in such terms by the propaganda of the Anglo-Dutch Wars, whether in the First Anglo-Dutch War earlier in the 1650s or the Second later in the 1660s. The Dutch quest for commercial supremacy was seen as of a piece with the machinations of 'the Austrian and Spanish faction'.[13] Thus the successful Orange party—helped by Jesuits, it was thought, to prepare the Dutch for absolute monarchy—might seem Spanish through and through. As for the Danes, in addition to abetting the Dutch, they had betrayed the Protestant cause in the Thirty Years War, it was claimed, by making peace with the House of Austria.[14] Nor did Friesendorff fail to remind the English that they had paid the Danegelt in times past.[15]

There is a telling balance in Marvell's list of expenses for reimbursement for the first year of his state service, 1657-8.[16] To the favoured Swedish envoys, he made over twenty visits. To the unfavoured Danish he made only four. Thurloe drafted a treaty of an Anglo-Swedish alliance not long after Marvell did Friesendorff's work. The Swedish king's daring winter campaign forced the Danes' consent by the end of February 1658 to the Treaty of Roskilde, which the English helped to broker. The consequence was that Skåne, the last of the Danish provinces on the eastern side of the Sound, was eventually ceded to Sweden. Marvell's secretarial duties that spring involved further Baltic work, including the drafting of instructions to the English

---

[12] *Burton's Diary*, vol. 3, 387-8: 21 Feb. 1658/9 (Neville).

[13] *Prose Works of Andrew Marvell*, 1:448; Steven Pincus, *Protestantism and Patriotism: Ideologies and the Making of English Foreign Policy, 1650-1668* (Cambridge: Cambridge University Press, 1996), pp. 190-1.

[14] *Prose Works of Andrew Marvell*, 1:442-4.

[15] Add. MS. 4459, fo. 187r: 'What spoyles it fetchd out of England ... exercising a piracy rather then a dominion over it even that Danish mony which at this day retains its name with you (the memory of which a singular providence of God seemeth to have preserved each to these times that by most just reason and with greater applause of the people it may be exacted against them) bearing sufficient witnesse.'

[16] London, Public Record Office, SP18/200/188; von Maltzahn, *Chronology*, p. 53.

envoy to the King of Sweden, then later serving as a go-between with the agent of the Elector of Brandenburg, as well as handling correspondence from Lübeck and communicating authorization for the export of gunpowder to the Duke of Holstein.[17]

With the Treaty of Roskilde, the Dutch were to be removed from the balance of power; but the Swedes soon overreached in attempting to improve on that success, thereby offering the Dutch fresh opportunity to project their power. So it followed that some months later in the summer of 1658, Marvell was ceremoniously greeting the Dutch ambassador in Cromwell's name (and this from the sumptuous Protectoral barge).[18] The ambassador Nieupoort came to protest that England should act as guarantor of the treaty it had helped to broker; he knew to play the Protestant card in dealing with Cromwell, who held the Dutchman in high esteem. When the Dutch then came to the relief of beleaguered Copenhagen, thus forcing the Swedes in 1659 to renew the terms of Roskilde in the Treaty of The Hague, we soon find Marvell at Whitehall translating from Latin a 'further agreement upon the Treaty at the Hague' then to be read and approved in what was left of the English Parliament.[19] In this complex run of international relations, the apocalyptic certainty of Cromwellian foreign policy had given way to the contingency of negotiating interests, economic and national.[20] After Oliver Cromwell's death, Richard Cromwell's succession marked the high point of Marvell's career in public service, which now included his election as a Cromwellian placeman to the English parliament, even as, in 1659, political and constitutional confusions were mounting. Soon that parliament was dissolved by the Army and now Marvell's status at Whitehall suffered owing to his association with the House of Cromwell, which was forced out of power.[21]

So Marvell, though it was not his only obligation, had a place at what we may term the Baltic 'Desk' at Whitehall. With him there was the blind Milton, although Milton, as ever, was a special case. Yet his Baltic connections too are considerable. In his service as Latin Secretary, Milton had a hand in many documents going out to and coming back from Sweden and Denmark in particular.[22]

---

[17] von Maltzahn, *Chronology*, pp. 50, 53, 55, 58 (Holstein was now alarmed by Swedish preparations; Thomas Birch, ed., *A Collection of the State Papers of John Thurloe*, 6 vols, 1742, vol. 6, p. 35).

[18] von Maltzahn, *Chronology*, p. 52.

[19] Oxford, Bodleian MS Rawl. A66, fo. 15; Kelliher, 'Some Notes on Andrew Marvell', 132.

[20] There has been a lasting debate over confessional solidarity versus trade rivalry as the causes of these conflicts, and concerning the Anglo-Dutch wars the recent swing has been to emphasize the political (Pincus, *Protestantism and Patriotism*), with still newer work considering trade anew (Bangor, Wales: 1670s Conference, 25 July 2007 session with Gijs Rommelse, Michel Reinders, David Onnekink). Nor is it novel to propose both, as Sir Charles Firth did a century ago; see the preliminary discussion in Michael Roberts, 'Cromwell and the Baltic', *English Historical Review*, 76 (1961), 402-5.

[21] von Maltzahn, *Chronology*, pp. 53-60.

[22] Robert Fallon, *Milton in Government* (University Park: Pennsylvania State University Press, 1995), pp. 100-11, 160-76.

We know from his Sonnet 18, to his former pupil, now friend, Cyriack Skinner, that he might wish relief from all the talk of 'what the Swede intend and what the French'—probably at the time when Karl X had come to the Swedish throne, enjoying military success in Poland in 1655 before it all went wrong in the winter of 1655-6. And the next year it seems to be Karl X's reckless military career that Milton has in mind when admonishing his sometime pupil, Richard Jones: 'The victories of princes, which you praise, and similar matters in which force prevails I would not have you admire too much... For what is remarkable if strong horns spring forth in the land of mutton-heads which can powerfully butt down cities and towns?'[23] Milton's misgivings about Karl X may have been aggravated by that warrior-king's departure from the example of Queen Christina. On her Milton had lavished praise in his *Defensio secunda*, this before her abdication and in part because she had at her court discountenanced Milton's adversary Salmasius after Milton's annihilating attack on him in the great first *Defensio*.[24]

About the Danes, Milton had more lasting suspicions still. Charles I's dynastic relation to the Danish throne had in 1642 led that desperate king to seek the assistance of his Danish uncle. When Charles I turned, as Milton put it, to warring upon his own subjects, the English king did so by sending 'an Agent with letters of the King of Denmark, requiring aid against the parlament; [which] aid was comming, when Divine providence to divert them, sent a sudden torrent of Swedes into the bowels of Denmark.'[25] This bitter resentment against the king's efforts once more 'to bring in ... our old Invaders the Danes upon us' sharpened Milton's denunciation of Charles I's attempts 'to gaine assistance from the King of Denmark'.[26] The Danes' close alliance with the Dutch in the 1650s much aggravated the fault. As a historian, Milton in the late 1650s took a dark view of the Danish yoke laid on England before the Conquest—the present occasion for thus recalling the Danish imposition has been overlooked by students of Milton's *History of Britain*—and he could fault Lund's own King Canute in censorious republican comment on the 'Court-Parasites' attending the monarchy of that day.[27]

Milton was of course no bad Latin Secretary to whom to turn in cloaking more secular interest in confessional terms. Whatever the impediment of his need in

---

[23] 21 Sept. 1656: thus translated from the Latin in *Complete Prose Works of John Milton*, gen. ed. D.M. Wolfe, 8 vols (New Haven: Yale University Press, 1953-1982), vol. 7, p. 493.

[24] William Riley Parker, *Milton: A Biography*, rev. Gordon Campbell (Oxford: Oxford University Press, 1996), pp. 387-8 and note, 409, 440-1.

[25] Milton, *Complete Prose Works*, 3:449.

[26] Milton, *Complete Prose Works*, 3:538, 541; 4:522.

[27] Nicholas von Maltzahn, *Milton's* History of Britain: *Republican Historiography in the English Revolution* (Oxford: Oxford University Press, 1991), pp. 168-73; Milton, *Complete Prose Works*, 5:257-367, 365-6.

blindness for an amanuensis, of which slow and insecure arrangement a Swedish diplomat complained,[28] here his usefulness is not in doubt. For if Cromwell eventually much complicated his foreign policy,[29] Milton was employed on translations that sound a simpler note, however accomplished their Latin. Throughout the state letters, the objectives still seem chiefly confessional ones, the public face of Cromwell and Thurloe's increasingly elaborate assessments of contending international interests. Prevailing in these public pronouncements is concern over any battle between Protestants, driven by the fear that 'Spanish Arts' might again divide and conquer them.[30] This becomes a frequent theme after the accession of the warlike Karl X in 1654. And most of Milton's letters the next year (1655) concern the attempt to rally Protestants against a common enemy, in this case the Duke of Savoy whose massacre in Piedmont occasioned so many stateletters as well as Milton's famous sonnet lamenting that confessional cleansing.[31] Milton's own long hopes of an international Protestant alliance, and recognition that they might not be realized, show in an earlier note of self-correction in his commonplace-book: 'From a league with just any Protestants, no matter which ones, not all things are to be hoped for.'[32] But in his state service, this reserve is not often expressed.

Hence the early success of the Karl X's attack on the Poles is viewed in apocalyptic terms, as Cromwell's Milton, or Milton's Cromwell, expressed them in a letter of congratulation. 'We do not doubt,' Cromwell attests, 'that the tearing away by your arms of the kingdom of Poland from the command of the Pope, as if from the horned beast, and the making of peace with the Duke of Brandenburg, will have great importance for the peace and advantage of the church'.[33] The next letter to the King of Sweden in the Miltonic state papers again emphasizes Cromwell's hope for 'a perpetual course of victories against all the enemies of the church', to which end a treaty was prepared for the Anglo-Swedish alliance of the spring of 1656, with which Milton assisted.[34] There might thus be

---

[28] Christer Bonde to Karl X (25 April 1656 n.s.), Michael Roberts, *Swedish Diplomats at Cromwell's Court*, Camden Society 4th Series, 36 (London: Historical Society, 1988), p. 282. Was this envoy at all placated by the letter praising his service that Cromwell in Milton's translation supplied, 30 July 1656?

[29] Roberts, 'Cromwell and the Baltic'.

[30] 178v.

[31] On May 25th 1655, letters went out to Sweden, Holland, Switzerland, and Denmark, insisting on the common Protestant cause; letters were also sent to the French to demand action on behalf of 'your allies and confederates who follow the reformed religion' and of French Protestants too (Milton, *Complete Prose Works*, 5:699-700).

[32] Milton, *Complete Prose Works*, 1:502.

[33] Milton, *Complete Prose Works*, 5:722 (7 Feb. 1655/6). I shall continue to quote from this translation, whatever the paradox of thus representing Milton's Latin, which itself translated Cromwellian English.

[34] Milton, *Complete Prose Works*, 5:732 (19 April 1656) and 733-4 (ca. 22 April).

some attempt to recall the Dutch to a common confessional purpose: later that summer, a state letter to the Dutch goes through the list of Spanish iniquities, now including the massacre in Piedmont since that violation might be claimed to have come at the Spanish behest, even as Cromwell seeks to stop the Dutch from troubling the Swedes, now engaged in the holy fight against 'the Pope's religion'. A contemporary state letter to Karl X, while bearing congratulations on the Swedes' victories over common enemies, soon addresses the Swedish/Dutch antagonism resulting from the disputed Baltic trade, but construes this in terms of 'the highest interests of Protestants'.[35] In the shift from confessional to interest politics, such a mixed idiom was common. 'The common bond of religion' might likewise be urged upon the Danes—again 'the highest interests of Protestants' are cited—but everywhere Cromwell-Milton saw at work 'the counsels of the Spaniards and of the Roman Pontiff'.[36]

In his confessional emphasis in these letters, Milton – with the government of the day – seems to refuse the new, more secular language of interest that now increasingly prevailed elsewhere. But the terms that Cromwell propounds, and Milton with him, in insisting on confessional solidarity belie the actual intricacy of Cromwell's later maneuvres. Milton's Cromwellian broadcasts favouring international Protestantism prove to be increasingly at odds with the more complex assessment of interests informing the messages conveyed through the back-channels of diplomacy.

II

Interest politics had come of age with the Treaties of Westphalia that concluded the Thirty Years War in 1648. The anarchic interplay of contending interests had seemed a baffling world set against the certainties of faith. But might the problem be not that people had been too much wedded to their own interests, but rather too little? If interest itself were seen as the common denominator in international relations, and if it were subjected to more careful analysis, might some order be imposed on this disorder after all? A more particular politics respecting interests at the local or national or international level could contribute to some better overall stability.

The new relativism marked a breach with the universalizing claims of earlier confessional politics. What is proclaimed here is not the reign of Christ but 'of market economies and sovereign politics,' nation vying with nation[37]—and

---

[35] Milton, *Complete Prose Works*, 5:754 ('Protestantium summae rei').
[36] Milton, *Complete Prose Works*, 5:777-9 (4 Dec. 1656).
[37] John Milbank, *Theology and Social Theory: Beyond Secular Reason* (Oxford: Blackwell, 1990), p. 5.

an inclination to religious toleration designed not, as with Milton, to foster an unencumbered dialogue for Truth, but rather to allow an agreement to disagree along the lines that Marvell affirms. This more passive toleration begins to resemble liberalism.

Continental diplomats, many of whom had played a part in establishing the Westphalian states-system, were surprised to discover in the 1650s how ignorant the English might be of those treaties. One English diplomat somehow kept calling the Treaty of Osnabrück the Treaty of Augsburg. And in London its terms seemed strangely unknown.[38] In the Westphalian invention of modern international relations the English had no part; they had had too many distractions of their own in the 1640s, not least in 1648 when the treaties were signed. But those long negotiations had proved something like a university course in international relations for many continental diplomats of that date.

Milton does not much use the word 'interest' and not at all in his poetry. Where he does use it in his prose the inflection is normally negative. For Milton, interest connotes what he terms a 'politick',[39] 'disjoynt' and 'privat', worldly self-concern,[40] apart from true religion or 'the Peoples good'.[41] In one of the divorce tracts, for instance, he compares 'the impunity of wickedness' with 'the duties of true charity; which preferrs public honesty before private interest'.[42] Elsewhere, it is the Jesuits' corrupt 'Church-Interest' that animates their murders of kings and magistrates.[43] That churchmen should ever resort to the language of interest Milton also deplores.[44] Moreover, his conception of public interest is that it is ideally indivisible, as when, very late in the second edition of the *Readie and Easie Way*, he adds a final fantasy of rectified commonwealth, imagining the removal of 'all distinction of lords and commoners, that may any way divide or sever the publick interest'.[45]

Even in the few places where Milton does come closer to interest analysis, the very exceptions prove the rule. He cites the king's interest as being at odds with that of the people, for example, but does so not to balance royal against popular concerns but to mock the king's self-aggrandizing ways. Correcting the king's avowal of his own and his children's interest, Milton's harsh rebuke is that 'All men by thir own and thir Childrens interest are oblig'd to honestie and justice: but how little that consideration works in privat men, how much less in Kings,

---

[38] Roberts, 'Cromwell and the Baltic', 410.
[39] *Complete Prose Works*, 1:574, 3:343.
[40] *Complete Prose Works*, 3:255, 383.
[41] *Complete Prose Works*, 3:307.
[42] *Complete Prose Works*, 2:467.
[43] *Complete Prose Works*, 3:316.
[44] *Complete Prose Works*, 3:319.
[45] *Complete Prose Works*, 7:461.

thir deeds declare best.'[46] The only true interest can be salvation, in this universalizing perspective. Milton also sneers at Charles I's self-indulgent professions of 'his own interests' even as that king faults 'the interest of Parties' in Parliament.[47] Elsewhere, Milton may in mockery speak as if from the perspective of others who think only in terms of 'interest' (the Scots, for example, or Irish Presbyterians), and again reveals his confessional frame of reference, as when he decries the King's going to war 'to the interest of Papists more then of Protestants.'[48] Milton did not succumb to the new fashion for viewing interests more positively, as something that rightly analysed and balanced might generate peace between nations and within them.

Marvell, by contrast, seems to have been all too ready to adopt this language. With the restoration of English Charles II to the throne in May 1660, this interest-politician had to apply his 'Italo-Machavillian' skills to a fresh set of challenges and opportunities. He reinvented himself as a busy Member of Parliament, eventually turning, in the ever longer periods between parliamentary sessions, to that career as a controversialist for which he became famous before his death in 1678. Here a significant feature is the language of interest-politics – both in positive applications, whether in national or international affairs, and in satirical mockery of those pretending to high-minded disinterest.

The effect is enhanced by Marvell's talent for ironic sympathy: he can represent his adversaries almost as if they were high-minded and not just high-handed— only then, of course, to expose such delusion as scarcely veiling the most naked private interest, privately conducted for private ends. In *The Rehearsal Transprosed* he differentiates sharply between the clerical and the Protestant interest. Similarly, in his twinned tracts of the mid-1670s, *Mr. Smirke* and the *Short Historical Essay*, Marvell can scourge 'the false and secular interest of the clergy'.[49] But if that ethical contempt for self-interest recalls Milton's hostile view—likewise Marvell's concern lest 'temporal Interests' interfere with any 'man's Eternity and Salvation'[50]—more telling is Marvell's readiness to dispense with these niceties.

And in the letters of Marvell the MP and London agent for Yorkshire concerns, following interest is just the way of the world. He very often considers issues in these terms, with the international application emerging – especially in the 1670s, as parliament came to play a more insistent part in foreign affairs. In Marvell's letters, he very often refers to personal, commercial, corporate, municipal, regional, and national interests, with the explanatory force of 'interest'

---

[46] *Complete Prose Works*, 3:357, see also 3:417, 478, 487.
[47] *Complete Prose Works*, 3:307, 417.
[48] *Complete Prose Works*, 3:319, 330, 493, 420.
[49] Marvell, *Prose Works*, 2:52, 129.
[50] Marvell, *Prose Works*, 2:147.

understood to be great regardless of whether he corresponds with friends, with the Hull corporation, or with the Hull Trinity House.

The discussion of national interests finds its fullest expression in Marvell's most influential work, *An Account of the Growth of Popery and Arbitrary Government*. From the opening sentence of the *Account*, the language of interest is pervasive, both where Marvell speaks in his own voice and where he ventriloquizes other parliamentarians speaking for England's interest. Thus Marvell's analysis of the Triple Alliance between Sweden, Holland, and England soon focuses on how this observed the interests of all three nations—and on this point he is happy to follow the influential analysis of national interests by François Paul de Lisola, which centred in a hostile assessment of French ambitions.[51] Again and again 'the Interest of England' finds emphasis.[52] At the same time, Marvell uncovers the operations of the French interest internationally or, closer to home, 'the French and Popish Interest' at work in the English court.[53] Revealing too is his use now of the phrase 'National Interest of Religion', in which the confessional is subordinated to the national, rather than vice versa. Interest alone might reliably measure national intention and action, as in the newly frequent proverb, 'Interest will not lye'.[54] And we may note that Marvell, who had in the 1650s translated the Swedish appeal for a war against Holland and Spain, in the 1670s became an avid proponent of Holland and Spain, and for the Dutch seems to have served as an informant or more.[55] For faced with French aggression, the Dutch interest and the Spanish interest and the English interest were now in his view one and the same. The still 'Italo-Machavillian' Marvell was keenly concerned with the contending interests poised in the post-Westphalian balance of power.

III

Milton's resistance to 'interest' facilitated his success as sublime poet, especially as English and then British tradition aestheticized his epic in the later seventeenth

---

[51] Marvell, *Prose Works*, 2:276. Lisola's influential works were variously disseminated in this period; see especially *The Buckler of State* (London, 1667) and the context of its English reception as described by Steven Pincus, 'From Butterboxes to Wooden Shoes: The Shift in English Popular Sentiment from anti-Dutch to anti-French in the 1670s', *Historical Journal*, 38 (1995), 333-361 [342].

[52] Marvell, *Prose Works*, 2:252, 336. In response the Crown too might study interest, as when it now claimed that the diversity of international interests at this date was not to be compassed by any alliance; Marvell, *Prose Works*, 2:327.

[53] Marvell, *Prose Works*, 2:289.

[54] Marvell, *Prose Works*, 2:328: compare Marchamont Nedham, *Interest will not Lie* (London, 1659); John Crouch, *A Mixt Poem, Partly Historical* [etc.] (London, 1660), p. 2; Richard Baxter, *The Difference Between the Power of Magistrates* [etc.] (London, 1671), p. 16; John Phillips, *Maronides or Virgil Travestie* (London, 1672), p. 70; John Smith, *Christian Religion's Appeal* [etc.] (London, 1675), bk 3, p. 48.

[55] K.H.D. Haley, *William of Orange and the English Opposition, 1672-4* (Oxford: Oxford University Press, 1953), pp. 57-8, 63; von Maltzahn, *Chronology*, pp. 150-4.

and in the eighteenth centuries, a valuation in great part adopted by the Kantian aesthetics that has since prevailed. By contrast, Marvell's 'interestedness' put him on the wrong side of history for quite some time. That was first overlaid by a Whig construction of his political disinterest. Only in the twentieth century did the success of Marvell's poetry come to outweigh this earlier reputation as a virtuous parliamentarian. But that came at a further cost, as this elevation followed from a Kantian valuation of Marvell's lyrics alone – that small portion of his work that might be set above any 'palpable design upon us' (in Keats's phrase).[56] Marvell's much-vaunted impersonality was celebrated by T.S. Eliot and by much subsequent criticism indebted to him. This disinterestedness has only recently been much tested by our revived study of his overtly political writing, especially the prose works that appeared in an edition from Yale University Press in 2003, and the satires, which canon has been expanded in the last couple of years.[57]

At the heart of Marvell's controversial writing lies its recognition of the interest at work in others' positions, whatever its occlusion of the interest at work in his own. His poetry too turned increasingly to promoting the specific at the expense of the universal, the particular over the general. Not that Marvell got there all at once. In the early 1650s we find him casting about and trying his hand at one discourse and another. Famously, this finds expression in the double perspective of 'An Horatian Ode', at once royalist and republican, or at least Cromwellian. In the early years of the Protectorate he persisted with an apocalyptic idiom, especially in writings aimed at Queen Christina of Sweden and calculated to draw her into a northern Protestant alliance with England.[58] Thus he supplied a Latin verse letter to the English embassy in Sweden with elaborate compliments to Queen Christina, urging on the Anglo-Swedish alliance and proposing a crusade against Rome, the Palatine, Austria and Spain; the queen is reported to have been charmed by the verses, which helped negotiations.[59] Marvell also supplied Latin epigrams for the portrait of the Protector sent to Christina. This apocalyptic register finds fuller expression still in Marvell's elaborate panegyric on *The First Anniversary of the Government Under His Highness The Lord Protector*, anonymously published in 1655. But it is the language of interest that became Marvell's more

---

[56] This finds fuller review in N. von Maltzahn, 'Andrew Marvell and the Prehistory of Whiggism', in *'Cultures of Whiggism': New Essays on English Literature and Culture in the Long Eighteenth Century*, ed. David Womersley (Newark: Delaware UP, 2005), pp. 31-61.

[57] Notably in the revived attribution to Marvell of the 'Second and Third Advices to a Painter' by George DeForest Lord and Annabel Patterson, for which see Nigel Smith, ed., *The Poems of Andrew Marvell* (London: Longman, 2003), pp. 321-22.

[58] For this idiom, see especially Margarita Stocker, *Apocalyptic Marvell* (Brighton: Harvester Press, 1984).

[59] Edward Holberton, 'The Textual Transmission of Marvell's "Letter to Doctor Ingelo": The Longleat Manuscript', *English Manuscript Studies, 1100-1700*, 12 (2005), 233-53; von Maltzahn, *Chronology*, p. 40.

enduring idiom. He was still capable of a lyric mode, as we know from his Restoration poem 'The Garden'. Even there, however, he is self-conscious about his removal from the world of competing concerns in which he was otherwise immersed. Posterity did not soon forgive him: until recently the view prevailed that, as one Victorian put it, 'the singer of an April mood, who might have bloomed year after year in young and ardent hearts, [became] buried in the dust of politics, in the valley of dead bones.'[60]

Milton, by contrast, remained Milton, if only up to a point. Posterity loved him, although it made sure in considerable part to aestheticize his epic. *Paradise Lost* came to define the sublime. Here his universalism found supreme expression. It is true that we can find local and topical references in the epic; its politics as published in 1667, or again in 1674, spoke directly to issues of the hour. But in the words of Samuel Johnson, no friend to Milton: 'the characteristick quality of [Milton's] poem is sublimity. He sometimes descends to the elegant, but his element is the great... it is his peculiar power to astonish... The poet, whatever be done, is always great... his work is not the greatest of heroick poems, only because it is not the first.'[61] For Milton the sublime had chiefly been a rhetorical category; by the late eighteenth century it had become an ontological one. The universalizing in Milton's poetics had had very palpable designs upon us, and was meant as no autonomous realm of the fictive. But once aestheticized, the epic could be accommodated first to the tastes of Addison's influential Spectator[62], then to the needs of continental theorists—Bodmer and Breitinger, for example—and eventually to the terms we find in Burke and in Kant. English Protestant nationalism laid claim to Milton's epic in ways that often betrayed its inspiration, as William Blake observed. And the Milton who refused to dwell on the interests of nations had generated a universalism that seemed applicable to the project of empire, in a way symbolized by Lord Macaulay's recommendation of Milton's epic in his 'Minute' on Indian education (1835). Its religious character kept *Paradise Lost* the stuff of Sunday reading well through the nineteenth century,[63] even as its also insurrectionary aspect increasingly captured imaginations.

More recently, however, the epic has become part of an educational project that professors of English in the twenty-first century continue to advance. This work proceeds even as the autonomous realm of the aesthetic comes under pres-

---

[60] Elizabeth Story Donno, *Andrew Marvell: The Critical Heritage* (London: Routledge & Kegan Paul, 1978), p. 262.

[61] Samuel Johnson, *The Lives of the Poets*, ed. Roger Lonsdale, 4 vols (Oxford: Oxford University Press, 2006), vol. 1, pp. 286, 288, 295.

[62] 'Addison neutered him', as Geoffrey Hill puts it, and 'got a nation's thanks': Geoffrey Hill, *A Treatise of Civil power* (Thame: Clutag Press, 2005), 'A Treatise of Civil power', stanza 22.

[63] For example in Barrington Harbour, Nova Scotia, in the 1820s: Benjamin Doane, *Following the Sea*, ed. Fred Scott and Marven Moore (Halifax: The Nova Scotia Museum, 1987), p. 5.

sure from the demands (not least in Canada) of multiculturalism, one of the major expressions of interest politics in our own day. When *Paradise Lost* was adopted by a literary tradition where an eventually Kantian emphasis on the autonomy of the work of art prevailed, the redescription of Milton's epic contributed to the longer redescription of religion as culture, to which we are heirs. The pacification of religious conflicts through the separation of church and state is usually cited as one of the achievements, perhaps the main achievement, of liberalism. A resulting concern is whether modern liberalism may, in its embrace of multiculturalism, have invited the revenge of the repressed in a way that erodes civil liberties even as it proposes to extend them. Or does multiculturalism too much aestheticize its subject—I almost wrote anaesthetize—in making it instrumental to nation-building? Either way, even a harmonious coexistence of distinct cultures puts into question any too transcendent a view of the literature of any one of those cultures. There may be nothing disinterested in the experience of the Sublime. Even those who side with Milton may find themselves at last in Marvell's world.

6

Paul Giles

Augustan American Literature:
An Aesthetics of Extravagance

My purpose in this paper is to outline possible ways of reading American literature of the seventeenth and eighteenth centuries, without of course claiming that this is anything other than a rough sketch of how such a map might be drawn. As Emory Elliott has observed, it is only since about 1970 that American literature of the pre-Revolutionary period has been taken seriously at all (6); the old canard that American literature began in the 1830s with Emerson has gradually been replaced over the past forty years by an increasing recognition of the historical complexity and aesthetic variety of this earlier work. Indeed, the term "early" American literature itself has come under critical scrutiny recently, since the very nomenclature seems to imply and to assume a subsequent cultural formation towards which pre-Revolutionary writing inevitably flows.[1] Much of the most significant work in this area was inspired first by Perry Miller's magisterial intellectual histories of the New England mind, and then, in the 1970s, by Sacvan Bercovitch's studies *The American Jeremiad* and *The Puritan Origins of the American Self*, the latter arguing for the nonconformist and apocalyptic temper of seventeenth-century Calvinist thought as the progenitor of nineteenth-century individualism and theories of American exceptionalism. Though Bercovitch's major critical contributions appeared some thirty years ago now, his scholarly legacy has become institutionalized through his role as general editor of the new *Cambridge History of American Literature*, which produced its first volume, on the period 1590 through 1820, in 1994. In this first part of the History, Bercovitch effectively finessed the problem of the eighteenth century by incorporating two substantial contributions, one from Robert Ferguson on the American Enlightenment after 1750, the other from David Shields entitled "British-American Belles Lettres," an account of polite literature written and circulated in the early-eighteenth-century colonies, drawing upon the brilliant work of textual reclamation in Shields's first book, *Oracles of Empire* (1990). The consequence of this

---

[1] On this topic, see De Prospo, Tennenhouse and, especially, Spengemann.

editorial strategy, however, was to leave the "Puritan origins" story largely intact. By locating Augustan American literature in the coffee-houses of Maryland and Pennsylvania in the reigns of Queen Anne and the first two King Georges, Bercovitch's trajectory implicitly reinforced the old legend of a cultural time lag in the colonies, whereby the artistic innovations of Pope and Addison were only given expression in America a generation or so later.

One argument I want to make here is that a conception of Augustan American literature might usefully be pushed back into the preceding century, thereby complicating the rather too neat sequence of development whereby seventeenth-century Puritanism is succeeded by a more worldly eighteenth-century idiom. Another argument, correlative to this, is that the cultural traditions of Britain and America from 1640 onwards were much more closely intertwined than is usually imagined, so that the idea of Augustan literature can be seen to operate on a transatlantic axis in the wake of the English Civil War. As David Norbrook has shown, when Oliver Cromwell was Lord Protector of the Commonwealth in the 1650s he deliberately associated himself with the model of Augustus Caesar, a parallel reinforced by the poet Edmund Waller, who iconographically celebrated Cromwell as the true heir of both the Roman emperors and the Stuart monarchs (306). Today we tend to associate the idea of Augustan England with Charles II's reign: Francis Atterbury, in his 1690 preface to Waller's *Poems*, asked rhetorically "whether, in Charles the Second's reign, English did not come to its full perfection; and whether it has not had its Augustan Age [Atterbury's words] as well as the Latin" (Womersley xv). But it is important to recognize how this image of Augustus was politicized and contested in the second half of the seventeenth century, and how there were claims for a republican interpretation of the Augustan narrative as well as a monarchical version. The New England community was heavily involved and invested in these debates: Sir Henry Vane, who succeeded John Winthrop as Governor of the Massachusetts Bay Colony in 1636, subsequently returned to England and became one of the parliamentary leaders who were then hanged upon the Restoration of Charles II in 1660, while two of Winthrop's own sons, Stephen and Fitzjohn, fought for Leveller regiments in England during the 1640s.

Despite all of this, the legacy of the English Civil War has tended to remain curiously obscure within the annals of the field now known as "early American Literature." There has been a certain amount of work on the importance of John Milton to an emerging republican tradition in eighteenth-century America, but the transatlantic cultural politics of the Restoration in the last decades of the seventeenth century have remained remarkably underexplored.[2] One obvious reason for this is the familiar emphasis on a spirit of American exceptionalism, which

---

[2]   On the reception of Milton in America, see Van Anglen and Stavely.

would seek to transform history into typology and geography into eschatology, thereby fulfilling the logic of John Winthrop's sermon "A Model of Christian Charity," which identifies America with a separatist city on a hill, in a prefiguration of the Book of Revelations. But such Biblical hypotheses were never universally admitted in seventeenth-century America, not even in the Puritan colonies. One of the regrettable things about our understanding of early American writing, I think, is that so many of its examples are taken from the rarefied Massachuetts Bay colony—Anne Bradstreet, Edward Taylor, and so on—when those in different locations tended to apprehend questions of the sacred and the secular quite differently. Indeed, one useful point of entry into Augustan American literature is to consider the significance of the word "plantation" itself. This is a word that Increase Mather did not care for, because he found it too redolent of the vulgar material world. "Let there then be no more Plantations erected in New England where people professing Christianity shall live like Indians," wrote Mather in 1676 (23); and again, this is Increase Mather in 1699: "Other Plantations were built upon a worldly Interest but New-England was founded on an Interest purely religious" (3-4). Yet that kind of deliberate sublimation of commerce into piety is precisely what we do not find in some New England writing of the mid-seventeenth century, for example in the anonymous work *Good News from New England*, published in London in 1648, which is interesting precisely because it positions itself textually between various boundaries: between old England and New England, between (as the punning title of the poem suggests) geographical location and scriptural revelation, and formally also between prose and poetry. All of this befits an environment of "mixt men" (5) with, as the poem says, "diversity of minds" (6), a scenario in which the "unlevel'd" nature of the landscape fittingly represents a world in which religion and profit keep house together (7). The author writes in his preface to the poem: "some Latin and Eloquent phrases I have picked from others, as commonly clowns used to do, yet be sure I am not in jest; for the subject I write of requires in many particulars the most solemn and serious meditation that ever any of like nature have done. Favour my clownship if I prove too harsh, and I shall remain yours."

This development of a style of "clownship" in early American writing can be seen as a stylistic counterpoint to the more familiar narratives of Biblical exegesis. We find a similarly humorous mood in Ebenezer Cook's poems *The Sot-Weed Factor* and *Sotweed Redivivus*, written in Maryland at the beginning of the eighteenth century. *The Sot-Weed Factor*, first published in London in 1708, chronicles the adventures of a tobacco merchant who comes over to Maryland from England, and the poem is organized around patterns of change, crossing and transgression, a movement across borders which is replicated formally in its transposition of epic to mock-epic. Many of the critical debates around the poem, such as they are, have centred on the issue of the kind of lesson the author was hoping readers might infer from his comic narrative, whether he is ridiculing the factor or merchant himself, or the Americans, or both (Egan 388); but this attempt to attribute a specific satiric impulse is of less interest than the way in which Cook's work adroitly imitates and manipulates the form of Samuel Butler's long poem *Hudibras*, published between 1662 and 1677. The point is that it is not just the form of *Hudibras* Cook is mirroring here: Butler's poem, with its colloquial language and clumsy rhymes, seeks to debase the high-flown rhetoric prevalent during the English Civil War, and the powerful effect of *Hudibras* derives from its dark, glittering cynicism, its description of Presbyterian synods (for example) as "mystical Bear-gardens" (91), and its frequently scatological demystifications of the idea of "inward Light" (93), so that all comes to appear, in Butler's phrase, "Arsie-versie" (84). The premise of *Hudibras* is of human culture as a mixed condition where spirit and matter are conjoined by an absurdist dynamic, and this pattern is replicated closely in *The Sot-Weed Factor*, where even the poem's language—"Wars of Punk" (27), the "ambodexter Quack" (29), and so on—recalls *Hudibras* directly. Just as Butler's poem looks back sardonically to the period in English history between 1648 and 1661 and describes religious rhetoric as a pretext for the acquisition of power and wealth, so Cook's poem deliberately evokes a heterogeneous world of Anglos and Indians, civic politics and economic profit, whose idiom is one of, as the poem says, "mixing things Prophane and Godly" (23).

For Cook, then, the idea of burlesque itself becomes a moral imperative, a way of following in the footsteps of *Hudibras* by deconstructing the idea of utopian phantoms and inscribing instead a material base for social culture. *The Sot-Weed Factor* consequently epitomizes John McWilliams's point about the proximity of epic to mock-epic in American eighteenth-century poetry: the idea of mock-epic was not to mock the epic, as such, but rather to ridicule human aspirations to epic status, so that the discrepancy between epic form and mundane content became a paradox on which Augustan American literature tended to thrive (67). We see this especially in Cook's later poem, *Sotweed Redivivus, or the Planters Looking-Glass*, published in 1730. Here the titular image of a looking-glass presages an aesthetics of diminution as Cook deliberately inverts Virgil's "Phoebian Fire," as the poem puts it (36), and shifts its scene to the humdrum world of Maryland trade politics, talking about the need for the colony to build up its wealth through global trade in agricultural commodities to replace the failing tobacco economy. In historical terms, Jack Greene has recently suggested that the colonial South was not peripheral to eighteenth-century America but was on the cusp of modernization in the way it was beginning to develop an international economy, so that it was rather New England, clinging as it did to its old myth of a redeemer nation, that was increasingly becoming the odd colony out. As Philip Gura has observed, it is worth thinking about the implications of this cultural and economic shift in relation to early American literature, where the traditional emphasis on the typological mission of the Puritan colonies has tended unduly to marginalize the different kinds of work being produced in other geographical areas (109).

This geographical association of Augustan American literature with the southern colonies would also be relevant to the writing of William Byrd II, who knew Wycherley and Congreve personally from the years he spent in London between 1715 and 1726 and who attempts to integrate the Addison model of civility within the rural conditions of Virginia and North Carolina. As with Cook, the whole tenor of Byrd's writing turns upon doubling and division, traversing a metaphorical line between England and America, official history and secret history, classical prototype and empirical reality. As a surveyor, his professional model of writing involves describing more literal boundaries but also a form of abstraction, whereby the rhetorical enclosure of space is played off in quixotic fashion against an acknowledged failure to encompass and map out the land. This introduces as well the problematic relation between Anglo-American and Native American culture at this time: Walter Mignolo has written about ways in which seventeenth- and eighteenth-century mapping was predicated upon "border gnoseology" rather than "territorial gnoseology" (11), upon identifying specific markers rather than attempting to encompass space for administrative purposes, and Byrd's structurally ironic narratives bring to light the yawning gaps between different kinds of epistemological assumptions in colonial America.

The world of Augustan American literature, then, differs in tone from that of the English cultural scene described by Paul Fussell in *The Rhetorical World of Augustan Humanism*, which primarily involves a conservative reverence for the authority of the past and acquiescence in the bounded circumference of custom, what Fussell calls "the closely circumscribed country of the humanist imagination" (300). Instead, the Augustan American idiom takes pleasure in bringing contraries into collision, in exploring incongruities between mind and matter. It is true that Fussell sees the idea of antithesis and conflict as an integral part of the eighteenth-century humanist dialectic, but Augustan American aesthetics tend to foreground this particular strain and not to vitiate the intensity of their paradoxical dynamic by establishing clear ethical distinctions between reason and passion. Byrd's dividing lines have less in common with those of Jonathan Swift or Samuel Johnson than with the more fluid lines of beauty developed by William Hogarth, who became very famous in America during his lifetime partly because of the way he delighted in transposing boundaries, in making contradiction itself into a generic principle; Mather Byles, Cotton Mather's nephew, kept a large collection of pictures from Hogarth prints, for example (Eaton 204). Ronald Paulson has written of Hogarth's pictorial method as taking scepticism to the edge of blasphemy through the way he redescribes theology as aesthetics—as in *The Harlot's Progress* (1732), described by Paulson as "a demystification of the mystery of the Virgin Birth" (1996:17); and this fractured visual style gets explicitly associated with the idea of America in Hogarth's etching of *Columbus Breaking the Egg* (1752), where it is the ability to think laterally that introduces new ways of seeing. In the latter picture, Columbus tells his doubting audience how it is possible to stand an egg on the table, and he confounds the expectations of his audience by breaking the egg in two to accomplish his end. Paulson also remarks on how what seventeenth-century theorists meant by travesty and burlesque is "something very like what Calvin meant by sacramental metonymy—making the incomprehensible comprehensible" (2003:22). The crucial point here is that the burlesque form in eighteenth-century America is not simply a flat mode of comic realism but also in its own way a metaphysical response to the disturbing interplay between epistemology and experience, between authority and insurrection. This is the same kind of hybrid style that we see also in John Gay's *Beggar's Opera* (1728) and in Handel's oratorios, both of which were very popular in eighteenth-century America.[3]

My point here is not just to adumbrate a hybrid Augustan culture centred on the colonies of the American south which might be seen as a complement to seventeenth-century New England Puritanism; rather, I want to push the argument to think about ways in which the narrative of New England literature itself changes if the south, rather than the north, were to become a discursive focal point. Although the history of the southern states today is identified closely with slave culture, we should not forget that slavery also flourished in the northern colonies during the eighteenth century, since it was not abolished in Massachusetts until 1783 (1784 in Connecticut); indeed, as John Donoghue has remarked, the extent of chattel slavery in New England, and even John Winthrop's own support of slavery for economic reasons, are understudied aspects of life in colonial New England, and this is something that a reverse geographical perspective, going from south to north and east to west, can help to redress (154). What one might call a Whig version of early American history was outlined in 1708 by the Somersetshire historian John Oldmixon, in his book *The British Empire in America*. Oldmixon sees America generally as an advantage to Britain, particularly in terms of its commercial possibilities, and he was particularly keen on Barbados and the Caribbean; however, though he draws heavily for his source material on Cotton Mather's *Magnalia Christi Americana*, published six years earlier in 1702, Oldmixon is quite scathing about the religious aspects of New England – dismissing the term "Antinomian," for example, as "too techni-

---

[3] On the popularity of Hogarth and Handel in America, see Silverman 12, 475. On the popularity of Gay in America, see Kate Keller 69. On the links between Hogarth and Gay, see Bender 87-136.

cal, or too much Cant, for the Gravity of History" (I, 76), and writing with sardonic humour about what he calls such "knotty Questions" as whether or not the "Grandchildren of Church Members had a right to baptism" (I, 109). Cotton Mather himself hated Oldmixon, of course, punningly castigating him in one of his letters as "Old Nick's Son" (Murdock 31). My purpose here, though, is not to take Oldmixon's side against Mather's, or vice versa, but rather to think about what happens to our understanding of Mather's major work if we were to read it within a transatlantic context, as an example of Augustan American style.

There is a certain heretical quality to such an approach, not only because it goes against the Bercovitch line of New England as what he calls "the American Israel," a protected space bound into an apocalyptic rhetoric of "New World promise" (1975: 75), but also because it cuts across the premise that the organizing principle of the *Magnalia* is "generational" (1975: 130), with Mather seeking to bind New England in a diachronic continuum across time. There is clearly a filiopietistic strand to the *Magnalia*, with Mather paying homage to his father Increase, to John Winthrop and to many others as he seeks to canonize New England history and institutionalize its legacy. But if the content of the text is filiopietistic, the form, I would argue, is primarily Augustan, ironically owing less to Increase Mather than to John Dryden, the arch-enemy of the Puritans, as Cotton Mather oddly imitates Dryden's official role as Historiographer Royal through a series of elaborate historical narratives that seek self-consciously to shape the world of New England into monumental artifice. It is, of course, not difficult to historicize Mather's work. Larzer Ziff and others have discussed it in relation to the political climate at the end of the seventeenth century, when the legal status of New England as an independent self-governing colony was a controversial and highly volatile matter; the old Massachusetts Bay charter was annulled by James II in 1683, leading to the institution of a royal administration in New England in 1686, before Increase Mather managed to negotiate a new, revised charter for the colony in 1691, in the wake of the Glorious Revolution in England. But, as Ziff says, "the push and pull between royal policy and New England policy" during the last twenty years of the seventeenth century were intense (208), and all this implies ways in which American literature of this time needs to be seen within the context of a British imperial imaginary, just as David Armitage has written about how "the ideological origins of the British empire" shaped political relationships at this time. To consider the *Magnalia* as immersed in the history of its times makes it in any case a funnier and sharper work. There are some brilliantly vivid vignettes in Book 3, describing the lives of New England clergymen: Mather talks, for example, about how Peter Bulkly cuts his hair very short and avoids "all novelties of apparel" while conducting his ministry (I, 401), while he also compares the more tedious preaching styles of those who wrote out their sermons in longhand with that of John Warham, who would talk extemporaneously from notes (I, 441). This is, among other things, a true guide to the daily practices of scholarship in the late seventeenth century. In Book 4, there is also a long discussion of the involvement of his uncle Samuel Mather with Cromwell's forces in London during the 1650s, how he went with Cromwell to Ireland in 1655 and died in Dublin after the Restoration.

One of the dominant themes in the *Magnalia*, then, is the tension between history and allegory, the strains and stresses involved in the struggle to bring temporal events into alignment with a providential pattern.[4] This precisely links Mather with Dryden, whose historical satires, "Absalom and Achitophel" and other works, play with both the analogies and the disjunctions between contemporary monarchs and mythological or Biblical archetypes. The whole idea of parallelisms is very important tropologically for Mather in the *Magnalia*: this is evident both at a microcosmic level—as when he takes delight in recounting how Samuel Stone was born in Hertford in England and died in Hartford in New England (I, 435)—and also at a macrocosmic level, as the motif of parallax, of moving backwards and forwards in time to create both temporal and spiritual conjunctions)—"hopeful Prolepsis," as Mather himself puts it (I, 53)—is one of the book's key concerns. In Book 4, he describes Samuel Danforth as an astronomer observing the "parallax" of a comet crossing the earth in 1664 (II, 63), and the black arts of astronomy and necromancy form an uncomfortable subtext throughout the whole work, as Mather is always pondering the question of how far parallels of all kinds might legitimately be pursued. At one point he quotes Increase Mather comparing Urian Oakes's appointment as President of Harvard to Samuel in the Bible becoming President of the College of Najoth, but he then goes on to cite Increase's reluctance to push this analogy too far: "And in many other particulars I might enlarge upon the parallel," he says, "but that it is inconvenient to extend such instances *beyond their proportion*" (II, 117). The rhetorical basis of the *Magnalia* is thus not so much typology as paradox: the author talks at one point about the "trials" of the New Englanders "in the days of their *Paroxisms*" (I, 123), and that notion of some kind of convulsive cutting across standard measures, deriving etymologically from the Greek *para* (beyond), is one of the author's recurrent concerns here.

Such play with perspective emerges partly from the author's readings in the Renaissance literature of exploration, the opening up of different temporal and spatial perspectives, and partly from the strong sense of geographical specificity apparent in his writings. The *Magnalia* opens, in fact, with a map of New England as its frontispiece, and this serves to link Mather with his rival Oldmixon, since both were acknowledging the relative situation of America in relation to

---

4 On this theme, see Arch 156.

wider global currents. Mather of course was asserting that, as he put it, "Geography must now find work for a Christiano-graphy of the entire Western hemisphere" (I, 41-2), while Oldmixon saw geography in a more aggressively secular sense, as conducive to the winds of trade and profit. But my point is that the *Magnalia* is in every sense a more capacious work than it has normally been assumed to be, particularly among those scholars, more numerous than they should be, who make assumptions about this major work without ever having read it properly. Mather deliberately invokes in his 1400 pages a world larger than he can encompass, and he plays with the illuminating disjunctions between enclosure and disclosure, between local teleology and ontological incompleteness. He talks at one point about what he calls the "meta-grammatising temper" of the preacher John Wilson (I, 319), and Mather himself might similarly be described as a "meta-grammatising" author, one whose style is inherently and reflexively self-contradictory, since he aspires to include material while acknowledging his own epistemological incapacity properly to order or control it. This is not unlike the principle of self-contradiction in Hogarth which, as I noted earlier, Ronald Paulson linked to the Calvinist conception of imperfect knowledge, and it links up as well with what Mather in one of his own diary entries, when contemplating the relative merits of praising Christ among the angels in heaven and preaching to mortals on earth, referred to as a quality of "sacred hilarity" (Levin 276). There is, in other words, a manic dimension to Mather's work which makes it characteristic of the peculiar tenor of Augustan American literature, where the comic insufficiencies of reason as an intellectual phenomenon are brought to light.

What I would argue, then, is that the Augustan tradition in American literature should not be seen as confined to belles lettres, interesting though such works in themselves might be. Part of the problem with interpretations of American Puritanism, as Lawrence Buell among others has pointed out, is the way in which our understanding of it has been shaped retrospectively by George Bancroft and the nineteenth-century Unitarians (217-8), thereby significantly underemphasizing the rationalist framework of early American literature and downplaying its involvement with the long transatlantic argument about republican liberty that followed in the wake of the English Civil War. There has been much discussion in intellectual history circles of transatlantic influences on American culture during the years leading up to the Revolution: J. G. A. Pocock, Bernard Bailyn, Quentin Skinner and others have outlined the long philosophical and political argument about republican ideology that followed the English Civil War and how this "neo-roman theory of liberty," as Skinner called it (55), eventually culminated in political independence for the United States. But alongside these more abstract conceptions of liberty there also developed in eighteenth-century America a parallel tradition of popular or lowbrow republicanism, which expressed itself aesthetically through literary forms of caricature, travesty or burlesque. In the second half of the eighteenth century, we see this oscillation between neoclassical structures and popular sentiment in the poems of Phillis Wheatley, a sentiment linked in her case to questions of slavery and abolition. We find it also in Timothy Dwight's more overtly politicized version of Augustan humanism in *Greenfield Hill*, a long poem he published in 1794, where the pastoral virtues of Connecticut become a levelling agent whose "pure, golden mean" (17) heralds the values of what Dwight calls "new Albion" (67).

The political poesis of American republicanism thus involves not a suppression of burlesque comedy, but rather its internalization and assimilation into a genre of structural demystification and, at times, reluctant inclusiveness. Hogarth is a ghostly presence in Dwight's 1788 poem *The Triumph of Infidelity*, published anonymously during Dwight's lifetime, whose explicit premise is satirically to obliterate the notion of fellow theologian Charles Chauncy that universal salvation might be plausible or even desirable. However, dedicated as the poem ironically is to Voltaire, and with textual details that evoke the spirit of Hogarth, who is actually cited at one point in the poem, what we find in *The Triumph of Infidelity* is precisely what the title of the work suggests: a triumph of disorder over order, or at least an implicit acknowledgement of the challenge posed by aesthetic paradoxes to assumptions of ethical or religious self-sufficiency: Chauncy, for example, is ridiculed in Hogarthian vein as a figure of "palsied age" (202), while another divine is said satirically to have "cheeks of port, and lips of turtle green" (199). One of the points about *The Triumph of Infidelity*, as with Mather's *Magnalia*, is thus the way in which the compulsions of caricature come into conflict with the Puritan tenets of plain truth, producing elements of comedy from a sense of epistemological insufficiency and the ontologically irreconcilable. In discussing Dwight's poetry, Karl Keller associated it with an idiom of what he called "wilderness baroque," involving "an aesthetic of outrageousness" and "extravagances surprising even to a modern sensibility" (201-3), and it is not difficult to see how Dwight's artistic investments draw him more closely into the realms of "infidelity" than he, as a church leader and pillar of the established order, would have felt comfortable with. The etymological derivation of "extravagance"—literally, wandering outside—exemplifies the manner in which forms of stylistic transgression became linked in the eighteenth century to the crosscurrents of geographical dislocation, and this suggests the way in which conceptual and territorial reshapings of early American culture are necessarily intertwined. This in turn testifies to the way in which much eighteenth-century American literature can be seen to position itself uncomfortably on the boundaries of Augustan humanism, whose parameters it reconstructs for its own particular intellectual purposes.

Works Cited

[Anonymous]. *Good News from New-England: with an Exact Relation of the First Planting that Countrey.* London, 1648.

Arch, Stephen Carl. *Authorizing the Past: The Rhetoric of History in Seventeenth-Century New England.* DeKalb: Northern Illinois University Press, 1994.

Armitage, David. *The Ideological Origins of the British Empire.* Cambridge: Cambridge University Press, 2000.

Bender, John. *Imagining the Penitentiary: Fiction and the Architecture of Mind in Eighteenth-Century England.* Chicago: University of Chicago Press, 1987.

Bercovitch, Sacvan. *The Puritan Origins of the American Self.* New Haven: Yale University Press, 1975.

----------. *The American Jeremiad.* Madison: University of Wisconsin Press, 1978.

----------, ed. *Cambridge History of American Literature, I: 1590-1820.* Cambridge: Cambridge University Press, 1994.

Buell, Lawrence. *New England Literary Culture: From Revolution Through Renaissance.* Cambridge: Cambridge University Press, 1986.

Butler, Samuel. *Hudibras.* Ed. John Wilders. Oxford: Clarendon Press, 1967.

Byrd, William II. *The Prose Works of William Byrd of Westover: Narratives of a Colonial Virginian.* Ed. Louis B. Wright. Cambridge, Mass.: Harvard University Press, 1966.

Cook, Ebenezer. *The Works of Ebenezer Cook, Gent.* In Bernard C. Steiner, ed., *Early Maryland Poetry.* Baltimore: Maryland Historical Society, 1900.

De Prospo, R. C. "Marginalizing Early American Literature." *New Literary History* 23 (Spring 1992): 233-65.

Donoghue, John. "Radical Republicanism in England, America, and the Imperial Atlantic, 1624-1661." Ph.D. thesis, University of Pittsburgh, 2006.

Dwight, Timothy. *The Triumph of Infidelity.* In Wells 183-209.

----------. *Greenfield Hill: A Poem in Seven Parts.* New York: Childs and Swaine, 1794.

Eaton, Arthur Wentworth Hamilton. *The Famous Mather Byles: The Noted Tory Preacher, Poet, and Wit, 1707-1788.* Boston: Butterfield, 1914.

Egan, Jim. "The Colonial English Body as Commodity in Ebenezer Cooke's *The Sot-Weed Factor.*" *Criticism* 41.3 (Summer 1999): 385-400.

Elliott, Emory. *Revolutionary Writers: Literature and Authority in the New Republic, 1725-1810.* New York: Oxford University Press, 1982.

Ferguson, Robert A. "The American Enlightenment, 1750-1820." In Bercovitch, ed., *Cambridge History I*, 345-537.

Fussell, Paul. *The Rhetorical World of Augustan Humanism: Ethics and Imagery from Swift to Burke.* Oxford: Clarendon Press, 1965.

Greene, Jack P. *Pursuits of Happiness: The Social Development of Early Modern British Colonies and the Formation of American Culture*. Chapel Hill: University of North Carolina Press, 1988.

Gura, Philip F. "Turning Our World Upside Down: Reconceiving Early American Literature." *American Literature* 63.1 (March 1991): 104-12.

Keller, Karl. "Literary Excess as Indigenous Aesthetic in Eighteenth-Century America." In Paul J. Korshin, ed., *The American Revolution and Eighteenth-Century Culture* (New York: AMS Press, 1986), 201-18.

Keller, Kate van Winkle, with John Koegel. "Secular Music to 1800." In David Nicholls, ed., *The Cambridge History of American Music*. Cambridge: Cambridge University Press, 1998. 49-77.

Levin, David. *Cotton Mather: The Young Life of the Lord's Remembrancer, 1663-1703*. Cambridge, Mass.: Harvard University Press, 1978.

McWilliams, John P. Jr. *The American Epic: Transforming a Genre, 1770-1860*. Cambridge: Cambridge University Press, 1989.

Mather, Cotton. *Magnalia Christi Americana; or, The Ecclesiastical History of New England, from its First Planting, in the Year 1620, unto the Year of Our Lord 1698. In Seven Books*. 1702. Ed. Thomas Robbins. 2 vols. Hartford, 1853.

Mather, Increase. *A Brief History of the War with the Indians in New England*. Boston, 1676.

----------. *A Brief Relation of the State of New England, from the Beginning of that Plantation to this Present Year, 1689*. London, 1689.

Mignolo, Walter D. *Local Histories/Global Designs: Coloniality, Subaltern Knowledges, and Border Thinking*. Princeton: Princeton University Press, 2000.

Miller, Perry. *The New England Mind: The Seventeenth Century*. New York: Macmillan, 1939.

----------. *The New England Mind: From Colony to Province*. Cambridge, Mass.: Harvard University Press, 1953.

Murdock, Kenneth B. "The *Magnalia*." In Cotton Mather, *Magnalia Christi Americana, Books I and II*. Cambridge, Mass.: Harvard University Press, 1977. 26-48.

Norbrook, David. *Writing the English Republic: Poetry, Rhetoric and Politics, 1627-1660*. Cambridge: Cambridge University Press, 1999.

Oldmixon, John. *The British Empire in America: Containing the History of the Discovery, Settlement, Progress and State of the British Colonies on the Continent and Islands of America*. 2nd ed. 2 vols. London, 1741.

Paulson, Ronald. *The Beautiful, Novel, and Strange: Aesthetics and Heterodoxy*. Baltimore: Johns Hopkins University Press, 1996.

----------. *Hogarth's Harlot: Sacred Parody in Enlightenment England*. Baltimore: Johns Hopkins University Press, 2003.

Shields, David C. *Oracles of Empire: Poetry, Politics, and Commerce in British America, 1690-1750.* Chicago: University of Chicago Press, 1990.

----------. "British-American Belles Lettres." In Bercovitch, ed., *Cambridge History I,* 307-43.

Silverman, Kenneth. *A Cultural History of the American Revolution: Painting, Music, Literature, and the Theatre in the Colonies and the United States from the Treaty of Paris to the Inauguration of George Washington, 1763-1789.* New York: Crowell, 1976.

Skinner, Quentin. *Liberty Before Liberalism.* Cambridge: Cambridge University Press, 1998.

Spengemann, William C. *A New World of Words: Redefining Early American Literature.* New Haven: Yale University Press, 1994.

Stavely, Keith W. F. *Puritan Legacies:* Paradise Lost *and the New England Tradition, 1630-1890.* Ithaca, N.Y.: Cornell University Press, 1987.

Tennenhouse, Leonard. *The Importance of Feeling English: American Literature and the British Diaspora, 1750-1850.* Princeton: Princeton University Press, 2007.

Van Anglen, Kevin P. *The New England Milton: Literary Reception and Cultural Authority in the Early Republic.* University Park: Pennsylvania State University Press, 1993.

Wells, Colin. *The Devil and Doctor Dwight: Satire and Theology in the Early American Republic.* Williamsburg-Chapel Hill: Omohundro Institute of Early American History and Culture-University of North Carolina Press, 2002.

Wheatley, Phillis. *Poems on Various Subjects, Religious and Moral.* London, 1773.

Winthrop, John. "A Model of Christian Charity." 1630. In Nina Baym et al., ed., *Norton Anthology of American Literature,* 2nd ed. New York: Norton, 1985, I, 37-50.

Womersley, David, ed. *Augustan Critical Writing.* London: Penguin, 1997.

Ziff, Larzer. *Puritanism in America: New Culture in a New World.* New York: Viking Press, 1973.

7

Simon Haines

English Bards and German Sages

This paper should be entitled English Bard and German Sage, since there is only space for one of each. So first a word or two of explanation. On a broader canvas my aim is to explore poetry or literature on the one hand, mostly but not all in English, and philosophy on the other, mostly but not all in German, from the Romantic era onwards: that is, from just after the time of Rousseau through to the period of modernism. This exploration is in terms of a model or models of the self persisting across time since the earliest European literature. Part of the object of this exercise is to try to find a way of talking about poets and philosophers alongside each other: an enterprise which philosophers tend to disapprove of more than literary-studies people do.

On the one hand, I believe, there are poets (Homer, Ovid, the Beowulf poet, Chaucer, Shakespeare, and in special senses Sophocles and St Mark) and philosophers (Aristotle, Thucydides, Boethius, Abelard, Ockham, Aquinas, Machiavelli, Hume) in whose work the self is presented as *passional* and *relational*: constituted first of all in emotions and interactions, or emotions *as* interactions: both "affective" and "intersubjective", as the jargon goes. Reason, will, thought and belief are aspects or orientations of a fundamentally passional self. Other selves are part of its constitution, while God, or faith, is something like a limit of its thought.

On the other hand, there are poets (Virgil, St Paul, the Augustine of *Confessions*, the Roland poet, Dante, Chrétien de Troyes, Rousseau) and philosophers (Socrates, Plato, Plotinus, Pico, Erasmus, Luther and most of the major 17th- and 18th-century figures from Descartes to Rousseau) for whom the self is a willing, choosing, deciding, reasoning or believing centre of being, often captured or determined by a single concept or idea, and embedded within a fabric of emotion, sense, imagination and memory. This makes other selves hard to reach or fathom, while a God of some kind is often in the centre, often is the centre, as well as being transcendently outside everything. This "inner" self is unchanging, something like a "soul", whereas the passional and relational self looks outward for its meanings and thinks of itself as changing or evolving: as a "life". The soul-centred view has become increasingly dominant, I believe, as time has passed, and I think it has had a tendency to devalue experience: to do over the millennia what Plato did to Homer, and substitute a conceptual model of the self for an experiential one. If all this sounds like a kind of anti-dualism on my part, then it is: but my argument is that some form of dualism goes a lot deeper and is a lot more prevalent in all our thought than standard anti-dualist accounts of cognition, say, tend to show.

Now the presiding genius of Romantic conceptualism was Rousseau, known to Kant, whose moral philosophy he inspired, not only as the author of the *Discourses, Emile* and the *Social Contract*, but also of *Julie*: as the great chronicler of the soul's search for *la source du sentiment et de l'être*, of the inner eye, and of the general will to equality.[1] But if Kant's *ethical* thought arose out of a deep assent to Rousseau, his metaphysics, at least at its creative core, arose out of his equally deep disagreement with David Hume. The Humean self has no core; it is dispersed through its affections and its associations: so dispersed, in fact, that famously it seems entirely to lack continuous identity and even agency. If the Rousseauan soul is all agency, the Humean self is all vacancy.

So one way to orient oneself in what can seem like a wilderness of philosophy might be to trace the passage from metaphysics to morals through the key junction point in Kant's greatest work, namely the *Transcendental Deduction* from the first *Critique*: "one of the most impressive and exciting passages of argument in the whole of philosophy", "the most important and central section of the whole Critique", according to two standard commentaries.[2]

The labyrinthine structure of the *Critique* is like a series of nested unequal pairs: at the top level are the two Doctrines, the main one, of Elements, where Kant develops his theory of knowledge; and a much smaller one, of Method, where he considers its implications for philosophy. Within the main Doctrine come a smaller first part, the *Aesthetic*, concerned with the mind in its more passive or receptive aspect, the sensibility, the intuition-receiving capacity, especially as it is formed by space and time; and a much larger second part, the *Logic*, which is about the understanding, the active, concept-forming aspect of the mind. The *Logic* in turn looks first at how the active, judging, concept-forming aspect of the mind works with the sensibility or passive, intuition-receiving aspect to make experience possible (this is the *Analytic*); and then at how the reason, understanding in its mechanical aspect, working alone, without sensibility, makes its various mistaken attempts to construct fictional entities or go beyond the bounds of

---

[1]   For this claim and those in the paragraph below as well as for the argument in the preceding paragraph, see Simon Haines, *Poetry and Philosophy from Homer to Rousseau: Romantic Souls, Realist Lives*, Palgrave Macmillan/St Martin's Press, Basingstoke/New York, 2005.

[2]   See P F Strawson, *The Bounds of Sense: An Essay on Kant's* Critique of Pure Reason, Methuen, London/New York, (1966) 1975, p. 25; A C Ewing, *A Short Commentary on Kant's* Critique of Pure Reason, University of Chicago Press, Chicago/London, (1938) 1967, p. 67.

what it can know (this is the *Dialectic*). And then of these two parts the *Analytic* itself is also divided into two: the basic "analytic of concepts", the exposition of the twelve key concepts or categories *of* experience as necessary *to* experience; and the "analytic of principles", showing how these concepts are always applied to intuitions or sense impressions, and never to things in themselves, which must remain unknowable simply because things are known to us only insofar as they are represented to us. Finally the analytic of concepts itself consists of a smaller "metaphysical deduction", setting out what Kant saw as the four main logical features of all judgments about objects (quantity, quality, modality, relation); and, at last, centrally, the larger "transcendental deduction". The heart of and clue to the labyrinth, that part of the *Critique* which according to Kant cost him the most labour in the first or 1781 version, and which he largely rewrote for the second edition of 1787, is that passage in which he sets out his theory of self-consciousness, of a single identical subject of experience, by considering it as the relation between the two types of representations (intuitions and concepts) that make up experience and the objects they represent.

I hope readers will forgive this rather painful mapping of territory no doubt familiar enough even to scholars of a more literary than philosophical turn; but it seems to me that the *Critique* in its very structure maps the punctual model of the self that I want to claim Kant expounds. And now we're coming to the clue to the clue to the labyrinth, the *cor cordium*, in Shelleyan phrase.

This passage is called "transcendental", in Kant's unusual use of the term, because it has to do with the necessary conditions of experience; it's about how the mind and objects alike *must* be in order for experience to be possible at all, even though we can't know this simply by empirical observation (precisely because these conditions transcend experience). And Kant calls it a "deduction" because it establishes not how the 12 concepts he sees as essential to all experience are derived *from* experience, as Locke and Hume tried to do (for Kant this was an absurd undertaking), but how these alone of all concepts must *enable* all experience, enable us to *synthesise* the welter of impressions, while being true independently of it, or true *a priori*. The whole *Critique* is about the possibility of these "synthetic *a priori*" judgements. Objects of sense must conform to these basic conceptual configurations of the mind, such as causality, for example, or necessity, or unity, or negation, in order to be objects for us at all. Hume had rightly said that you will look in vain for causality *in* objects (no matter how often you look at one billiard ball striking another you won't see the actual *cause* of the second one's movement), and so he sceptically denied its very existence. Yet as he did not see, but as Kant now argues, causality is a concept that originates in the understanding, but is nevertheless part of how we must think of objects *as objects*. They wouldn't be part of a world of objects for us unless we brought this concept, and others like it, to them, or them to it, more accurately. This bringing of intuitions under concepts is what Kant calls *judging*. Indeed the very word *Kritik* is rooted in the Greek *krisis*, which means precisely judgement, as all literary critics know very well.

So it's the *activity* of bringing the impressions under the concepts that actually makes experience possible. Here's a crucial passage, in Kant's rather forbidding terminology, from the first edition of the Deduction:

> If therefore I ascribe a synopsis to sense, because it contains a manifold in its intuition, a synthesis must always correspond to this, and receptivity can make cognitions possible only if combined with spontaneity. This is now the ground of a threefold synthesis, which is necessarily found in all cognition: that, namely, of the apprehension of the representations, as modifications of the mind in intuition; of the reproduction of them in the imagination; and of their recognition in the concept. (A97)[3]

Let's try to translate this translation. Knowing the world, having experience of it, is a three-fold process. First, the mind is passively modified by impressions or "intuitions" which come to us successively in time but nevertheless seem to hang together as impressions of a spatial world. Second, these impressions are retained or reproduced by the imagination, which "hangs on" in this way to earlier impressions even while we are experiencing later ones: so that the whole can in fact *seem* whole even though it came to us only in bits. And now third, and crucially: when we recognise, or *re*-cognise, these moments, as belonging together *as* something, we are conscious of them as *one* object, and conscious of them *as recognised by one consciousness*. This recognition, crucially, is a *spontaneous* act of that single consciousness: what Kant in the second edition of the Deduction repeatedly calls an "act of the *spontaneity* of the power of representation" (B130, 132).

So the all-important third part of cognition has us not only actively bringing the intuitions under concepts, recognising them as objects in a world, but also has us recognising *ourselves*. Here is Kant again: "the original and necessary consciousness of the identity of oneself is at the same time a consciousness of an equally necessary unity of the synthesis of all appearances in accordance with concepts" (A108). The concept of "an object", in other words, or more critically the active applying of a concept to an impression, involves the necessity of self-consciousness and self-identity. We need both, along with all the other categorical concepts such as causation, to have experiences at all. "Only because I [can]

---

[3] Immanuel Kant, *Critique of Pure Reason*, trans. and ed. Paul Guyer and Allen W Wood, Cambridge University Press, 1998, p. 228. Hereafter I follow the convention by which A numbers refer to 1781 pages and B numbers to 1787 pages, both being given in standard modern editions. I use the Cambridge translation throughout.

ascribe all perceptions to one consciousness can I say of all perceptions that I am conscious of them" (A122). This integration of the two ideas of spontaneous activity and of identity, incidentally, even leaks back up the perceptual chain into the imagination, the second link, which looked at from the conceptual side, as it were, rather than the intuitive side, looks not simply reproductive but actually *pro*ductive, an active, synthetic or "spontaneous" (B151) faculty, an intermediate capacity of blending multiple intuitions into single objects, which "is determining and not determinable". "Insofar as the imagination is spontaneity, I also call it productive" (B152). The nature of this "transcendental imagination" is controversial in the commentary but obviously of great importance for aesthetics and the theory of art (as in Coleridge's famous passage in the *Biographia*); and it serves to illustrate how important the idea of spontaneous activity is in Kant's whole account of cognition.[4]

To return to his own famous, indeed world-changing, words: "thus we ourselves bring into the appearances that order and regularity in them we call nature . . . the understanding is itself the legislation for nature" (A125-6). This understanding, which is, remember, a "*spontaneity* of cognition", arises directly out of the "faculty of concepts"—or of judging ("they come down to the same thing", says Kant at A126 and B150). Judging, the use of the concept faculty, is "an action of the understanding", an "act of its self-activity", "an act of the *spontaneity* of the power of representation" (B130). And combination of the manifold of intuitions has to be an act of a spontaneous understanding *capable of grasping itself as a single understanding*. An object can only be grasped as an object by such a mind. "I am conscious of myself not as I appear to myself, nor as I am in myself, but only *that I am*" (B157); this is not "intuition" but active thought, and active thought implies a self-aware thinker. In the second edition of the *Critique* this self-aware spontaneity is called "the pure apperception", "original apperception" or "transcendental self-consciousness" (B132). It is the necessary condition or ground for grasping all my intuitions as mine and combining them as an experience of whole objects. The understanding is once again called "spontaneity" (B150). Through its active synthesising categorical force we make the inchoate swirling intuitions of a who-knows-what ("there is a pain in the room"[5]) into the coherent perceptions of a self-conscious person. At the heart of the Kantian account of experience is a legislating, cognising, categorising self-consciousness: and at the heart of all *that* is the notion of *spontaneity*.

---

4   I found Terry Pinkard's *German Philosophy 1760-1860: The Legacy of Idealism*, Cambridge University Press, 2002, pp. 19-44 ("Human Spontaneity and the Natural Order"), immensely helpful in making sense of these passages.

5   The helpful Dickensian example, from Mrs Gradgrind on her deathbed, is used by Roger Scruton, *Kant*, Oxford University Press, 1982, p. 32.

Now this is a good moment to recall, as Kant does not, nor as far as I know do any of his commentators (this being perhaps the kind of thought that occurs to literary types more than to philosophers), that the root of the German and English words *Spontaneität* and *spontaneity* is the Latin *sponte*, the ablative form of a defective noun *spons* which only exists in the ablative and genitive. *Sponte* means "of free will", "of one's own accord", "of one's self", "voluntarily", "willingly". *Italiam non sponte sequor*, Aeneas tells the furious and incredulous Dido, justifying himself (unsuccessfully) on the grounds that his own will has become merely a vessel for, and thus identical with, that of Jupiter (a submergence of a human will in the divine Will which bears an uncanny resemblance to Augustine's account of the process, or condition, in *Confessions*).[6] *Sponte deum* was a traditional expression meaning "by the gods' will". The verbal root is *spondere*, to bind, engage, or solemnly or sacredly promise or pledge oneself; this was derived in turn from a Greek verb *spendo*, to "pour out", as in a libation: the sense of libation crops up a good deal in Latin usages of *spondeo*. This isn't part of the same concept-family as *voluntas* or *sua voluntate*, with their core senses of willing, choosing, desiring. *Sponte* is more like a sacred commitment, a pledging or pouring out of the self.

This is a paper about Kant's first *Critique*, not his second (1788); about pure not practical reason; about epistemology not ethics. But they can't in the end really be separated, nor did Kant think they should. The Kantian free will, heir of the Augustinian *liberum arbitrium*, is the archetype of the non-derivative, self-generating, autonomous self.[7] The free will "must be viewed as also giving the law to itself", writes Kant in the *Groundwork of the Metaphysic of Morals* (1785).[8] Inevitably, however, he is also thinking about this in the first *Critique*, whose two editions straddle the writing and publication of the *Groundwork*. In the section of the *Critique* called the Third Antinomy, freedom of the will is defined as "an absolute causal *spontaneity* beginning from itself" (A446/B474), and is set outside the natural world of causation, as belonging to the transcendental realm of things in themselves, in which the moral agent must see himself as belonging. The *autonomous* self-legislator of Kant's ethics is continuous with the *autogenous* self-knower of his epistemology. Autonomy in morals is not of course the *same* capacity as spontaneity in cognition; autonomy shares ancient volitional ground with *voluntas* and *arbitrium*, whereas autogeneity takes us back more to the Renaissance self-making of Pico della Mirandola and others. God tells Adam in Pico's *De hominis dignitate* that He made him *ut tui ipsius quasi arbitrarius*

---

[6] See Virgil, *Aeneid IV*, lines 305ff., and Augustine, *Confessions*, Books 7-8.
[7] See Pinkard, p. 46.
[8] In Immanuel Kant, *Practical Philosophy*, trans. and ed. Mary J Gregor, Cambridge University Press, 1996, p. 82.

honorariusque plastes et fictor, in quam malueris tute formam effingas: "so that you may make yourself into whatever shape you choose, as a matter of choice and honour, as it were, the moulder and maker of yourself".[9] As *if* a matter of choice and will: but the self-making is really deeper than this; it's a *spontaneous* matter, more fundamental than choice, referring to the capacity for self-determination prior to the actual legislating for oneself. Nevertheless Kant's (and Kantian) ethics, just like his epistemology, notoriously depends upon a kind of event horizon, over which we cannot see and yet from the far side of which issue imperatives arising from reasons.

So at the heart of Kant's philosophy, epistemology and ethics alike, is a model of the self, insofar as it is active, as *spontaneous*: as at its centre an ultimately mysterious, creative, self-generating, pouring-out, fountain-like sacred core, like that dimensionless originary point out of which the universe is nowadays believed by scientists to have emerged. And it's this that interests me, as having so much in common with that ancient punctual model of the self I mentioned above, traceable alike in Plato, Rousseau and many others between and since. Ultimately, in both philosophy and literature, this spontaneous self, adapted and exalted by Kant's successors, was to place an enormous burden on the twin human ambitions to know the world and be the good, since in the end the spontaneous self will appear as the source of both the world and the good. Herder, Hamann, Schleiermacher, Schopenhauer and Kierkegaard all articulated or objected to various versions of this existential problem, this burden of angst at the levels of responsibility and of uncertainty incurred by a self which has to do everything for itself, and yet which does not really know what the sources of its power are.

And now for our English bard. William Wordsworth is notoriously anxious, of course, about the hiding places of his power, which sure enough deserted him completely after the age of 35 or so. But his poetry until then is a more or less continual effort to recover that original source. The famous "spots of time" from *Prelude* 12, with their "renovating virtue", reside chiefly in "those passages of life that give/Profoundest knowledge how and to what point/The mind is lord and master—outward sense the obedient servant of her will".[10] The most gifted or imaginative amongst us, those who are by "sensible impressions not enthralled", do indeed live in this "world of life", "for they are powers: and hence the highest bliss/That flesh can know is theirs,—the consciousness of whom they are" (*Prelude* 14). These people are those in whom the imagination, what Kant would have called the productive imagination, is most developed as "that glorious faculty/

---

[9]   Giovanni Pico della Mirandola, *De Hominis Dignitate* (1486), ed. and trans. Eugenio Garin, Firenze, 1942, p. 106.
[10]   Quotations are from the 1850 *Prelude*.

That higher minds bear with them as their own", "another name for absolute power/And clearest insight" (14). Here is the Wordsworthian analogue for Kantian spontaneity. Even though it is awakened by outward scenes, this *spontaneous imagination* is lord and master of outward sense, of intuition, and ultimately, perhaps, of Nature herself.

As we know, the *Prelude* more or less explicitly and *Tintern Abbey* more or less codedly tell the story of the breakdown or loss of this power and its eventual recovery. In the summer of 1793 Wordsworth was the father of an illegitimate child and the abandoner of both that child and its mother; he had no prospect of income; he was a recent witness to the destroyed hopes of liberalism in France, and a potential victim of both French revolutionary terrorism and the resultant reactionary repression in Britain; he was himself a near-vagrant, having just crossed on foot a Salisbury Plain filled with images ancient and modern of darkness, misery and sacrifice; and worst of all, perhaps, he had been led to the verge and indeed over the edge of breakdown by a moral philosophy which had at first seemed to offer new hope for disappointed liberals, but quickly came to represent for him all that was arid, abstract and destructive of spirit in philosophy in general. And so when he eventually reached the valley of the Wye he was, in the famous phrase from "Tintern Abbey", "more like a man/Flying from something that he dreads, than one who sought the thing he loved". What this story alludes to as the hidden heart of the whole Wordsworthian story, much more interesting and deeply hidden than any E P Thompson-type account of political "apostasy", is that the *natural* sublime of Snowdon or the Alps, the "something far more deeply interfused" suggesting an unfathomable depth both in the cosmos and in the poet's own mind, or better still the natural beauty of the Wye, are what the spontaneous imagination can connect to, can half create and half perceive: while the unbearable *human* sublime of the Revolution with its dizzy raptures on the one hand and its "never heads enough for those that bade them fall" on the other, or the quieter human beauty of love with Annette or even friendship with Coleridge and Dorothy, are what it cannot accommodate. Wordsworth's spontaneous imagination soars into the egotistical sublime in its interactions with the natural world, but is sucked into the egotistical *abîme*, to conflate Keats and Derrida, in its dealings with the human world.

The most celebrated occurrence of the word "spontaneous" in Wordsworth is in prose, of course, not poetry: at the point in the Preface to the *Lyrical Ballads* where he tells us that "all good poetry is the spontaneous overflow of powerful feelings". As John Stuart Mill pointed out, this was a description that did not apply very accurately to Wordsworth's own poetry, and for the good reason which Wordsworth himself articulates in that same Preface: that he thought long and deeply about the feelings before writing the poems, thus bringing the intuitions under the concepts, as one might say in Kantian vein. But even if that poetry cannot be said to *be* a spontaneous overflow, it is certainly *about* such moments: as in "Simon Lee", for example, where the action of the younger narrator in chopping through the tree root causes a spontaneous overflow of tears and gratitude in the old huntsman; or in "The Two April Mornings", where old Matthew stops short beside his daughter's grave and for some reason does *not* wish the blooming stranger were his. Coleridge, of course, more famously, has the same idea in mind in the *Rime of the Ancient Mariner*, where there is simply no accounting for the two crucial moments when the mariner shoots the bird and blesses the snakes. These are spontaneous acts. He blesses them *unaware*; a spring of love gushes spontaneously from his heart, like a prayer or a pouring out, as in a libation; the word "blessing", too, is etymologically connected with blood, and specifically with the idea of sacrifice in praise of God.

The difficult but critical connection between the Kantian spontaneity of the *understanding* and this Wordsworthian (and Coleridgian) spontaneity of *affection* is that both, for reasons partly locked up in the root sense of spontaneity itself, depend on a notion of pouring out or pledging the self: and even more, of an inexplicable, sacred, mysterious or even dangerous *source* of this activity. The very notion of a solemn engagement or giving of the self to a *sacred* cause, or more radically of the self *as* such a cause, implies something ineffable out of which all its activity proceeds, or may suddenly cease to proceed, as happened in Wordsworth's (or indeed Mill's) breakdown. And this is as true of the formidably schematic and rationalist Kantian self as it is of Wordsworth's sentimental empiricism. At the heart of both, I believe, is a kind of black box which there's no looking into, something of a different kind from the rest of the self: but out of this different and opaque centre emerge real imperatives, indeed all moral life. I'd like to call this almost the definitive Romantic manoeuvre, the step back from Enlightenment materialism or rationalism, the reserving of a special innermost corner of the self that the new science and philosophy can't get at. Whether your model of the self is basically rational like Kant's or basically passional like Wordsworth's, the move is the same. It's a non-negotiable withholding of the self from a perceived determinist scrutiny.

In the end, however, this spontaneity is by its own definition rather arbitrary. Resistance to determinism is really all it is. Such an account of the spontaneous self just says: there's a reserved bit you can't explain, can't get into, which also happens to be the most important bit. Of course in a sense this is a Lutheran and Augustinian move, but it isn't, say, a Thomist one: so it can't be identified with Christianity *per se*. On the other hand, the trick it performs is still very close to Cartesian dualism, although of course without Descartes' final recourse to God. Kant calls his black box, the mysteriously humming generator at the heart of all experience, the "spontaneity of understanding"; Wordsworth calls it "gratitude" or just "feeling"; Coleridge calls it "blessing"; St Paul, to change the epoch or paradigm, calls it "grace". The historical Romanticism of 1780-1830 perhaps differs from earlier manifestations of the same intellectual and moral habit in that what it grew out of and reacted against was the science and philosophy of the 17th and 18th centuries: it *was* that reaction. The keener the peculiar gaze of the Newtonian or Cartesian eye, the Galilean telescope or the Benthamite pan-opticon, the more dogmatic the resistance to its perceptions, the more private, far off, secret and inviolable the inner self, the more work it must do, the greater the moral burden it must bear, and of course bear alone, since of its nature it is out of contact with any other inner self. It is the solitary observer, knower and chooser; it bears the terrible burden of *knowing* that all that makes sense of the world and makes it non-contingent—is itself. This is a heavy and a weary weight all right. Other people are at best ends in themselves, therefore things in themselves, unknowable things rather than the sources of all our knowing. The Romantic generations were the first in history to feel that ancient tendency to dualism quite like this, to experience life without God like this: and in doing so they created modernity.

8

Birgitta Berglund

Dramas of Regeneration: The function of children and childbirth in Jane Austen's novels

Chapter 19 of *Pride and Prejudice*, containing Mr Collins' proposal to Elizabeth Bennet, is a wonderfully comic piece of writing and a favourite with many readers. However, present-day readers, and particularly young readers, often miss part of the sharpness of the comedy, as anybody in the habit of teaching the novel can testify. The fact that there was a very real risk that a girl like Elizabeth might have to marry a man like Mr Collins escapes most students today completely, and they see the proposal scene and Mr Collins himself as just wonderfully absurd.

When I teach the novel to first-year university students, I usually ask them to consider the following questions: 1/ Why does Elizabeth turn down this proposal of marriage? 2/ How many times does she actually say no? 3/ How can it be that Mr Collins does not seem to understand or accept her rejection? (Chapter 20 starts with the sentence "Mr. Collins was not left long to the silent contemplation of his successful love…".) My students find the first question frankly idiotic, the obvious answer to them being "She doesn't love him"; but I ask them to bear with me and consider *why* Elizabeth does not love Mr Collins and why we agree that it is impossible that she will ever marry him. This elicits the answer that Elizabeth is a bright, independent and pretty young woman who would never fall in love with a stupid, clumsy and pompous man like Mr Collins. (Some students also point out that Elizabeth and Mr Collins have entirely different conceptions of class and society, as shown in their different attitudes to the greatness of Lady Catherine de Bourgh.)

The second question (How many times does she say no?) is slightly more difficult, but a careful reading of the scene shows not only that Elizabeth actually says no an astounding five times, but also that she does so in no uncertain terms. My students then start to feel that it really is a bit of a mystery that Mr Collins does not take it in. He is admittedly stupid, but nobody could be *that* stupid. He does speak English, after all, and he obviously manages to function as a clergyman. He should be getting the message. Nor is he blinded by love. Mr Collins came to Longbourn with the express intention of choosing a wife among the Bennet sisters, first decided on the eldest, changed his mind when informed by Mrs Bennet that Jane was already spoken for, and after Elizabeth's rejection proposed and got engaged to her best friend instead. He was never in love with Elizabeth and cannot have imagined that she was in love with him. A further reading of the proposal scene, now concentrating on Mr Collins' responses to Elizabeth's five-fold "no", together with some discussion of the possibilities – or rather lack of possibilities – for a penniless young woman in the late eighteenth century, makes the students see that the crucial factor here is not love but money.

The nature of an entail, which Mr Bennet finds so difficult to explain to his wife, is the pivot on which the plot in *Pride and Prejudice* turns. It is the fact that Longbourn is entailed on a male heir that makes the situation of the Bennet sisters so precarious, Mrs Bennet so desperate for her daughters to marry, and Mr Collins so certain that Elizabeth will accept his proposal – and he is not afraid of pointing this out to the object of his desire: "My situation in life", he says, "my connections with the family of de Bourgh, and my relationship to your own, are circumstances highly in my favour; and you should take it into further consideration that in spite of your manifold attractions, it is by no means certain that another offer of marriage may ever be made to you. Your portion is unhappily so small that it will in all likelihood undo the effects of your loveliness and amiable qualifications (ch. 19)".

Mr Collins' lack of tact is mind-boggling; but, as students will be starting to realise at this point, his arguments, far from being stupid, make perfect sense and also give Mr Collins such a trump card that for Elizabeth to turn down his offer might indeed seem quite mad. By accepting marriage to Mr Collins, she would not only secure her own future, but also that of her mother and sisters. How many young women would have been able to turn down such an opportunity? Would Jane Bennet, for instance, had she been asked first and had there been no Mr. Bingley? (Probably not, is the general verdict of my students.) Would Elizabeth herself, if her father had joined forces with her mother in pressing her to accept? Perhaps, but there would have been nothing comic about the situation.[1]

That money is a key issue in all of Jane Austen's novels is a universally accepted truth, and so is the fact that the subject of money is intimately connected with the subject of marriage. Characters marry, or try to marry, for money (like Charlotte Lucas and Miss Bingley); they are prevented from marrying because of lack

---

[1] In the latest film version, this is actually spelled out to the audience by making Mrs Bennet use exactly these arguments in trying to make Elizabeth accept the offer. Elizabeth is also shown to be quite upset and unhappy about the situation. Unfortunately this attempt at giving a twenty-first-century audience an understanding of the circumstances and assumptions of the time is somewhat marred by Keira Knightley as Elizabeth crying defiantly: "You can't make me do it!" As if they couldn't.

of money (like Colonel Fitzwilliam); or they marry despite the lack of money and live to regret it (like Lydia and Mr Wickham).

However, I would claim that the subject of money is also closely connected to the idea of children and childbirth and that this is a state of affairs that may be more difficult to discern for a modern reader. What to us is the accepted way of attaining financial security – i.e. to perform well in school and at university, so as to qualify for a career within a prestigious and well-salaried profession – is not the obvious or natural way for a character in a Jane Austen novel. For women it is not an option at all, of course, but even for men it is an uncertain path. Although some of Austen's male characters are self-made men – Mr Gardiner in *Pride and Prejudice*, Mr Weston in *Emma* and Captain Wentworth in *Persuasion*, for instance – money is, on the whole, inherited rather than earned by work. It is the aim of this paper to show that the idea of inheriting an estate or securing it for one's children is quite as important as that of marrying into one, and that this is a concern which to some extent underlies or drives the plot in all of Jane Austen's novels, making the topic of childbirth a much more important one than might appear at first sight.

If we return to *Pride and Prejudice* to begin with, the crucial fact is that if Mrs Bennet had given birth to a son, as everybody assumed she would, the question of whom the Bennet girls would marry would have been a far less pressing one, and Mrs Bennet need not have worried about who would take care of her in her old age.

There is also another possibility, however. One of Mr Bennet's infuriating responses to his wife's quite understandable worries about the future is: "My dear, do not give way to such gloomy thoughts. Let us hope for better things. Let us flatter ourselves that *I* might be the survivor (ch. 23)." He might very well be, in fact. At a time when medicine was still more guesswork than science, a considerable number of women as well as men died before their time. The most common cause of death for women in fertile ages was of course childbirth.[2] That would not be a risk for Mrs Bennet as we meet her in the novel, since she is obviously past child-bearing age; but there were numerous other diseases which were lethal at the time, and which might quickly and unexpectedly kill an otherwise healthy

---

[2] Ruth Perry claims that at least 10 per cent of fertile, married women died in childbirth. This is based on her study of the Bills of Mortality in London 1657-1758 (Ruth Perry, "The Veil of Chastity: Mary Astell's Feminism", *Eighteenth-Century Fiction* 8, 2 (January 1996), 193-250). The numbers were not uniform, though. According to Rosemary O'Day, "It was more common for marriages among the peerage . . . to be dissolved by the death of a wife than of a husband. High mortality rates among aristocratic women seem to have been associated with childbirth and, especially, with intervention in childbirth. The rate of such deaths actually appears to have increased after 1750 as male medics began to assist female midwives." (Rosemary O'Day, *The Family and Family Relationships, 1500-1900*, London: Macmillan, 1994, p. 95; O'Day refers to Lawrence Stone and Jeanne C. Fawtier Stone, *An Open Elite? England, 1540-1880* (Oxford: Clarendon Press, 1984), p. 95.)

person. That this was the case, Jane Austen herself had the opportunity of seeing in her immediate family circle: of the five Austen brothers who married, all lost their first wives at fairly young ages; three died in childbirth and two in other diseases. Four of her six novels also contain widowed fathers whose wives have died young: General Tilney in *Northanger Abbey*, Mr Dashwood in *Sense and Sensibility*, Mr Woodhouse and Mr Weston in *Emma*, and Sir Walter Elliot in *Persuasion*.[3]

Let us speculate a bit: *If* Mrs Bennet died, Mr Bennet might remarry, and a new and younger wife might produce the longed-for heir. In fact, if concerned enough about his portionless daughters, a widowed Mr Bennet might remarry with that specific intention, quite apart from the perfectly natural wish for a more congenial partner in life than his first wife. Second marriages were certainly not unusual either in life or in literature; and although the idea of a woman remarrying upon the death of her husband was to some extent frowned upon, no such restrictions applied to men.[4] To return to the Austen family, three of the Austen brothers remarried upon the death of the first wife, and two of them fathered a new set of children with the second wife. This also happens in several of Austen's novels, and it is something that usually has important implications for their plots. In *Sense and Sensibility*, Mr Dashwood has thus married a younger woman[5] after the death of his first wife; in *Emma*, Mr Weston remarries and starts a new family in his middle age; and in *Persuasion*, finally, the mere idea that rich and good-looking Sir Walter Elliot might marry the redoubtable Mrs Clay – or any other young and fertile woman – is enough to worry not only Anne Elliot, who does not relish the idea of such a stepmother, but above all the present heir of the estate, Mr Elliot, who can clearly see the implications for his own future of such a marriage.

In fact, Mr Elliot is in exactly the same situation in relation to Kellynch as Mr

---

[3] The younger Mr Elliot in *Persuasion* is also a widower, although without children.

[4] Men who were widowed were two to three times more likely to remarry than women in the same situation. This was presumably to some extent at least because widowers, particularly with young children, remarried in order to obtain a housekeeper, whereas a woman, if she was economically independent, could manage the household herself with the help of servants, so that there was less incentive for her to remarry. However, 'there was also social and religious criticism of widows remarrying', especially if they had children (Robert B. Shoemaker, *Gender in English Society 1650-1850*, London and New York: Longman, 1998, p. 137). Some husbands even made stipulations in their wills which would make it disadvantageous for their widows to remarry (ibid., p. 138). (See also O'Day, *The Family and Family Relationships*, pp. 114-115.) This double standard is commented on by Austen in *Persuasion* in relation to the possible remarriages of Sir Walter Elliot and Lady Russell: "That Lady Russell, of steady age and character, and extremely well provided for, should have no thought of a second marriage, needs no apology to the public, which is rather apt to be unreasonably discontented when a woman does marry again, than when she does *not*; but Sir Walter's continuing in singleness requires explanation" (ch. 1).

[5] Mrs Dashwood is not yet forty at the death of her husband, and since Elinor, the eldest child, is then nineteen, she must have been barely twenty when she married Mr Dashwood, then a widower with a young son.

Collins is to Longbourn: he is a relatively distant relative, personally unknown to the family, who will inherit the estate because its present owner has fathered daughters only. Like Mr Collins, Mr Elliot also rather suddenly makes contact with the family and starts courting Anne Elliot for very much the same reasons as Mr Collins courts Elizabeth Bennet – albeit with considerably more tact and charm. His prime attraction to Anne, one that actually makes her consider such a marriage for a brief moment, is indeed his situation as the heir of the estate, and the idea that if she married him she need not lose her home – exactly the consideration that Mr Collins counts on as a strong argument in his favour with Elizabeth.

However, Mr Elliot's reasons for courting Anne go further than Mr Collins' clumsily stated but on the whole honourable idea of making amends for his situation as heir presumptive by marrying one of the daughters (or simply of finding a young woman who is not likely to turn down his proposal). Mr Elliot's main objective is to infiltrate Sir Walter's family in such a way that he can make sure that the widower is not tricked by a cunning and attractive young woman into a second marriage which might result in a son. That Sir Walter is not averse to the idea of a second marriage is clear from the beginning, as we are told that although his official explanation for remaining single is that it is for the sake of his daughters, his real reason is wounded pride, as he had "met with one or two private disappointments in very unreasonable applications" (ch. 1). The emphasis on the vain Sir Walter's excellent physique also serves as a reminder that this healthy and good-looking fifty-four-year-old could easily be envisaged as remarrying and producing an heir.

Children are intriguingly elusive presences in all of Austen's novels, but one way in which they are particularly interesting and important is within an economic framework, as heirs of estates. This is an aspect of childbirth that would have been present in the minds of readers of Jane Austen's day in a way which we do not appreciate today; and it would particularly be the case with readers belonging to her own class, the often impecunious country gentry with more children than estates to go round. The difference between the birth of a child (in particular the birth of a son) and a state of childlessness could mean the difference between affluence and destitution, between a family stepping up or sliding down the financial ladder.

It is the lack of a son that makes the Bennet women's situation so precarious and gives Mr Collins his great expectations. Likewise, it is the childlessness of the unnamed uncle and late owner of the Norland estate in *Sense and Sensibility* that makes for the expectations of the Dashwood family. It was upon the death of his sister, who acted as his housekeeper, that the old man invited into his home his nephew Henry Dashwood, "the legal inheritor of the Norland estate, and the person to whom he intended to bequeath it" (ch.1). Mr Dashwood is thus provided for by his uncle's lack of a son and heir, and it is Mr Dashwood's intention in his turn to leave the estate to his own wife and daughters. However, he is prevented from doing so by the existence of another child – his own grandchild, in fact: Mr Dashwood's son from his first marriage is the father of a little boy of four, and because this little boy has won the affections of Norland's late owner, Mr Dashwood only inherits the estate for the duration of his own life, after which it passes to little Harry.

It is this child who sets the plot of the novel in motion. If it had not been for him, Mrs Dashwood and her daughters would not have been reduced to genteel poverty on Mr Dashwood's death; they would not have moved from Sussex to Devonshire; and Marianne would never have come in the way of Mr Willoughby and Colonel Brandon. The existence of a son and heir is thus as important to the plot of *Sense and Sensibility* as the lack of one is to *Pride and Prejudice*.

Emma is not a novel so obviously built around the idea of inheritance, but there are nevertheless very similar implications and concerns. At the beginning of the novel, Mr Knightley, the owner of Donwell Abbey, is in a position similar to that of the owner of the Norland estate in that he is a rich and childless uncle to his younger brother's children – a situation which is particularly important to the eldest boy, who is obviously regarded as the heir of Donwell. It is significant that when Mrs Weston first suggests to Emma that Mr Knightley might be in love with Jane Fairfax, Emma reacts with horror on her nephew's account: " 'Mr Knightley and Jane Fairfax!' exclaimed Emma. 'Dear Mrs. Weston, how could you think of such a thing? – Mr. Knightley! – Mr. Knightley must not marry! – You would not have little Henry cut out from Donwell? – Oh, no, no, Henry must have Donwell' " (ch. 26). When she thinks through the idea later, it is still this aspect that is uppermost in Emma's mind: "Her objections to Mr. Knightley's marrying did not subside. She could see nothing but evil in it. It would be a great disappointment to Mr John Knightley; consequently to Isabella. A real injury to the children – a most mortifying change, and material loss to them all" (ibid).

It is certainly true that Emma does not know herself, that she is mistaken about her own feelings, and that her real objection to this marriage is the fact that she is herself in love with Mr Knightley. Even so, I would claim that it is significant that Emma's (and I would suspect many nineteenth-century readers') first reaction to the suggestion of a new marriage is what the marriage in question would mean to the families involved on either side, and that this is closely connected to the idea of children and inheritance. If Mr Knightley were to marry, he would most certainly father children, and the birth of even one child at Donwell Abbey would rock the economic boat of his brother's family.

Later, when Emma is herself engaged to be married to Mr Knightley, Austen returns to this aspect with an ironic comment on Emma's change of attitude: "It is remarkable, that Emma, in the many, very many, points of view in which she was now beginning to consider Donwell Abbey, was never struck with any sense of injury to her nephew Henry, whose rights as heir expectant had formerly been so tenaciously regarded" (ch. 52). To a modern reader this might perhaps seem to indicate that Emma's earlier considerations were far-fetched and not to be regarded seriously. However, this is not necessarily the case. The irony should be seen as directed at Emma's cheerful and perfectly natural selfishness, which makes it quite acceptable for little Henry to be robbed of his inheritance when it is on the behalf of Emma herself rather than Jane Fairfax. That the child *is* robbed of his expectations by the marriage of his uncle is still a fact, though, and one that Emma is perhaps not entirely indifferent to.

Nor, apparently, are the inhabitants of Highbury, since one reaction to the news of the engagement is, significantly, the suggestion that instead of Mr Knightley moving in with Emma and Mr Woodhouse at Hartfield, they should all move to Donwell Abbey and leave Hartfield to the John Knightleys. The implication seems to be that since Emma's future children will be the heirs of the Donwell estate, she should make amends by resigning whatever claims she might have on Hartfield to her sister's children. As for Emma herself, at the end of the novel we see her rejoicing at the birth of a daughter to Mrs Weston because this makes possible thoughts of a future marriage between one of her nephews and the little girl. It is easy to laugh at this as merely another example of Emma's match-making propensities and proof of her not having changed very much after all. However, there is more to this idea than that. Since Frank, Mr Weston's son from his first marriage, has been formally adopted by and made the heir of his rich relatives, the Churchills, it seems clear that little Anna Weston will be the sole heiress of her father's moderate fortune. (It is implied, although not openly stated, that Mrs Weston's age makes it unlikely that she will have more children after this one.) With one nephew inheriting Hartfield and the other marrying into Randalls, Emma need have no qualms about having injured either of them by her marriage.

Staying with *Emma*, I would further like to suggest that the frequent references to Mr Woodhouse's frailness and his being old before his time are there partly to stress the fact that in this case there is no risk of a second marriage to a younger woman. When Emma exclaims to Harriet Smith: "I believe few married women are half as much mistress of their husband's house as I am of Hartfield; and never, never could I expect to be so truly beloved and important; so always first and always right in any man's eyes as I am in my father's" (ch.10), she is explaining her own disinclination to marry. However, the statement also serves to demonstrate her father's lack of inclination in this respect. The stress throughout the novel on Mr Woodhouse's childlike devotion to his younger daughter, as well as his comic aversion to marriages which break up family circles, function to assure readers that this is a widower who will not remarry, and that Emma's queen-like status as mistress of Hartfield will not be threatened by a stepmother and a young brother.[6]

I began these reflections with Mr Collins' proposal to Elizabeth Bennet, and I should like to return to it by way of conclusion. Mr Collins may be clumsy, tactless and selfish, but he is not quite as stupid as students may think at first; and when it comes to economic matters he is quite astute. A man who knows exactly not just how much money the woman he intends to marry owns and how much she is likely to inherit, but also how it is invested,[7] will also be well aware of his own economic prospects; and with a little Bennet boy being born at Longbourn they would definitely dwindle. This gives a further edge to his wish to secure one of the Bennet girls in marriage. It may be seen not only as a way of making amends for his situation as heir presumptive, or of finding a young woman who is not likely to refuse him: married to Elizabeth and part of the Bennet family circle, Mr Collins would stand a much better chance of inheriting the Longbourn estate, and Mr Bennet's motives for remarrying in the event of his first wife's death would be much weaker, since instead of securing the estate for his offspring he would in fact be robbing his favourite daughter of it.

All of the above may be considered idle and frivolous speculations, a parlourgame along the lines of "What if...?" However, considerations like these would have been uppermost in the minds of readers belonging to Jane Austen's time and class, readers to whom children and childbirth were not only literally matters of life and death but also crucial to the long-term economic success or failure of entire (extended) families. If we do not pay attention to them, we miss a layer of meaning in her novels. To return once more to *Pride and Prejudice*, we are told towards the end of the novel that Mrs Collins is expecting a baby. This circumstance, easily passed over as an incidental detail by present-day readers, is a fact highly pregnant with meaning to the characters involved: as the reading public of two centuries ago would have appreciated, Charlotte's fertility seals the inevitability of the Bennets' loss of Longbourn.

So, to conclude: Consider the little children – for they shall inherit the estate.

---

[6] Otherwise, what would have been more natural than for Mr Woodhouse rather than Mr Weston to marry Miss Taylor?

[7] "I am well aware . . . that one thousand pounds in the 4 per cents. which will not be yours until after your mother's decease, is all that you may ever be entitled to," he informs Elizabeth during the proposal (ch. 19).

9

Lawrence Buell

Fictive Nation-Building on the Grand Scale: Contested Templates for "The Great American Novel"

This essay is an interim report on a long-term study of the chimera of the great American novel—the dream either of writing it or of seeing it written.[1] My project has three main facets: a historical review of commentary on the subject (a story with a distinct beginning, several middles, and no end); a formalist examination of several dozen aspirants or nominees, organized in terms of a typology of recurring structural patterns; and a nation-and-narration metaperspective conceptualizing "American" narrative as, in broadest terms, part of a world system inflected by what Pascale Casanova calls the "Herder effect": the postulate that each nation shall speak in its own voice, within and against which even determined cosmopolitans like Joyce and Beckett must contend.[2]

This might seem a distinctly unfashionable project. First, it might seem to be out of phase with the recent Americanist push to think "beyond" or "outside" the confines of nationness that has been an energizing force behind many of the papers in the section of the conference where this one was first delivered, including Professor Giles' essay in the present volume. Beyond this, the topic of great American novelism *per se* may well seem quaintly paleolithic, a relic of the bygone precritical past. Indeed, during its nearly 150-year history, critical elites have repeatedly disparaged it as naive, quixotic, shallow, jingoistic, market-driven, etc.—a stream of deprecation that continues down to this day. "Aside from [irritating] the literati, does the Great American Novel, a monumentally 19th century concept, serve any higher purpose?"—so begins one recent manifesto.[3]

---

[1] I am grateful to colleagues both at the IAUPE triennial conference in Lund and at the Dartmouth Institute for American Studies for their responses to previous drafts of this essay, to the National Endowment for the Humanities for fellowship support, and to my excellent research assistants: William Pannapacker, Jared Hickman, Brian Distleberg, Christopher Le Coney, and Jamie Jones.
[2] Pascale Casanova, *The World Republic of Letters*, trans. M. B. DeVevoise (Cambridge, MA: Harvard University Press, 2004), 77ff.
[3] Alan Williams, "Whatever Happened to the Great American Novel? (Part Deux)," *Simon Magazine*, 10 May 2007.

In fact, the dream of the GAN—first satirically reduced to its acronym by none other than Henry James[4]—has been killed off not once but at least twice. First by quickly degenerating into a media cliché—on the same level, one late-19th-century critic observed, as "the great American sewing-machine, the great American public school, [and] the great American sleeping car."[5] It was killed off again with the rise of academic American literary studies in the middle half of the 20th century, in a string of scholarly articles dismissing it as naively amateurish age-of-realism hubris, "faded into the limbo of literary lost causes."[6] Moving more slowly through the epochs from then to now, we find a bad-tempered equivalent of the "escalator effect" with which Raymond Williams metaphorizes the history of pastoral nostalgia, each generation fancying that the one before lived a life closer to nature.[7] Great American Novel commentary, by contrast, plays itself through as a discourse of repeated *dis*-enchantment: each generation seeing the one before as more gullible than itself.

Yet the legacy of detraction proves the durability of the irritant. Neither critical nor internal skepticism ever kept American writers from attempting big national fictions, then or now. "Every American novelist," Maxine Hong Kingston has written, secretly "wants to write the Great American Novel."[8] She wrote this during the runup to *Tripmaster Monkey,* her most ambitious novel. Consider too the spate of Year-2000 fictional tomes that aspired to sum up the century, or at least the half-century, such as John Updike's *The Beauty of the Lilies* and Don DeLillo's *Underworld.* As my colleague Louis Menand remarked to me, although no self-respecting reviewer today would ever praise a new book as the long-awaited great American novel, it is hard to think of a major US novelist who has not given it a try. The persistence in the face of skepticism and mockery of desire for a preeminent text—whether past, present, or future—that might encapsulate U. S. national experience reflects an entrenched quasi-understanding—however problematic—among authors, critics, publishing industry, and readers at large to read the national through N number of a perhaps infinitely extending series of putative master narratives. This alliance is reinforced every time some journalist compares Lyndon Johnson, Richard Nixon, or George W. Bush to Captain Ahab stalking the white whale.

As to the first objection, the obsolescence of the nation-focus, my aim is to

---

4   James to Howells, 5 December 1880, *Henry James Letters*, ed. Leon Edel (Cambridge, MA: Harvard University Press, 1975), 2: 321.
5   James L. Allen, "The Great American Novel," *Independent* (July 24, 1891): 1403.
6   George Knox, "In Search of the Great American Novel," *Western Review,* 5 (Summer 1968), 64.
7   Raymond Williams, *The Country and the City* (New York: Oxford University Press, 1973), 9-12.
8   Maxine Hong Kingston, "Cultural Mis-readings by American Reviewers," *Asian and Western Writers in Dialogue: New Cultural Identities*, ed. Guy Amirthanayagam (London: Macmillan, 1982), 57-58.

treat the centripetal forces at play in the light of the migratory character of the preferred tropes and plot strategies, as well as the fascination with the animating idea itself. Broadly speaking, the conception of "a" great national novel would seem to be one, though hardly the only inevitable, outcome of "the national longing for form," as Timothy Brennan has called it, in a context of acute anxiety about cultural coherence and legitimation, such as gripped the postcolonial Anglo-American intelligentsia that first gave rise to the GAN idea.[9] Why a similar discourse developed among creole elites in some Latin American countries but not others,[10] or why there should be no equivalent for the 19th century German literary history of Alessandro Mazzoni's *I Promessi Sposi* (1842) despite the analogous condition of a populace culturally interknit striving to realize itself as a unified country, may forever remain something of a mystery. For now, suffice it to say that even though there is probably no *precise* equivalent to the GAN discourse tradition elsewhere, U. S. literary-cultural history is hardly unique in its fascination with fictional narratives that promise to sum up the national essence, nor by the same token must an inquiry into such lead to naive reaffirmation of national literary autonomy.

Often it is impossible to specify when a concept is born. But in this case we can: in a short essay of January, 1868 by New England man of letters and Civil War veteran John W. De Forest,[11] author of a new novel that clearly tried to model his idea, *Miss Ravenel's Conversion from Secession to Loyalty* (1867)—one of those historically noteworthy but intractably subcanonical texts that keep getting rediscovered and then falling out of print.

De Forest envisaged a work that would capture "the American soul" through portrayal of "the ordinary emotions and manners of American existence" *via* a "tableau" that would grasp the full geographical and cultural range of national life, with the amplitude of a Thackeray, a Trollope, a Balzac, or a George Sand. To date, he argues, American fiction has been overwhelmingly "local" or sectional; moreover its best fiction writer, Hawthorne, captures "little but the subjective of humanity." The closest approximation so far is Harriet Beecher Stowe's *Uncle Tom's Cabin* (1852), which despite glaring defects *did* at least have "a national breadth to the picture, truthful outlining of character, natural speaking, . . . drawn with a few strong and passionate strokes, not filled in thoroughly, but still a portrait."

De Forest risked self-contradiction in taking for granted that there *must* be

---

9   Timothy Brennan, "The National Longing for Form," *Nation and Narration*, ed. Homi K. Bhabha (London: Routledge, 1990), 44-70.

10 See Doris Sommer, *Foundational Fictions: The National Romances of Latin America* (Berkeley: University of California Press, 1991).

11 J. W. De Forest, "The Great American Novel," *The Nation*, 6 (9 January 1868): 27-29.

such a thing as *an* "American soul," although the literary evidence to date, by his own testimony, argued the contrary. He was myopic in postulating that regional and national writing must be antagonistic projects. So too his assessment of *Uncle Tom's Cabin,* which shows scant interest in slavery and racial division except as issues now resolved, much less in the possibility that a black novelist (say) might see things differently from a white one. Such limitations mark him as the product of a particular background and time: a white Anglo-American Yankee writing in the immediate aftermath of the war, with fictional realism coming into ascendancy, long before the critical establishment began to take serious notice of a body of narrative writing by writers other than white Protestant.

Myopic—yet prophetic too. Critical calls for an autonomous national literature dated back to the Revolution—but no substantive theory of what might constitute *national* fiction had congealed, partly because of the regional fissuring De Forest deplores. With the war behind and completion of territorial conquest and hinterland settlement in sight, the GAN was also (for the first time) a real possibility. It was, in short, the leading literary edge of what historian Nina Silber calls the "romance of reunion" between northern and southern whites—and, beyond that, a leading literary edge of a broader, century-long push toward consolidation of the nation as a literary, cultural, and political unit.[12] Also pivotal was prose fiction's rising critical prestige stateside. Nina Baym, who has studied this aspect of antebellum criticism most closely, argues (rightly, I think) that the emergence of the GAN idea presupposed a greater acceptance of prose fiction as a high art form,[13] although Cooper, Sedgwick, Hawthorne, Poe, Melville, Stowe, and others helped make this possible. Significantly, even after much sleuthing, I have managed to unearth only two isolated antebellum references to "the great American novel," the earliest an advertisement for a London penny edition reprint (1852) of—fortuitously—*Uncle Tom's Cabin* that simply touts its runaway best-seller status.[14]

De Forest's essay was no less consequential for its concurrence with a rising tide of high nationalist theory abroad. This was the eve of Ernest Renan's seminal

---

[12] Nina Silber, *The Romance of Reunion: Northerners and the South, 1865-1900* (Chapel Hill: University of North Carolina Press, 1993); Paul Giles, "The Deterritorialization of American Literature," *Shades of the Planet: American Literature as World Literature,* ed. Wai Chee Dimock and Lawrence Buell (Princeton: Princeton University Press, 2007), 39-61.

[13] Baym, personal correspondence.

[14] Harriet Beecher Stowe, *Uncle Tom's Cabin: The Great American Novel, to be completed in six weekly numbers, price one penny each Saturday, August 7, 1852* (London: Vickers, 1852). The prefatory "A Few Words to the British Reader" characterizes *UTC* as "the most interesting and startling work of the age. . . . The work has produced, and is producing, such a sensation as no book ever produced before in America or in Europe." This comports with the general promotion strategy for the book on both sides of the Atlantic; cf. Michael Winship, "'The Greatest Book of Its Kind': A Publishing History of *Uncle Tom's Cabin,*" *Proceedings of the American Antiquarian Society,* 109.ii (1999): 309-332.

premodern manifesto, "What Is a Nation?", which defined "a nation" as "a living soul, a spiritual principle," entailing "the common possession of a rich heritage of memories" and the will to preserve "the undivided inheritance which has been handed down."[15] That personification of nationness as living soul is the remote ancestor of the most influential treatise on nationalism of recent times, Benedict Anderson's *Imagined Communities*,[16] a book sharply critical of Renan yet by the same token providing even greater reinforcement for the great-national-novel idea. The contrast between Renan and Anderson I especially have in mind is of course Anderson's theory of nations as acts of collective imagination rather than as primordially "there." This model has in turn been criticized as overblown, but the effect has been to intensify attention toward the historic role of literature and the arts in the work of nation-building. Through an Andersonian prism, nations, as one critic puts it, start to seem to "depend for their [very] existence on an apparatus of cultural fictions in which imaginative literature generally [and the rise of the novel particularly] plays a decisive role."[17] De Forest himself would never have made such big claims about the *American* novel, which for him barely existed. His view, like Renan's, was that national fiction presupposed an "American soul," not that fiction was a nation-building force. He shows no interest in *Uncle Tom's Cabin's* social activism, much less its possible role in touching off the Civil War. Yet he takes the notion of nation-building and fiction-building as intertwined projects to a new plane of affirmation that has never ceased to haunt later novelistic and critical practice.

The GAN idea soon entrenched itself as a term of reference in criticism, reviewing, and book promotion, despite the skepticism it provoked.[18] Though used much more as an impressionistic epithet than as a theory definable with any precision, at least three connotations quickly took hold.

First, GAN discourse commingles retrospect with anticipation, typically stipulating that the GAN remains unwritten albeit some previous named effort points the way. When a specific claim *is* lodged, except for publisher advertisements of new titles, the novel in question is usually at least a decade old, and often far older. Second, GAN discourse therefore correlates broadly, though unevenly, with evolving canon theory, increasingly appropriated over time, but never monopolized, by the professoriat. On the one hand, GAN discourse is a far more open,

---

[15] Mazzini, "To the Italians" (1871), in Vincent Pecora, ed., *Nations and Identities* (Oxford: Blackwell, 2001), 157; Ernest Renan, "What is a Nation?" (1882), in *ibid.*, 174, 175.

[16] Anderson, *Imagined Communities: Reflections on the Origin and Spread of Nationalism*, rev. ed. (London: Verso, 1991); cf. p. 15.

[17] Timothy Brennan, 49.

[18] The fullest review of late-19th-century primary sources is Charles A. Campbell, Jr., "'The Great American Novel': A Study in Literary Nationalism," Ph. D. Diss., University of Minnesota, 1951.

participatory, discourse than the academic, as evidenced during the early years by contributors' columns in newspapers and magazines and in our own time by internet blogs. When I googled "great american novel" while drafting this essay I got 2,660,000 hits—many of them redundant, of course. On the other hand, both late-Victorian readers at large and turn-of-the-21st-century bloggers have been regularly swayed, even against their intuitive judgments, by critical authority, as for instance with those today who accept *Moby-Dick* as a possible GAN while confessing that they do not much like or understand it.

A third constituent is the paradox of the one and the many. Although the mythical GAN is regularly hypostasized as a singular, unique "the," more often than not it is deployed *de facto* as a plural category: a top five, for instance, as with the much-publicized 2006 *New York Times* poll of the best American novels of the past quarter century.[19] (The winner was Toni Morrison's *Beloved*.) This pluralization comports with the typical disputes, starting with De Forest himself, over criteria. Should regional fiction be disallowed? Frank Norris, for one, argued the opposite. Should the setting necessarily be American? Edith Wharton argued the contrary.[20] Must it be a realist mimesis? Although most authors and readers seem to have thought so, especially through the 1930s, many objected from the start, anticipating the now-discredited but hardly defunct correlation proposed first by D. H. Lawrence and F. R. Leavis and then by Lionel Trilling, Richard Chase, and Leslie Fiedler, of romance as the mark of American fictional difference—a claim sometimes made for Latin American narrative as well.[21]

So even though the GAN has typically been deployed as a labeling device, it also implies at least a rudimentary conceptual matrix, an incipient critical problematic, and not merely for the score of novels most commonly so named by those who play the game, but also as a basis for mapping the whole, massively complex ever-changing flow of narrative discourse in U. S. literary history.

Several templates or recipes—not mutually exclusive—seem to facilitate, though hardly ensure, GAN status. The most obvious and reliable is to have been subjected repeatedly to a series of memorable rewritings (in whatever genre or media) such that the text seems to assume a kind of master-narrative status, whether or not it aspired to such to start with. *The Scarlet Letter* is perhaps the

---

[19] A. O. Scott, "In Search of the Best," *New York Times Book Review*, 21 May 2006, 16-19.

[20] Frank Norris, "The Great American Novelist," *The Literary Criticism of Frank Norris*, ed. Donald Pizer (Austin: University of Texas Press, 1964), 122-124; Edith Wharton, "The Great American Novel," *Yale Review*, 16, n.s. (1927): 646-656.

[21] For Latin America, see for example Edouard Glissant, *Caribbean Discourse: Selected Essays*, trans. J. Michael Sash (Charlottesville, VA: University Press of Virginia, 1989), 105. For a critical history of the England: novel, US: romance hypothesis (from a standpoint sympathetic to the distinction), see G. Richard Thompson and Eric Carl Link, *Neutral Ground: New Traditionalism and the American Romance Controversy* (Baton Rouge: Louisiana State University Press, 1999).

most striking premodern case in point, both despite and because it is arguably at least as much a "diasporic" or "Atlantic-world" narrative as an "American" one, despite having traditionally been treated by Americanists as a designedly fictive myth of national/Puritan origins.[22] Recipe/template two might be called the romance of the divide (or divides), fictions of sectional and/or ethnic division that instantiate that division in the form of a family history and/or heterosexual love affair, which thereby becomes a national synecdoche. De Forest's *Miss Ravenel* builds upon this trope, although by far the most influential pre-modern fiction is *Uncle Tom's Cabin*. Template three is a narrative centering on the lifeline of a socially paradigmatic figure (traditionally male, but diminishingly so), whose saga tilts on the one side toward the picaresque and on the other toward a plot of personal transformation, spiritual or material or both—or the failure of such. Here the fiction that has become the text of commonest reference is *Huckleberry Finn*. An expanded variant of the socially representative protagonist's saga, indeed arguably a category of its own, is the saga of the paradigmatic family, like Gertrude Stein's *The Making of Americans* and John Steinbeck's *Grapes of Wrath*. A fourth template is the constellation of a heterogeneous assemblage of individuals, often though not always in a confined space around a common task, but almost always involving a high degree of scene-shifting geographic mobility, who taken together image the promise and/or the failure of democratic possibility. Here *Moby-Dick*, with its complex ideologization of the shipboard microcosm, today stands preeminent. That *The Scarlet Letter, Uncle Tom's Cabin, Huckleberry Finn,* and *Moby-Dick* have been cited in latter-day lists of possible GANs more often than any other premodern fictions confirms the ongoing influence of critical canonization (in Stowe's case, recanonization), ratified by school syllabi and artistic recyclings at various levels of sophistication from pop to avant-garde, in shaping public memory of what counts as monumental in the distant past if not the near distance.[23]

These encapsulations, terse and formulistic as they are, should substantiate why a Great-American-Novel project must be transnational—and also transgeneric. Recipe number three, especially, cannot be understood without taking into account picaresque and *Bildungsroman* traditions, not to mention such nonfictional prototypes as slave narrative, conversion narrative, and its secular counterpart and successor, Franklinesque stories of success (*or* failure)—none of whose provenances is wholly cisatlantic. But it is especially the contestedness, the messiness, with which what I have lumpingly called the templates or recipes are

---

[22]   See my "Hawthorne and the Problem of 'American Fiction': The Example of *The Scarlet Letter,*" *Hawthorne and the Real*, ed. Millicent Bell (Columbus: Ohio State University Press, 2005), 70-87.

[23]   A symptomatic instance is the Wikipedia entry for "Great American Novel" (1 June 2007): http://en.wikipedia.org/wiki/Great_American_Novel

implemented in practice that I wish to concentrate on in the final section of this essay, with *Huckleberry Finn* as my case in point.

Luckily for me, of the four putative pre-20th-century great American novels just named, *Huckleberry Finn* is the novel whose canon history has been analyzed most searchingly, above all by Jonathan Arac, who demonstrates that its "hyper-canonization" was problematically catalyzed by an influential group of American critics after World War II—among whom he singles out especially Lionel Trilling and Leo Marx. These critics, according to Arac, reinterpreted what was in the author's own day read as a bad-boy story in the comic regional picaresque vein as a work of high moral seriousness and national-political vision, starring a liberal hero who revolts against the regime of plantation slavery by which he has been conditioned (a regime these critics implicitly equated with the communist menace), when he decides in that memorable thirty-first chapter to "go to hell" rather than betray Jim.[24]

Although Arac is by no means the first scholar to dissent from the mid-century apotheosis of *Huck Finn*,[25] he argues with unequaled thoroughness and erudition against the problematic "mythicization of history" entailed in *Huck Finn's* displacement of *Uncle Tom's Cabin* as *the* definitive classic national anti-slavery novel, "despite its having been written at a time when slavery did not exist and was defended by no one," despite Huck's prevailing deference to the regime of slavery apart from his one act of shamefaced defiance, and despite the fact that late-19th-century readers rarely if ever seem to have taken the novel as a serious engagement with issues of slavery or racism.[26]

Arac's analysis of this retro-fitting of *Huck Finn* helps explain why the first GAN contenders to bear distinct marks of its influence date only from the 1950s: Saul Bellow's *The Adventures of Augie March*, Ralph Ellison's *Invisible Man*, and J. D. Salinger's *Catcher in the Rye*. Beyond this, it helps make at least partial sense of the somewhat perplexing fact that the template of the Great American Novel as socially-representative protagonist-biography-centered fiction seems to have crystallized fully a mere generation before, with the concurrent publication in the mid-1920s of Fitzgerald's *The Great Gatsby*, Theodore Dreiser's *An Ameri-*

---

[24] Jonathan Arac, Huckleberry Finn *as Idol and Target: The Functions of Criticism in Our Time* (Madison: University of Wisconsin Press, 1997), 108-183 *et passim*. For the textual moment in question, see *Adventures of Huckleberry Finn*, rev. ed., ed. Victor Donyo (New York: Random House, 1996), 273. (Here and elsewhere I cite the expanded edition of *HF* based on the rediscovered manuscript of the first half of the novel.) For *Huck Finn's* perceived significance in its own time as a "bad-boy" novel, see especially Steven Mailloux, *Rhetorical Power* (Ithaca: Cornell University Press, 1989), 100-129.

[25] For an early example, see William van O'Connor, "Why Huckleberry Finn is Not the Great American Novel," *College English*, 17 (October 1953): 6-10, which observes *inter alia* that "Twain sometimes loses sight of Huck's moral sensitivity" (7).

[26] Quotation from Arac, 93. Mailloux, *Rhetorical Power*, also remarks on the two latter points.

can Tragedy, and Sinclair Lewis' *Babbitt*, central to all of which is the device of measuring the focal figure's moral worth as he attempts to live out the American dream of material success. Perhaps the full efflorescence of the template might have something to do with the intertwined emergence between the two world wars of the U. S. as a dominant world power and of American literature and American studies as organized, coordinate academic fields.[27] Some such interlinkage seems implicit in Arac's critique of the canonization of Huck's moral individualism as part and parcel of a broader mid-century critical "nationalization of literary narrative" empowering a "national first-person subject" that privileges the "imaginative space of psychological interiority" to the neglect of the imbrication of personal with social.[28] These strictures are broadly congruent with the widespread diagnosis by other revisionist American critics of the past twenty years of the valorization of free-standing individual interiority as the glory of "free" America, contra Soviet Russia and German National Socialism, as a hallmark of much so-called "cold war criticism."

On the other hand, pre-1920s American fiction (not to mention autobiography) hardly lacked for attempts at protagonist-centered plots centered on representative American figures with more or less emphasis on psychological interiority and relatively little commitment to rendering social geography at the national level. A few examples that spring to mind include Henry James's *The American* and *Portrait of a Lady*, W. D. Howells' *The Rise of Silas Lapham*, Stephen Crane's *The Red Badge of Courage*, Robert Herrick's *Memoirs of an American Citizen*, and the one Wharton novel the author seems to have considered a GAN project, *The Custom of the Country*, featuring the murderously innocent parvenue Undine Spragg. If none of these or other such books won acclaim as GAN candidates, it was not because the trope or template of the individual exemplar lacked cultural capital. On the contrary, as Sacvan Bercovitch has shown, it dates back to early colonial times.[29] Why then could not *Huckleberry Finn*, in principle, have achieved GAN status sooner than the mid-20th century?

In point of fact it did, and rather quickly too, although not for most critics—even the critical *doyen* of his day, William Dean Howells, Twain's admirer and close friend, esteemed *Uncle Tom's Cabin* much more highly than *Huckleberry Finn*; and the grounds on which the latter was praised by its enthusiasts had nothing to do with the issue of the protagonist's moral heroism. Consider the very first claim on behalf of *Huckleberry Finn* as the GAN, lodged in 1891 by

---

[27] On this point, see David R. Shumway, *Creating American Civilization: A Genealogy of American Literature as an Academic Discipline* (Minneapolis: University of Minnesota Press, 1994).

[28] Arac, 212-213, 135.

[29] Sacvan Bercovitch, *The Puritan Origins of the American Self* (New Haven: Yale University Press, 1973).

Scottish man-of-letters and folklorist Andrew Lang, best known today for his many compendia of fairy tales. Lang admired the "unrestrained sense of humor" and deliciously vivid droll meanderings through "towns full of homicidal loafers" that the Cold War critics euphemized. Indeed, he went so far as to praise *Huck Finn* on that same account as "an historical novel . . . more valuable . . . to the historian than 'Uncle Tom's Cabin,'" precisely because "written without partisanship, and without 'a purpose,'" by reason of its pseudo-autobiographical comic picaresque.[30] Here Lang stakes out a position precisely opposite that of Arac's liberal critics. American satirist H. L. Mencken, who as a boy first delightedly read the book at about the time of Lang's essay, later followed suit in much the same terms (though without recourse to the "GAN" label), acclaiming *Huckleberry Finn* as "one of the great masterpieces of the world," fully equal to *Don Quixote*, "the greatest work of imagination that These States have yet seen"; and praising Twain as the first American writer "to immerse himself willingly and with gusto in the . . . life of his time and country" and "to understand the common man of his race."[31]

The sharp divergence between these assessments and those of the Cold War critics discussed by Arac arises partly from their presumption of a different GAN template: that of the shifting heteroglot assemblage, broadly in keeping with De Forest's supposition that the GAN would be a work of panoramic realism. This is a telling instance both of the potential convergence or overlay in practice of what I earlier described simplistically as a menu of discrete possibilities, and of how the sense of what the defining template is may shift over time. An even more crucial difference between the turn-of-the-20th-century and the mid-20th-century encomia, however, is their divergent view of the importance, to put it crudely, of high moral seriousness as a requisite of the GAN. Arac concentrates mainly on the irony of the scene of white adolescent *angst* in a novel invested mostly in the re-creation of bygone antebellum white culture (and Huck as a figure therein) having been singled out by the mid-20th-century liberal critics as *the* classic exposure of slavery. This is an entirely understandable critique from the standpoint of our present dispensation of critical race studies, from which perspective it seems self-evident (*vide* the *New York Times* 2006 poll) that a GAN might be written from "the margins" as well as from "the center"—an unthinkable prospect for De Forest's generation and doubtless also Twain's own—and the authority of "the center" to speak for "the margin" seems deeply suspect. But Arac's project does

---

30 Andrew Lang, "The Art of Mark Twain," *Illustrated London News*, 14 February 1891, 222. For an antithetical mid-20th-century assessment of much of what Lang praises, see William van O'Connor, *op. cit.*

31 H. L. Mencken, review of Albert Bigelow Paine's *Mark Twain: A Biography* (1912), *H. L. Mencken on American Literature*, ed. S. T. Joshi (Athens, OH: Ohio State University Press, 2002), 24, 33, 29.

not allow him directly to take up the question of novelistic tone *per se* as a (dis) qualifying element. Can a raffishly satirical work written from the perspective of a shrewd and good-hearted but indolent juvenile slacker, whose chief strategies for coping with a toxic dominant culture are evasion and (when trapped) accommodation, really be a GAN? That in effect is precisely what Lang and Mencken claimed. But is this sustainable? After all, what kind of national self-image is that?

Here it may be instructive to glance back at the protagonist-centered fictions mentioned earlier from the 1920s and 1950s. Most of the protagonists are quite venial (Lewis' Babbitt, Dreiser's Clyde Griffiths, Bellow's Augie, Salinger's Holden Caulfield most conspicuously); all the novels take a wryly if not caustically satirical view of dominant American culture; and all three of the 1950s texts—*Augie March, Invisible Man,* and *Catcher in the Rye*—are in different ways comic masterpieces. All this would tend to suggest that the GAN is at least as receptive to stories of failure as to tales of success and to veniality as to heroism, and hardly unreceptive to comic satire, clowning, and even "outrageous" ribaldry. (Think here also of *Moby-Dick* and *Gravity's Rainbow.*) To be sure, *Invisible Man* and *Catcher,* if not *Augie,* also suffuse a degree of moral striving alien to the Twainian world as represented by Lang and Mencken. But here it is revealing to enlist Ralph Ellison against himself, as it were. On the one hand, no liberal critic of his day urged more strongly the milestone significance of *Huckleberry Finn*'s "image of black and white fraternity," both despite and because of the minstrel-show reduction of Jim that Ellison confessed made him wince ("a white man's inadequate portrait of a slave").[32] On the other hand, Ellison also insisted—also with frequent reference to *Huckleberry Finn* as a touchstone—on the importance of not overlooking, as Lionel Trilling and other contemporary critics had, Henry James's cryptic allusion to "the American joke," which Ellison, almost as cryptically, suggested might have been "the objective of the American novel all along."

Elsewhere Ellison explains what he himself takes to be the origin and core of this joke. It arises from "the declaration of [a separate] American identity", which perforce "meant the assumption of a mask" and with it "an ironic awareness" of the discrepancy "between appearance and reality" in a culture defined as mobile, self-invented, full of possibility. Theatricalism is therefore culturally paradigmatic; the United States "a land of masking jokers"; and "verbal comedy" a crucial way "of confronting social ambiguity," especially around issues of race.[33] Accordingly, when Ellison paid tribute to Twain as an inspiration for his own writing in

---

[32] Ralph Ellison, *Collected Essays,* ed. John Callahan (New York: Modern Library, 1995), 89, 112.
[33] *Ibid.,* 718, 107-108, 109, 607.

the preface to a re-issue of *Invisible Man* thirty years after its first publication, he played both cards at once, as it were: both the moral-earnestness card (Huck and Jim on the raft as an ideal image of democratic inclusivism) and the comic-satire card ("Twain had demonstrated that the novel *could* serve as a comic antidote to the ailments of politics").[34] Even though Ellison's overall assessment, as with his commentaries on other white American canonical authors from Melville to Faulkner whom he admired, finally came out sounding more Trillingesque than Menckenian, it did at least allow—as did *Invisible Man* itself to a much greater extent—that satire, even farcical exaggeration of the most grotesque kind, might indeed be a crucial ingredient of the GAN.

---

[34] *Ibid.*, 483.

10

Dinah Birch

Writing and Teaching: Victorian Education and Literature

Education, the subject of my paper, is something that mattered to Victorian writers of every background and every kind of aspiration. That is a fact we all recognise, for education was the means by which the Victorians affirmed and communicated their values, and as such it was a crucial channel of political and cultural power. But it was also a vigorously contested site of debate, as shifting balances of influence expressed themselves in radical changes throughout educational systems, institutions and ideologies.[1] I will explore some of these far-reaching tensions and creativities through the work of two very different figures: Charlotte Brontë and Matthew Arnold. Both were major authors who experienced a serious and sustained involvement with teaching and with schools. Their writing could hardly be more distinct, their backgrounds more different, or their ambitions more divided. Yet both found their voices through their work in Victorian education. They were sometimes sharply critical of the practices they encountered, and of the assumptions that lay behind those practices, but they continued to express their own identities as writers most fully within the energies of pedagogy. These energies were, I want to suggest, more directly associated with the preoccupations and strategies of the literature of the period than we have often recognised. Perhaps because those who study Victorian literature are

---

[1] Accounts of this revolution include Robert Anderson, *British Universities: Past and Present* (London: Hambledon Continuum, 2006); T. W. Bamford, *The Rise of the Public Schools* (London: Nelson, 1967); Pauline Fletcher and Patrick Scott, *Culture and Education in Victorian England* (London: Bucknell UP, 1990); Dinah Birch, *Our Victorian Education* (Oxford: Blackwell, 2007); J. F. C. Harrison, *Learning and Living* (London: Routledge and Kegan Paul, 1961); John Hurt, *Education in Evolution* (London: Hart-Davis, 1971); John Roach, *A History of Secondary Education in England, 1800-1870* (London: Longman, 1986); Sheldon Rothblatt, *The Revolution of the Dons: Cambridge and Society in Victorian England* (London: Faber, 1968); Gillian Sutherland, *Elementary Education in the Nineteenth Century* (London: Historical Association, 1971); Neil J. Smithser, *Social Paralysis and Social Change: British Working-Class Education in the Nineteenth Century* (Berkeley: University of California Press, 1991); W. B. Stephens, *Education in Britain, 1750-1914* (New York: St Martins Press, 1998); David Vincent, *Literacy and Popular Culture* (Cambridge: Cambridge UP, 1989); David Wardle, *English Popular Education 1780-1975* (Cambridge: Cambridge UP, 1976).

commonly also professionally involved in teaching, scholars are inclined to over-look the impact of the experience of education on intellectual and literary iden-tity. It is the air we breathe, and we hardly notice it. Though my paper focuses on tracing this deep-rooted association through the writing of Charlotte Brontë and Matthew Arnold, it is a link that is by no means limited to their work. An engagement with education could take many different forms, but it represents a literary pattern that repays critical attention in a wide swathe of Victorian writing at its strongest and most creative.

Because education has such a central part to play in intellectual formation, it cannot easily be separated from other foundational codes of cultural iden-tity. Here gender is especially important, and throughout the nineteenth century conflicts in the interpretation of educational purpose are deeply rooted in its divisions. All Victorian social functions define themselves in terms of gender, but none was more deeply split along its antagonistic lines than education. To put the issue in its simplest terms, it clearly matters, fundamentally, that Charlotte Brontë was female and Matthew Arnold was male. But the dissemination of gen-dered values within education is also decisively shaped by the pressures of class interest. Though both Arnold and Brontë emerged from what might broadly be defined as a professional middle class, Arnold's family was more deeply rooted within that class than the Brontës. Charlotte's social status was not quite as secure as that of Matthew Arnold, and it was largely dependent on Patrick Brontë's reso-lute efforts. Behind the definitions of both gender and class lies the determining influence of religious authority. This is essential here, as always when we think about Victorian education. Arnold and Brontë were the children of ordained ministers in the Church of England. Matthew Arnold did not become a Chris-tian writer, but the model he developed for cultural criticism and for education is firmly located within the established values of the Anglican Church. Char-lotte Brontë, on the other hand, maintained her firm-minded Christian faith throughout her life. It was of a very particular kind – fiercely Protestant, with a bedrock of self-determination that profoundly influenced her understanding of the function and purpose of education.[2] These three essentials – gender, class, and religion – are not disconnected. They are bound up together, throughout the work of Brontë and Arnold, as they are in all nineteenth-century educational thinking and action.

In the case of both Arnold and Brontë, these pervasive cultural factors were reinforced by family circumstances. Charlotte Brontë's work as educationalist

---

[2] Marianne Thormählen's important work on the Brontë family, in *The Brontës and Religion* (Cam-bridge: Cambridge University Press, 1999) and *The Brontës and Education* (Cambridge: Cambridge University Press, 2007), sheds much invaluable light on this association.

and writer had its beginnings in her early experiences as the child of a teaching family, as did Matthew Arnold's. Brontë's parents had in fact first met through their work in schools. The heroic story of Patrick Brontë's using his work as a teacher and tutor to lever himself from his lowly position as the son of a small-scale farmer in County Down to become an undergraduate at St John's in Cambridge, and then perpetual curate at Haworth, is a familiar one, and it is very remarkable.[3] It certainly seemed so to Charlotte Brontë. Born in 1816 (she was six years older than Matthew Arnold), she lost her mother at the age of five. Her two elder sisters, Maria and Elizabeth, died in 1825, and she grew up as the eldest surviving child. She identified strongly with her father's ambition, enterprise and charisma. Education had given him power, and it was the basis of his financial and social status both within the family and the community. Patrick Brontë had founded his own small school in Ireland, at the age of sixteen, astonishingly – and it had been the first step in his hard-fought rise into the middle classes. Charlotte Brontë saw no reason why she and her sisters should not follow the same path to success. Planning her strategy, she thought of a continental expedition to acquire the qualifications that would forward her professional aspirations, since entry into Oxford or Cambridge was not possible for a woman. She wrote to her aunt, Elizabeth Branwell, mooting the idea of establishing a school which would be run by herself and her sisters, in the hope of persuading her to fund the proposed trip to Belgium:

> These are advantages which would turn to real account, when we actually commenced a school; and, if Emily could share them with me, we could take a footing in the world afterwards which we can never do now. I say Emily instead of Anne; for Anne might take her turn at some future period, if our school answered. I feel certain, while I am writing, that you will see the propriety of what I say. You always like to use your money to the best advantage. You are not fond of making shabby purchases; when you do confer a favour, it is often done in style; and depend upon it, 50L., or 100L., thus laid out, would be well employed. Of course, I know no other friend in the world to whom I could apply on this subject except yourself. I feel an absolute conviction that, if this advantage were allowed us, it would be the making of us for life. Papa will, perhaps, think it a wild and ambitious scheme; but who ever rose in the world without ambition? When he left Ireland to go to Cambridge University, he was as ambitious as I am now. I want us ALL to get on. I know we have talents, and I want them to be turned to account.[4]

---

3   For an account of Patrick Brontë's early life, see Juliet Barker, *The Brontës* (London: Weidenfeld and Nicolson, 1994), pp. 2-3.
4   Charlotte Brontë to Elizabeth Branwell, 29 September 1841; *The Letters of Charlotte Brontë*, ed. Margaret Smith, 3 vols (Oxford: Oxford University Press, 1995-2004), 1, pp. 268-9.

This is a characteristically bold statement, and a revealing one. Brontë sees education as an activity that will make her and her sisters for life. A financial vocabulary is noticeable here, as she talks of turning talents and advantages to account, using resources to the best advantage, the laying out and employment of money. And it is very much a family venture that she describes – with, noticeably, the exception of her brother Branwell, whose drinking had already made it clear that he was not suited to following his father's disciplined example. Given that the school was to operate from Haworth Parsonage, Branwell's unruly and unpredictable presence there was one of the reasons for the school's failure to come into being. The fact that her sisters, Emily and Anne, and her father were not quite as keen on the project as Charlotte was another reason, for though Charlotte envisaged this as a way for the whole family to progress in the world, there is no doubt that she was the driving force behind the scheme. Though her plan did not come to fruition, the determined bid for independence that it represents is a central preoccupation in her books. As many critics have remarked, notably Marianne Thormählen in *The Brontës and Education*, Charlotte writes persistently and almost obsessively about schools and teachers, and about women finding the means of self-determination though the business of teaching – Frances Henri in *The Professor*, Jane Eyre, Lucy Snowe in *Villette*. Here, Charlotte was responding to a strongly marked pattern among women of her generation and social situation. The founding and running of small independent schools could offer such women real financial independence and autonomy, together with a measure of cultural authority. This was a different matter from serving as a governess, though the two activities were often linked, with the same women being involved in both – as the fictional Jane Eyre acts as a governess, and later finds solid satisfaction in her work as a teacher in Morton.

However, Jane Eyre remains a fiction, and "The Misses Brontë's Establishment for The Board and Education of a Limited Number of Young Ladies", as it was described in the prospectus Charlotte had printed, did not, as things turned out, become a reality.[5] Charlotte Brontë's letters make it clear that she found the day-to-day demands of teaching wearisome, especially as she encountered them in the oppressive circumstances of a governess working in private homes, or as a pupil-teacher at Roe Head. For all her interest in schools, finally Charlotte Brontë was more interested in her writing, and in the challenges of the education performed in her fiction. She transferred her educational and professional ambitions from the institutional to the literary. Though her novels often draw on her thinking about day-to-day experiences or theories of teaching, that thinking

---

[5]   The prospectus is reproduced in Barker, *The Brontës*, facing p. 685; see pp. 439-41 for an account of the sisters' plan to open a school.

is not what readers have primarily carried away from her fiction. What we remember is the novels' treatment of the relations between men and women, often hostile and competitive relations, but also intensely romantic. 'Reader, I married him'[6] must count among the most familiar lines in the history of the Victorian novel, and it comes from Jane Eyre, the best-known of all governesses. But that line is not about teaching.

What Charlotte Brontë's writing often does, I would argue, is to modulate her engagement with the enterprises of pedagogy into the gendered dynamics of the erotic. She understood that they were closely connected, for both rested on the exercise of power. Even in the difficult circumstances in which Brontë encountered them, the processes of teaching confer power. This is a central reason for Brontë's engagement with the identity of the teacher – it allowed her to claim that independently forceful and ambitious spirit represented by her father. But an assumption of power is not part of a conventionally defined feminine identity, and the power of the erotic also rests, for Charlotte Brontë, in the subservience of the passively submitting female, in relation to a dominant male – the man she would call 'Sir', or 'Master' – Crimsworth, Rochester, Paul Emanuel, Louis Moore. In Brontë's fiction, we find a strangely shifting and doubled pattern of assertive or even recalcitrant women shadowed by an almost masochistic pleasure in submission. Clearly, the frustrated love that Brontë conceived for Monsieur Heger, her Belgian teacher, has much to do with this pattern. But for both personal and broadly cultural reasons, the dynamics of the school became the fictional site where these contested values were defined and resolved. In Charlotte Brontë's writing, the school is the place where teachers, governesses, employers and pupils confirm their status, sometimes in unexpected ways, and often because they also become lovers, or spouses, or partners in business. Sometimes they become all three together, as happens in *The Professor*, and in a different and less fulfilled way in *Villette*. This is a condition which Brontë's fiction celebrates.

Matthew Arnold, notoriously, had little time for Charlotte Brontë. 'Why is *Villette* so disagreeable? Because the writer's mind ... contains nothing but hunger, rebellion and rage.'[7] Arnold's verdict on Brontë's final novel in 1853, the year of its publication, has long been remembered, and is often quoted. A characteristic moment of male resentment, readers might think. But Arnold's animosity amounts to more than careless prejudice. The grounds of the antagonism run deep, and their strongest roots are to be found in education. What was Brontë hungry for, what was she rebelling against, what was filling her with rage? To

---

6   Charlotte Brontë, *Jane Eyre*, ed. Michael Mason (Harmondsworth: Penguin Classics, 2003), p. 498.
7   Matthew Arnold to Arthur Hugh Clough, May 1853, *The Letters of Matthew Arnold*, ed. Cecil Y. Lang, 6 vols (Charlottesville and London: University Press of Virginia, 1996-2001), 1, p. 262.

some extent, it was the settled assumption of privilege and primacy represented by Matthew Arnold's early educational experiences. For Arnold, as for Brontë, education meant power, and education was where the central contests of his generation would be settled. And Arnold, again like Brontë, was primarily influenced in his educational thinking by an exceptionally powerful father – Dr Thomas Arnold, the charismatic and passionately Christian historian, theologian and reforming headmaster of Rugby School. But the models of education represented by those two paternal figures, Thomas Arnold and Patrick Brontë, were sharply different. Born in 1795, Thomas Arnold went to Winchester, then Corpus Christi, Oxford. Ordination into the Anglican Church was a natural destination for him, rather than the hard-won social triumph that it was for Patrick Brontë. The headmastership of Rugby, which he took on at the age of 32, was a very different matter from working in the small schools with which Patrick had been associated as a young man. Thomas Arnold, who was appointed to the post without interview, accepted it because it offered a significantly higher salary than the professorship of modern history at the new University of London, for which he had also been a candidate.[8] Success came more easily to Thomas Arnold. He moved in different circles.

Patrick Brontë's career as an educator had been a triumph won against the odds. It affirmed the possibility of success for the outsider. Charlotte understood it as such, and used Patrick's example as a model for her own struggle as a female outsider – Romantic, Protestant, responsible for her own identity. For Thomas Arnold, education worked, or should work, from the inside rather than the outside. It meant, as he developed it at Rugby, the reinvigoration of the Anglican Church as a force for the inclusive purification of the heart of the nation. But its model for inclusiveness was always incomplete, for the idealised education that he advocated was designed only for young men. Thomas Arnold had no experience of education as something that might be available on equal terms for boys and girls, and it was an idea that remained alien to him. His own schooling had been all-male; so too had been his university education, and like all nineteenth-century public schools Rugby admitted no girls. In fact Thomas Arnold immediately ended the tradition of boarding-houses run by women at Rugby – 'dames' houses', as they had been called – and replaced the women's long-established pastoral role with that of male tutors. Mixed education was conventional only for the lower social classes. Education rigidly divided by gender identity was a marker of middle-class status throughout the nineteenth century, and beyond. Under Thomas Arnold's leadership Rugby School, rising in prestige as it did,

---

[8]   Michael McCrum, *Thomas Arnold: Headmaster* (Oxford: Oxford University Press, 1989), gives a full and sympathetic description of Arnold's early life, and his work at Rugby School.

became a still more exclusively masculine institution, both in its values and in its membership. It was within that exclusively male tradition – Rugby, where he was a schoolboy, and then Balliol College in Oxford – that Matthew Arnold's understanding of education was first formed. Its substance was classical, as it was for all boys of his class and generation, but its context was Anglican. What it meant for him was a proper balance, stability, continuity – a cool and rational impartiality that he was later to identify as a necessary contemporary Hellenism. Detached analysis, not personal struggle, was the point of education for Arnold. It was a sense of over-heated and perhaps feminine emotional energies that he recognised and deplored in Charlotte Brontë's *Villette*.

The experience that was to challenge and then gradually to revise Matthew Arnold's pedagogic understanding was a lifetime of committed work in education. Having won a fellowship at Oriel College Oxford as a young man, he found that it demanded an intellectual and religious conformity that he could not sustain, as he moved away from his father's committed Anglicanism. Like Charlotte Brontë, he needed to work to earn a living. Again like Brontë, he turned to education for the new avenues of financial and professional opportunity that it provided for the middle classes. He did not become a teacher, but in 1851 he took on, at the age of 29, the work of an inspector of schools, a salaried job in which he laboured steadily for 35 arduous years. It was an extension of the family business – almost all the male Arnolds had serious jobs in education.[9] This was work that amounted to very much more than a gentleman's hobby. For many of those years, Arnold had special responsibility for Nonconformist schools, not especially grand ones, often with both girls and boys as their pupils. What he saw there often struck him as narrow, mechanical, and reductive.

Without losing his faith in the balanced clarity of Hellenism, Arnold came to believe that the energies of feeling were after all necessary to the functions of education. Literature – the thinking that could 'make us feel'[10] – became essential to what he believed education should do, and his polemical work in a stream of publications about educational reform is at its most engaging and humane in its insistence that such work, an education that would include the education of feeling, should be available for all children, whether male or female, rich or poor. Arnold was scathing about the imaginative poverty of what those in charge of state education envisaged as an adequate training for the children whose schools

---

[9] Park Honan, *Matthew Arnold: A Life* (New York: McGraw-Hill, 1981) gives the most detailed account available of Matthew Arnold's professional career and his complex relations with his family, while Stefan Collini, *Arnold* (Oxford: Oxford University Press, 1988) is shrewd on the complex development of Arnold's critical thought.

[10] Matthew Arnold, 'Memorial Verses: April 1850', in *The Poems of Matthew Arnold*, ed. Kenneth Allott (London: Longmans, Green & Co., 1965), p. 229.

he inspected, and was vehement in his insistence that the imaginative resources of literature should be equally available to children of all social classes. National education, in the liberal vision which developed from Arnold's years as a school inspector, must amount to something more than utilitarian instruction. In 1886, the year of his retirement, he insisted that it must be 'a training of all to all which is human. And when our attention has once been called to the matter we may go further, and consider how entirely the popular education actually now given, in England at any rate, often fails to awaken and train not only the sense of beauty, but the soul and feeling generally.'[11]

This was a broader version of Thomas Arnold's Anglican ideals – a model for education that would at its best be generous and invigorating. But it was also a continuing expression of his father's membership of a social élite. Matthew Arnold's criticism often took the form of institutionally sponsored work in prestigious formats – like his 1861 study of 'The Popular Education of France', commissioned by the government, or his piece on the educational uses of 'Literature and Science', first delivered as the Cambridge Rede lecture of 1882. His interventions in the cultural direction of the nation were grounded in professional experience, but they were also based on a firmly articulated authority. Brontë's contribution, which was as potent and as durable, could not be made through those formal channels. It was necessarily framed within the complex and sometimes covert analysis of her fiction, a medium that allowed scope for a woman in a relatively isolated position to find her own public voice. Charlotte Brontë and Matthew Arnold can be seen as radically opposed, at odds in their different and divided experiences of education, and in their interpretation of those experiences – opposed for reasons that are closely bound up with gender, class, religion. And yet an unexpected current of continuity develops in their thought, as they constructed models of education that allow for both intellectual and emotional development and fulfilment, for thinking in balance with feeling. Their direct and sustained experience of schooling was crucial to the substance and intensity of their mature writing. They are a reminder that for those interested in Victorian culture, educational history and literary history are not separate subjects.

---

[11] Matthew Arnold, 'Common Schools Abroad' (1886), *The Complete Prose Works of Matthew Arnold*, ed. R. H. Super, 11 vols (Ann Arbor: University of Michigan Press, 1960-77), 11, pp. 89-90.

11

Elisabeth Jay

British Writers and Paris, 1840-1871: a research project in outline

In January 1863, John Bellows (1831-1902), a Gloucester printer, was summoned by her family to see his fiancée who lay dangerously ill in Arendal, on the Norwegian coast. Having discovered that the summer ferry route from Hull to Christiansand did not operate during the winter, he packed 'some books and newspapers in Norsk' to practise the language, together with some 'pasties' because he had no idea what and where he would eat again, and set off on what was to prove a twelve-day journey, travelling by night and day by train, ship, coach, and sled in extreme conditions. When Bellows finally arrived he found his fiancée dead, and within three days he set off on the return journey. On his return to Dover he had travelled two thousand miles in three weeks, passing through six customs points on his journey, changing currency as and when he could, without access to handy guides to acceptable rates of exchange. Nevertheless, ever the good tradesman, Bellows was determined to profit from his experience. A committed Quaker, Bellows had acquired the habit of working for the Bible Society on Sunday afternoons, distributing Bibles on the Gloucester docks; in the process he had met sailors of many nationalities and developed a real interest in languages.[1] On this trip he acquired sufficient familiarity with Swedish to realise that the Danes and the Swedes used mutually intelligible dialectal variants, but he lacked the fluency necessary to express his bereavement. The bulkiness of the Danish dictionary he had taken with him led him to the conclusion: 'one cannot unpack a portmanteau for the sake of a word'. Moreover he resented the fact that, having no French, he felt that he was prey to being rooked by the French guides who seemed ubiquitous at stations along the route.[2]

For the next ten years, Bellows worked unstintingly as a lexicographer while con-

---

[1]   [E. Bellows], *John Bellows: Letters and Memoir edited by his wife* (London: Kegan Paul, Trench Trübner & Co. Ltd, 1904), p. 9. Interestingly, this account, by the woman he subsequently married, makes no mention of a former engagement, nor does it list her husband's account of his Scandinavian journey in the list of his writings.

[2]   Bellows' phlegmatic account of this emotional voyage is to be found in *A Winter Journey from Gloucester to Norway* (London: Trübner & Co; Gloucester: John Bellows Steam Press, 1867).

tinuing his printing business. The Oxford-based German philologist Max Müller helped him to produce his *English Outline Vocabulary for the Use of Students of the Chinese Language* in 1868. Bellows next mastered French and in 1873 – with the aid of the Parisian printers, the Beljame brothers – produced the first French pocket dictionary, containing 340,000 words.[3] The book, measuring 4 x 2 inches, demanded innovative printing processes, being printed by hand in diamond type on especially thin paper. The expanding market that Bellows had identified resulted in six thousand copies selling rapidly, and a further thirty reprints being made between 1915 and 1947. *The Times* called his pocket dictionary 'a gem of typographical art' and Mark Twain referred to it as 'the church of the gratis lesson'.[4]

I came upon this 'tale of the printer of Gloucester' whilst reading systematically through the three hundred or so entries in the *New Oxford Dictionary of National Biography* which appear when the words 'Paris' and 'writers' as well as the dates '1840-1871' are entered in the search facility. I should explain why I have chosen these dates to frame my research, since to a French historian the fact that they lie across, rather than in line with, changes of political regime may seem curious. 1840 was the date when Thackeray – a key figure in my project – published his *Paris Sketch-Book,* a volume that self-consciously distinguished itself from the tea-party prattle, as he dismissively referred to it, of women travel writers like Lady Sidney Morgan and Frances Trollope (respectively authors of *France,*1817; and *Paris and the Parisians,* 1835),[5] and adopted the stance of the urban flâneur, just then coming into vogue in Paris (see Louis Huart, *Physiologie du Flâneur* (1841)). Taking 1871 as my end date allows me to convey British reactions to the Franco-Prussian siege, the Commune, and the second siege, a series of events that seemed to bring to an end the reign of Paris as the tourist capital of Europe. In December 1870 Annie Thackeray, who had spent much of her adolescence in Paris and considered France a second home, wrote to a friend that in the current turbulent circumstances, Paris was 'farther away than India'.[6] Indeed it must have seemed as if Franco-British relations, which had so flourished in the meantime, would revert to the condition operating at the start of the century, when there had been a political embargo on cross-Channel travel.

Ever since the days of the Grand Tour, Britain's upper classes had been just as

---

[3] A privately printed memoir by his son tells how the manuscript of the dictionary narrowly escaped destruction during the siege of Paris when the next-door house was shelled. After the city had fallen, the Commune granted a permit for the removal of the manuscript to a place of safety. J.E. Bellows, *John Bellows, 1831—1931: A Biographical Sketch and Tribute* (n.p., 1931), p. 11.

[4] *New Oxford Dictionary of National Biography.*

[5] W.M. Thackeray, 'On Some French Fashionable Novels', in *The Paris Sketch Book*, The Biographical Edition of the Works of William Makepeace Thackeray, ed. A. Ritchie, 13 vols (London: Smith, Elder, 1898-1901), v (1900), 80-97 (p. 82).

[6] H. Ritchie (ed.), *Letters of Annie Thackeray Ritchie* (London: John Murray, 1924), p. 144.

likely to cross paths in Paris as in London; but the advent of rail and steamship travel in the 1840s began to make Paris accessible not only to the families of wealthy middle-class bankers and merchants, such as the Ruskins, the Barretts, and the Brownings, but to the lower middle classes. Catherine Gore's 'silver-fork' fiction gained fresh sustenance from her husband's posting in 1832 to the British Embassy in Paris: this enabled her to pose as a satirist while also providing a useful handbook for the socially aspiring to the ways in which the aristocracy comported themselves in Paris. Increasingly, successful artists and writers, from Wilkie Collins's father to Elizabeth Gaskell and Charles Dickens, saw a visit to Paris, and acknowledgement in its salons, as both reward and gauge of their achievements, and were often keen for their children to acquire the fluency in French which their own upbringing had not afforded. (Dickens was to find Collins's endless boasting of adolescent familiarity with Paris irritating, and never himself lost the English accent with which he came to speak the language.)

One of the first questions my project poses is what it was that had made Paris so peculiarly attractive to British writers at the very time that London was attracting waves of émigrés from mainland Europe. The cost of living was obviously one factor: shabby-chic gentility, or the furnishings of bohemian life, seemed easier to achieve in Paris than in London. Moreover, French journalists, who had even secured representation in the Chamber of Deputies, seemed to enjoy enviable influence, prestige and wealth, bearing little of the taint of 'Grub Street'. (Walter Bagehot and John Delane, future editor of *The Times*, first developed their interest in political matters in Paris, although they had arrived as banker and medical student respectively.) In Britain, the 'taxes on knowledge' proved a drag on the wheel of cheap print until the tax on paper was finally removed in 1861. The chance of working in Paris, therefore, as the correspondent for one, or indeed several, British newspapers, appealed to talented but impecunious British writers. The sheer number of *NODNB* entries recording this as the first rung on a career ladder merits investigation, although Thackeray's picture in *Pendennis* (1850) of the political and economic influence potentially exerted by these reporters needs to be balanced by his rather more sober assessment of the risks that this toehold on a career in print carried: 'My poor friend A'Beckett's death has shocked me', he wrote in 1856 of a fellow reporter in Paris. 'He has left no money and hasn't insured his life—Down from competence and comfort goes a whole family into absolute penury. One boy 1/2 through the University, and likely to have done well there I believe – another at a public school, daughters with masters, and mamma with tastes for music and millinery. What is to happen to these people? Had I dropped 3 years ago my poor wife and young ones would have been no better off.' [7]

---

[7] *Ibid.*, p. 53.

Paris's reputation as a printopolis, and as the nerve centre of a centralised system, gave residents and visitors a sense that they had their finger on the cultural pulse of a nation in ways never quite possible in Britain, where learning and publishing were more dispersed around the ancient Scottish and English universities. And yet, to what extent did the Paris that Britain's writers sought out reflect and feed their prejudices and those of their various readerships?

'I see a beautiful city and a brilliant people rising from this abyss'.[8] These words, attributed by Dickens to Sydney Carton at the foot of the scaffold, suggest something of the ambiguous reputation Paris enjoyed in mid-nineteenth-century British imagination. It was variously perceived as the literary and artistic centre of Europe, the fount of rational intellectualism, the heartland of European revolutionary socialism, the incarnation of immorality in the theatre and fiction, a mecca for fashionable shopping, and an invitation to debauchery. Those who first encountered Paris's parks and fountains as children were enchanted by them; but Dickens, who first visited Paris as an adult, never ceased to see it as both 'wicked and detestable' and 'wonderfully attractive',[9] offering decorous family outings alongside the louche night-time world of gambling dens and cheap dancing halls which he explored, in furtive 'Don Giovanni' or 'Haroun Al-raschid' style, with Wilkie Collins.[10] There is no doubt that the demonic energy and vaunting ambition seen in Paris's building programme, and culminating in the grandeur of Haussmann's series of orchestrated vistas, appealed to Dickens. Between 1852 and 1869 entire enclaves were to be swept away: 20,000 houses were demolished and 43,000 built. The sheer scale of planned demolition and construction work dwarfed the piecemeal scars on the urban landscape effected by railway construction in London. Paris's purposeful frenzy was in strong contrast with the vested interests that resulted in Parliament approving only 2 out of 19 proposed London railway termini, or the slow completion rates which meant that the earlier parts of developments, such as Bloomsbury, were already decaying before the last parts were built. [11]

French politics continued throughout this period to be a touchstone for English radicals and conservatives alike, but I am more interested in the cultural influences Paris exerted as easier and cheaper travel enabled freer access. By 1856 the upwardly mobile Isabella and Sam Beeton, who had both learned French at

8   C. Dickens, *A Tale of Two Cities*, Oxford Illustrated Dickens (1859; London: Oxford University Press, 1970), p. 357.
9   M. House, G. Storey, K. Tillotson *et al.* (eds), *The Letters of Charles Dickens*, 12 vols (Oxford: Clarendon Press, 1965-2002), iv, 669.
10 *Letters of Charles Dickens*, viii, 623.
11 Information derived from P. Mansel, *Paris Between Empires, 1814-52: Monarchy and Revolution* (London: Phoenix, 2001), p. 423; and J. White, *London in the Nineteenth Century* (London: Jonathan Cape, 2007), pp. 39 and 72-73.

school, thought a honeymoon in Paris appropriate to their station and swiftly networked their way into a French artisanal world of printing, fashion, and cookery. Isabella unabashedly translated French articles on these matters for that wide reading public in England who craved information on the latest French fashions while deploring their manners and morals. Exposure to contemporary French print culture in turn developed in some writers a keen sense of the different kinds of censorship operating over time on either side of the Channel. Siting a fictional seduction or adulterous liaison in Paris somehow satisfied British readers that such goings-on were rendered safe by taking place beyond the *cordon sanitaire* provided by the British coastline. Conversely, Paris's Bohemian artists' circles, or the poetry of Baudelaire, provided a satisfying source of inspiration for writers as intent on shocking their English audience as Swinburne and the aesthetes. The hypocrisy, or doubleness, of which Thackeray has so often been accused stemmed, I think, from his being forced to consider how to relay his observations as a Parisian theatre-goer and journalist to a British readership; and his notorious caution as editor of the newly-launched *Cornhill* (where he refused to print Barrett Browning's sexually satirical poetry) is entirely in keeping with his sense of the cultural distance between London and Paris. It was Thackeray's capacity to switch perspectives so rapidly that – while it disturbed some readers – won him the admiration of George du Maurier, another writer whose education had veered between Paris and England.

Despite the extension to the copyright act in 1844 that granted the same right to foreign authors as that enjoyed by their British counterparts, a fine trade seems to have developed in rummaging through French bookstalls and attending the uncensored French theatre in search of melodramatic plots that could be adapted for British tastes (and this is an area where I should particularly appreciate help in finding further specific examples).

Other aspects of Paris's cultural influence could be more openly acknowledged: the national pride that sponsored the artistic collections of the Louvre, and the government-subsidised conservatoire and opera, provided epiphanic for youthful writers such as Ruskin, Browning, and Henry James, whilst inspiring pre-Raphaelite painters and providing an example for the Eastlakes to follow in effecting their purchases for the National Gallery in London.

For some Francophiles, such as Matthew Arnold, Clough, and Browning, it was the intellectual debate and informed European viewpoints they encountered in Parisian salons that increasingly influenced the way in which they viewed and wrote of England. Indeed, I have wondered whether the relative neglect that some of these writers' work suffered in the mid-twentieth century has derived from a persistent feeling that they had become 'semi-detached' from dominant English concerns and attitudes, causing their work to be at best inaccessible and at worst suspect to a British readership once again cut off by war and its after-math from regular contact with French culture.

The tendency to parcel books and taught courses by author, genre, or topic, coupled with post-colonialism's focus on empire, has tended to divert attention from Britain's interaction with its nearest European neighbour. In the broadest sense, most British writing about Paris could be described as travel writing; but even when defined more narrowly, a host of letters, diaries, journals, memoirs, articles, essays, and guide books were produced. Queen Victoria was following fashion when, having paid a formal visit to the Grande Exposition of 1855, she published her journal account. By the time Thomas Hardy ventured to Paris, hoping to combine his honeymoon with some research for his next book, Murray's Handbooks provided a menu of 'must-see' tourist attractions, including the morgue and Père-Lachaise cemetery, for novice sightseers.[12]

Setting up a household in Paris might involve hiring tutors and governesses as well as additional servants. It is perhaps unsurprising that a standard element in the novels of sensation popular in the 1860s was the hiring of a governess or maid who, once admitted to the bosom of the family, turned out to have falsified references or good reason for 'jumping ship' abroad. The notoriety of English-born actress-courtesans such as Cora Pearl (born Eliza Crouch) stood proxy for sadder tales, as is suggested by the picture, drawn by Barrett Browning in *Aurora Leigh* (1857), of lowly-born Marian Erle, raped and transported to a Paris brothel, who escapes into service as a lady's maid only to be sacked when her pregnancy becomes evident. George Eliot, who, despite Lewes's Francophile enthusiasm, re-mained obstinately averse to Paris after her first visit in 1849, cautiously recorded that a ten-day trip in 1865 to Haussmannian Paris had begun to dissolve her old dislike; but then she wrote, 'it must be confessed that the Paris of today is another Paris than the one I used to detest'. [13] Nor did this slight unbending prevent her from using Paris as the appropriate site for castigating the moral myopia of scientific men in the story of Lydgate's infatuation with the French actress Laure, who had used a stage performance to rid herself of a tiresome husband.[14] One of the changes Eliot doubtless approved was the way in which Haussmann's re-routing of Parisian thoroughfares had cut right across the 'boulevard du temple', known colloquially as the 'boulevard du crime' on account of the melodramatic shockers performed at its numerous theatres. Of course, this episode also posi-tions Lydgate, despite his determination to experience the best of French medical education, as still essentially a spectator, a flâneur, an outsider to Paris *intime*.

---

[12] Thomas Cook and Baedeker swiftly followed suit with their own guides.
[13] G.S. Haight (ed.), *The George Eliot Letters*, 9 vols (New Haven, CT.: Yale University Press, 1954-787), iii, 362 and viii, 333.
[14] G. Eliot, *Middlemarch* (1872), ch.15.

In looking at the experience of British writers in Paris, one of the aspects I shall consider is the networks through which they accessed it. In one sense Paris, which expanded at less than half the rate of London over the course of the nineteenth century, may have seemed more 'manageable', more 'homely'; but just as the French in nineteenth-century London proved reluctant to assimilate, so the English set up their expatriate camp in the maze of narrow streets and alleys behind the Champs Elysées, many of which were swept away by Haussmann's reforms. The lives of this pre-Haussmann generation were bounded (save for the occasional festive trip out to St. Cloud) by the British Embassy at the lower end of the rue du Faubourg St Honoré, walks in the Tuileries gardens, and the reading room afforded by the English-language bookseller Galignani, whose newspaper *The Messenger* kept them up-to-date with English news and gossip; based at 3 rue de Rivoli, Galignani's premises were also handy for the Hotel Meurice at no. 228, where wealthier visitors, like Ruskin or Dickens, would put up for a day or two while searching for longer-term lodgings. The English colony's religious needs were supplied by the nearby Temple Protestant de l'Oratoire du Louvre and its accompanying école, where the likes of Annie and Minnie Thackeray were entrusted to Pastor Adolphe Monod's strict instruction. The numbers of English expatriates were swelled by Irish writers and their families, both Roman Catholic and Protestant, who, in the long tradition to which Joyce and Beckett were to prove heirs, preferred Paris to London as a more congenial place of exile.

The British continued to be attracted both by the ample supply of apartments afforded by successive governments' building projects and by the favourable conditions of the trade treaty concluded with Britain in 1864. Many who came to Paris already had relatives working there in banking or commerce; this was true, for instance, of Thackeray and the Brownings. The British Embassy formed a further social nucleus: many of its staff managed to combine their official tasks with parallel careers as writers or diarists. The Marquess of Normanby (ambassador in 1846-52), with four romantic novels to his name, an interest in amateur theatricals, and a liaison with the actress 'Atala Beauchêne', was just one of the many who published a journal describing his experience of Paris in the ferment of 1848.[15] Personal inclination, then, as much as professional duty encouraged these literary diplomats to entertain their compatriots, or to host events such as the enormously successful charity readings from *David Copperfield* that Dickens gave in January 1863. In the mid-1860s, the embassy staff included at least two poets famed equally for their literary ambitions and their womanising: Julian Fane and Wilfrid Scawen Blunt. The itemised sexual conquests recorded in Blunt's diary included, *inter alia*, the simultaneous conquest of the ambassa-

---

[15] Constantine Phipps, *A Year of Revolution: from a Journal kept in Paris in 1848* (1857).

dor Lord Cowley's daughter, Feodorowna, and the English courtesan Catherine Walters (professionally known as 'Skittles'), whose own tally included both the heir to Chatsworth and the reigning French Emperor. Such illicit liaisons, often domesticated by the acquisition of a 'love-nest', suggest that the exoticism of national difference might have played its part in encouraging intimacy.[16]

A question remains, however, as to how far British writers penetrated French literary circles. One or two close friendships were formed: for instance, Joseph Milsand – a renegade Protestant convert from Dijon – became one of Robert Browning's best friends and served to introduce both Browning and Ruskin to a French readership; but he was not Parisian by origin, nor an avid attender of salons. Gender division played a great part in the kinds of encounter to be enjoyed. Thackeray's thumbnail sketch of a soirée at the home of the President of the Chamber of Deputies would seem to confirm this: 'I could just as well have fancied these places before going but it is as well to have seen – a hall, a crowd of lackies, and antechamber; a great groom of the chambers who shouts out your name, about a hundred gentlemen in black coats, and a dozen ladies – voilà tout, but it will spin into 6 pages or so, & looks well in a book.' [17] Elizabeth Barrett Browning, who regarded Parisian salons as 'the shop window of the world', accounted Robert 'a prince of husbands' for allowing her to attend George Sand's Sunday salon along with 'the crowds of ill-bred men who adore her…betwixt a puff of smoke and an ejection of saliva.' [18] The reputation of these French gatherings, where men far outnumbered the bold women who attended, and talk was of the freest, was one that Mrs Humphry Ward could still draw upon for *Robert Elsmere* (1888) to suggest their sexual and intellectual frisson. On the whole British women writers seem to have preferred the salons run by their female compatriots, such as Mary Mohl, Lady Elgin, or Lady Ashburton, who between them entertained a range of European literati.

I hope that these brief examples will have conveyed something of the way that my project serves to complicate stereotypical accounts of mid-century Victorian writers as preoccupied by British concerns and solely governed by the sense of a repressive Victorian morality. I plan eventually to organise the evidence of individual writers' encounters with Paris so as to convey the way in which, taken together, they suggest the webs of meaning and value that comprise cultural history.

---

[16] Napoleon's visits to Skittles in the relaxed surroundings of Biarritz court life took place under the English *nom de plume* of 'Captain Jones'. Elizabeth Longford, *A Pilgrimage of Passion: the Life of Wilfrid Scawen Blunt (1840-1922)* (London: Weidenfeld and Nicolson, 1979), p. 34.

[17] G.N. Ray, ed., *The Letters and Private Papers of William Makepeace Thackeray*, 4 vols (London: Oxford University Press, 1945-46), i, 359.

[18] Quoted in R. Gridley, *The Brownings and France: a chronicle with commentary* (London: Athlone Press, 1982), p. 121.

12

Susan McCabe

Bryher's Archive: Modernism and the Melancholy of Money

Asked in an interview "Do you see yourself as a Modernist writer?", the well-known poet and H.D. biographer Barbara Guest responded with this compelling tale of the archive:

> "Modernism is actually over. That is, it's become part of the world… people are now afraid of Modernism. I'll tell you a story. When I was writing my little biography of HD, I spent many months [in the late 1970s] in the Beinecke … There were all HD's papers in the basement, literally on the basement floor. I think I had been the first one to go through some of them since HD had died. And there was a large pouch among the boxes, and one day it turned out that this pouch had one million dollars in it."
>
> "In cash?!?!" asks the interviewer
>
> [Firmly.] "Cash. It had just been sitting there for who knows how long. It was left them by Bryher, a very wealthy woman, to help cover preservation costs."[1]

Bryher was the "apparition" I pursued during my Beinecke Fellowship at Yale, when I launched upon a first full-length biography of Annie Winifred Ellerman (1894-1983), who at fifteen changed her name to one of the wildest of the Scilly islands. She was the daughter of Sir John Ellerman, who rose from relative poverty to a baronetcy and was the wealthiest man in England when he died in 1933 and bequeathed her a vast legacy, mostly built upon his shipping lines and partly on munitions income from World War I. During his lifetime, Sir John dominated British periodicals, owning *The Times of London*, *The Illustrated London News*, *The Sphere*, and *The Tatler*, to name several. Bryher, for her part, diligently and quietly fashioned and funded alternative ventures, including *Contact Press*, *Life & Letters To-Day*, and *Close Up*. But these were not her sole achievements, and,

---

[1]   Kevin Killian and Susan Gevirtz, Interview with Barbara Guest, "The Problem with Beauty," *Small Traffic Press Newsletter*, Berkeley: Summer 2003, 5. The interview took place following upon Guest's 2003 Lifetime Achievement award.

as Margaret Atwood observes, "few twentieth-century women's lives were more interconnected with their own era, and few others displayed her edgy bravery and intellectual curiosity, but she is little known today."[2]

The Beinecke's boxes, over 185 boxes solely devoted to Bryher's correspondence and writings, contained no pouches of cash. The truth of Guest's story is that Bryher's money fuelled (and preserved) a significant portion of modernist culture. Money also allowed her to rescue others threatened by poverty or political danger. Bryher was an active participant in shaping many of the twentieth century's major historical movements—cinema, psychoanalysis, modernist poetics. Why, then, was Bryher given such a "basement" depiction by Guest in her interview and her groundbreaking biography *Herself Defined*, which cast Bryher as the Imagist poet's life-long companion? The towering H.D., "with her long feet and hands, her luminous probing eyes," has indeed overshadowed Bryher.[3] In Guest's influential treatment, Bryher is both regressed and controlling; with every inch Guest concedes, she pathologizes further: "[Bryher] also had—regardless of the manipulations, the tantrums, the schemes, the need to program everyone's life, and despite her eternal childhood—the good fairy's gift of common sense. The bad fairy made her a permanent child. Sadly her capabilities could not prevent her from remaining forever a child in a world of adults" (115). Lawrence Rainey further claims that Bryher damaged H.D.'s career by "cocooning" her.[4]

Like any biographical subject, Bryher raises contrary reactions. But the unusual extent of disparagement, neglect and discounting of Bryher has more to do with her transgressive "husband" role in curating modernism than with her actual character. Guest's patronizing assessments misgauge what Bryher gave, as well as her collaborative role in H.D.'s life: "H.D. could never take without giving" (106), and what she gave was "the gift of her genius, of her creativity, her temperament, her instability, her sorcery" (114).

Pound could don the role of impresario of the new poetry, but Lowell and Bryher—with their intrusive money—faced immediate criticism. In a less common reaction to Bryher, E. Marek claims that a "characteristic modesty" eclipsed Bryher's "extensive role" in broadly supporting modernist writers.[5] This short

2   Review of *Visa for Avalon*, "After the Last Battle", *New York Review of Books*, 7 April 2005 (52.6), 38-9.

3   Barbara Guest, *Herself Defined: The Poet H.D. and Her World* (New York: Doubleday, 1984), 14.

4   *Institutions of Modernism: Literary Elites and Public Culture* (New Haven: Yale University Press, 1998), 12.

5   *Women Editing Modernism: 'Little Magazines' & Literary History* (Lexington: The University Press of Kentucky, 1995); see pp. 101-37. Georgina Taylor likewise reveals a counter-public sphere that flourished among women modernists between 1913 and 1946 (with H.D. at the center) where "new ideas emerged through a process of interaction" primarily through the little magazines (*Little Review, Poetry, The Egoist*); *H.D. and the Public Sphere of Modernist Women Writers, 1913-1946* (New York: Oxford University Press, 2001).

piece overviews the virtual money trail that crisscrosses Bryher's triangular collaborations, whose unusual character to some extent accounts for her curious absence in literary histories. The archive uncovers gifts and attachments, diverse and strange: among them, a washing machine too large to fit in Dorothy Richardson's window, a pair of monkeys for her adopted child, a cottage for Edith Sitwell, and the premature publication of Marianne Moore's first book of poems. Moore, whom she nicknamed Pterodactyl, felt like a "naked gosling" after Bryher's ambiguous act of generosity.[6] In the gift, "'obligation and liberty intermingle'," as Karin Cope amplifies in a study of Stein's literary collaborations. Cope reminds us that in the 18th century, the Latin word collaborare—"to work together"—meant the work of a couple, taking on its negative connotations of compromise much later, during World War II.[7] Bryher cultivated "aesthetic erotic conjunctions," complicated by her money, melancholic desire, and gifts—both tangible and creative.

Janet Malcolm eloquently describes the biographer's predicament as a form of looting:

> The biographer at work, indeed, is like the professional burglar, breaking into a house, rifling through certain drawers that he has good reason to think contain the jewelry and money, and triumphantly bearing his loot away. The voyeurism and busybodyism that impel writers and readers of biography alike are obscured by an apparatus of scholarship designed to give the enterprise an appearance of blandness and solidity… The transgressive nature of biography is rarely acknowledged.[8]

Bryher's archive doubles as transferential loot. In 1936, Bryher wrote to H.D.: "I'm fundamentally interested in dirt and politics," yet we may still wonder how much dirt control she exerted in her bequest to the Beinecke of H.D.'s and her own papers (along with the proverbial pouch).

As a child, Bryher traveled all over the world, including to Egypt where she studied Arabic and rode her first camel when she was nine. She watched the fireworks of the Queen's Jubilee from her window as a child; at five years old, she attended the Paris Exhibition in 1900. She had a persistent childhood fantasy to run away to sea and become a cabin boy. In 1909, with the birth of her brother John, her parents married, revealing to her that she was illegitimate. Bryher's father offered to legitimize her, but she perversely refused. Illegitimacy became a mark of character for her. The following year Bryher was sent to Queenwood, a

---

[6]   To Bryher from Marianne Moore, 7 July 1921 in Moore's *Selected Letters*, ed. Bonnie Costello (New York: Penguin, 1997), 164.

[7]   *Passionate Collaborations: Learning to Live with Gertrude Stein* (Victoria, Canada: ELS, 2005), 13.

[8]   *Silent Woman: Sylvia Plath and Ted Hughes* (New York: Random House, 1993), 9.

boarding school, where she suffered what she termed a "violation of spirit."[9] Bryher lived through World War I, saw the gas lamps cleaned and relit on Armistice Day, predicted war, lived through the Blitz and wrote poignantly of the ruins. Bryher suspected she had Jewish ancestry on her father's side, but she could never verify her suspicion.[10] Through her meeting with Havelock Ellis (upon H.D.'s recommendation), Bryher discovered she was "a girl only by accident."[11]

When Sylvia Beach met Bryher, she admitted: "I couldn't keep my eyes off Bryher's: they were so blue—bluer than the Blue Grotto in Capri. More beautiful still was the expression in Bryher's eyes. I'm afraid that to this day I stare at her eyes."[12] Bryher inspired fixation; she could also become quite fixated herself. She appeared at H.D.'s cottage in Cornwall in 1919, after memorizing *Sea Garden*, recommended to her by Amy Lowell, her lifeline correspondent during World War I. She had completely absorbed the sharp and violent landscapes of withheld passion in poems like "Oread" with its "Whirl up, sea—," the sensuous remaking of Greek settings caught up in flux. At twenty, Bryher wanted to wear doublet and hose like a page-girl but was still living at home at the stuffy mansion at 1 Audley Street; she longed to leave the damp and dead atmosphere of London after the Great War. The entire world seemed to have fallen apart. To the older poet Lowell across the Atlantic—to whom she was still "Miss Ellerman"—she confessed that she was "going suddenly to pieces."[13] Bryher's own crisis somewhat alarmed H.D., for Bryher talked about drowning herself. (H.D.—no paragon of mental health—preferred the method of throwing herself from a cliff.) It was indeed a period of concussive shocks. The archive does not reveal Bryher as solely pragmatic, the way critics often portray her, but rather as one who continually craved new experience and adventure.

By 1920, Bryher had cut her hair and fallen in love with and cared for H.D., who had been betrayed by the poet's then husband Richard Aldington and was pregnant after her affair with Cecil Gray. Bryher supervised H.D.'s recovery from pneumonia, installed six-month-old Perdita at Norland Nursery in Kensington, and then whisked H.D. off to Greece. The couple took Havelock Ellis with them to Corfu, arriving on the Borofino, one of Ellerman's ships. A kind of snapshot from the period, H.D. described Bryher as "not wholly gracious" and as a

---

[9] *Heart to Artemis: A Writer's Memoirs* (New York: Harcourt, Brace & World, 1962), 118.
[10] When Bryher asked Freud if "he didn't think [she] was a Jew," he flatly denied this possibility. She found his answer "dreadfully disappointing," and continued to think of herself as a small David fighting the giant Goliath of fascism (Bryher to Kenneth Macpherson, 31st March 1933). In Susan Stanford Friedman, *Analyzing Freud: Letters of H.D., Bryher, and their Circle* (New York: New Directions, 2002), 163.
[11] Bryher to H.D., 20 March, 1919 (Beinecke Rare Books and Manuscript Library).
[12] *Shakespeare and Company* (New York: Harcourt, Brace and Company, 1956), 101.
[13] Bryher to Lowell (11 October, 1919). Houghton Library, Harvard University.

"tiny Aphrodite," with "tiny, improbable hands," picking among seaweed and fishnets.[14] In a Corfu hotel room, Bryher and H.D. shared visions—"a series of strange experiences," "a series of light pictures" traced on their hotel bedroom wall. H.D. was the primary seer, but couldn't "go on" without Bryher; when H.D. retold the experience to Freud, he called it symptomatic of grave mental disorder, part of her sexual deviance.[15] I invoke H.D. and Bryher's early relationship as emblematic of Bryher's distinctive role as rescuer and rescued—and the curiosity of a kind of honeymoon which, given the social constraints, and given the pair's life-long triangulation of mediating desire through others, looked more like a séance for the "apparitional lesbian."

After Greece, H.D. and Bryher went to America in 1920 with infant and nurse, and when they returned to London in 1921, Bryher was married to the bisexual poet Robert McAlmon. By then Bryher had written three autobiographical novels as well as a critical book on Lowell's polyphonic poems, and (prematurely) published Moore's poems. This was an unusual narrative for any woman. To some extent, it can be explained by Bryher's money: she could support a woman, a baby and a man, as well as numerous artistic and political enterprises. In the mid-twenties, Switzerland became her home base, but she shuttled between Paris, London, Vienna and New York. She underwent psychoanalysis with an eye to becoming a lay-analyst, and paid for many of her friends to have "p-a," as she called it, insisting that the new science could help stem the historical turn to fascism by rehabilitating the individual's unconscious.

Bryher sponsored and edited *Close Up,* the first film journal in English (1927-30), later publishing several articles by Moore and Stein and debut translations of Sergei Eisenstein along with her own pieces that warned of the rise of Nazism. During the late thirties, she worked for the British government undercover, using her house in Switzerland as a "receiving station" for refugees fleeing Germany. (Walter Benjamin was among those she aided.) In the 1950s and 1960s, during her extremely productive belated career, she wrote fourteen favorably reviewed historical novels.

This is a very truncated overview of Bryher's varied life. Fostering an international modernism, she was a kind of "female Pound" and became an "ambassador," what H.D. called the "secondary function of the poet" (*Heart to Artemis* 155). The recipients of her funds, however, were a quite different set from those of the curatorial Pound; she supported Jews, emigré(e)s, women writers, artists, bookstore owners and pensioners.

---

[14] H.D., "Hedylus" in *Contact Editions*, 1925 (UCLA Rare Manuscript Library).
[15] *Tribute to Freud* (New York: Pantheon, 1956), 76.

Who was this girl who was really a boy, and who began to emerge in the archival light through her diverse attachments and projects? The archive portrays Bryher alternately as rescuer, dominatrix, and poet manqué, both wild and puritanical. She took on the roles of majordomo, bookkeeper, economist, mother, analyst, father, Resistance fighter, and novelist. In 1927, Bryher took the extraordinary step of legally adopting H.D.'s child, Perdita, who depicts her as both the more temperamentally even of her two mothers and as a "hippo with the whip." In many situations she assumed the role of presiding super-ego, as in the 1930 avant-garde film "Borderline," which she edited with H.D. and Macpherson and where she played a hotel manageress. She also acted within another historic triangle (with Paul and Eslanda Robeson). With her short hair and cigar and her piercing eyes, she keeps the books and indicts the film community's racists.

Bryher's longest intimate relationship was with H.D., yet many of her attachments were triangular. First, she mediated her emerging poetry aesthetic through Lowell and H.D., then tested her sexual identity with H.D. and Ellis; she pitted Moore against McAlmon; later she mediated her analyst's and his wife's relationship; at other times, the objects of her mediation were H.D. and Perdita. Like H.D., she often needed a third person, publishing vehicle, or program (like psychoanalysis) through whom/which to deflect her deepest emotions. Her first marriage, undertaken to allay her parents' anxieties, turned out to be rather inconvenient because of McAlmon's addictions. Bryher and McAlmon, however, engendered *Contact Press* which published key modernists, including James Joyce, Edith Sitwell, Stein, Mina Loy, Djuna Barnes, William Carlos Williams, and Bryher herself. After her divorce in 1926, she married bisexual Kenneth Macpherson and lived with H.D. in a ménage à trois. H.D. had a brief affair with Macpherson, but the three continued to collaborate on film projects.

The Melancholy of Money

Bryher's wealth and illegitimacy—her double sense of restitution and loss—leads to a revelation of sorts: *money clarifies and clouds.* Melancholia, as Freud speculated, works in an "economic sense"—the melancholic cannot "substitute" for the lost object and, in short, the melancholic "ego turns against itself with all the ammunition supplied by an identification with the abandoning object."[16] Her endeavors were shadowed by a sense of ego loss. Already in analysis with Hans Sachs, Bryher met Freud in 1927 and subsequently funded H.D.'s treatment

---

[16] Freud, "Mourning and Melancholia" (1917). In *The Standard Edition of the Complete Psychological Works of Sigmund Freud* (24 volumes), trans. James Strachey, Volume 14 (London: Hogarth Press, 1955), 242.

(yet another triangle) during 1932 and 1933. Studying Freud's many economic metaphors, Bryher well understood the balance sheet of introjections and projections; the column of giving and taking; expelling and intaking; and the hydraulics of income and expense in an emotional and political sense. Bryher's expenditure never matched her income. H.D. noted Freud's "courageous pessimism" in the face of political disaster; so too Bryher, another great melancholic, predicted again and again, Cassandra-like, world crisis.

Bryher knew well the melancholic collection of things that could never suffice. Monnier translated Bryher's *Paris 1900* and later sent it to Benjamin to give him some idea of the woman who was helping fund his escape from the Nazis. In it she remembered going to the Exhibition, and later recounted:

> So perhaps the age, as it felt itself dying, flowered into an immense jungle of tiny and useless possession? Surely modern art was born …? After walking all between jeweled thimble cases and Fragonard pictures reproduced on bead bags so tiny they could not even hold a handkerchief, thousands of people must have longed for blank walls and straight lines. (*Heart to Artemis* 26)

Bryher understood the nineteenth century "terror of a blank wall" that motivated the hysteria of Flaubert's Madame Bovary; her own response was a Bauhaus home, distinctively bare and drafty. Another response included shoring up everyday life, keeping a daily record book of luncheons, teas, sunbaths, walks, raids, haircuts and "pricks" (inoculations), and turning money and "dirt" into art. In the back of her 1940 diary, she scrawled: "who should be caged the analyst the patient or both?" She was probably referring to Walter Schmideberg, Melanie Klein's son-in-law and Bryher's long-time analyst and friend, and eventually her "patient": in fact she financed his treatment. Walter (nicknamed "the Bear") became increasingly dependent upon her, much to his wife's satisfaction; all the same he did manage in 1935 to pinpoint the crux of her vulnerability and melancholy:

> All the analytic ointment I can give you in a letter is that because you fear that everything dear to you would be taken from you, you rather give it up yourself; and that the fact that you sacrificed these things only increases the feeling of having lost so much, and the fear of having to lose more still.[17]

The Bear and Bryher corresponded over a twenty-year period until his death from alcoholism 1954 at Kusnacht, the same sanitarium where H.D. had been institutionalized.

---

[17] Walter Schmideberg to Bryher, 1935 (Beinecke Archive).

H.D's memoir of her analysis refers to Freud's notion of epiphanies as "striking oil." It is not a little ironic that the industries of Bryher's family lubricated H.D.'s poetry and therapy. The phantasmal bag of money that Guest stumbled over had enormous literal consequences for modernism. But gifts can backfire, so that Bryher's talent and generosity are often construed as a will to power. Bryher was 82 years old and perhaps losing her memory when Guest visited her. Complaining that "there was no major revelation" about H.D., Guest declares herself stymied: "I do not know what she believed she was shielding. I wish she talked openly to me. This book might have been different spelled from her own lips" (x). I take Guest's remarks that "within the chambers of the life" she examined "lay another nautilus" as an invitation of sorts to to spell out a narrative founded upon Bryher's extensive archive and its dormant overlapping, triangular collaborations.

In Bryher's novel *January Tale*, her main character digs a hole to hide his silver while contemplating "flight" and the sacking of Exeter: what can be kept and saved? The "gifts" that are given to those in power do not buy peace. For Bryher, 1940 was in some ways a replication of 1066—her Eldred suffers from a kind of pre-traumatic anticipation, driven by Bryher's melancholy vision:

> A blight prowled over the things he loved, everything seemed about to end, in a clash of soundless blades…. Ending, ending, what was ending? What were these battle sights that he noticed round him but which his companions seemed not to see? Was it the doom of the world? Why did he keep saying to himself, The berries will rot, there will be no paths for the swine to dig for acorns, family will be set against family for countless generations.[18]

How does one stop the sense of a blight destroying "the things [one] loved"? Out of a life of unconventional investments and preemptive losses, the cosmopolitan and multilingual Bryher helped fashion an international modernism. Her experimental life prompts a rethinking of literary and artistic legacies, the unwritten history of "illegitimate" marriages and friendships, triangular desire and alternative modes of collaboration.

---

[18] *This January Tale* (New York: Harcourt, Brace & World, 1966), 79.

13

Michael Bell

Magical Realism Revisited

In the late twentieth century various forms of the marvellous became popular in fiction around the world, including Britain, and in explaining the genesis and meaning of this development the phrase 'magical realism' has played a large but possibly misleading part. The most popular version of the story is that in the 1960s a group of Latin American novelists devised a mixture of 'magic' and 'realism' which subsequently extended to almost all parts of the globe. 'Magical realism' draws on pre-scientific folk belief to subvert the 'Western' commitment to scientific reason, itself associated with both imperialism and a history of realist representation, so that the new genre is intrinsically oppositional and progressive. García Márquez' *One Hundred Years of Solitude* (1967), as the most popular, substantial and summative work in this mode, was the principal source from which magical realism became a dominant form in late twentieth-century fiction world-wide. Yet while there is considerable truth in this story, and writers from around the world, such as Salman Rushdie, have acknowledged the importance of García Márquez' example, this broad-brush account obfuscates a number of important questions and occludes a significantly different history.

To understand the wider recovery of the marvellous in world fiction, it is first necessary to question the assumption of a mainly Latin American influence. The new sympathy for the marvellous has broader bases, and wider sources. As signs of a more general cultural change, for example, one might note over the same period a new interest in Shakespeare's late romances, or the widened appreciation of opera as a dramatic form. It may be, in other words, that García Márquez is less a cause than a harbinger of change. That would not, of course, reduce the interest of his case. To be the symptomatic index of a deep-lying cultural shift suggests a more profound order of significance than being the instigator of a literary fashion. Likewise, some of the conscious rationales of 'magical realism' may have an *ex post facto* aspect, and an ideological thrust, which miss some of its underlying cultural meaning.

We should also note the unstable equilibrium in the very concept of 'magical realism.' It is often said that the *proprium* of the genre, in contradistinction to the fantastic, is that elements of the marvellous are naturalised, treated as unremarkable, in the narration.[1] But of course it is often hard in practice to determine when this occurs, or if indeed it can truly be said to occur at all in respect of the reader's response to even the most apparently naïve narration. For even if neither characters nor narrator baulk at the marvels, the reader, by the very logic of the genre, must be aware of them. Not surprisingly, therefore, even Wendy Faris's classic study of the form serves partly to reveal its elusiveness.[2] Meanwhile, the phrase itself is as elusive as the genre it seeks to define. In oxymoronic formulations of this kind, it is always a delicate matter to determine where the principal emphasis lies. To what extent is magical realism *opposed* to realism or a form *of* it? Much discussion of the genre emphasises, or assumes, the former while other commentators note the ultimate importance of the containing category of realism as it is expanded and enhanced, but not exploded, in this genre. Since the familiar story has been well told on many occasions, I don't rehearse it here but propose a different rationale for 'magical realism' by first revisiting what the 'marvellous' meant in an earlier Latin American writer, Alejo Carpentier.[3]

Because the term 'magical realism,' after some nonce usage in European art history, came into general use as a literary generic term in the Latin American context, it was affected by the gravitational pull of a neighbouring phrase '*lo real maravilloso*' (the marvellous real, or reality). This was notably expounded by Alejo Carpentier in the prologue to his 1949 novel *The Kingdom of This World*. Carpentier records how, on visiting Haiti after a decade in the Paris of the surrealists, he was overwhelmed by the 'surreal' quality of the Caribbean and Latin American landscape and history. Here the anti-rational devices of the surrealists were starkly revealed to him as formal games still essentially within the world of western rationality. In being merely oppositional they were still defined by it. By contrast, the story of the eighteenth-century slave uprisings inspired partly by African tribal beliefs, or that of Henri Christophe with his fantastic redoubt of Sans Souci, were marvels of history. The phrase *lo real maravilloso*, therefore, refers to a *reality* whereas 'magical realism' refers to a literary *mode*. And 'marvel' similarly refers to the natural, just as 'magic' implies some departure from it. These expressions are, therefore, quite distinct in their meanings and claims; but Carpentier's argument, which was squarely based on a regional specificity, has coloured the use of the English phrase so that an ethnographic exceptionalism became part of the meaning of the sub-genre.

---

[1] Amaryll Chanady, *Magical Realism and the Fantastic* (New York: Garland, 1985).

[2] *Ordinary Enchantments: Magical Realism and the Remystification of Narrative* (Nashville: Vanderbilt University Press, 2004).

[3] See Wendy B. Faris, *Ordinary Enchantments*, Wendy B. Faris and Lois Parkinson Zamora, eds, *Magical Realism: Theory, History, Community* (Durham and London: Duke University Press, 1995); Stephen M. Hart and Wen-chin Ouyang, eds, A *Companion to Magical Realism* (Woodbridge, Suffolk: Rochester, NY: Tamesis, 2005).

'Magical realism,' that is to say, has acquired such a meaning *de facto* without any intrinsic connection with Latin America. At the same time, Carpentier's prologue, illuminating as it is for the creative impulse behind the book, is actually quite two-dimensional as compared to the work itself. *The Kingdom of This World* is a poetically concentrated meditation on history in which the experience of the marvellous is ethnographically relativised as part of Black African culture, and is ultimately assimilated into the narrative as a form of artistically sustained mythopoeia.[4] However deadly and duplicitous the European category of the aesthetic is shown to be, it remains the basis of the book's own utopian affirmation. The book is consciously a work of *literature*, of literary *art*. Likewise, while the book owes much of its local power to the communal imagination of the black slaves, it is squarely in the tradition of European Enlightenment in seeing slavery itself as an intrinsic, that is to say a universal, not a merely local and relative, evil.

It is difficult, and ultimately unimportant, to determine how far Carpentier may have been conscious of a gap between the rousingly simple reality claim of his prologue and the literary complexity of his actual achievement. The gap itself matters, however, because it separates a direct claim about reality from the significance of an artistically created world. And that matters in turn because the claim of an ethnographically specific experience is a common rationale for valorising 'magical realism' as a challenge to 'Western' rationality. Such a claim, although offered as a compliment, actually makes such works vulnerable to the charge of unreflecting sentimentality. I say 'unreflecting' because the rationality sometimes labelled 'Western,' and thereby contaminated with imperialism and other evils, is also the very universalism on which the moral standpoint of the book is at the same time likely to depend. García Márquez, for example, has been a Marxist throughout his mature life and therefore a child of the Enlightenment And I say 'sentimental' because such a viewpoint seeks to enjoy a moral high ground on a simplified basis. But that is what Carpentier, in this classic and founding instance, notably avoids. If his prologue comes close to making such an argument, the book itself does not.

When I have called Carpentier's novel 'poetic' this does not imply a tendency to purple writing but rather a way of focusing, with a near-anthropological detachment, on metonymic moments which become radiantly iconic concentrations of historical experience. And with this thought we may return to the instability of the phrase 'magical realism' as reflecting an instability in the underlying notion of realism which the phrase 'magical realism' both exacerbates and occludes. A common argument for magical realism is that it subverts or expands

---

[4]   For a discussion of this, see Michael Bell, *Literature, Modernism and Myth* (Cambridge: Cambridge University Press, 1997), pp. 182-95.

the protocols of a more traditional novelistic realism, itself associated in turn with philosophical assumptions underwriting the political possession – and the scientific understanding – of the world. There is an important measure of truth in this. Several Hispanic writers of the region turned to the example of Cervantes, who is commonly accredited with founding European novelistic realism on mocking the marvellous in the form of medieval romance but, as Borges and others have insisted, Cervantes rather found in *Don Quixote* a cunning means of indulging his affection for it. In this respect, he represents a route back to the pre-Cervantean marvellous, and Carpentier in his prologue comments on the cultural ambiguity of a Cervantean episode in precisely this spirit. But there repeatedly creeps into the rehearsals of this account an assumption that 'realism' is a naively mimetic form, seeking to encapsulate reality objectively in language. It is one thing for writers such as Borges, within his fictions, to promote such a reductive conception of realism; but others, whether scholars or general readers, should not be drawn into taking such ideas too literally. Of course, the reality *effect* is crucial to much nineteenth-century fiction, hence the weight of the term 'realism,' but it is necessary every so often to remind some readers, including academics, that realism itself is only a literary convention. The great works of nineteenth-century realist art doubtless inform us about human experience; but, despite their occasional rhetoric or rationalisations as in Balzac's 'All is true,' they do so, no less than Dante or Greek tragedy, through literary means.[5] All literary art affects us, in Nietzsche's words, as 'a concentrated image of the world.'[6] In this respect, the assumed internal polarity in the phrase 'magical realism' has to be significantly reconfigured. The 'magical' and the 'realism' are both equally literary. Hence, along with the notions of 'magical realism' as either critiquing or expanding realism, one can also see it more directly and pertinently as foregrounding the literariness of the narrative. 'Magical realism' has origins beyond the ethnographic, and it often flaunts a specifically literary pedigree.

This may initially appear a banal and circular reduction in so far as literature is a minimal and general category as compared to magic and realism. But it is sometimes the obvious that is at once most important and most overlooked. In the late twentieth century, despite the *de facto* popularity of literature, and specifically of fiction, it became a deeply problematic category, and especially under the pressure of political thinking on a geo-political scale. In a pedagogical volume entitled *Literature in the Modern World*, designed to introduce students to advanced, globally-conscious thinking about literature at the end of the twentieth century, the editor includes an excerpt from Terry Eagleton arguing the ideolog-

---

[5]   The phrase occurs at the opening of *Le Père Goriot* (1835)
[6]   *The Birth of Tragedy*, trans. Walter Kaufmann (New York: Random House, 1967), p. 135.

ically-oriented arbitrariness of literary judgements. Literature, Eagleton suggests, is merely what a given set of people at a particular time find valuable or judge to be fine writing, and the supposed specialness of literature is a mystification.[7] His argument has a structural similarity to Margaret Thatcher's notorious assertion that there is no such thing as society. Many observers saw this as a wicked dishonesty because it used the literal truth that there is indeed no such *thing* as 'society' to obfuscate the fact that every one born on to the planet is governed by a network of socio-economic relations which are man-made and a matter of political responsibility. As a popularising Marxist, Eagleton reveals with unusual candour the damaging pressure to which the category of the literary has been widely subjected within the academy. Although literary fiction remains buoyant in so far as it continues to sell, and is popular across a wide spectrum of readers, there is a question as to *how* it is read or what it is read *as*.

The literary has been a threatened category, if not at the level of practice, then at the level of understanding, and the notion that nineteenth-century realist writers practised a naive literalism is itself a symptom of its general occlusion. Imaginative writers like Carpentier and García Márquez, who have strong political and historical views, are for that very reason impelled to create a literary density within their fiction, which is why it may be an important underlying impulse of 'magical realism' more generally to foreground and affirm the literary as such. To take the sub-genre in this way is to deflect its meaning from premodern ethnographic exceptionalism and to see it rather as the expression of a highly sophisticated universality. That also explains why 'magical realism' has characterised widely different writers around the world, irrespective of influence from a single regional centre.

In this respect, Mikhail Bulgakov's *The Master and Margarita* provides an illuminating comparison. First published with the Khrushchev thaw in 1966 from a manuscript which had survived the author's death in Stalinist Russia in 1941, its publication was almost contemporary with *One Hundred Years of Solitude*; yet its particular brand of 'magical realism' emerged from a completely different history, both literary and political. Both works use the Bible as a significant structural model within which to mobilise magically realist effects. Indeed, on a world-historical scale, the Bible is the most influential work of 'magical realism' in a colonial context, although this fact is commonly overlooked for the very feature that makes it so interesting a case: its peculiar status of having survived into modernity with a large readership for whom the magical elements are a matter of literal faith. Bulgakov and García Márquez exploit this fact in different ways,

---

[7] *Literature in the Modern World*, 2nd ed., ed. Dennis Walder (Oxford: Oxford University Press, 2004), pp. 31-2.

but in both cases it ultimately serves to foreground the meaning of their own literariness.

Several chapters of Bulgakov's novel consist of the Master's novel, which he has actually burned, telling the story of Christ and the imperial official, Pontius Pilate. Where James Joyce's fictional opening of the twentieth century took a Jew as its everyman figure, Bulgakov, in the latter half of the century, made Pilate the modern archetype. Pilate, the hand-washer, if not the moral centre of the book, is the centre of its moral significance. Unlike many of the real functionaries or bystanders in twentieth-century history, this Pilate is eternally tortured by the thought of his missed opportunity. And Pilate's moral cowardice is central because it figures forth that of the Master, who has imagined him, and through that of the writer as such. But, although the Master has destroyed his own work, in the magical world of Bulgakov's fiction 'Manuscripts don't burn,' and the work survives the personal weakness of its creator.[8] Moreover, this work is a specifically literary one in multiple contrast to the familiar Biblical story which claims a veracity both historical and super-historical. Not only is the Master's novel narrated from Pilate's rather than Christ's viewpoint, and the characters given unfamiliar names, but Christ, known as Yeshua ha-Nosri, is presented in entirely secular terms. Yeshua repeatedly warns his disciple, Matthu Levi, the Evangelist Matthew, that he misunderstands and misrepresents his master. The proverbial value of the phrase 'Gospel truth' is subverted by an alternative history envisaged through the literary imagination. Meanwhile, the entirely secular conception of Yeshua/Christ in the Master's novel is in ironic contrast with the story of modern atheistic Moscow in which it is embedded, for this relates the grotesque mayhem created by a group of supernatural demons. Here again, however, the devils are deflected from traditional Christian figures and have an essentially literary provenance. Indeed, the whole Moscow story is an *hommage* to the moral imagination of the nineteenth-century Russian novel. It is not only strewn with allusions from Pushkin to Tolstoy, it uses the grotesquerie of Gogol and the psychological imagery of Dostoevsky to explode the spiritual vacuity of Soviet Russia. If Bulgakov's novel had drawn on a literal religious faith, the effect would be more narrowly reliant on it. As it is, the literary imagination is felt as an enduring spiritual power and an historical resource.

Although *One Hundred Years of Solitude* draws more evidently on the folk imagination for its mediation of Biblical motifs, this also occurs through overtly literary means: Cervantes's signature device of the foreign historian. A major episode in the story of Macondo is the memory sickness which may be thought of as the shift from myth to history, the moment in which the communal memory

---

8 *The Master and Margarita*, trans. Mirra Ginsburg (London: Picador, 1989), p. 300.

becomes dependent on writing. The townsfolk initially seek to stay the loss of memory by the mechanical means of putting name labels and instructions on everyday items, and then they start to produce an 'imaginary reality, one invented by themselves, which was less practical for them, but more comforting.'[9] After these rather desperate veerings between mechanical records and flights of imagination, José Arcadio starts to construct a memory machine: a wheel turning thousands of cards reminiscent of a nineteen-sixties computer. But just as José Arcadio has written some fourteen thousand cards it is rendered redundant by the arrival of a mysterious, decrepit old man who eventually proves to be Melquíades. The focus veers in mid-sentence, and the memory machine itself quickly fades from the memory of most readers as the narrative goes on to tell how Melquíades cures the memory sickness with his magic potion.

Only at the end of the novel does the conjunction of Melquíades and the memory machine become significant. For Melquíades's true remedy for the memory sickness is not the potion but the written narrative he produces in the timeless zone of the chamber to which he retires. The timeless room combines a Nietzschean superhistoricism, the capacity to escape 'presentist' illusions, with the traditional 'once upon a time' of fiction.[10] So too, although within the world of the novel Melquíades's manuscript is a chronicle – the simplest and most factual form of history – within the novel which we read *as* a novel, it is the purest fiction. And as an internal image of the novel itself, it preserves the ambiguities signalled at the moment of its birth. What does it mean for a novel to be a memory machine? Is this a reductive image, exposing its mechanistic limitations, or a positive one suggesting how it transcends the mechanics of its medium? The embedded chronicle images the novel's own ambiguous status as history and fiction, in which its considerable power as each is inseparable from the other. Most notably, the memory of the banana-company massacre, echoing the original memory sickness, disappears from the official history, and even from collective memory, but is revived, in a more mythic than historically accurate form, by virtue of the fiction. Fiction may be a deviation from history, or a concentration of it as meaning. As the latter, however, it may not be transparent, and interpretation, or a lived experience of history, may be necessary before its meaning can be appreciated. Hence, the final deciphering only when the experience has been lived is a resonant symbol, in Michael Wood's words, of what literature knows.[11] It knows in a mode of the open secret, both transparent and opaque. In

---

[9] *One Hundred Years of Solitude*, trans. Gregory Rabassa (New York: Harper, 1970), p. 46; *Cien Años de Soledad* (Buenos Aires: Sudamericana, 1967), p. 124.

[10] This notion was developed in *The Uses and Disadvantages of History for Life*, the second of the *Untimely Meditations* (1874).

[11] *Literature and the Taste of Knowledge* (Cambridge: Cambridge University Press, 2005).

this respect, the populist literary charm of the book is itself part of the seductive illusion from which the Buendías need to awake in their sleep-walking through history. Literary formal self-consciousness is the figure, and the means, of historical awareness.

The archetypal Anglophone work of magical realism in the postcolonial vein is Salman Rushdie's *Midnight's Children* (1982) which, like *The Master and Margarita*, has other sources antedating García Márquez. Günter Grass's *The Tin Drum* (1959), for example, is a major structural and thematic influence; and, as a reversal of the German *Bildungsroman*, it is itself a book of dense literary-historical allusion. Rushdie's novel creates a formal self-consciousness designed, in his case, to negotiate the problematic nature of representation in both its mimetic and its political senses. The narrator, Saleem Sinai, is constantly cast, by himself, by others, and by circumstances, as a representative of the collective Indian experience after Independence. Yet his capacity to embody the national history is continually ridiculed, and his magical property of being able to enter telepathically the consciousness of individuals all over India gives him what is referred to as the 'illusion of the artist.'[12] Indeed, all the magic children mentioned here are artists figuring the art of the book in which they appear. Insofar as Saleem is specifically the Balzacian artist whose dramatic narrative expresses the national experience, the comparison is as ambiguous as the memory machine. Does it mean that India cannot be represented as nineteenth-century France could? Or that, for a late-twentieth-century, postmodern and postcolonial consciousness, this was always an impossible ambition even in Balzac's time? No doubt both implications are in varying measure present, and are made equally irrelevant, because the narrative uses the incapacity of Saleem to achieve more implicitly the representativeness that is apparently denied. The overt literariness of the work pre-empts the literalistic objections to which it could be vulnerable at the level of history while constantly putting into imaginative orbit highly concentrated iconic foci of the national experience. Once again, it is specifically as literature that the text is able to embody a history, or to become what Fredric Jameson calls a 'national allegory.'[13]

Rushdie holds the historical tragedy and the fictional fantasy in a testing tension, but magical realism is peculiarly susceptible to short-circuiting the relationship and slipping into coyness or sentimentality – a danger which García Márquez saw in *One Hundred Years of Solitude* after its extraordinary success. Once again, sentimentalism may arise not from the genre as such but precisely from

---

[12] *Midnight's Children* (London: Pan, 1982), p. 174.
[13] Fredric Jameson, 'Third World Literature in the Age of Multinational Capitalism,' *Social Text*, 15 (Fall, 1986), 65-88.

its too easy privileging of an exceptionalist viewpoint, an exceptionalism which may be ideological as well as ethnographic. For many readers, the privileging of female sensibility in Isabel Allende's *The House of the Spirits* (1982) or Laura Esquivel's *Like Water for Chocolate* (1993) allows the magic to become rather soft focus. *Nights at the Circus* (1984), by Salman Rushdie's friend Angela Carter, is open to the same objection even though it offers an internal critique of contemporary strains of feminism. The strength of Carter's novel lies in its being so self-consciously literary in challenging the influentially masculinist conceptions of art associated with Goethe and Joyce. Like *Midnight's Children*, it approaches that characteristic late twentieth-century sub-genre of the rewritten classic for which Jean Rhys's *Wide Sargasso Sea* (1966) remains the magnificent exemplary case. The note of indulgence in Carter's novel arises not from its feminism *per se* but from its too easy collusion of magic and exceptionalism, while the power of Rhys's short novel, like Carpentier's, derives from its broader sense of historical tragedy enveloping Rochester as well as Antoinette, and from its narrative containment of the exotic and the oneiric as experienced by the characters within the sober historical realism of the novel itself.

In whatever mode, the discipline of the real is vital, and it continues at all times to find expression in the traditional form of realism. Over the period in which magical realism has flourished, there have been writers of equal if not greater power, such as Anita Desai on India and John McGahern and William Trevor from Ireland, whose works have achieved the enigmatic transparency of literary transformation the more effectively for observing the protocols of realism. In this respect, it is useful to compare the South African novelist, J. M. Coetzee.

Until *Elizabeth Costello* (2003) and *Slow Man* (2005), Coetzee's fiction had stayed principally within the protocols of realism, yet it has always been pervaded by a metafictional concern for the modes of meaning and responsibility peculiar to imaginative literature. Coetzee is remarkable for the rigour with which he thinks of major historical questions strictly within, or through, the category of literature. He repeatedly refuses to translate the moral substance dramatised in his work into general discursive opinion. His *Foe* (1986) ranks with *Wide Sargasso Sea* as a rewritten classic, but along with *The Master of Petersburg* (1994) it reflects on the tortuous truth conditions of imaginative writing. Coetzee's case makes clear that, although I have deprecated the tendentious, the category of the literary is far from apolitical. Indeed, the contemporary forms of the marvellous seem often to insist on the literature's own oblique mode of intervention. Hence, although we may properly think of them as inhabiting different fictional universes, Coetzee and García Márquez have a deeper commonality in making self-conscious the vital, yet untranslatable, mode of meaning known as literature.

While I have emphasised the literary as a positive mode of meaning, Coetzee's case also suggests more negative and political reasons why a globally-conscious, postcolonial fiction in the late twentieth century should wish to emphasise its own literariness. The early twentieth-century generation of European modernist writers, most of them in some sense post-Nietzschean, frequently turned to myth as a primordial category whose functional modern counterpart is imaginative literature. The aesthetic is modernity's equivalent of the mythic world-making.[14] Such a privileging of aesthetically constructed myth was largely progressive in spirit, as Joyce and Mann especially exposed the arbitrariness of all philosophical systems. But to a later generation around the world the universalistic claims of these writers seemed Eurocentric, and it became more urgent – while recognising the mythic nature of every worldview, both individual and cultural – to question the hegemonic power of myth. If human beings are indeed mythopoeic animals, they have to adopt a more relativistic, quizzical and postmodern relation to myth. As the Francophone Caribbean novelist, Edouard Glissant, put it in 1973: 'The main difficulty facing national literatures today … is that they must combine mythification with demystification, this primal innocence with a learned craftiness.'[15] The difference in spirit is evident between D. H. Lawrence's *The Rainbow* (1915) and *One Hundred Years of Solitude*. Both invoke Genesis to tell a modern regional history through a generational family saga, but Lawrence's high seriousness contrasts sharply with García Márquez' playful populism. Where Lawrence draws on a deep structure in English sensibility, García Márquez plays with the folk imagination without sentimentally endorsing it.

In this respect the fictional marvellous in late twentieth-century fiction is politically distinct from modernist mythopoeia, and its analytic or generic difference can be focused through Nietzsche's remarks on literary response in *The Birth of Tragedy*:

> Whoever wishes to test rigorously to what extent he is related to the true aesthetic listener…needs only to examine sincerely the feeling with which he accepts miracles represented on stage: whether he feels his historical sense, which insists on strict psychological causality, insulted by them, whether he makes a benevolent concession and admits the miracle as a phenomenon intelligible to childhood but alien to him, or whether he experiences anything else. For in this way he will be able to determine to what extent he is capable of understanding myth as a concentrated image of the world that, as a condensation of experience, cannot dispense with miracles. (*BT*, 135)

---

[14] See *Literature, Modernism and Myth*.
[15] *Caribbean Discourse: Selected Essays*, trans. J. Michael Dash (Charlottesville, VA: University of Virginia Press, 1989), p. 100.

Nietzsche instances the marvellous in fiction as an index of the aesthetic response through which modern man comes closest to the experience of myth. But, as in Bulgakov, miracle in itself is not myth in this aesthetic sense: literal belief in the miracle would be as far removed as scientific positivism from a properly aesthetic response. The miracle occurs under an aesthetic condition equally separate both from the spectator's life world and from ethnographic identification. But whereas Nietzsche, as a proto-modernist, wished to recover the mythopoeic *through* literature, the magical realist typically seeks to deconstruct the mythopoeic *as* literature. Both are internal transformations of the Enlightenment.

Western literature has a long tradition of Gothic, romantic and fantastic writing which critiques internally the cultural tendency to instrumental reason, and magical realism can be seen as a contemporary manifestation of the same internal balancing. But the most radical cultural critique has always been that of the literary imagination as such, for which the implication of Wendy Faris's phrase 'ordinary enchantments' could be reversed. Enchantment can too easily become merely ordinary, and magical realism may offer a fatally clichéd short cut; but it remains the *proprium* of the literary imagination to achieve the enchantment of the ordinary. That is why magical realism is best understood as a signature of the literary as such.

14

Donald Anderson

Necessary Lies: The expedient blurring of fact/fiction in creative writing

"Writing is not apart from living. Writing is a kind of double living. The writer experiences everything twice. Once in reality and once more in that mirror which waits always before or behind him." [1] So says Catherine Drinker Bowen, and I believe her. Memory and imagination are our only resources. Our stories are remembered or imagined, or, more likely, remembered *and* imagined. "It's a poor sort of memory," Lewis Carroll's Queen says, "that only works backwards." [2]

Mind and brain studies agree upon one thing: there is no agreed-upon model of how memory works. Daniel Schacter tells us we can trust, though, that a good model for how memory works must be consistent with the notion that memories are constructions made in accordance with present—yes, *present*—needs, desires, influences. As such, our memories are accompanied by feelings, convictions, emotions. Furthermore, the experts say, memory involves an awareness of memory. [3]

Jean Piaget, the great child psychologist, claimed that his earliest memory was of nearly being kidnapped at the age of two. He remembered sitting in his baby carriage, from where he watched his nurse defend herself against the kidnapper. He recalled scratches on the nurse's face and a police officer with a short cloak chasing the kidnapper off. The policeman swung a white baton. The rub against this story is that the event had not occurred. Years after, Piaget's nurse confessed that she'd fabricated the story. Piaget later wrote that he must have heard, as a

---

[1] Quoted in *Creativity and the Writing Process*, edited by Olivia Bertagnolli and Jeff Rackman (New York: John Wiley & Sons, 1982), p. 101.
[2] Lewis Carroll, *The Annotated Alice* (New York: Clarkson N. Potter, Inc., 1960), p. 248.
[3] Quoted in "Memory," *The Skeptic's Dictionary*, edited by Robert Todd Carroll <http://skepdic.com/memory.html>. For fuller coverage, see Daniel L. Schacter, *Searching for Memory: The Brain, the Mind, and the Past* (New York: Basic Books, 1996).

child, the account of this fabrication and projected it into the past in the form of a visual memory. It was, then, a memory of a memory, only false.[4]

Studies have indeed shown that there is no significant correlation between the subjective feeling of certainty a person has about a memory and that memory being accurate.[5] And other studies support that we often construct our memories after the fact, and that we are susceptible to suggestion when we fill in the gaps.[6] In the scientific literature, a confabulation is a fantasy that has unconsciously emerged as a factual account in memory. A confabulation may be based partly on fact or be a complete construction of the imagination. But confabulation is not just a deficit of memory. It is something anybody might do—*need* to do—and *does*. Experiments suggest that confabulation may be a routine activity for healthy people—the manner in which we justify our everyday choices.[7]

Eyewitness accounts in court are, as a matter of course, granted less force than circumstantial evidence. Given the susceptibility of memory, it's a reasonable approach to approaching the truth. It may even be dishonest to assume you always know when you're being honest.

James McConkey writes in *The Anatomy of Memory*:

> [I]magination and memory are so interconnected (PET scans, for example, show that the same areas of the brain are affected, whether we imagine or experience something), it might at first glance seem handy to connect the two names with a hyphen, in the manner of certain present-day marriage partners. But in this case memory is no doubt the dominant partner, and must provide the family name. Still, there is a dalliance between the pair, one necessary for literature.[8]

McConkey, a memoirist and fiction writer himself, goes on to point out that the work of Marcel Proust certainly suggests that "memory, through imagination, can impose a value beyond that of the actual experience."[9]

In the teaching of creative writing I feel obligated to raise the issue of accuracy, factual and emotional. Novelist Russell Banks once said to me that if all we wanted from one another was information then all we'd need to do is exchange drivers' licenses. What we need from one another, he said, is useable emotional

---

4   Ibid.
5   Ibid.
6   Ibid.
7   Helen Phillips, "Mind fiction: Why your brain tells tall tales," <http://www.newscientist.com/article.ns?id=mg19225720.100&print=true>.
8   *The Anatomy of Memory*, edited by James McConkey (New York: Oxford University Press, 1996), p. 124.
9   Ibid.

data, and mere facts are hardly sufficient. And thus follows a vital early disillusionment for writers: *Just because something happened to you does not necessarily make it art. You may have to invent—mint, hatch, spark, beget!*

According to Helen Phillips, "some experts argue that we can never be sure about what is actually real and so must confabulate all the time to try to make sense of the world around us."[10] Sounds to me like what writers do, and *why*.

A few years back I was flying to Florida for Spring Break. I had that day finished classes and was taking a night flight from Colorado to South Florida. My wife was already there. I had a layover in Cincinnati. It was about 7:00 pm. The sun had set and it was rainy and cold. At the end of the terminal I spied a Starbucks. Just what I need, I thought: a 50-krona cup of coffee. I started that way.

At the counter, ahead of me, was a dwarf. My reaction was as yours might have been. It made me think of words like *Well, now* or *Oh*! My reaction was compounded by the fact that the little woman was lovely, shockingly gorgeous. I felt confused and affronted. Brainless. What right had I to decide that this dwarf did not look as she should have?—like *I* expected her to? Something felt wrong. What was it? I knew I would have to write about the experience to understand the least of it. The essay was published in the *North American Review* (290. 3&4, 2005, 76-7). It was listed under Nonfiction and titled "Stunted."

The woman was so small—the height and size of a three-year-old—that the clerk behind the Starbucks counter in the Cincinnati Airport didn't see her. When the clerk asked for my order, I, along with a hand gesture, said, "I believe she was first." Was I trying to pretend it was normal for a grown person to be 30 inches tall? The clerk— bless her heart—then leaned over the counter. To be fair, it was a wide counter, though I don't think higher than standard.

"Oh," the clerk said. "What would you like?"

"A small latte," the dwarf said.

The clerk, taller than I, was a thin black girl with straightened hair. She was kind and probably some years younger than the white dwarf below her.

When the clerk set the latte on the counter to reach for the money, she inadvertently set the cup beyond the dwarf's reach. The clerk handed over the change, then asked for my order. I pointed at the cup.

What was I feeling? Shame? Fear? Pride? Generosity? What I knew for sure was that whatever the feeling was, it was anchored in an awkward self-centeredness. What did this woman's growth have to do with me?

The clerk saw she had to push the latte closer, and she did. I ordered a small latte.

---

[10] <http://www.newscientist.com/article.ns?id=mg19225720.100&print=true>.

I didn't want to give the impression that my body could absorb more liquid than the dwarf's. Besides, how to utter Starbuck's word for small: *tall*?

The woman had to reach as high she could to remove the plastic lid from her cup to add sugar. She'd moved down the counter, sliding the capped cup toward the stirrers, the honey and sugars. I was worried she'd pull the hot cup over onto her head—her uplifted face—and had to resist helping. Craning, she managed to add raw cane sugar, stir the coffee, and replace the lid. When she headed off in her little beige London Fog, navy slacks, and kid's clogs, I noticed her hands were the size of a woman's, strong and dexterous enough to hold her latte and to maneuver her rolling luggage. If her clothes were doll-size, her pull luggage wasn't.

For her height and size her head was, as seems the case for dwarves, disproportionate. Too large, of course, but in this case—her case—only slightly. And her features were fine, not distorted. Her long hair was tended and highlighted professionally with streaks of blond.

I boarded my plane. Late that night, I told my wife about the little woman and her latte.

What I've just reported is factual. It is, as best as I recall, what happened in the airport. I did, that night, tell my wife about the dwarf. What Ellen said—and it is *all* she said—was this: "She was probably going to a conference." I needed dialogue, so I wrote some.

[Late that night, I told my wife about the little woman and her latte.]

"She had glorious hair—really—I have to say," I say to Ellen. "A little kid's voice but a grown-up's hair. Luxurious. And she was neat and urbane in her kid's clothes, her little purse."

"You don't have to feel bad for her," my wife says. "Why do you feel bad? You feel bad, don't you? You do."

"Well, God," I say, "I think of Marnie racing her bike in that mountain thing in Moab." Marnie is one of our daughters. As the local joke goes, you can tell she's from Boulder, Colorado: She owns a $500 car, but pedals a $3,000 bicycle made from space-age metals.

"When I saw the little woman walking away," I say, "pulling that suitcase her size, I thought about Marnie talking about her bike's composite frame, the composite shifters, titanium gears, step-in pedals."

I say: "Her feet lock into her pedals like ski boots. That little woman will never ride a mountain bike. They don't make good bikes that small. She'd have to buy a tricycle for Christ's sake—a Goddamn Big Wheel or something. You know?"

"Why is this personal?" Ellen asks. "Is this personal?"

"I don't know."

"Dwarves attend conferences. I've read about this," Ellen says. "They have dwarf stores for clothes and furniture. Car stuff. A lot of dwarves drive cars." Then: "Dwarfism is treated as a disability. There are lobbies for this. 'Little People' lobbies. And: *conferences*. She was probably on her way to a conference. They meet at these places, fall in love, marry, have babies."

"What kind of babies? Regular or small?"

"Regular," she says.

"Why would they be regular? A bald guy's son is usually bald. Big noses run in families. A son of an alcoholic is an alcoholic risk. A fat woman's mother is generally large, right? You think I didn't check out your mother?"

I should tell you that my wife heard me read this essay at a conference in Key West. After my reading, she said, "I didn't say those things." "I know," I said, "but you should have." And there you have the hazard—on both sides—of having a writer in the house. In my defense, there were people in the audience who know both Ellen and me, and who said, "Sounds just like you, Ellen." I should report too, I suppose, that Ellen was not amused.

Because I was still trying to understand what I was writing about in "Stunted," I continued to write dialogue. In fiction or nonfiction, what I'm after as a writer is *emotional* accuracy not *factual* accuracy. I hope that is a notion that makes sense and is the worthy goal I believe it to be.

["A fat woman's mother is generally large, right? You think I didn't check out your mother?"]

My wife is a slender woman who smokes cigarettes. She walks four miles a day. Power walks. To stay fit, is what she says, and to keep on smoking. My wife buys cheap filtered menthols she stubs out when half puffed. It stunts your growth, she says. I call her E sometimes instead of Ellen.

"You should quit, E," I say.

"You *like* tiny women," she says, lighting up. She raises a kitchen window and sticks her head close. She is a polite smoker insofar as she keeps smoke out of people's faces and houses, even her own.

"Why wouldn't dwarves bear dwarves?" I ask. And when Ellen doesn't answer: "What would a dwarf do with a four-year-old who could knock her over?"

Ellen blows smoke out the window then swivels her head. "What makes you think all dwarves are actors or circus freaks?"

"I think that?"

"Do you?"

I say that every few years you read in the paper about dwarf tossing or such. "You don't remember Cuomo signing legislation banning dwarf tossing and dwarf bowling in New York bars?" We'd lived in New York for a few years.

"Dwarf bowling?" E says.

"Yes."

"Bowling?"

"They strap them on skateboards and fire them down the lane." Then: "As I understand it, they do wear helmets and the pins are plastic."

I clamp shut because I suddenly remember seeing on TV some little folks wrapped in Velcro clothes. They were hung like pictures on Velcro walls. I don't recall whether they were tossed at the walls, but, in any event, I don't bring it up.

"Bars and bowling alleys," E says. "I take it they throw dwarves in bars."

"Liquor's involved," I say. "It would have to be, right?"

"You tell me," E says.

"Some dwarves have sued for the right to be tossed and bowled." I nod my head to enforce the point.

"Claiming what—the right to make a living?"

"So, maybe there should be a right? I mean, who stops 300-pound blubber boys from squashing skinnier backs and wide-outs? Why isn't that illegal? Pitchers fire balls at batters' heads. We're not talking hockey or Tyson eating Holyfield's ear. Consenting dwarves," I say, "wear sturdy little helmets and padding, and when they're tossed, they land on mattresses—no, usually a pile of them."

"Consenting? Did you say *consenting*?"

"I did." Then: "I say if a man wants to juggle hatchets, let him do it."

"Where would you draw the line," E asks, "chainsaws, grenades, white phosphorus? White phosphorus," she says, "reacts rapidly with oxygen, catching fire at 10 to 15 degrees above room temperature. Dangerous enough, Ace?"

My wife takes a drag on her cigarette. She blows smoke into the room then shoots me a look. It's the look I imagined on the writer Annie Dillard's face a few years back.

A technique I hope I usefully apply when I write is to get more than one ball in the air to juggle. Juggling one ball seems pointless (and is the reason, I believe, that topic sentences are overrated!). Once I get more than one ball—a few balls—in the air, I try to relate them and then work to catch them. If you're lucky as a writer, you then manage to string the caught balls together, to link them like a necklace—something that appears as fundamental, desirable, and whole.

James McConkey, whom I quoted earlier, was a favorite professor of mine at Cornell. His autobiographical meditations (contained in his memoir *Court of Memory*) is a non-fiction masterpiece, and I am partial to his argument that imagination is not separate *from* memory—in fact, is a faculty *of* memory. It is imagination's work to link remembered material, to find pattern, and in so connecting, to make meaning.[11]

[My wife takes a drag on her cigarette. She blows smoke into the room then shoots me a look. It's the look I imagined on the writer Annie Dillard's face a few years back.]

I've never met Ms. Dillard, but have taken pleasure in her work and had just finished her book, *For The Time Being*. It's hardly a book in an obvious sense of unity and purpose. It is a loose yet rich federation about human abnormalities, sand, clouds, numbers, China, Israel, God, evil, archaeology, and life-size Chinese clay soldiers and their horses—thousands of them sculpted for, then buried with the Emperor Qin to honor and protect him for the past two thousand years. The clay soldiers and their mounts were a whole new idea. It had been the practice to bury an emperor's living army with him when he passed.

In the book, Dillard not only covers a variety of human abnormalities—noting, in particular, mentally deficient bird-headed dwarves—but a variety of human cruelties as well, such stunted acts as the flaying of the 85-year-old Rabbi Akiva for teaching Torah. The Romans, more than 100 years before Christ, stripped the Rabbi's living flesh to its bones with horse currycombs, all the while the Rabbi singing Shema, *Hear O Israel, the Lord our God, the Lord is One.*

When I talk about the look on the writer's face, I'm thinking of a look that must have accompanied a one-sentence paragraph three-quarters of the way into the book. Dillard, a smoker, notes: *Do you think I don't know cigarettes are fatal?*

In her book, for every heartening note such as 17th-century Jews who so respected books that when books wore out, they were buried like a person, there *is* a person like Joseph Stalin who took the long view: "One death is a tragedy; a million deaths are a statistic." Or Mao who told Nehru that the atomic bomb was nothing to be afraid of. Or a Ted Bundy who, with an invested sense of chilled proportion, is able to explain his serial killings: "I mean, there are so many people."

When I finally get into bed, Ellen is asleep. I lie on my back, eyes wide. What I see is my dwarf careening down a boulder trail in Utah. It's a full-size bike. There are metal extenders strapped to her feet and locked into her pedals. At times, as she flies down the trail, she's airborne. In this picture I'm painting, my dwarf is unhelmeted, her streaked locks like some nation's flag. But, as my eyes adjust to the bedroom's dark, my picture dissolves. I'm past 60 and I lie on my back thinking about college some 40 years before and the fraternity I joined. It was a group known for drinking and reliable and current exam files. The president of the fraternity didn't live in the house on Greek Row. He bought one of his own, a three-story deal where he lived with eight

---

11 See "Court of Memory: an interview with James McConkey," by Donald Anderson, EPOCH 43.3 (1994), 273-288.

roommates who covered his mortgage each month. I was one of the renters. "Grog" Greer was, during his junior and senior year, the Bareback Bronco Riding Champion in collegiate rodeo. He was better known, though, for the annual Frat Bash, which featured competitive dwarf tossing.

"Imagination," McConkey has written, "is rightly seen as the creative power, the power that enables us to see affinities, to link disparate materials together in our search for a structure or form that will satisfy a personal sense of truth."[12] I did live with a cowboy at Utah State University who was a champion rider and who owned enough funds and foresight to buy a house he lived in for free, and from which, upon graduation, he garnered a profit. I leave it to you to decide whether or not he sponsored dwarf tossing. Does it matter? What is the point of "Stunted": verifiable fact or sensed truth?

Although he is writing about war in *The Things They Carried*, Tim O'Brien was also writing about story—pursued and useable "truth." *The Things They Carried* is a testament to the power of story while it is, at the same time, a meditation on the elusiveness of truth and the shiftiness of memory.

> In any war story, but especially a true one, it's difficult to separate what happened from what seemed to happen. What seems to happen becomes its own happening and has to be told that way. The angles of vision are skewed. When a booby trap explodes, you close your eyes and duck and float outside yourself. When a guy dies, like Curt Lemon, you look away and then look back for a moment and then look away again. The pictures get jumbled; you tend to miss a lot. And then afterward, when you go to tell about it, there is always that surreal seemingness, which makes the story seem untrue, but which in fact represents the hard and exact truth as it *seemed*.[13]

And then:

> True war stories do not generalize. They do not indulge in abstraction or analysis.
>
> For example: War is hell. As a moral declaration the old truism seems perfectly true, and yet because it abstracts, because it generalizes, I can't believe it with my stomach. Nothing turns inside.
>
> It comes down to gut instinct. A true war story, if truly told, makes the stomach believe.[14]

---

[12] Ibid.
[13] Tim O'Brien, "How to Tell a True War Story," *The Things They Carried* (New York: Broadway Books, 1998), p. 71.
[14] Ibid., p. 78.

O'Brien is hardly thrashing about facts here; he is sifting emotions—anger, ardor, love, grief, despondency, sentiment, shame, sorrow. At the end of "How to Tell a True War Story," from which I've been quoting, O'Brien (the character? the real person?) complains about people—particularly women—who complain about his war stories, his "true" stories:

> All you can do is tell it one more time, patiently, adding and subtracting, making up a few things to get at the real truth. No Mitchell Sanders, you tell her. No Lemon. No Rat Kiley. No trail junction. No baby buffalo. No vines or moss or white blossoms. Beginning to end, you tell her, it's all made up. Every goddamn detail—the mountains and the river and especially that poor dumb baby buffalo. None of it happened. *None* of it. And even if it did happen, it didn't happen in the mountains, it happened in this little village on the Batangan Peninsula, and it was raining like crazy, and one night a guy named Stink Harris woke up screaming with a leech on his tongue. You can tell a true war story if you just keep on telling it.[15]

"Absolute occurrence is irrelevant," O'Brien states earlier. Absolute occurrence does not constitute the truth a true war story depends on. "A thing may happen and be a total lie; another thing may not happen and be truer than the truth."[16]

It's a commonplace—isn't it?—that most fiction is, on some level, *true*, though perhaps not striving for this condition as assiduously as nonfiction. But both forms are after—aren't they?—what we call willingly a *larger truth*. It's mushy, though, because truth with a capital T is hardly universal or given to convincing verification. Facts can be checked and confirmed, of course, but absolute truth remains in debate—which is why in courtrooms we lower our aim for a "reasonable" truth. Acknowledging such may be also why we have witnessed the rise of *creative nonfiction*, a term as bewildering, perhaps, as it is accurate. Fiction and nonfiction writers share more than they don't, and face (as they ransack memory and imagination) the same holy mess in their constructions. Why wouldn't they reach for the same problem-solving contraptions: dialogue, description, plot, detail, characterization, point of view, image, metaphor?

Metaphor—that old instrument of perception—is the very heart of whatever gifts a writer has to offer and whatever gifts a reader is prepared to receive, and yet is in fact a small lie. No metaphor is factually true, but we accept, if not believe, them. I think of Graham Greene: ". . . innocence is like a dumb leper who has lost his bell, wandering the world, meaning no harm."[17] Or David Keplinger:

---

[15] Ibid., p. 85
[16] Ibid., p. 83.
[17] Graham Greene, *The Quiet American* (New York: Penguin, 1996), p. 37.

"The smell of a man's hat—an old man's hat—is like the nostril of a horse."[18] I think of Jean Cocteau, who, in coming upon stacks of Marcel Proust's notebooks after Proust's death, characterized them as "watches ticking on the wrists of dead soldiers."[19] Metaphor, in all its variations—similes, and the like—become the little lies we live by. Welcomed lies that stay.

In Harriet Doerr's semi-autobiographical novel, *Stones for Ibarra*, there is a chapter in which the American Sara Everton takes Spanish lessons from an older Mexican nun. The novel takes place in Mexico. Sara is blessed with a busy imagination, from which place she constantly invents the nun's former life. Simultaneously, she works to imagine a future for her husband who has contracted terminal cancer. This novel captures as well as any I've read those twins: Memory and Imagination.

> "Where were you born?" asked Sara.
>
> "For your next lesson please write a paragraph on an event of the coming week," said the nun.
>
> As simply as this, without method or rules, the line of skirmish was drawn between the two women, one resolved to close off the past, the other to reject the future.[20]

Because the nun has shut the door to her past, Sara feels compelled to invent it. What else is she to do? In controlling the past, Sara appears to feel more secure in imagining a future which contains a cure for her husband. Richard senses what Sara is doing and calls her on it. Sara parries the way a writer might. After one particularly extravagant slice of the nun's former life, Richard examines his wife's face:

> "Are you sure this is what Madre Petra told you?"
>
> Sara thought of the convent *sala*, its sparse furnishings, the nun's seamed face, her crippled hand.
>
> "It's what I heard her say."[21]

And then later:

> "Is that what the madre told you? In those words?"
>
> "Almost," she said.[22]

---

[18] David Keplinger, *The Prayers of Others* (Kalamazoo: New Issues Poetry & Prose, 2006), p. 9.
[19] William C. Carter, *Marcel Proust, A Life* (New Haven: Yale University Press, 2002) p. 809.
[20] Harriet Doerr, "Parts of Speech," *Stones for Ibarra* (New York: Penguin, 1984), p. 88.
[21] Ibid., pp. 90-91.
[22] Ibid., p. 92.

Tobias Wolff concludes his first story collection with a story entitled "The Liar." The character of interest in this story is a 16-year-old who confabulates. The stories he tells are fake tragedies, such as his mother suffering from appalling disease. James is an accomplished liar. He is good at what he does. In one of the deft set pieces in recent fiction, James conscripts a neighbor kid to help him move his father's body into an upstairs bedroom. James' father has died on the couch after a prolonged illness. James is proud that his father has "died well"—that is, as Wolff puts it, without complaining or overly inconveniencing those who are to be left behind.

> He died downstairs in a shaft of late afternoon sunlight on New Year's Day, while I was reading to him. I was alone in the house and didn't know what to do. His body did not frighten me but immediately and sharply I missed my father. It seemed wrong to leave him sitting up and I tried to carry him upstairs to the bedroom but it was too hard, alone. So I called up my friend Ralphy across the street. When he came over and saw what I wanted him for he started crying but I made him help me anyway. A couple of hours later Mother got home and when I told her that Father was dead she ran upstairs, calling his name. A few minutes later she came back down. "Thank God," she said, "at least he died in bed." This seemed important to her and I didn't tell her otherwise. But that night Ralphy's parents called. They were, they said, shocked at what I had done and so was Mother when she heard the story, shocked and furious. Why? Because I had not told her the truth? Or because she had learned the truth, and could not go on believing that Father had died in bed? I really don't know.[23]

Wolff finishes "The Liar" with James on a bus, traveling to spend time with his elder brother. The bus breaks down, and James, given a chance to confabulate, takes it. He can't seem to help himself, but put yourself on the stalled bus and see if you don't welcome this weakness. The bus is stuck and a friendly fat woman is passing around cold fried chicken.

> The wind was blowing hard around the bus, driving sheets of rain against the windows on both sides. The bus swayed gently. Outside the light was brown and thick. The woman next to me pumped all the people for their itineraries and said whether or not she had ever been where they were from or where they were going. "How about you?" She slapped my knee. "Parents own a chicken ranch? I hope so!" She laughed. I told her I was from San Francisco. "San Francisco, that's where my husband was stationed." She asked me what I did there and I told her I worked with refugees from Tibet.

---

[23]   Tobias Wolff, "The Liar," *In the Garden of the North American Martyrs* (New York: The Ecco Press, 1981), pp. 167-168.

"Is that right? What do you do with a bunch of Tibetans?"

"Seems like there's plenty of other places they could've gone," said a man in front of us. "Coming across the border like that. We don't go there."

"What do you do with a bunch of Tibetans?" the woman repeated.

"Try to find them jobs, locate housing, listen to their problems."

"You understand that kind of talk?"

"Yes."

"Speak it?"

"Pretty well. I was born and raised in Tibet. My parents were missionaries over there."

Everyone waited.

"They were killed when the Communists took over."

The big woman patted my arm.

"It's all right," I said.

"Why don't you say some of that Tibetan?"

"What would you like to hear?"

"Say 'The cow jumped over the moon.'" She watched me, smiling, and when I finished she looked at the others and shook her head. "That was pretty. Like music. Say some more."

"What?"

"Anything."

They bent toward me. The windows suddenly went blind with rain. The driver had fallen asleep and was snoring gently to the swaying of the bus. Outside the muddy light flickered to pale yellow, and far off there was thunder. The woman next to me leaned back and closed her eyes and then so did all the others as I sang to them in what was surely an ancient and holy tongue.[24]

As you know, Tobias Wolff is a memoirist as well as a fiction writer, and his prefatory note to *This Boy's Life* is, well, memorable. "I have been corrected on some points," he says, "mostly of chronology."[25]

Also my mother thinks that a dog I describe as ugly was actually quite handsome. I've allowed some of these points to stand, because this is a book of memory, and memory has its own story to tell. But I have done my best to make it tell a truthful story.[26]

Memory has its own story to tell. How to improve upon that except to finish with

---

[24] Ibid., 174-175.
[25] Tobias Wolff, *This Boy's Life* (New York: The Atlantic Monthly Press, 1989), p. vii.
[26] Ibid.

Wolff's last two sentences? They read: *My stepfather used to say that what I didn't know would fill a book. Well, here it is.*[27]

My earliest mentor, the novelist Alfred Kern, would say, "Art and life are different. Of course they are. If they weren't, we wouldn't need art. What is art," he would go on, "but a remaking of the world over into forms more acceptable to us?" Writers value the world by describing it, by *re*-creating.

Perhaps like you I've felt comfortable, accustomed with the thought of word as concept made flesh, but why not the William Gass perception: "It's not the word made flesh that we want in writing . . . but the flesh made word"?[28] Gass puts it this way too:

> . . . every loving act of definition reverses the retreat of attention to the word and returns it to the world. The landscape which emerges from the language which has made it is quite as lovely, vast and curious, as rich and prepossessing, as that of the deity who broke the silence of the void with speech so perfect the word "tree" grew leaves and the syllables of "sealion" swallowed fish.[29]

Or Diane Ackerman, who has written: "We inhabit a deeply imagined world that exists alongside the real physical world. Even the crudest utterance, or the simplest, contains the fundamental poetry by which we live."[30] And so we are back to where we started: *Writing is not apart from living. Writing is a kind of double living.*

Aristotle's notion that History accumulates but only Poetry unifies is a notion we can subscribe to. Art grants access to a larger world, allows us to live other lives, allows us to examine the quality and meaning of our own lives. Whose very earliest recollections do not include the request, Tell Me a Story? The human race needs stories. We need all the experience we can get. Before we made fire, before we made tools, before we made weapons, we made images. Lies apart—willed or not—Art, at its deepest level, is about preserving the world.

---

27 Ibid.
28 William Gass, *On Being Blue: A Philosophical Inquiry* (Boston: David R. Godine, 1976), p. 32.
29 Ibid., p. 87.
30 Diane Ackerman, *An Alchemy of Mind* (New York: Scribner, 2004), p. 219.

15

Jürgen Schlaeger

Selves for the Twenty-First Century

The following is not so much a scholarly contribution as an extended thought experiment. I am offering here a kind of second reading of the close connection between identity formation and narrativity that most scholars still consider to be essential for an understanding of selves, even under postmodern conditions.

Life-writing is more popular than ever. At first sight this looks very surprising, for in the postmodern condition the position that personal experience has an authority of its own because it is the authentic experience of an individual self, and, what is more, because such a self may even be seen as giving people something exemplary in one way or another, seems to have become untenable. No modern biographer can repeat Boswell's claim to have Johnsonized the land for the treatment of his own subject. It would be absurd to state that Glendinning has Trollopized, or Holroyd has Shavianized English culture. But somehow, this loss in the general significance of a particular life has not diminished the attractiveness of the genre. On the contrary, as stated above, life-narratives have gone from strength to strength on the book market, and have attracted a continuously growing readership.

Maybe, and that would be one explanation, life-writing has earned it as an antidote to the postmodern condition. The rise to power of life-writing could then be seen, to a large extent, as a reaction to cultural forces and pressures that postmodernists have dramatized into a universal condition of selves in post-industrial globalized societies.

Indeed, compared with the images of our culture and of the selves in it which postmodernism projects, much life-writing appears, in spite of its often complex strategies for reconstructing a life, as fundamentally reactionary, conservative, perpetually accommodating a constantly changing multiple-choice situation, new theories of the inner self, to a personality-oriented popular mainstream, thus helping to defuse the subversive potential of postmodern lifestyles and strategies for self-fashioning by providing an endless stream of counter-models with their promise of showing the way to a fulfilled life.

If it is true that the self, in the words of the American sociologist Christopher Lasch, is under siege because "commodity production and consumerism" have created "a world of mirrors, insubstantial images, illusions increasingly indistinguishable from reality" (Lasch 1984, 30), then life-writing could indeed fulfil the function of a safe haven. Individualized selfhood implies a personal history, friends, family, networks, a sense of place and time, a public or common world to which one can relate oneself or against which one can define oneself. When such certainties recede into the shadows, there is bound to be a need for compensation; and life-writing serves such a need – even in its more salacious, unashamedly voyeuristic forms, it underscores what has been called a "strategic humanism".

As I have pointed out, however, the compensation theory only works on the assumption that all life-writing ultimately projects a unified, unmistakable and identifiable self. And while much of the fantasizing about such an ultimately indivisible self may explain the popularity of the genre (including the contemporary celebrity cult) with a general reading public, such an assessment does not account for a parallel development alongside it: a development which eventually produced the curious reversal around the turn of the millennium, when life-writing also seemed to become the darling of minds who think and conceptualize themselves in postmodern terms as fractured, hybrid, layered and multiple.

I have a feeling, a hunch, that there is more to this new postmodern fascination with life-writing than meets the eye, and that an analysis of the situation will uncover a number of skeletons in our intellectual cupboards beckoning to be laid to rest, or, at least, to be buried in style.

My claim would be that there has never been a period in European history in which – culturally, not philosophically, speaking – the subject, the individual, the self was conceptualized as simple, unified or monolithic, not as slippery, contradictory or complex. On the contrary, to the extent that it has moved centre-stage in our attempts to understand ourselves and our world, the self has always been conceived of as multifaceted, incalculable, endlessly diversified, always shifting and morally dubious and, as a consequence, difficult to represent and difficult to control. Shakespeare's early modern tragic heroes provide ample evidence for this. But even before the Renaissance, in the medieval Christian anthropology, man was considered as fundamentally split, torn apart by conflicting forces, always in doubt as to what end lay in wait for him on the Day of the Last Judgement.

Here is an example from a period in which a belief in the self as unified and whole is said to have been still firmly in place:

> But in truth this "we", which looks so simple and definite, is a nebulous and indefinable aggregation of many component parts which war not a little among themselves,

our perception of our existence at all being perhaps due to this very clash of warfare, as our sense of sound and light is due to the jarring of vibrations. Moreover, as the component parts of our identity change from moment to moment, our personality becomes a thing dependent upon the time present, which has no logical existence, but lives only upon the sufferance of times past and future, slipping out of our hands into the domain of one or other of these two claimants the moment we try to apprehend it. And not only is our personality as fleeting as the present moment, but the parts which compose it blend some of them so imperceptibly into, and are so inextricably linked on to, outside things which clearly form no part of our personality, that when we try to bring ourselves to book, and to determine wherein we consist, or draw a line where we begin or end, we find ourselves baffled. There is nothing but fusion and confusion. (Butler 1877, 64)

This is what Samuel Butler wrote in *Life and Habit* in 1877. That in the case of personal identity there "is nothing but fusion and confusion" is not really convincing evidence for the belief of many Victorian intellectuals in the unity of the subject as something that could or should be achieved. I will return to what Butler has to say about the inextricable link between outside things and selfhood.

If what I have tried to demonstrate has some plausibility to it, then the question arises: what were the intellectual and cultural reasons for setting up the unified subject as a straw-target? A short answer might be that just as distance tends to beautify, the unified subject has become valuable through its unattainability, desirable through its absence.

However, I will leave the answer to this question to another paper and move on to skeleton number 2. (Number 1, for clarity's sake, was the unified subject and closure in matters of identity in general.) Myth number 2, and here I am getting closer to my selves for the twenty-first century, arose around the belief that the sense of self – whether fragmented or unified or whatever – is inextricably linked to narrativity. I believe that this apparently indissoluble marriage between conceptualizing the self and narrativity, still an almost universal conviction, is now breaking up.

The statement that life is only a life if and when it is told, when it has become a text, even if the manner of telling is no longer straightforwardly linear, being multifaceted and highly self-reflexive, is based on many centuries of a cultural development that was dominated by print-culture, by narrative, by the novel; but time has moved on and what has been seen as indispensable and unquestioned for a long time may now turn out to be yesterday's consensus, in spite of Charles Taylor's recent reaffirmation of narrativity as central to the sense of self. (Taylor, 1992, 50ff.)

My argument in this part of my paper is based on Galen Strawson's "Commentary" on "A Fallacy of our Age" published in the *Times Literary Supplement*, October 15, 2004. This is a short version of a paper he gave to a conference of psychotherapists.

Strawson embarks on his argument by quoting examples from the current creeds in matters of the self:

> "Self is a perpetually rewritten story", according to the psychologist Jerry Bruner: we are all constantly engaged in "self-making narrative" and "in the end we become the autobiographical narratives by which we 'tell about' our lives". Oliver Sacks concurs: each of us "constructs and lives a 'narrative' [and] this narrative is us, our identities". A vast chorus of assent rises from the humanities – from literary studies, psychology, anthropology, sociology, philosophy, political theory, religious studies, echoed back by psychotherapy, medicine, law, marketing, design […]: human beings typically experience their lives as a narrative or story of some sort, or at least as a collection of stories. (Strawson 2004, 13)

Strawson calls this "the psychological narrativity thesis":

> It is a straightforwardly empirical thesis about the way ordinary human beings experience their lives – this is how we are, it says, this is our nature – and it's often coupled with a normative thesis, which I'll call the Ethical Narrativity thesis, according to which a richly Narrative outlook on one's life is essential to living well, to true or full personhood. (ibid.)

The two theses produce, according to Strawson, "four possible positions":

> 1) […] one may think the empirical psychological thesis true and the ethical one false: one may think that we are indeed deeply Narrative in our thinking and that it's not a good thing.
>
> 2) […] one may think the empirical thesis false and the ethical one true. One may grant that we're not all naturally Narrative in our thinking while holding that we should be, and need to be, in order to live a good life.
>
> 3) […] one may think both theses true: all normal human beings are naturally Narrative and Narrativity is crucial to a good life. This is the dominant view in the academy, followed by the second view. It leaves plenty of room for the idea that many of us would profit from being more Narrative than we are, and the idea that we can get our "self-narratives" wrong in one way or another.
>
> 4) […] one may think both theses are false. This is my view. I think the current dominance of the third view is regrettable. It is not true that there is only one way in which human beings experience their being in time. There are deeply non-Narrative people

and there are good ways to live that are deeply non-Narrative. I think the second and third views hinder human self-understanding, close down important avenues of thought, impoverish our grasp of ethical possibilities, needlessly and wrongly distress those who do not fit their model, and can be highly destructive in psychotherapeutic contexts. (ibid.)

What Strawson defines as two distinct ways of experiencing one's life and what he classifies as two distinct types of human beings – "Narrativists" and "Episodics" – are not, I think, anthropological but cultural categories. The link between a sense of the self and narrativity is not an anthropological universal, but an option that has been forged over centuries by and in a particular print-dominated culture. One could think here of the role of the novel, of diaries and autobiographies as models, as cultural practices which provided an ever-expanding range of blueprints for looking at and conceptualizing one's own life, as something that, as Taylor has it, "necessarily has temporal depth and incorporates narrative." (Taylor, 1992, 50)

Such a historicizing of the bond between narrativity and the self leaves open the possibility that this bond may become weaker and will finally break, that narrative continuity is not the only option for forging an identity, for understanding the self. Signs are on the horizon that such a weakening is happening, although it would be foolish to deny that narrativity is still in a very strong position indeed. One could say that the age in which knowledge of the self, and maybe any kind of knowledge, is shaped by the writing and reading of books, i.e. by the sequential structure of language, is slowly and irrevocably being replaced by an age dominated by the spatial structures of visual perception.

To clarify what I mean, I would like to go back to Butler's *Life and Habit*, in particular to the passage in which he talks about the close links between self-experience and things outside the self. What Butler implies is that life and the self as we see it are always not only temporally but also spatially positioned, and this is exactly what Strawson claims for his episodics. They think of their existence in terms of a sequence of time spaces, i.e. spatially rather than temporally.

This observation leads me to my general thesis: texts, especially those that deal with lives and selves, have definitely become more spatial. The rise of intertextuality as a critical category and the popularity of such key metaphors as fields and networks, domains, architecture, even structure, also point to a shift towards spatialization.

I think this whole development has to do with the fact that the concept of a time-line spreading from the past through the present into the future has changed radically. One could claim that there has been a dramatic inversion of the time-flow: from the future into the past. The present has expanded massively in the process. And how can it do that? By becoming more spatialized. The present is no longer a fleeting moment of transition between a past and a future, but an extended space in which future and past are made to serve present concerns. As the authors of a book about *Zeitpraktiken* have put it:

> By privileging the present as decisive for the structuring of our time-experience, new and different opportunities for developing new time-practices have been opened up. Contrary to the still dominant orientation on the past and the future, the present is emphasised as the dimension of time in which we are not only constantly forced to make choices but in which the future as well as the past are 'happening'. Such a highly charged present guarantees a high measure of sensibility over against more and more complex temporal relationships, but it also becomes the central stage for all problems. (Hörning, Ahrens and Gerhard 1997, 167-168; my translation, J.S.)

The authors of this study of time as a cultural category attribute this development to the influence of the modern, particularly the visual, media. However that may be, there is a distinct impression that our postmodern attitudes to the traditional aspects of time create an imaginary space-time, a stereo-Dolby-time with something similar to an acoustic surround-sound-effect, an effect in which the past and future are arranged in a three-dimensional field around the present and not two-dimensionally in a before and after.

As examples of this non-narrative, spatialized type of life-writing, I would like to discuss briefly a number of texts by Iain Sinclair and Peter Ackroyd. Significantly, they all deal with lives in pre-eminently urban, i.e. spatial, surroundings.

When Iain Sinclair's *Lights Out for the Territory* appeared in 1997, it caused quite a stir in the already densely populated market of books about London. The reviewers described it as "a riot of a book on London", as the "effusions" of a "sublime archaeologist of the present", as "one of the most remarkable books ever written on London" (quotations from the 1998 Granta Books edition, cover and first inside page). Although most of the pieces it contained had been published separately before, their cumulative effect was tremendous.

Indeed, Sinclair's book is more than just another piece of city literature, more than just another literary appropriation of London from a flâneur's point of view. It is not a work of fiction, at least not ostensibly so. Superficially, it is a journal with notes, thoughts, and pictures of walks about London, as well as records of visits to a large number of places in different areas and the train of remembrances, thoughts and images that these visits evoked.

Lights Out for the Territory contains reminiscences of films and reviews of poems, as well as fragments of autobiography and of character studies of people as diverse as Lord Archer and the Kray brothers. The actual experience of walking

the city is only loosely and intermittently interwoven with the imaginary journeys undertaken, so to speak, along the road. References to films and poems
about the city, to historical, biographical and autobiographical episodes of city
life, are never introduced as mere additions to or illustrations of a main text, for
there is no main text – only an assortment of subtexts barely held together by
what Sinclair calls their "quest". As a text, the book is completely hybrid, a fractal
composition of different types of discourses strung together on the determination of the author to go through with it, however multidirectional, endless and
ultimately aimless it may seem.

For Sinclair and his photographer companion Marc Atkins, there is no physical London to explore district after district, street by street. Everything they encounter is already encrusted with layers of myths, episodes, histories, remembered impressions, stories, texts, pictorial appropriations by graffiti, paintings
and films. So the two city explorers move about, not as highly individualized
observers in a physical reality structured by time and space, but in ever-changing
configurations of after-images and imaginary projections, in a world of past and
future made present in which their selves no longer provide the principle of order
and perspective.

Implicitly, Sinclair claims to convey by these representational strategies a quality of life in the city which no urbanistic discourse is able to communicate. In
a sense he thereby fulfils Clifford Geertz's conviction that "to know a city is to
know its streets" (Geertz 1983, 167) in a synaesthetic interplay between spaces
and minds. The text thus presents itself as a contribution to an entirely new type
of literature which the Reaktion Books publishers defined as "Topographics" in a
new series – a series in which Atkins' and Sinclair's next book *Liquid City* was to
appear. They define this project in the following way:

> Topographics features new writing about place. Embracing both the cultural and the
> natural, the city and the wilderness, it appraises the geographies people inhabit, visit,
> defend, destroy – and overlook. The reverse of travel literature, the books in this se-
> ries do not depend on a journey to supply a plot. Instead they mingle analysis with
> anecdote, criticism with original expressive writing, to explore the creative collision
> between physical space and the human mind. (Publisher's note on the book jacket of
> Atkins and Sinclair, 1999)

This collision clearly produces a spatialization of the mind – a self that is not only
inextricably bound up with the physical environment, but also moves within the
stereo-effect of a co-presence of past and future.

Liquid City contains a selection of the photographs Marc Atkins took through
their walks in London and new texts by Iain Sinclair which further intensify the

visionary perception of London he had created in *Lights Out*. In terms of London discourses, Sinclair's strategy could be defined as an intertextual and intericono-graphic practice, a thick description without the professional anthropologist's desire to be exact, systematic and explanatory.

In terms of life-writing, it is a highly episodic interpretation of an endless number of lives shaped by the city and of the city shaped by an endless number of people. Crucial in this practice is a reversal of the direction of meaning-as-signment. Existing city realities are not only alluded too, added on to, discussed, rejected, extended and arranged so as to make that piece of city reality more vis-ible, more plausible, historically profound and personally significant, but inter-pretations, comments, episodes in people's lives and events are read back into the space of the city so insistently that the physical reality of the city becomes a kind of objective correlative for the intended stereo-effect which combines time and space as dimensions that penetrate each other in multiple directions.

Lights Out is not an exercise in topographical analysis, nor is it a sophisticated city-travelogue; it is, to use Kevin Lynch's key concept, a practice of multiple "imageabilities". However, their readability does not, as Lynch claims, depend on the ideal of a city which guarantees stability and order; it lies in the city's charac-ter as a source of endless projections and interpretations (Lynch 1969, 9-12).

Sinclair develops a radical writing practice. His literary strategies are designed to deconstruct time as the major principle of order. He is not moving in a phys-ical environment that then stimulates and associates meaning or beckons for interpretations; he moves in a highly complex and chaotic field of meanings, pictures, voices, memories, which he randomly strings together and attaches to observations, occurrences, physical details along his journey. No principle of se-lection, no system of priorities can be discovered. In his approach to representing the experience of his city, he is a true specimen of Strawson's episodics. During this quest the past becomes an optional landscape. The future cannot be called on "to describe the geography of a present divorced from its memory traces." There is no "[fixing] the future to rewrite the past" (Sinclair 1997, 77).

In the territory of the city, such clean divisions of labour between past, present and future do not exist and refuse to make sense. One might say that for Sinclair the past is as present as the future. There is a level time-space in his book that refuses to be structured in any simple linear way. If there are connecting net-works, links or webs, they are subterraneous, out of sight, magical, shamanistic, grids of forces beyond rational comprehension. "We were convinced", he writes, that London

> was mapped by cued lines of energy, connecting buildings with natural geological and
> geographical forms; making paths available down which the more tedious laws of time

could be aborted. Now there was another, wilder system in play: the improvisations of the dog. The retreats, spurts, galloping loops and pounces of the stalker. (Sinclair 1997, 85)

A similar strategy for creating a kind of stereo-time-space can be observed in *Rodinsky's Room,* an investigation into a mysterious life, written jointly by Rachel Lichtenstein and Iain Sinclair and first published in 1999. The reconstruction of the protagonist's life is achieved by an interpretation of the room he had inhabited and not by piecing together a life-story. "Emotionally the trick of the thing was to strip him of his history and to translate him directly into the substance of the room that had housed him" (Lichtenstein and Sinclair 1999, 67).

Making the lives of individuals readable through the physical surroundings which embody a sort of amalgam, a co-presence of past, present and future, is no longer dependent on narrativity in the traditional sense. Similar techniques can also be observed in much of Peter Ackroyd's writings. A particularly telling example is his *London. The Biography,* published in 2000.

At first, Ackroyd's *London. The Biography* seemed to constitute a backtracking from the most advanced presentations of London as the product of endless processes of subjective signification. But at a second glance, Ackroyd's own philosophical and theoretical background is seen to support another interpretation (see Ackroyd, 1976). It was not the wish to construct a coherent history of London in the traditional way that led him to pick a model of representation in which the city figures as a person with a life, but his conviction that a city as physically massive as London cannot be adequately depicted as a magma of idiosyncratic discourses; that its physical presence throughout the centuries and its uncanny power to influence people's lives, to make them and break them, its presence like an incalculable force of nature, makes some recognition of its physical presence beyond time unavoidable; that a "picture" of what the city is and what it has meant and still means to millions that inhabit it as a special place with special life styles, special risks and special opportunities, necessarily requires a discourse that takes due notice of the dual nature of the city as "flesh and stone" alike. Mind and matter are spatially bound up with each other in special ways in a big city like London, and to sacrifice most of it to the flow of time would, for Ackroyd, miss the whole point, would deprive the city of its defining characteristics. This is why he draws on a broad range of different discourses, a range that allows him to convey both the historical aspects of city reality and its character as an "endless fecund source which can offer alternative realities and different experiences" (Ackroyd 2000, 380) in a forceful co-presence that is detachable from the time-line of history.

Ackroyd's treatment of time and space forms a telling example of the strategy with which he achieves the intended interaction between "flesh and stone", mind and matter. On opening the book his readers find a tabular chronology of the city, listing major dates and events, and a series of maps showing London in the various stages of its development. In view of what is to come, this can be interpreted both as an attempt to give the reader some basic historical orientation and as an easy way of getting these basic facts out of the way before he embarks on showing, at great length, how irrelevant this information is for a deeper understanding of what London is. Ackroyd uses time and space as loose scaffoldings for constructing his "biography". He begins at the beginning ("From Pre-history to 1066") and finishes in the present. London and the geographical position it occupies also seem to provide a reliable spatial framework when he places everything he has to tell within its confines or relates it to the city's location on the river near the Sea, at the crossroads of important trade routes etc. Whether he talks about "London as Theatre" (chapters 13-19) or "Voracious London" (chapters 32-42), he always associates what he has to say with the physical city. In this way he strengthens the impression of his subject as an entity that has a time-independent physical presence. But the temporal and spatial coherences and identities he creates are quickly broken up into and supplanted by fragments of legend and story, individual biographies, views and experiences. Thus the time structure of past, present and future is transformed into a curious simultaneity. "The nature of time in London is mysterious. It seems not to be running in one direction" (Ackroyd 2000, 661). London, the place, the city, combines a very practical sense of time as money with a timelessness in its capacity to survive disruptions and revive traditions that often seemed to have been on the brink of disappearing.

Equally, London in Ackroyd's *Biography* appears very distinctively as a place, a geographical location with the City of London as its hub, but at the same time he declares it to be "so ubiquitous that it can be located nowhere in particular" (Ackroyd 2000: 734). Just as in Sinclair's *Lights Out*, places and spaces become mere signs for what is absent. The "fallacious nature of space" (Lively 1991: 210) in the city becomes apparent when Ackroyd invokes a genius loci for certain parts of London which is designed to give them a unique colouring and tradition (cf. chapter 51, "Where is the Well of Clerkenwell?"). He frequently connects observations of the physical reality of a locale with its prehistoric past, with legends and stories, with its modern development, and often finds or states deeper continuities beneath a surface of disruption and change. But these continuities are never something stable and specific; they are as often as not fluid, imaginary and mythical. Whatever happened in the city commercially, architecturally, politically and culturally, it is for Ackroyd something that seems to happen in and to a kind of body, to an "organic being" (Ackroyd 2000: 670), "a truly living thing"

(Ackroyd 2000: 595), an entity which has a life of its own, whose "true history" is of a London "which lives and moves beneath the incidents and events of public record" (Ackroyd 2000: 91). But in spite of such statements in which he imagines London as a living entity, he always insists that it is ultimately hidden, mysterious, guided not by rational planning but by dark pagan forces. So Ackroyd manages to construct his London as a space organised by "essential continuities" which allow for limitless diversification, endless renewal, breathtaking human greatness and shocking human depravity. His vision is almost Manichean: London is the city of light as well as the city of darkness.

Ackroyd's gift as a teller of tales, the richness of the book in anecdotal detail, the local colour and the continuous intertwining of stories, facts, and historical personalities prevent the chapters from congealing into unspecific generalities. The general and the particular, just as the continuous and the discontinuous, the role of individuals and the agency of the darker and more permanent forces, are kept in a delicate balance, so that the London whose biography Ackroyd is writing remains as mysterious as a complex human being about whom we know many things, but whom we find difficult to understand completely. As one of his reviewers rightly pointed out: "Ackroyd's vision is ultimately mystical, with London as a kind of Eternal City … London, as presented here, is a kind of religion, as this book is its sacred text" (Baker 2000: 14). The city comes to life through a strategy that shifts the burden and significance of human agency from its inhabitants to a spatial construct which pays for its significance and its semantic inexhaustibility with narrative continuity.

The question is, are we all – as a result of this fundamental reversal in the relationship between bios and topos, the "fusion and confusion" which Butler imagined when he ruminated about the relationship between personal identity and "outside things" – are we all moving towards the life-concept of Galen Strawson's "episodics" as entities that are spatially spread out over time and life spaces, rather than narratively embedded? As I have pointed out earlier, narrativity as a basis for conceptualizing and rooting individual lives and as an indispensable ingredient for most life-writing is still going very strong, but the stereo-time effect created by more spatialized forms of life-writing will continue to put pressure on narrative acts of selving in the 21st century.

Bibliography

Ackroyd, Peter (1976), *Notes for a New Culture. An Essay on Modernism*. London: Vision.

Ackroyd, Peter (2000), *London. The Biography*. London: Chatto and Windus.

Atkins, Mark, Sinclair, Iain (1999), *Liquid City*. London: Reaktion Books.

Baker, Phil (2000), "The Bell Ringer of Lost London", *Times Literary Supplement*, 24 January, 14.

Butler, Samuel (1877), "Life and Habit", in: *The Shrewsbury Edition of the Works of Samuel Butler*. Vol. IV. Henry Festing Jones (ed.).

Geertz, Clifford (1983), *Local Knowledge*. New York: Basic Books.

Hörning, Karl H., Daniela Ahrens, and Anette Gerhard (1997), *Zeitpraktiken: Experimentierfelder der Spätmoderne*. Frankfurt/M.: Suhrkamp.

Lasch, Christopher (1984), *The Minimal Self: Psychic Survival in Troubled Times*. New York: Norton.

Lichtenstein, Rachel, and Iain Sinclair (1999), *Rodinsky's Room*. London: Granta.

Lively, Penelope (1991), *City of the Mind*. London: Deutsch.

Lynch, Kevin (1969), *The Image of the City*. Cambridge, MA: MIT P.

Sinclair, Iain (1997), *Lights Out for the Territory*. London: Granta.

Strawson, Galen (2004), "A fallacy of our age", *Times Literary Supplement*, October 15, 13-15.

Taylor, Charles (1992), *Sources of the Self: The Making of Modern Identity*. Cambridge UP.

16

Ihab Hassan

Changelings in Janglish: Or, How Australian Is It?

And what see I on any side but
the transmigrations of Proteus?
Ralph Waldo Emerson, "History"

Australia is still revealing itself to us. We oughtn't to
close off possibilities by declaring too early what we have
already become.
David Malouf, Plaque on Circular Quay

I

The New Literatures are glaringly plural; so are their janglish examples. All those accents, cadences, patois. All those authors with strange names (like mine). All those oral traditions—songs, myths, folktales—crowding into print. Is it still literature, and is it still English? Or has the imagination without borders gone berserk as texts cross every meridian with a click?

Queries dissolve into queries; passion and prejudice are rife; but in particulars begin our responsibilities. That is why I will linger in this paper with the Australian example of David Malouf. But I must begin with a personal note, propaedeutic to my thesis.

*

The only subject I failed in school was Arabic; the first prize I ever won was for English; I speak every language with an accent. What does it all mean? Perhaps I am a kind of changeling, a changeling at heart. The idea, though speculative, takes me directly to the matter at hand.

I think a "changeling effect" informs the New Literatures, an inner transformation or imaginative mutation, shaping traditions nearly everywhere. I think

of the New Literatures as metaphors of identity; I think of them as tropes troping older tropes. (Mita Banerjee called it the "Chutneyfication of History".) The
suggestion is at least plausible as a way of perceiving certain processes in this
postcolonial moment—perceiving even what we glibly call globalization.

I will return to this suggestion. For the moment, though, I want to remark on
some afflictions in our field.

*

The task of the intellectual, the late Edward Said believed, is to speak truth
to power. Certainly. But the task of the intellectual is also to speak truth to
himself—to himself and herself and the whole intellectual tribe. Otherwise, partisanship rather than commitment reigns. (I distinguish between those two concepts thus: commitment recognizes its own truth as well as the truth of others;
partisanship admits only to its own verity.) And partisanship skews understanding, limits sympathy, coarsens language. Who has not wearied of the rhetoric
of grievance, the ham-handed moralism, the bristling slogans of cultural and
postcolonial studies?

But that is a partial view itself. Some scholars, like Kwame Anthony Appiah,
have rarely yielded to current shibboleths. His "new cosmopolitanism," fallible
and pragmatic, attentive to individuals as well as to groups, moves with a limber
step. And it knows how to interrogate itself. (What does drinking Coca-Cola tell
us about a person's soul, he asks?) That is a task we owe ourselves.

A tradition of *ichtahad* (self-scrutiny) once thrived in the various medieval
caliphates. But the weight of history has smothered that tradition in emergent
societies. Nor is self-criticism obvious in Western, postcolonial discourse, where
Orientalism and Occidentalism often seem like twin characters in a shadow play.
Meanwhile, unheeded, the literary imagination goes it way, following the rich
transmigrations of Proteus.

Let us look closer.

II

Admittedly, the issues of the New Literatures are the issues of the world. It will
not suffice for me to particularize with the Australian example. I will need a still
narrower entry into my subject: namely, the figure of the changeling again.

The changeling—a shift in origins, a displacement of language, a cultural
transumption—contains the issues of identity and imagination. These two
terms, identity and imagination, *because* they are not quite antithetical, may pry
our topic loose without locking us into a dead dichotomy.

Ah, but what is imagination, you ask? The constant play of signifiers, as poststructuralists claim? A flame burning at the summit of mind, "the region of the metaphor of metaphor (110)," as Gaston Bachelard believed? The divine or es- emplastic faculty of Blake or Coleridge? We do not really know. I prefer to think of the imagination as motion, migrancy, transformation—metaphor, from *meta- pherein*, implies transfer—a knack of seeing otherwise, "wrong" identification, if you wish. More, in moving away from things as they are—that's imagination too—we die to some essential things, including our own identity.

Strange, that idea, that chimera of identity. Identity with what exactly? Some in- ner truth? Some external norm? How often do these coincide in our postmodern, postcolonial world? In any case, identity is mysteriously made, not simply "con- structed" like a garden scarecrow or Lego skyscraper. An element of self-creation gives it a unique character. Nevertheless, in extremity, identity will choose the Iron Maiden over the Proteus; it abhors Changelings of every kind. (Think of begrimed Gemmy, in Malouf's *Remembering Babylon*, who clambers over a fence separating a farm from the outback, stuttering: "Do not shoot. I am a B-b-british object" (3), and is held in the white community with fear, hatred, and contempt.)

*

So how is all this pertinent to the New Literatures? It is doubly pertinent. The New Literatures, as I have said, trope on the forms and themes of British and American literature, with which they share a common language. But the New Literatures also reconstitute imaginatively the theme of identity itself, the iden- tity of their characters as well as their own collective identity as literatures.

Of course, nationalism and especially fundamentalism run counter to this troping tendency. Hence the famous fatwa, which Naipaul tastelessly called an extreme form of literary criticism. *Fundus*, fundamentalism: look it up, you'll meet basics and bottoms, first principles and animal posteriors. They provide the etymology, if not ontology, of the incandescent terror and idealism in our midst.

But let's not simplify: literature itself contains the germ of fundamentalism. In the beginning was the Word, John said, and the Word was with God. What could be more fundamental than the Logos? Well, that was then, you say. Not really. Fatwa, like other edicts, bulls, ukases, fiats, decrees, impose their will on reality. That's also called the totalitarian lie. But it's not just totalitarianism. Even the magus of deconstruction—I mean the late Jacques Derrida—recognized that the letter is inherently ethnocentric, imperialist. (Never mind that he badly pre- dicted the end of *clôture*, the end of the book, the inauguration of "writing.")

The imperial letter becomes literal, congeals into a canon. But even canons melt—and are recast. The Same returns altered in the shape-shifting flow of time. In new, postcolonial societies, however, this dialectic without synthesis be- tween identity and imagination is fraught with menace. The mass-soul, as Elias

Canetti put it, "foams like a huge, wild, full-blooded, warm animal in all of us, very deep, far deeper than the maternal" (411). The mass-soul smothers fantasy, play, humor, imagination—and the individual spirit.

Of course, each postcolonial society is unique, and the case of Australia is genially different.

III

I come closer to the particular now by asking: How Australian is it, how Australian is Australian literature? The question, mindful of its mild absurdity, reflects the irony back upon itself.

We know that postcolonial societies gaze compulsively at themselves in the mirror of history, eager to win approbation, eager to confirm their self-esteem. Australia, a brash, successful society bursting at its creative seams, blends strut and cringe in projecting its image for the world to see.

But on what would an Australian identity really rest? The voyages of Cook; convict Transportation; the colonial experience; the outback (sometimes called the "Never, Never, Back of Beyond"); Aboriginal history; the travels of Leichhardt, Burke, and Wills; the exploits of Ned Kelly; Gallipoli; the ethos of mateship and the fair go; the tyranny of distance; the idea of the lucky country (beer, barbie, and beach); the newest immigrants (mostly Chinese); Crocodile Dundee; the millennial Sydney Olympics; the debacle of the Tampa; the vernacular of the larrikin and swagman; or the emu, kangaroo, wombat, galah, bandicoot, and gum tree?

No doubt, all these enter the Aussie myth of identity, inhabit the underside of its self-awareness, with various degrees of skepticism and belief. Mythic Australia—shimmering always like a giant Ghost Gum—continues to haunt writers, even those who try to exorcise it with postmodern ironies. Classics like Henry Lawson's "The Drover's Wife" still seem unappeased, echoing in Russell Drysdale's eponymous painting and Murray Bail's story, echoing again in Inga Clendinnen's Boyer Lectures of 1999, *True Stories* (of these later).

For my purpose here, I need to touch only on Aboriginality, emblematic of the larger question of cultural identity.

*

Colonial societies, once oppressed by imperial powers, seem to have perpetuated oppression by turning against minorities within; but no minority has fared worse than Australia's Aborigines. No wonder, then, that the modern Australian conscience has obsessed about its indigenes in order to comprehend, redeem, or vindicate the past—that is, to legitimate itself.

The Mabo High Court decision of 1992 marked a turning point in Aboriginal rights. But the law has failed to alter the lives of "blackfellas" on the streets of Darwin or Alice Springs. Hence the "black armband," worn metaphorically by some writers, especially historians. The symbol of grief and penance is apt but requires nuance.

In his 1980 Boyer Lectures, *The Spectre of Truganini*, Smith argued that a culture needs to "put down firm ethical roots in the place from which it grows" (10); it cannot live off the principles of another culture, though it may challenge or modify them. The premise allows Smith to see all the ambiguities—sometimes sheer paradoxes—of the Antipodean condition, without ever condoning genocide.

Two decades later, Inga Clendinnen took up the same theme in her own Boyer Lectures. She remarks: "there remains a scar on the face of the country, a birth stain of injustice and exclusion directed at the people who could so easily provide the core of our sense of ourselves as a nation…" (102).

But how many Australians, I wonder, believe this national ideal? How many of the immigrants of the post-Whitlam years? And what does the ideal practically mean? That collective guilt and right recall create a decent society? That the revived debates about Reconciliation, the Stolen Generation, and a Prime Ministerial Apology, can serve as foundation for moral and political acts?

I feel unqualified to answer these queries; I am more confident in saying that the genocide of Native Americans does not provide the "core sense" of my own citizenship in the United States. But these are deep matters, hard to reason, easy to rationalize.

Before leaving the history wars—which go back to Manning Clark and Geoffrey Blainey and the Australian Bicentennial—I want to note their curious after-effect: a revival of the old Platonic-Aristotelian quarrel between History and Poetry, the truth of fact and the truth of the imagination. Historians and novelists have squared off, each side claiming the loftier ground; more precisely, each side claiming the steadier view of the horrors of history. The issue remains: who speaks of atrocity better, the historian or the novelist? Or is there really no poetry after Auschwitz? (In this intellectual joust, Clendinnen herself has challenged the novelist Kate Grenville, and skirmished with Norman Mailer and J. M. Coetzee.)

But the point is obvious without martial metaphors: in contesting its past, Australia is also changing its white identity. I say changing, not shedding. This is also a kind of troping, ethnic and genetic troping.

*

The shifts and changes, however, go beyond race. The Anglo-Celtic heritage remains vital—it's claptrap to say otherwise—but like all strong cultures, that heritage knows how to adapt, adopt, and sometimes refuse what comes its way. Thus a classic essay like Manning Clark's "Tradition in Australian Literature," written in 1949, may appear quaint to younger writers, a bit like Abel Tasman's seventeenth-century map of the Antipodes, on the floor of the Mitchell Library in Sydney, showing a phantom continent, unfinished, lopsided, grotesque, with the Gulf of Carpentaria an open jaw about to devour Celebes to the west and New Zealand a stiff-nippled breast floating into the Pacific to the east.

If this seems too fanciful to learned minds in the ancient city of Lund (apparently founded by Sweyn Forkbeard, not Canute the Great), then let me focus on one work, one iconic image morphing through the years. I mean Henry Lawson's story, "The Drover's Wife" of 1894.

*

The story does not escape clichés about grit, self-reliance in the bush, its mean pleasures and exorbitant solitudes. But the story also limns a mother's love, facing down evil, all those black, slithering snakes in a stringy-bark shack. What is it all about? Is it the Australian thing, toughness and fortitude, or something universal? In any case, it's nothing you'll ever see in Sussex or Kent.

Now cut to Russell Drysdale's famous painting, "The Drover's Wife" (1945). No children, no snakes here; bare, spindly trees; a wagon, a horse, an ant-like man in the far distance; hard, blue sky above the red earth. The rest is the woman, hulking in the foreground, with her suitcase and shadow. As in Lawson's story, the sense of bleak, clumsy endurance comes through; the big feet press firmly on the ground. One wonders how a woman could stand so full in such a spare, ungiving space—where did the fat on her body, her legs, come from? But the real difference between story and painting is loss: the eyes in the small face, half-hidden by the sadly tilted hat, the eyes have a thousand-yard stare. Right over the viewer's head. Do they express bewilderment, resignation, old hope, terminal loss? Where is the woman going with her suitcase, her back to the puny man? Right out of the frame? And what else from the bush is going out with her? Myself, I think this lumbering woman with small head and shaggy dress stands up front, at once curvaceous and columnar, saying: I'm here, I *may* be Australia, but I'm really just me. Is that what the picture really says?

Questions again, and questions are what Murray Bail proffers us in *his* story, "The Drover's Wife." Bail is sly, knowing, ironic, secretive, acutely intelligent, gruffly urbane, always sere. That's a distance from Lawson. Watch him go at Lawson through Drysdale. (No need here to invoke postmodern reflexivity or intertextuality; writerly cunning will nicely do.)

In Bail's story, a dentist speaks: that's Hazel there, my former wife, he confides—why do they say she's a *drover's* wife? Bail, ever the trickster, is at it from the start: "There has perhaps been a mistake—but of no great importance—made in the denomination of this picture" (25), the author writes. A "mistake made"? By whom? "Perhaps"? "Of no importance"? And where did Drysdale find the dentist's wife to pose? Come off it now, Bail.

This is not the place for a fussy *explication de texte*. The point is that Bail's smart narrative takes up an icon of Australian culture, wraps it in ambiguities, casts upon it a hundred lights and shadows—and ends by reaffirming it somehow. The trick is in Bail's flickering realism, a style of enigmatic banality, which undermines the world of common appearances without quite erasing it. That person there in the picture is Hazel, a real person, the dentist avers.

Real in what sense? And does she—or doesn't she?—elope with a drover? And why would she elope at all? Because she feels "in her element in the bush," and the silence of the drover "woos" her? Because, unlike her husband, the dentist, she likes snow on Ghost Gums, and enjoys chopping wood and killing snakes. She is "Australian" alright, "the silly girl." In brief, the stereotypes somersault back on their feet; reality wavers, but only for a moment; and even those bush-flies, absent in Drysdale's picture, make their way back into the story. That's "a serious omission," the dentist grumbles, deadpan. "It is altering the truth for the sake of a pretty picture…" (30).

Is Bail kidding us, or what? Not entirely. The tacit pain in the tale, the husband's loss and wife's loneliness, put reality back into place. And so, beyond all ironies, the Drover's Wife lives. Though her mystique may mutate in history or flicker in language, it won't disappear.

But what could be more enduring in Australia than the mystique of the gum tree? Bail won't let it be. In his beguiling romance, *Eucalyptus*, the author feels obliged to say on the first page:

> But *desertorum* (to begin with) is only one of several hundred eucalypts; there is no precise number. And anyway the very word, *desert-or-um*, harks back to a stale version of the national landscape and from there in a more or less straight line onto the national character, all those linings of the soul and the larynx, which have their origins in the *bush*, so it is said, the poetic virtues (can you believe it?) of being belted about by droughts, bushfires, smelly sheep and so on; and let's not forget the isolation, the exhausted shapeless women, the crude language, the always wide horizon, and the flies (1f).

What is this Calvino-like passage doing here at the commencement of an Australian fairy tale called after the ubiquitous gum? Repudiating the stereotypes by perpetuating the archetypes, no doubt, troping the tropes and unsettling the scene.

I will resist the temptation to advert to the master of allegory and displacements down under, Gerald Murnane. Instead, I will hurry to tarry with David Malouf.

IV

Malouf—Malouf and that crabby bloke from Bunyah, Les Murray—are the preeminent Australian writers of our time, and in my view candidates for the Nobel Prize. Moreover, Malouf is a compelling example of how the imagination tropes on nature, history, and the human heart to create a metaphoric world, mysteriously intimate.

Like all great artists, Malouf eschews ideology in his work. "I don't have very strong opinions because I don't think a writer can afford to," he said in a recent interview in the *Weekend Australian*. "I think opinion is pretty much the death of thinking. And it's certainly the death of trying to understand how other people think and feel" (4). That is why his novels, like poetry, work so close to the edge of things, the fringe of feeling, the silence crumbling into articulation.

*

So how does Malouf engage the issues of identity, cultural nationalism, postcolonial reaction, and all those topics so dear to scholars in our field?

In his essay called "The South"—the South here is not *Terra Australis*, but the "real" south, up north, Italy if you wish—Malouf writes:

> On a soft, sunlit morning in March 1959, just a few days before my twenty-fifth birthday, I stood at the rails of an Italian liner, the Fairsky, and after a five-weeks sea-voyage…saw the Bay of Naples open before me, and utterly familiar in the distance the dark slopes and scooped-out cone of Vesuvius—all just as I had always imaged it, like the breaking of a dream (119).

It is the imagination that liberates Malouf from Australia, but also, later, from the Europe he had pre-imagined. Malouf does not feel "born" gliding into the Bay of Naples, as the expatriate, Peter Conrad, feels, riding his first red double-decker, crossing Waterloo Bridge. The grandson of Lebanese immigrants is at home in his "dream," whether in Italy or Dacia, whether in Europe or Australia. Where's the betrayal of identity here?

*

Let us turn now to *Johnno* (1975), the first, most autobiographical, and distinctively "Australian" of his novels. What does it reveal about identity? The author himself, in a preface he wrote a quarter of a century after completing the work in Italy, gives some clues. The first clue concerns the place of composition:

> The apartment [in Florence] was low-ceilinged but cool, and at number 23 next door (there was a plaque) Dostoevsky, exactly a century before, had written *The Idiot*, looking out on the same view of the grand, rusticated front of the Pitti Palace, the cypress

tops of the Boboli Gardens, and on the ridge above, airily theatrical against the Tuscan sky, the lemon-pale, villalike façade of Forte Belvedere. If Dostoevsky, closing his outward eye on these splendid evocations of Italy, could imagine so darkly the snow-bound avenues of St. Petersburg and the swarming bridges across the Neva, surely I could look in the same direction, I thought, and catch a view of Brisbane, my weatherboard, sub-tropical hometown, with its mangrove-choked river, rain-swollen and sluggish, and on every hilltop the unmistakable outline of bunya and hoop-pines (vii).

Here the writer's inner eye trains itself to penetrate, not only memory, not simply setting, but the haze of everything inessential to the vital core—penetrate, I insist, without ever slighting the sensual world. This makes for a figurative, if not allegorical, book. Thus Malouf again:

> *Johnno* is a book about reading and interpretation, which is what links it with much else that I have written; about how we read and misread words, events, feelings, people, including ourselves, and how we are shaped not only by what happens to us but by what we have read; as if fiction, rather than being a mirror of life reorganized, were a blueprint for how lives themselves may be shaped (xi).

A book about books, Malouf says, not by Australian authors, mind you, not even by English authors, but by the likes of Dostoyevsky, Nietzsche, Rimbaud, and Lermontov. For both Johnno and Dante (the narrator), cultures are permeable, characters are fluid; for Dante especially, the fabric of existence allows for "parallel lives, alternative fates". Colonial experience is never binding; and though Australia remains the "necessary" place, the path to it leads through Europe, forth and back, back and forth. "What an extraordinary thing it is, that I should be here rather than somewhere else… Why Australia? What *is* Australia anyway?" (52), Dante asks at one point. But that has nothing to do with expatriation. "An extraordinary denomination," expatriation, the narrator remarks later in the novel. "What did it mean? It seemed too grand to fit anything I felt about my position" (128).

It means that Malouf himself inhabits such denominations imaginatively. And means that, though Johnno drowns himself in the Condamine, Australia abides, "more loud-mouthed, prosperous, intractable than ever."

*

Take now *An Imaginary Life*, published three years later. I have always considered that work, more than a novel, a consummate fable of our age of migrancy and exile. And I have always considered Ovid's *Metamorphoses* a ludic myth of myths, a diapason of identities, Proteus as the worker of Creation. In reinventing Ovid, then, David Malouf may have found his true subject, his necessary angel; and in writing *An Imaginary Life*, he may have also written part of his own imaginary autobiography as a parable of identity and change and cosmic reconciliation. In the wastes of Dacia—that is, in Australia—language eerily sings.

The wild Child in the story speaks no language, neither Latin nor the barbarous tongue of the Getae, but only the gutturals of God, only "the language of the spiders." The Child is the old poet's tutor: Ovid must pass through and beyond words. For if language is the house of identity, the immensity of the steppes obliterates every habitation; exile is home. Ovid knows—I mean Malouf knows—that imagination brings you finally to the brink of Nothing. "I have smelled [that is, intuited] my way to the very edge of things, where Nothing begins" (27), Ovid says.

Nothing: that is the solution to the problem of identity. Get lost.

*

But I have overleapt myself; I have suddenly reached the far horizon of my topic. Yes, the changeling is really the child of no one, no thing; and the process of troping on tropes leads to the void. But that is a horizon I want to limn, not assert. Our topic is less mystical than worldly: self-dispossession is only its very last stage.

The plight of the protagonist, we must now recognize, is also that of the poet in the face of power: playful Ovid against solemn Augustus, the pen seeking the chink in imperial might, the empire striking back at itself. But in Malouf's case, the catch-phrase acquires ambiguity and resonance, as if Ovid had *sought* to free himself by fleeing Rome. In allegorical terms, it is as if the colonial writer, in order to free himself from imperial Britain, had first to pass through not only Britain but all Europe before returning to Australia.

*

If *An Imaginary Life* is a spiritual autobiography presented as a fable of displaced identity, what, then, is Malouf's real memoir, so plainly, so tantalizingly, named *12 Edmondstone Street*? Does it finally give away the "identity" of David Malouf? Hardly. For in that brief, luminous text, the moments of self-perception come with visionary remembrance, epiphanies of imaginative recall, presaging Malouf's future life in art. The figures in the carpet are all waiting there.

If the Old Country means anything to Malouf, it is the silence of his grandfather, who could speak no English, his dignity looming against the opacity of Lebanon. Did I say silence? The old man holds court in a corner table of the family store, regaling his compatriots with stories his grandson could not understand: "Listening at the edge of the circle, with my chin resting on the bent cane back of a chair, I would get so lost in the telling that I almost understood: not the words but the tune" (5).

Malouf's own father, born in Brisbane, is a clean-cut Catholic, shy and reserved with his son, who volunteers at St. Vincent de Paul and plays League on Saturday afternoons. Malouf's mother, London born, brings England to 12 Edmondstone Street, keeps Australia out, well beyond her verandah's lace. So, naturally, Malouf and his sister play Australian toughs, out of earshot: "Him and me done it this arvo. I betcha we did" (33). I see no great revelations of a writer's identity in these circumstances; I see more in the domestic landscape of Number Twelve.

Topographies show contours, borderlands. Such limits matter to a writer, the fierce flip-flop of inside-outside. The sleeping arrangements require Malouf and his sister to sleep on a verandah, beyond their parents' bedroom window, a small, nocturnal exile he desperately resents. "A verandah is not part of the house. Even a child knows this…," Malouf says. "Each morning I step across the threshold and there it is, a world recovered, restored" (20f).

But what better borderland than the dark, dank space below Brisbane bunga-lows, a forest of creosote-brushed posts, a black sky with cracks, through which the secret life of the house sifts: "There are no clocks down here. There is not even language… To come down here, up under the floorboards and the life of rooms, is to enter a dream space…" (47). Indeed, the work of David Malouf may owe far more to verandahs and under-floors than to all the cedars of Lebanon.

Imagination, however, dwells in the body, the body of Malouf and the world's. Flesh tingles, objects breathe. It is a sensuous, sensual space, the space of this writer's childhood, suffused with libido, the libido of poesis and of vivid recall. This body, the "experiencing mind-in-the-body," Malouf says, serves as a limit to what we can know of reality—a limit but also a door. Hence: "We have only to dare one last little blaze of magic to pass through" (66).

Passing through or taking a "different train," bound to another, "unnamable destination," as Malouf puts it in a later, darker episode of his memoir. This, I suggest, is the changeling effect. This is also the destination of all serious artists, exchanging closure for the openness of existence, in puzzlement or play. But the wounds of experience, though they may change or fade, never leave the soul im-maculate.

V

I approach my conclusion now by reverting to my subtitle. The question, "How Australian Is It?", lives uneasily in the imaginary space between the concreteness of culture and the universality of the human condition. I want to close, therefore, with a key text that inhabits that space: David Malouf's own Boyers Lectures of 1998, *A Spirit of Play*.

For Malouf, Australia at the start of the third millennium is a "raft" on which people have scrambled, "a new float of lives in busy interaction" (7). It is also an ancient continent to which Europeans brought, as a kind of gift to the land, a way of seeing *it*, not simply in itself but also as "it fitted into the rest of the world." (An interesting idea this: call it colonialism if you wish, but it has been much more than that.) And so, if Aborigines are a land-dreaming people, late-comers share a sea-dreaming. This makes for a "complex fate"—the phrase, of course, is Henry James's about Americans—makes for multiple allegiances to different worlds, multiple tensions between cultures and environments, which Australians need not scramble to unify. Thus "identity" becomes a confident way of being in the world, rather than some anxious definition. No cringe or scratchi-ness necessary, a level gaze at the world.

A Spirit of Play ends with a plea for Falstaff, for the festive, motley, carnival as-pect of existence, say Gay Mardi Gras in Sydney, a civic, erotic occasion of toler-ance and laughter, mockery and release, death too (in the form of AIDS), which must stalk every feast. "Finding a place for Falstaff," Malouf concludes, "acting imaginatively in the spirit of lightness he represents, is the way to wholeness; and wholeness, haleness, as the roots of our language tell us, is health" (116).

Health, yes, but also death I insist, death and rebirth, both warp and woof, the loom of being. Death, the ultimate displacement, which inhabits every meta-phor, the change of one identity into another. For identities dissolve where hu-man beings attain their fullest destiny, and that is the fate of the best of the new literatures. Changelings in Janglish? No, a new music creeping to us over distant waters, a rich sound, of which I have reproduced here only a few notes.

Works Cited

Appiah, Kwame Anthony. "The Case for Contamination." *The New York Times Magazine*, January 1, 2006: 28-37, 52.

Bachelard, Gaston. *The Psychoanalysis of Fire.* Trans. Alan C. M. Ross. Boston: Beacon Press, 1964.

Bail, Murray. *The Drover's Wife and Other Stories.* Melbourne: Text Publishing, 1998.

Bail, Murray. *Eucalyptus.* New York: Farrar Straus and Giroux, 1998.

Banerjee, Mita. *The Chutneyfication of History.* American Studies Monograph, Series, 95. Heidelberg: Winter Verlag, 2002.

Clendinnen, Inga. *True Stories.* Sydney: ABC Books, 1999.

Indyk, Ivor, ed. *David Malouf: A Celebration.* Canberra: Friends of the National Library of Australia, 2001.

Malouf, David. *An Imaginary Life.* Sydney: Picador, 1980.

Malouf, David. *Johnno.* New York: George Braziller, 1997.

Malouf, David. *Remembering Babylon.* London: Vintage, Random House, 1994.

Malouf, David. "The South." *Heat,* 1, New Series. Newcastle: University of Newcastle Press, 2001.

Malouf, David. *A Spirit of Play: The Making of an Australian Consciousness,* Sydney: ABC Books, 1998.

Malouf, David. *12 Edmondstone Street.* Melbourne: Penguin, 1986.

Neill, Rosemary. "An Imaginative Life: Interview with David Malouf." *Weekend Australian,* September 30-October 1, 2006: 4-5.

Smith, Bernard. *The Spectre of Truganini.* Sydney: ABC Books, 1980.

17

Ihab Hassan

Notes on Literary Theory in an Age of Globalization: Or Blackbirds Skimming the Void

When the blackbird flew out of sight,
It marked the edge
Of one of many circles.
Wallace Stevens, "Thirteen Ways of Looking at a Blackbird"

Forget the blackbirds for now. The question is: how many ways are there of questioning theory in our age? And if beauty is in the eye of the beholder, and the earth wobbles under the weight of six billion beholders, what is beauty then? Or is beauty unmentionable in academe, despite the indiscretions of some scholars—Elaine Scary, Fred Turner, Charles Jencks, among others—who have recently taken the name of beauty in vain?

Again, forget beauty and the blackbirds; think of geography. Thomas Friedman went home one day and said to his wife, "Honey, I think the world is flat" (5). He was echoing a technocrat in Bangalore who said to him, "Tom, the playing field is being leveled" (5). Leveled or flattened, they both meant the world is very round: interactive, interdependent, instantaneous, contemporaneous—and viciously fractious withal.

The Taliban vandalize priceless Buddhist statues; thieves armed with computers loot Aztec and Assyrian treasures; fatwa establish new guidelines for literary criticism; and the great museums of the world wrangle with governments, with history itself, about the patrimonies of art. This is a nasty condition, both flat and round. What kind of literary theory, what kind of aesthetics generally, can emerge from a world that defies Euclidean and non-Euclidean geometries with every diurnal spin?

The answer to these real and mock queries seems lost in partisanship and prejudice, abrasive ideologies and slick skepticism. Sane critics may look for a way out in ideas of pluralism, eclecticism, hybridity, and cosmopolitanism, recently propounded by Kwame Anthony Appiah. Sooner or later, though, these ideas crash on the realities of our time, on ethnic violence, economic volatility, and empires in decline, as Niall Ferguson argues in *The War of the World*. Above all, they crash on the obdurate self, on self-interest without borders. Is there a way out?

*

World history tends to abstractions that art can flesh. Last year, the Louvre Museum sponsored an ambitious, multi-disciplinary event called "The Foreigner's Home." Toni Morrison served as presiding spirit. She chose Géricault's painting of 1819, "The Raft of the Medusa", as an icon of her theme. For her, the distraught sailors struggling to stay afloat provide a haunting—perhaps also melodramatic—image of millions in search of new homes, wandering about, as she put it, "like nomads between despair and hope, breath and death" (7).

Imagine the tempestuous sea, seething with monsters; imagine the splintered, overloaded raft and shredded sails, tossed about, without destination; think of them symbolizing our collective destiny. What kind of art can emerge from this wreck, what kind of criticism or aesthetic theory? Morrison's answer is: look to the individual human body, a choreography of blood and bones. In a sea of distress, she says, "you have the body in motion and you have the obligation of seeing the body as the real and final home" (7).

The phrase resonates: "the body as the real and final home." The body not only as a political or aesthetic entity, the refuge of exiles who sew their lips and artists who mutilate their genitals, but also as the locus of experience, an epistemological ground, waiting to be worked, waiting to be known, leaking away its life. Can this sense of a death-heavy body serve not only art but also theory in an age of diaspora and division? Or does that sense, sooner or later, hit a dead end despite the brilliant efforts of thinkers like Bataille and Leiris? Death and the body: perhaps they can teach theory to accept its own transience, to refrain from systematizing the irrational, to acknowledge desire even as it opens itself to the void.

I will return to these issues. For the moment, I am tempted to remark that diverse and relative beliefs—in the West, at least—manage only to paint a Benetton rainbow over the wretched Raft of the Medusa.

*

Here's the D-word, diversity, dreadful in its glibness. Why dreadful? Because the issue goes beyond different cultural norms and sundry moral or aesthetic judgments; it affects the human capacity for responding itself.

I have stood frozen before certain objects in galleries around the world, feeling that no experience I've had at the Metropolitan or Uffizi, at Karnak or the Parthenon, can help me cope with what appears before me. I don't simply mean the shock of the new; I also mean the profound, and ultimately inexplicable, threat of otherness. And I also mean the paradoxical temptation of indifference. You end by asking yourself: do I really have to deal with this? Do I care?

Admittedly, our perplexity nowadays—Herbert Grabes aptly calls the phenomenon the "aesthetics of strangeness"—is partially due to the radically disjunctive legacy of modernism, postmodernism, and assorted avant-gardes in the last hundred years. But haven't we inured ourselves to the various avant-gardes by now? Haven't we absorbed their shock? We actually live their scandal, or, rather, we let the media, if not our servants, live it for us. In any case, the arts continue to create their audiences somehow—with the possible exception of contemporary music.

But the difficulties of aesthetics today, of literary theory as well, are due to something larger than catachrestic modernism and paratactic postmodernism: that is, a collision, not only of styles, values, and expectations, but also of radical assumptions of being. Call it ontological diversity, a clash not of civilizations but of ways of being and breathing in the world. *And yet, that may be precisely the creative moment in globalization, before homogenization sets in, before differences freeze into lucre or flare up into rage.*

Can this be the present task of theory, to grasp the creative moment of difference, of ontological diversity itself? A leap of empathy, you might say, a recklessness with all we know and are. A way of grasping the moment out of time, the *kairos* of aesthetic globalization. That may be too much to ask. In the end, most of us most of the time will fall back on habit, hypocrisy, or the common balm of indifference. At best, we try to translate—the etymology of the word implies transport, carrying something across—translate the different languages of being in this world, in other worlds too. And why not? As the poet James Merrill put it: all life is translation, and we are all lost in it.

So, theory as pragmatic translation, mediating ontological diversity, moving between art and abstraction—right brain, left brain—between creation and consumption: is that the best we can hope for?

*

The alternative to translation may be fundamentalism, absolutism of one kind or another.

Just for grim fun, I try to imagine a Fundamentalist Aesthetic. Would it issue fatwa in the name of Yahweh, Christ, or Allah, but probably not the Buddha? Or, more philosophical, would it invoke Plato and hail Hegel? Or perhaps, more equable still, it would claim Universal Reason, dormant since the Enlightenment, as final arbiter. And if Fundamentalist Aesthetics discovers a heretic here or a deviant there, what then? Would it call the SWAT of Art or Taliban of Theory to expunge the miscreant from creation? I shudder, though part of me, part of us all, yearns for the simplicity of fundamentalism.

All fun aside, literary theory demands a semblance of articulation, a gesture toward generalization, as the arts do. Once, the Bible, or Shakespeare, or the myths and archetypes of the world, or the Freudian Unconscious, or the Marxist version of History, or powerful concepts like mimesis, or the basic structures of language itself, provided frames of generalization. But now, general principles, pragmatic "universals," however soft, dare not breathe their name in academe.

Yet universals, not Platonic but empiric, abound. For instance: languages; human emotions; marks of status; ceremonies of birth, marriage, and death; gods, spirits, taboos, and rituals; not to mention the sixty-seven socio-biological practices that E. O. Wilson calls, in *Consilience*, "epigenetic rules." In other words, cultures and individuals not only vary infinitely; their variations also follow patterns; and even chaos seems to follow complex rules. Without self-revising rules, no theory would carry conviction, and no aesthetic response would share itself with another.

*

I will return to the word "conviction"—yes, my theme is recursive—but now, I want to brush base with Kantian philosophy, and so relate pragmatic universals—call them generalizations, if you prefer—to the more traditional concerns of theory.

From the New Critics of the forties to the poststructuralists of yesteryear, theorists have nodded toward Königsberg, whether to adapt, adopt, or reject the *Critique of Judgment*. Improbably, I want to allude to Kant by way of Walter Benjamin. It's just a hint, really, from his murkily-written essay of 1917, entitled "Program of the Coming Philosophy."

Benjamin wants to derive from Kant an epistemological concept of experience. "A concept of knowledge gained from reflection on the linguistic nature of knowledge," he writes, "will create a corresponding concept of experience which will also encompass realms that Kant failed to truly systematize" (49). And what is experience for Benjamin? It is simply "the uniform and continuous multiplicity of knowledge" (49).

There is a chicken-and-egg effect here, one that would fail to trouble a resolute pragmatist, who would give no priority to knowledge or experience. But Benjamin is more than halfway to pragmatism anyway, and his Neo-Kantian project might well serve to critique the arts. An epistemology of experience would allow effective generalizations, a basis for judgment. Grounded in experience, it would also acknowledge the body—Morrison's "real and final home"—and make a place for death among its abstractions. Still, one thing lacks for me here: a fiduciary principle, a working idea of trust, which would apply to the arts.

*

This leads to the core of my essay. An epistemology of experience, relying on pragmatic principles, depends less on metaphysical truth than on human trust. This trust, as William James shows in *The Will to Believe*, depends on another's trust, just as our faith "is faith in someone else's faith…" (9). Hence the self-defeating character of radical relativism, of extreme particularism. Hence, too, the innate sterility of fundamentalism, which spurns human trust in favor of fiats, ukases, edicts, writs, and gospels of every kind.

The fiduciary principle I invoke here, this idea of trust, is also the trust on which knowledge rests and by which knowledge is shared. Call it the epistemic contract; call it the aesthetic compact as well. Without this tacit compact, the artist cannot create, let alone communicate; without it, the aesthetician cannot theorize; without it, the critic or reader or viewer falls silent. This trust, I would argue, has a spiritual character.

Why on earth spiritual? Because trust comes from self-bracketing, self-emptying, self-dispossession, comes ultimately from what theologians call *kenosis*. Trust is a quality of attention to others, to the created world, to something *not* in ourselves. "All mean egotism vanishes…I become a transparent eyeball. *I am nothing, I see all*" (10). That's the vision of the Man at Concord, perhaps the vision of us all when we profoundly trust. The Woman at Amherst went farther:

> By homely gifts and hindered words
> The human heart is told
> Of nothing—
> "Nothing" is the force
> That renovates the World. (650)

Emily Dickinson might as well have said: Nothing is the force that renovates Trust. Nothing—that notional mother of death—is the force that renovates Creation, yes, but Nothing also underwrites our faith in symbols and representations. Silence, absence, and the void cradle language, cradle Being itself. (Paul Valéry once quipped that though God made everything out of nothing, the nothing shows through.) This intuition, central to both modernism and postmodernism—from Heidegger to Derrida, from Kandinsky to Bill Viola, from Webern to Cage—is spiritual in nature because it touches the ultimate mystery of existence. What does it really mean: "I exist"? No one knows. Not René Descartes. Not Dr Johnson, who used to stub his toes on stones.

*

At this point, we might pause to catch our breath. So far, we have looked for a basis of theory—and by implication of art—in a globally fragmented age. The search brought us to soft universals, pragmatic generalizations, which underwrite all human discourse, a tacit compact of trust. Trust, I suggested, comes from self-dispossession, ultimately, a gift of giving oneself to the void. In the beginning was the Word, and the Word was with Nothing. Is this blasphemy? Is it mysticism?

I would rather think of it as an expression of our common faith that language, as a symbolic structure, rises arbitrarily from brute experience—from nothing, so to speak—to enable all the glorious ambiguities of human communication. Oh, it's better than that: on a good day, language also creates for us a home-made world, in which we all trust and share. Somehow, against all odds, ours remains an answerable world.

The issue, then, is not only linguistic but also fiduciary, a quotidian miracle. But *can trust underwrite theory in a radically diverse and globally fractious age*? I am uncertain, and uncertain also that these notes can unfold all the meanings of trust, all its aspects and degrees. But I know that literary theory in a time of contested globalization will not find legitimacy in sectarian politics or fundamentalist dogma, not in cultural identity or transcendental philosophy. In what, then, beside pragmatic trust?

*

Might the vaunted universality of art underwrite theory and widen trust in the world? That "universality" was equivocal from the start. It is most convincing in the case of traditional music—the beat of foot, the pulse in the artery, is nearly ubiquitous—and most arguable in the case of literature, which embeds itself in the mother tongue.

I turn to literature precisely because its case is the most equivocal. I turn, inevitably, to Shakespeare. But this is a particular Shakespeare, touched by the hyperbolic brilliance of Harold Bloom. As we know, Bloom believes that Shakespeare's plays read us, comprehend us; we all live within *them*, Eli, Bushman, Patagonian, Londoner, Cairene, and Hairy Ainu alike. This seems extravagant until we recall the passional scope of the Bard's plays, which seem to excite, all at once, the lymphatic system, hypothalamus, amygdala, and neocortex, flashing even in the transparent eyeball of the visionary. (The conceit may not seem implausible to a neuroscientist like Susan Greenfield, who claims, in *The Private Life of the Brain*, that emotion is the most basic form of awareness.)

Specifically, for Bloom, Fat Jack and the Prince of Denmark reveal the most comprehensive consciousness in literature. Be that as it may, the two characters—could anyone include both in a modern play?—emerge as prodigious charismatics. They also share a deep vein of nihilism, which contributes, paradoxically, to their universality. Having plumbed the depths, they saw Nothing there, and that's what we all see in our rare moments of unflinching clarity. "Our thoughts are ours, their ends none of our own." The lines are the Player King's, scripted by Hamlet, acknowledging that the universe doesn't give a fig for us.

I think Bloom—his penchant for psychomachia aside—is right in his intuition that Hamlet's universalism derives from his enigmatic indifference to everyone and everything, shading into nihilism. For this quality, I would add, I trust Hamlet—yes, trust him—because he sees everything, cares about nothing, not even about himself. Because he is a center of a terrible lucidity and indifference in the world. Can this indifference, this kenotic quality, suggest a premise of literary theory in the global age? Or does kenosis serve only the elect?

Indifference and lucidity, when they are so richly embedded in the world as they are in Shakespeare's plays, surely define noble attributes of the critical mind, if not of theory itself. They clear the doors of perception and invite, not compel, assent. Thus they help create the condition to which theories aspire when theories aspire to trust.

*

I seem to have cornered myself into the position that aesthetics generally, and literary theory in particular, have something to learn from great art. (I can hear Gotthold Lessing grumbling and tossing in his deep grave.) Learn nihilism or what?

Learn more than nihilism, I think. Theory can take a hint from the inexhaustible range of human emotions, sensual impressions, and artistic forms.

A good theorist will be as inward with the aching human body—the mortal "body as the real and final home"—and with the human mind and heart, as any poet or novelist. A good critic will know how to follow the "inner momentum of a poem," as Helen Vendler does in *Poets Thinking*, rather than some extraneous thesis. (We can all do with a fix of "negative capability" now.) Best of all, both theorist and critic will find a way to withdraw tactfully sometimes, or at least turn aside, mindful of Cage's insight that the best criticism of a work of art is another work of art.

These hopeful notes point toward a pragmatic theory, a theory nearly but never quite as wide as the world, a theory that trusts in imagination and play without insistence on itself. Theory is fading fast, anyway, smiling at us like the Cheshire Cat. So why not let theory fade even if we must coax back the Cat someday?

*

I have mentioned John Cage in haste, and want now to adduce him as a slant parable, a personal memory rippling out in circles across the surface of our subject.

Cage melds Western vanguards with Eastern precepts, Dada with Zen. Yet, the man remains an American original. Like his father, a California inventor, Cage recalls the down-home, crackpot anarchism and creativity of the New World. In him, American Puritanism, Transcendentalism, and Pragmatism—the pragmatism of James and the pragmatism of Suzuki—all find ludic affinities. In him, laughter and creation, self-heedlessness and commitment, chance and order, all meet. In his spirit, if not in his music exactly, the human spirit, whatever its tribe, renews itself.

In short, Cage serves as a particular case—call him eccentric, if you wish—of the aesthetic compact, global in reach yet singular in persuasion, practical like chopping wood, playful like a child, loony like a Zen fool, spiritual without benefit of theology. His chance operations and aleatory techniques are exercises in kenosis, attempts at emptying the self, and so earn—grudgingly, I admit—our trust. It's all contained in a remark he once made to me in mock exasperation: "Don't you see, Ihab, that when you've delivered a judgment, that's *all* you've got!" His jaw then dropped in that soundless, goofy laugh of his.

*

I may be utopian to think that art can inspire aesthetics, that kenotic trust can underwrite vanishing theory. Yes, it's a far ideal, like Rumi's ideal in "Infidel Fish":

> In this world full of shape,
> There you are with no form. (166)

Can we hope for a diaphanous theory, unafraid of its affinities with silence, death, the void? Is that possible? Is it useful? Or are the lineaments of that ideal already part of our arts, like a vanishing blackbird making the last circle visible in the sky?

This I know: an essay of this kind will never catch the thirteenth blackbird in full flight.

*

In this last section, all the blackbirds now invisible at the edge—the edge not of the topic but of my sight—I want to avoid closure and think against myself.

I realize that before Thales of Milesia ever drew breath, the claims of the particular and the aspirations of the universal had quarreled, and continue to quarrel still. Perhaps theory, then, should renounce the hope of becoming a global theory, satisfied to become, instead, a set of local practices, each looking over its shoulder at other practices, all of them aware of the great world.

I realize also that I may have put too heavy a burden on trust as a theoretical principle. Perhaps a weaker version of it can do us for a while, something combining dispassion with empathy, something ready to translate itself, to risk its own assumptions, to let go when ripeness calls.

And I realize that I have spoken of spirit often without ever defining it. In

Wittgenstein's sense, spirit is everything we mean when we talk about it. (*Webster* gives 25 definitions of the word.) But spirit is also more specific in my usage because it comes to us in the guise of self-dispossession, a way of suspending our wants to look and watch.

Finally, I realize how glib the tongue grows when it speaks of spirit, skimming the abyss. True self-dispossession demands, as Eliot said in *Four Quartets*, "A condition of complete simplicity / (Costing not less than everything)" (39). Who can afford simplicity at this exorbitant price, the obverse of the terrible simplicity of fanaticism, the antithesis of rooted self-regard?

What I have offered, then, is neither theory nor assured ideas, only hints and queries, in twelve perspectives—no, not thirteen. The possibilities, I hope, sketch a pattern, trace the fissures in our thinking about literary theory today. In the end, we cannot theorize literature completely without denying the essential shadows in ourselves. The "snowy mountains" and the "indecipherable cause," as Wallace Stevens put it, will remain, and this is also something readers need to know.

Works Cited

Benjamin, Walter. "Program of the Coming Philosophy." *The Philosophical Forum*, 15,1-2 (1983-1984): 41-51.

Bloom, Harold. *Shakespeare: The Invention of the Human.* New York: Riverhead Books, 1998.

Dickinson, Emily. *The Complete Poems.* Ed. Thomas H. Johnson. Boston: Little, Brown, 1960.

Eliot, T. S. *Four Quartets.* New York: Harcourt, Brace, 1943.

Emerson, Ralph Waldo. "Nature." *Essays and Lectures.* New York: Library of America, 1983.

Ferguson, Niall. *The War of the World: Twentieth Century Conflict and the Descent of the West.* London: Penguin, 2006.

Friedman, Thomas. *The World Is Flat: A Brief History of the Twenty-First Century.* New York: Farrar, Straus and Giroux, 2005.

Grabes, Herbert. *Einführung in die Literatur und Kunst der Moderne und Postmoderne: Die Ästhetik des Fremden.* Tübingen: Narr, 2004.

Greenfield, Susan. *The Private Life of the Brain.* London: Penguin, 2002.

James, William. *The Will to Believe and Other Essays in Popular Philosophy.* New York: Dover Publications, 1956.

Morrison, Toni. "The Foreigner's Home." Lecture at the Louvre Museum, Paris, November 15, 2006. Excerpts quoted by Alan Riding, "Entr'acte: At the Louvre, Toni Morrison hosts a conversation on exile." *International Herald Tribune*, November 15, 2006, p. 7.

Rumi, Jelaluddin. *The Soul of Rumi: A New Collection of Ecstatic Poems.* Ed. and trans. Coleman Barks. San Francisco: Harper Collins, 2002.

Vendler, Helen. *Poets Thinking.* Cambridge: Harvard University Press, 2004.

Wilson, E. O. *Consilience: The Unity of Knowledge.* New York: Random House, 1998.

18

Helen Vendler

The Future of English: The Future of the Lyrical Imagination

These days, the media constantly remind us of the status of English as a world language. And in spite of vague predictions of universal translation machines, English is certain to be, for the immediate future, the language of scientific and business communication. But we must not forget, in the midst of all the clichés about Global English, that people learning English for practical purposes will never possess English as a mother tongue. Nor will most possess English as Conrad or Nabokov did, as a second tongue raised to literary power. And although it is true that we may render our students less provincial by expanding the geographic range of the Anglophone literature that we teach, the argument for deprovincializing them comes phrased, for the most part, in ethical or political terms: we will become more hospitable to others if we recognize that world literature in English, rather than English or American literature, is our mandate; we will support, as citizens, a more benevolent foreign policy if we diminish the estrangement from the foreign that is endemic in all nationalisms. Aesthetic terms are generally absent from these arguments, as is any consideration of the effect on the curriculum of expanding our mandate. And it is always forgotten, in the ethical argument for enlarging student sensibilities, that the sustained study of the past is one of the best ways to deprovincialize students, to make them realize that their personal cultural assumptions are both arbitrary and temporary.

Since everything added to a curriculum entails something subtracted, we need to ask how to give at least as much weight to aesthetic claims as to social desirability. For instance, works from "world English" that are added to the undergraduate curriculum are rarely poems, and even more rarely works of past eras; rather, they are works of fiction or drama by twentieth-century authors. We have been silent on the aesthetic grounds, if any, for the increasing insertion of contemporary works at the expense of the past. And we do not ask to what extent the presence of poetry in the curriculum has been diminished by the geographical, ethical, and political shifting of values in higher education.

We learn from our professional organizations that enrollments in literary studies have fallen and are falling. Increasingly, in the United States, our offerings in "English" timidly respond to consumer preferences. Cultural studies have in many universities displaced literary study; and the undergraduate records of our Ph.D. students are more likely to show courses in film studies, ethnic studies, or gender studies than courses in poetry. For all these reasons, poetry, formerly central to literary education, seems especially threatened in the curriculum, and as a teacher of poetry, I both grieve at its gradual disappearance and seek an altered mandate that will preserve the lyric imagination as an indispensable part of all undergraduate and graduate study.

Although we as professors all do research as scholars and critics, I want here to recall our primary and greatest mission in higher education: the training of the next generation of literary authors, and especially poets. (Later I'll come to our responsibility for the training of literary readers.) It is no secret that young poets (and young novelists, too) benefit from following a serious curriculum in poetry and language. From Harvard alone, with its emphasis on poetry and classical and foreign languages, sprang, in the twentieth century, T. S. Eliot, Wallace Stevens, Robert Frost, Robert Lowell, Adrienne Rich, John Ashbery, Frank O'Hara, and Robert Creeley (as well as many other poets less celebrated). In the long run, cultures are remembered, after all, less for their politicians, their generals, or their businessmen than for the creative works they bequeath to the future—works by poets, dramatists, novelists, painters, sculptors, architects, composers, and philosophers. We as a profession exist to call attention to past and present authors and to train new ones. We engage ourselves in research, writing, and teaching primarily in order to perpetuate literary works, and to reveal the originality in them of imagination and language. There is no major author who has not in youth been an omnivorous, if eclectic, reader; and the authors of tomorrow depend on us to lead them into the green pastures that will nourish their emerging talent. They depend on us, too, to encourage them in the study of another language, since, as they read, they come to realize that most major authors of England and America (like the major authors of Europe) have been bilingual (at least as readers), familiar with one or more classical or modern literatures not written in their native tongue. Such well-schooled authors write powerfully in part because they know precisely, from etymological roots, what a word means and what its connotations are—a knowledge lacking in monolingual readers unless, like Emily Dickinson, they take their lexicon as their daily companion.

How good are we at training the authors of tomorrow? Although literacy is supposedly attained by primary schooling, literary literacy is left, at least in the United States, to us, the third-level instructors. We have few secondary schools that develop literary literacy in English, let alone in a foreign literature, and so our students arrive in our classrooms with almost no interior access to literature through memory and affection. They would not have the resources to praise, with George Herbert, "Lovely enchanting language, sugar cane, / Honey of roses." In spite of Herbert's accomplishment in writing poetry in Latin and Greek as well as in English, his heart was with the verbal plenitude and literary possibilities of his mother tongue. As he says in his sonnet "The Son" (which relishes the pun, unique to English, on the astronomical "sun" and the heavenly "Son"):

> Let foreign nations of their language boast,
> What fine variety each tongue affords:
> I like our language, as our men and coast;
> Who cannot dress it well, want wit, not words.

The preference for one's mother tongue may be irrational, but it remains true that only in the mother tongue can poets write lasting and influential poetry. Rilke's scores of poems in French do not equal his poems in German; and Brodsky's poetry in English—for all his prose competence in the language—is feeble. Even in the case of Nabokov, a marvelous pasticheur, the poetry in English, though more than competent, does not equal in originality the English prose. There is, even in the case of genius, an obstacle to writing poetry in words that are unconnected with early Oedipal passion and the concomitant first acquisition of language.

Will there be authors and readers in our future if our students do not become lovers of language, relishing its taste on the tongue, feeling in every word a unique sensation and weight? The love of language arises at two significant moments—when, for the first time, a student hears a tone, a syntax, a rhythm, that makes him realize that language can be both arresting and solacing; or when a student hears replicated, in language, a contour already mentally present in his mind but never previously articulated in his reading. The first *coup de foudre* is perhaps independent of content: musicality of collocation and grace of cadence can be detected even when hearing poetry read in a language not one's own. But the second reason is not independent of content: it depends on an incoherent but strong awareness in the student of some emotional, imaginative, or intellectual insight that he does not yet have the vocabulary or the rhythm to express. As Emerson said, when our thoughts speak to us from an author's page, they acquire an alienated majesty. The student learns that his own thoughts are indeed majestic. This is such a powerful realization that innumerable adolescents have been won to literature by a single such moment.

As a reader, one can joyously recognize the power of words enacting a contour of experience without feeling a drive to replicate that power, just as one can listen to music without desiring to become a composer. Nonetheless, students must grasp, at least partially, the peculiar impulse of literary composition if they are to understand how literature both imitates and necessarily reshapes its life-origins. How can we make real, to students, the mimetic appetite of the author and the equally necessary departure from transcriptive mimesis? And how can our students be brought to differentiate adequate from inadequate aesthetic representation? Keats, in his Induction to *The Fall of Hyperion*, distinguishes the poor dreamers whose unuttered dreams are permanently and silently stifled by "sable charm / And dumb enchantment" from dreamers whose imagination can successfully find expression in language. He pities, he says, fanatics and savages who

> have not
> Trac'd upon vellum or wild Indian leaf
> The shadows of melodious utterance.
> But bare of laurel they live, dream, and die;
> For Poesy alone can tell her dreams,
> With the fine spell of words alone can save
> Imagination from the sable charm
> And dumb enchantment. Who alive can say
> "Thou art no poet; may'st not tell thy dreams"?
> Since every man whose soul is not a clod
> Hath visions, and would speak, if he had lov'd
> And been well nurtured in his mother tongue.

It is up to us to ensure that the nascent authors of the twenty-first century are "well nurtured in [their] mother tongue," and are brought to love it. The future of the lyric imagination is—at least in part—in our hands.

I speak not only of those of us who are teaching literature in English to students whose mother tongue is English, but also of those who are teaching English literature to students who may eventually write poetry in their own maternal language. We all know how indispensable it has been to poets writing in English—from Chaucer to Heaney—to have read poetry in languages other than their own; it is equally indispensable that young poets in Russia or Germany or Poland or China read great poetry written in English. But if poetry is not included in the English-language curriculum, will youthful readers find it by themselves? Most will not. And of course, until recently, foreign poetry thought to be "bourgeois" was banned from Marxist countries. I recall speaking to a Chinese university professor just after China was opened to the West. He had received his Ph.D. from a first-rate American university, writing a dissertation on Keats. In my naïveté, I asked him whether he had been teaching Keats in China. He looked at me, pitying my incomprehension, and said gently, "Sometimes I have felt able to use a line from Keats to illustrate a point of syntax." We have no such official ban in place in the United States, but we have an informal cultural ban on poetry that has caused its virtual suppression from elementary and secondary education, and has now increasingly deleted it from post-secondary education, even in our departments of English. The distrust of literature and its sister arts is a legacy from our dissident founders, who tendered to consider the arts as the diversions of a dissolute elite: I am told that it took a full vote of the Board of Trustees of Swarthmore, in 1879, to allow a piano to be installed on campus.

Poetry has sunk from attention for other reasons as well. The social practices that nurtured poetry in the past—hymn singing, choral recitation, memorizing poetry, learning classical languages—have largely vanished from the modern child's world. Popular songs have neither the sublimity of hymns nor the linguistic ingenuity of canonical poetry. With the absence of training in the classical languages, the knowledge of etymology is disappearing; and even if etymological roots are taught, as they sometimes are, in spelling lessons, the root has no emotional power for the student because it has not been encountered in a line of Virgil or a passage from Catullus. Because we, in the universities, cannot replace those past social practices, it is all the more important that we familiarize our proto-poets with the principal glories of English poetry. What they need above all, these proto-poets, is a training of the ear, which comes from a training in regular rhythms. As Eliot said, accomplished free verse is constantly adverting to traditional line-lengths and cadences. A curriculum consisting largely of modern free verse robs the student's ear of the inherited rhythmic practice of formal verse.

Poetry itself will not die, but in our day the traditional poem may vanish, as the Polish poet Zbigniew Herbert foresees in his poem called "Wagon." Herbert has read that even the Emperor participates in the Japanese yearly competition in traditional poetry, and he imagines the centenarian Hirohito—who formerly composed anything from "acts of pardon" to "elaborate tortures"—writing a poem—"the venerable tanka"—on the competition's set theme, "a wagon." Hirohito's tanka, reticent and self-contained, devoid of either pity or hope, with "no false posturings," is, says Herbert, "different / from the glibly lachrymal / handiwork of modernity / full of triumphal howling." "I wonder," Herbert continues,

> I wonder
> with an aching heart
> what will be the fate
> of traditional poetry
>
> will it pass away
> after the emperor's shadow

perishable

negligible[1]

I wonder, with Herbert, what kind of poetry can be produced by young monoglot authors unacquainted with the rhythms and forms of pre-twentieth century poetry (not to speak of the rhythms of the Bible), unable to read in a second language, and having only a vague demotic sense of the meanings of words. Even the monolingual Whitman and Dickinson had sedulously read formal poetry of the past, from the Psalms through Shakespeare to Tennyson and Barrett Browning. They had absorbed all sorts of structural and generic forms along with verse forms, and, as James Merrill says, "Form's what affirms."

Merrill puts that aphorism into a witty segment of his long Arabian Nights sequence, "The Thousand and Second Night." Part 4 of the sequence offers a parody of a class in which a professor is teaching the opening segment of the sequence. The professor not only begins pedantically (with empty remarks on pentameter quatrains and abstractions of theme), but also huffs and puffs evasively as he responds to students, fobbing off their desire for ethical relevance by an aphorism which he dimly knows to be true—"Form's what affirms"—but which he cannot convincingly defend. Here is the desiccated professor, mischievously ventriloquized by Merrill:

> Now if the class will turn back to this, er,
> Poem's first section—Istanbul—I shall take
> What little time is left today to make
> Some brief points. So. The rough pentameter
>
> Quatrains give way, you will observe, to three
> Interpolations, prose as well as verse.
> Does it come through how each in turn refers
> To mind, body, and soul (or memory)?
>
> It does? Good. No, I cannot say offhand
> Why this should be. I find it vaguely satis—
> Yes please? The poet quotes too much? Hm. That is
> One way to put it. Mightn't he have planned
>
> For his own modest effort to be seen

---

[1] Zbigniew Herbert, *The Collected Poems, 1956-1998*, tr. and ed. Alissa Valles (NY: HarperCollins, 2007), 450-52.

Against the yardstick of the "truly great"
(In Spender's phrase)? Fearing to overstate
He lets *them* do it—lets their words, I mean,

Enhance his—Yes, what now? Ah. How and when
Did he "affirm"? Why, constantly. And how else
But in the form. Form's what affirms. That's well
Said, if I do—[*Bells ring.*] Go, gentlemen.[2]

If this is the wrong way to teach poetry, what would be the right way? In the poem under discussion in that airless classroom, "The Thousand and Second Night," Merrill accuses himself of being emotionally paralyzed, "Cold and withdrawn." Appearing normal to others but to his own view a "vain / Flippant unfeeling monster," he recalls the "thousand and one nights" of his past erotic life—"They were grotesque."[3] What professor, facing a group of students who have read this wrenching meditation on the abject humiliations of eros, would begin by speaking of pentameters? Merrill does not offer a counter-example of a better class, but we can imagine that it might begin by evoking the griefs of the poem, might suggest the difficulties of putting such interior disquiet into imaginative form, and might comment on the allusion to *A Thousand and One Nights*: what happens, asks the title of Merrill's poem—"The Thousand and Second Night"—when Scheherazade's voice falls silent? Imagining that emptiness might bring students into the atmosphere of the poem.

Our restoration of poetry to a central place in our classrooms will serve no purpose unless our students are led to perceive its intrinsic function, which is, as Merrill says in the poem "Processional," to alchemize language, change LEAD to GOLD. Although, he concedes, life's motion sometimes declines from better to worse, it can nonetheless go in the other direction, just as a "demotic" drop of water may be temporarily elevated to a "Mandarin" snowflake, or—and here Merrill descends to a word game, "word golf," which challenges the player to transform one word into another by changing one letter at a time—

Or in three lucky strokes of word golf LEAD
Once again turns (LOAD, GOAD) to GOLD.[4]

Merrill reminds us, too, that poetic words, once memorized, infuse them-

---

[2]   James Merrill, *Collected Poems*, ed. J. D. McClatchy and Stephen Yenser (New York: Alfred A Knopf, 2001), 184-85.

[3]   Ibid., 180-81.

[4]   Ibid., 583.

selves into students' very being. So words sank into his being when he and his schoolmates (in an all-male secondary school) acted in Shakespearean plays, in which he was cast, at various times, as a Herald, Puck, Goneril, and Prospero:

> And that flushed, far-reaching hour came back
> Months of rehearsal in the gymnasium
> Had led to: when the skinny nobodies
> Who'd memorized the verse and learned to speak it
> Emerged in beards and hose (or gowns and rouge)
> Vivid with character, having put themselves
> All unsuspecting into the masters' hands.[5]

The students have put themselves into their schoolmasters' hands with no notion that they will become, interiorly, the characters whose speeches they speak; but as they recite their parts they have put themselves into the master Shakespeare's hands as well.

Seamus Heaney, in "The Real Names"—another poem about schoolboys acting in plays by Shakespeare[6]—makes a similar claim for the power of lines of Shakespeare memorized and acted out. If our classrooms are to quicken the sensibilities of future poets, our students must learn by heart, be nurtured in and by, the poetry of their mother tongue. We must encourage them to feel form before learning technical terms for it. An *ottava rima* stanza feels different from blank verse; a multi-stanza poem feels different from a single-block sonnet; a poem in the present tense has a different atmosphere from a poem in the imperfect; a poem in the third-person plural is worlds away from a poem in the first-person singular. The speech acts of a poem confer a form of their own: the "inner weather" (in Frost's words) generated by, say, an address to a god is not the weather of an elegy, just as an elegy cannot display the benign warmth of an epithalamion. It is these "auras" of the genres that we need to teach, especially by having students recite aloud, singly or collectively, poems they have studied; and, in spite of their protests that they are not good at memorizing, urging them to internalize, if they can, their favorite poems. If we adopt these means, we will not be failing our future poets—or novelists: we know that Faulkner, like so many other proto-novelists, composed and even published poems before he wrote his novels.

A contemporary workaday English used for transactional, commercial, and

---

5 Ibid., 422.
6 Seamus Heaney, *Electric Light* (London: Faber & Faber, 2001).

instrumental purposes will take care of itself, and is not—although we all spend time training our students to write acceptable prose—our primary concern. Our concern is to transmit, explain, and preserve the art of literature—its genres, its overlapping and evolving structures, its linguistic reaches, its aesthetic energies—so that our young Anglophone writers are well nourished in their mother tongue, and young writers from other countries can borrow what they need from our poetry. We cannot let the teaching of literature be subdued into dumbness and indifference, even if the cultures in which we live prize our results less than those of science and technology. We all share a wonder at the explosion of twentieth-century science; no woman, certainly, would choose to have been born before the twentieth century. But we need to claim art's profound difference from the sciences, and affirm the necessity, to any culture, of the production and the study of art.

The sciences evolve with spectacular rapidity towards better states of themselves; but poetry does not. It changes, of course, as it throws up new forms of genius; in the seventeenth century there was no Wordsworth, as in the nineteenth century there was no Stevens. But Marvell is as brilliant today as he ever was, and so is Keats. Literary changes are additive and imaginative, not progressively evolutionary, and they consequently represent a type of excellence (in the mind and imagination) different from that of the natural sciences and their accompanying technologies.[7] The arts and their adjunct disciplines are different, too, from the social sciences. Training in the creation of, and the response to, any art aims at a delicacy of medium and a boldness of the imagination which are not the explicit aims of training in the social sciences. So we must continue to declare, often in the face of public incomprehension, that if we do not have imaginative artists refreshing our sensibility and our language, our culture and idiom will petrify. We must invite the public to imagine a thought-experiment in which all the literary and artistic ventures of the English-speaking imagination never occurred, in which there had been no Shakespeare and no Dickinson, no Constable and no Eakins, no Dowland and no Ives. A world so culturally deprived cannot be the one we desire for our children's future. It is up to us, in the field of literature, to perpetuate authorship and a relish in authorship, even if in the current inhospitable environment we must remind ourselves, with George Herbert, that "We are the trees whom shaking fastens more." The arts will not suffer extinction, nor will the study of the arts.

For Eliot, every individual talent developed in the matrix of tradition, and

---

7   The Harvard *Gazette*, the official organ of the Faculty of Arts and Sciences, does not think of what humanists do as "research." Although they are eager to disseminate the new findings of scientists and social scientists, they decline to report on our published results, saying (in the words of one staffer) "We don't do book reviews."

could be understood only in the light of the tradition from which it arose. But the preservation of the art of the past, so natural (in Eliot's mind) for the understanding of the new, has been thought by some to be politically limiting. I recall having to be the respondent, at a conference in Ireland in 1971, to a paper by Raymond Williams. Since Williams had not sent me the paper beforehand, I had no time to mull over the shock of what I heard him say that day. He was arguing against our teaching the works of any traditional authors at all, because, he said, they insensibly subdued the minds of students to feudal ideas. In the past, he continued, he used to exempt Shakespeare, until he realized that even though Shakespeare's plays were often skeptical of established thought, they nonetheless—by not imagining democracy or socialism—reinforced and ratified monarchy and a stratified society. He ended by saying that he would now discard Shakespeare from the curriculum, too. I asked, more as a rhetorical question than a real one, what authors he would then teach in his literature classes at Cambridge? He answered sincerely, "The Beatles." And he would not be moved from that position.

The poets themselves have always known that they could not have given birth to their new poetry without a profound relation to tradition—tradition in its living sense. But what do we mean by a "living" tradition? Wallace Stevens considered that question in a 1945 poem called "Tradition,"[8] in which he attempts various definitions of the concept. As Stevens begins to seek a visual form that would satisfy his sense of tradition, he asks whether the appropriate image would be something like Rodin's "The Thinker." No, says Stevens, repudiating any form of fixed wisdom. Perhaps, he thinks, tradition can be equated with memory: after all, Mnemosyne was the mother of the Muses. But he discards this speculation as well, since it yields nothing but the "secondhand". Is tradition, he wonders, the embodied archetype of human experience, "the final form / To which all other forms, at last return, / The frame of a repeated effect, is it that?" This suggestion dies, as a more frightening question is posed: is tradition finally useless, an unintelligible past inscribed in an arithmetic we have forgotten, an alphabet we cannot learn?

All these definitions of tradition are too remote to represent Stevens's living sense of tradition. Finally, searching for the elusive image that would stand up under his inquiry, he finds it. However, he does not immediately name its source in a classical text, but rather describes what it would look like as an image held in the mind:

> It has a clear, a single, a solid form,

---

8   *Collected Poetry and Prose* (New York: Library of America, 1997), 595-96.

That of the son who bears upon his back
The father that he loves, and bears him from
The ruins of the past...
                    The son restores
The father. He hides his ancient blue beneath

His own bright red. But he bears him out of love,
His life made double by his father's life[.]

At last Stevens concedes his Virgilian and neo-classical sources, suggesting that the form tradition wears is that of Aeneas seen by Nicolas Poussin.

The incantation that follows issues from a son who lost his own father: Stevens' father refused to attend his wedding, and Stevens never again saw his father or entered his father's house. Because Stevens knows the severity of the loss of the Oedipal father, of a warmly continuous family line, his filial attachment to a living tradition is both wistful and insistent:

The father keeps on living in the son, the world
Of the father keeps on living in the world
Of the son. These survivals out of time and space
Come to us every day.

We hope to enkindle in our students this living and filial sense of tradition, so that they know we sustain the past out of love, as Aeneas bore Anchises out of the ruins of Troy. Our students, however much they may know of contemporary work, cannot be bearers of the linguistic and imaginative continuity of human experience unless they become aware—in the ever-eclectic way of young writers—of the works of literary predecessors, in and out of their own mother tongue. Tradition is a burden, as Stevens's image explicitly declares, but it is a burden borne willingly.

If this is so, then we make a wretched mistake in cutting great swaths of past literature from the curriculum in order to make room for the relatively unsifted contemporary. The contemporary, after all, cannot be understood in such artificial isolation. And any desirable ethical results (the enlarging of the students' awareness of other minds and other cultures) cannot be brought about—in the particular domain of the arts—by excluding the aesthetic as the chief motive and reward for creation. Just as ethical results, for the writer, are attainable only through a perfecting of technique that will give his passionate belief a lasting form, so ethical results for students can be obtained only by their internalizing literature as an art—and not as an art of pentameters, or of desirable political ends, but as an art of the imagination symbolically reconceiving human experience, making Rome rise out of Troy's ruins.

In a late poem, "The Sail of Ulysses," Stevens claimed that "The mind renews the world in a verse, / A passage of music, a paragraph / By a right philosopher."[9] It is to renew the world of our students that we teach verse that has itself renewed the tradition from which it comes. Stevens said in a late letter, "My own way out toward the future involves a confidence in the spiritual role of the poet, who will somehow have to assist the painter, etc. (any artist, to tell the truth) in restoring to the imagination what it is losing at such a catastrophic pace, and in supporting what it has gained."[10] "What it has gained": while not refusing the elegiac, Stevens asserts that ridding the imagination of superannuated ideas that no longer compel belief, and discarding forms that have lost contemporary flexibility is, in the long run, a gain. But it will be a gain only if the old beliefs are not forgotten, but rather transformed; if the old forms are not dismissed, but rather transmuted.

English as a profession is, then, to be in the future what it always has been, informally and formally: the nurturer of writers who will find original words and forms for contemporary experience, and the nurturer of readers who will value those writers' originality. As we know from living through the twentieth century, when imagination is forced underground the expressive impulses of human beings will not be very long denied; writers spring up, at great cost, to reclaim—often in ingenious unpunishable forms of allegory and symbol—their right to free thought and its symbolic articulation. Without tradition, where would the oppressed poets of the past century—in Germany, Northern Ireland, Hungary, Poland, Greece—have found their devastating allegories and their powerful symbols? Without tradition, how would their readers have been able to interpret those allegories, those symbols? It is natural that one of our responsibilities as teachers of literature is to transmit the great stories created by the human imagination—the Greek myths, the epic events of the Hebrew Bible, the parables of the gospels, the fairy-tales and legends that come flooding our way from South America or India or Japan. But insofar as we are teachers of poetry, our mandate is to illuminate the indispensability to great literature of original language and imaginative form. By revealing the many strategies invented by poets to enact imaginative thought—strategies of genre, symbol, structure, cadence, speech acts, tone, syntax, rhythms, and rhymes—we can nurture our students in the memorable new and its inheritance from, and transgression of, the memorable old. There will always be arguments about the new; and the old is often difficult to teach to the young. But if we are to nourish the poets of the future, we must

---

[9]   Ibid., 465.
[10]   *Letters of Wallace Stevens* (New York: Knopf, 1966) 340 (June 1, 1939, to Henry Church).

give them the past in all its abundance, symbolic and linguistic. "How but in custom and in ceremony / Are innocence and beauty born?" asks Yeats. We are the midwives of that birth by which innocence and beauty are renewed in contemporary language out of the custom and ceremony of the past.

I do not discount our second function: to create readers. "To have great writers, there must be great audiences, too," said Walt Whitman. Our students who will become mothers and fathers, scientists and stockbrokers, physicians and lawyers, may because of us become also the readers who will understand and praise the writers of their moment. We need to offer, and to examine, the works of first-rate writers because mediocre authors are not convincing, do not sustain the mind, and do not inspire more reading. Mediocre voices do not leap off the page and become living beings; it takes a great strategist of language to bring about that miracle. If our students once see how it deepens their emotional lives to encounter them on a living page, they will not have to imitate the poor ghosts, in Stevens's poem "Large Red Man Reading,"[11] who, not having been aware that their feelings could be imaged in words, creep up after death to hear the poet read "from the poem of life":

> There were those that returned to hear him read from the poem of life,
> Of the pans above the stove, the pots on the table, the tulips among them. . . .
>
> *Poesis, poesis,* the literal characters, the vatic lines,
>
> Which in those ears and in those thin, those spended hearts,
> Took on color, took on shape and the size of things as they are
> And spoke the feeling for them, which was what they had lacked.

The genres of literature—poetry, drama, fiction—intersect, as we know, with several scholarly disciplines (history, sociology, political science, philosophy, and so on); but although such disciplines may inform our understanding, they are not themselves literary creations, and they are not intent on delighting as powerfully as they instruct. It is up to us to keep always in mind our principal obligation— to nurture through literature the writers and readers who will animate and alter the consciousness, and with it the conscience, of their era. At every moment we should be asking ourselves whether our assignments and our classroom lectures will enhance the eager powers of the potential writers and readers before us, so that they will encounter the past borne towards them as an illumination by which to judge and understand the present.

---

[11] *Collected Poetry and Prose,* 365.

As for our intellectual life beyond the classroom, our immemorial scholarly and critical work—pursued no longer in the scriptorium but rather on the computer—permits us to rediscover that transporting experience of solitude in the company of art that revives our early adolescent joy in what Emily Dickinson called "this consent of Language / This loved Philology."[12] Out of that early transport comes all that we do.

---

[12] *The Poems of Emily Dickinson*, ed. Thomas H. Johnson (Cambridge, MA: The Belknap Press of Harvard University Press, 1965), #1651, "A Word made Flesh is seldom."

19

Elizabeth Closs Traugott

The State of English Language Studies: A Linguistic Perspective

1. Introduction[1]

In 2006 there was much discussion among linguists and members of the public, including the *New York Times*, about a claim that Núñez and Sweetser made in *Cognitive Science* regarding the spatial metaphors used to express future time in Aymara, a language of Bolivia and Peru. In this language, the future is "behind," and the past "in front." Of course, this is not unique to the Aymara; they are not aliens (as some surmised), but have simply conventionalized as their norm what we also sometimes use metaphorically, as in Marvell's *at my back I always hear time's winged chariot hurrying near*, or only marginally, in grammatical constructions such as *The meeting was moved back a week*. Was it moved earlier or later? If later, then the "future is behind" metaphor is being used—a very understandable one, since the future is unknown and what is behind our back is also unknown.

I have been asked to talk about the state of English studies from the point of view of linguistics and language arts. I take linguistics to be the study and theory of what it is we know as users of a language (unconsciously or not), and language arts to be the pedagogical study and teaching of language. Since I know more about linguistics than language arts, I will focus on linguistics, especially directions it has been recently been taking in the US and the English-speaking world. For better or worse, linguistics has in the last half century been situated in the English-speaking world, and therefore much that happens in English linguistics is what happens in linguistics (though hopefully that will change). The recent past and present are reasonably clear, but the future is murky, very much in the unknown space behind me. One thing is clear about the recent past, however:

---

[1] Many thanks to Marianne Thormählen for inviting a plenary talk on language studies. I am grateful to Anne Curzan and Merja Kytö for comments on some issues raised in this paper, and to members of the IAUPE audience who asked challenging and important questions, especially Carol Kaske. Liz Coppock helped me access some of the electronic data bases.

what was marginal only a decade or so ago has become or is becoming mainstream, and is encouraging new avenues of work.

Since we all use language, and, unlike blood, it is "out there" to be heard and seen, we all in some sense feel we are experts on it, and we might wonder why it needs to be studied in systematic detail. Although other animals clearly have communicative systems, humans appear to be unique in being able to talk about the future and about hypothetical ideas. If we are to understand ourselves as thinkers, creators, and communicators, an analytic approach to this unique ability will enhance our ability to define ourselves, and to fully appreciate the role of language in human life.

Much of what we know about language is unconscious. We know that we can say *I'd like to use the edition you have*, and that we can reduce *you have* in *I'd like to use the edition you've assigned*, and we also know we cannot reduce it in *I'd like to use the edition you've*, in the sense that we would not say it. We have learned complex rules like this without explicit instruction, and for the most part are totally unaware of them. This raises important questions about the brain, and how we acquire this kind of knowledge. Linguistics attempts to answer such questions, by analyzing language much in the same way as the medical and physical sciences seek to understand the nature and chemistry of blood or of the ozone. When things go wrong, as in autism, or brain damage, linguistic analysis can help those seeking to provide a remedy. Furthermore, in the current world where language is so important across cultural, gendered, and other potential divides, the study of language, its power and its limitations, is an essential ingredient in comprehending social dynamics.[2]

Because language affects so much of what we do and who we are, linguistics is a bit like an octopus, with tentacles stretching out in all kinds of directions (though eight arms turn out not to be nearly enough!). Obvious connections that come to mind include the following—this is not meant to be an exhaustive list, but simply to suggest how inter-disciplinary the linguistic enterprise is:

- pedagogy (including native and second language teaching); the tradition of grammar-teaching goes back to the Greeks, Romans, and Sanskrit scholars of millennia ago,
- literature (a major factor in the development of linguistics in Europe; here the connection to philology and understanding of earlier literary texts is important, an enterprise that has now shifted, along with "literature", to the study of texts in general),
- anthropology (a major factor in the US, with work on American Indian languages; much of this is now concerned with cross-linguistic typology, language and culture, and language endangerment),

---

[2] For fuller discussion of the issues, see Curzan and Adams.

- sociology (e.g., the interaction of language, ethnicity, race, and gender; workplace discourse),
- forensics (language as evidence in criminal investigations),
- philosophy (both logic and ordinary language philosophy, and the issue of utterance meaning vs. sentence meaning),
- psychology and cognitive science (language acquisition, common ground, intelligence),
- computer science (information retrieval, parsing, etc.; artificial intelligence; models of evolution),
- neuroscience (physiological brain studies, using MRI, and PET scans, etc.),
- genetics (is there evidence of language-dedicated DNA?).

The potentials are enormous, but we need to find better ways to get the various separate tentacles better networked with each other and better attached to the disciplines. As I will explain later, I think we may in some cases be getting closer to being able to do so than we have been.

2. Twentieth Century Linguistics

Since everything arises out of or in reaction to something earlier, to situate my discussion, I start with a brief glimpse of twentieth century linguistics and language arts.

One of the striking things about twentieth century linguistics is that there were two dominant figures, one at the beginning, Ferdinand de Saussure, and another in the middle, Noam Chomsky. Their influence beyond linguistics, on the thinking of the time, was, and still is, enormous, Saussure's especially in the humanities and social sciences, Chomsky's in computer science, and recently neurosciences. Though neither man necessarily invented the intellectual paradigm he is associated with, they nevertheless found ways to develop the discourses that shape ideologies. Inevitably, their work had far-reaching institutional implications. Saussure established linguistics as an autonomous discipline: "the only true object of study in linguistics is the language, considered in itself and for its own sake" (230). Harris (xii) points out that there is no evidence that Saussure himself said this, but his pupils who were his editors, Charles Bally and Albert Sechehaye, did, and this ideology lasted well into the late twentieth century and is still alive. While agreeing in principle, Chomsky also inspired the creation of larger-scale cognitive science groups, of which linguistics is just one member.

Saussure was a distinguished historical linguist by training and practice, but his legacy has been construed primarily as a synchronic one. I will mention a few of his key hypotheses, because, although they are well-known, I will come back to them one way or another.

- Synchrony vs. diachrony. Saussure distinguished system as something stable, accessible only from the idealized perspective of an atemporal viewpoint ("synchrony"); to him diachrony was identifiable with individual changes, not with systems. The perspective that pays no or little attention to time and dynamic emergence became one of the hall-marks of structuralism in the twentieth century.
- Langue vs. parole. Langue is famously the shared homogeneous system, the abstract rules of the game. Parole is the actual moves of the game (utterances). His interlocutors are mirror images of each other, homogeneous in thought and all else.

Figure 1. Symmetric communication (Saussure 11)

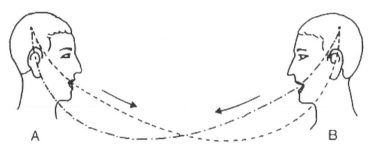

- The basic unit of langue is the sign: a meaning-form pair that is a mental entity; it is also arbitrary, and discrete. "The essential feature of Saussure's linguistic sign is that, being intrinsically arbitrary, it can be identified only by contrast with coexisting signs of the same nature, which together constitute a structured system" (Harris x).

Chomsky's *Syntactic Structures* was published exactly one hundred years after Saussure's birth, in 1957. He rejected the central role of meaning and of social factors that had driven Saussure's and many of his followers' view of language. Instead of langue and parole he proposed:

- Competence vs. performance. "Competence" is the language capacity, the system internalized by the individual language-user: "Linguistic theory is concerned primarily with an ideal speaker-listener, in a completely homogeneous speech-community, who knows its language perfectly" (Chomsky 1965, 3).
- Cognition vs. communication. Rejecting the behaviorism of the first part of the century, especially in the US, and Saussurean notions of language

as social contract, Chomsky took a cognitive turn and focused attention on the study of mind and brain. The mind was conceived as a computer, and theories were valued by their internal consistency rather than their faithfulness to empirical data.

- Privileging of child language acquisition. Chomsky insisted that the important question was how a child comes to learn a language. Assuming that input to the child is skewed and inadequate for learning, he concluded that much of language must be innate. The study of UG and I-language—universal (innate) grammar and internalized competence—came to be privileged over that of E-language—externalized language or usage.
- The core of the language capacity is syntax, most especially the system that underlies our capacity to produce and understand an infinite set of new sentences. Structures are all basically similar: they are XP's (minimal, binary branching phrases, such as are illustrated in Figure 2 for the abstract structure underlying *He discussed the problem with John on Monday*).

Figure 2. An example of branching XPs (Cinque 146)

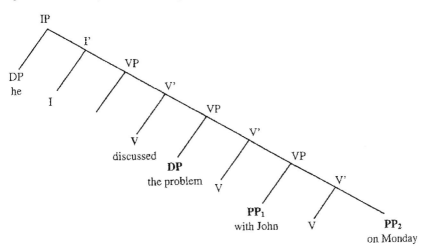

The effect of Chomsky's theory was enormously exciting not only in linguistics, but in computer science and artificial intelligence as well, where huge successes emerged using syntax as the basis for computerized parsing and production, and in psychology and cognitive sciences, where the study of the mind came to dominate.

Initially it was exciting for the language arts too. In the late sixties and early seventies, literary stylistics benefited from the study of the syntax of novelists and poets (see essays collected in, e.g., Carter and Freedman). There were also pedagogical texts like Roberts, based on his *Roberts English Series*, which was used from grade school through college. But in the end Chomskyan generative grammar proved disastrous for the language arts, at least in the US. For one, it was not directly relevant to language teaching, since it was concerned with UG and competence, but teachers are concerned with performance. For another, if one takes the logic of individual innate capacity for language too far, or becomes discouraged by the technicalities of formalisms, one can end up saying a) one doesn't need to learn any other language as one's native language is the only one that one can really know, b) one doesn't need to learn grammar, because it is innate. When I started teaching in California in 1964, every potential teacher of English was required to take a course in the structure and history of English. By the end of the 1970's most school districts had dropped that requirement. Linguistics lost social value in the educational arena while gaining considerable kudos in the technical one.

3. Twenty-first Century Linguistics

Rapid forward to the present century. There have been social shifts toward discourses about diversity. It is a time when the public demands a voice. This is a time of *American Idol*, and of YouTube, a time when the British Library spent the month of May working with Microsoft to collect a time-capsule not of "official history" but of "a democratic resource": representative email (*New York Times*, 29 May 2007). It is also a time when in the sciences and engineering tiny units are matched with huge abstract structures, as in nanotechnology, or in cosmology where the current microphysical world is linked with the big picture of fourteen or more billion years since the big bang. Linguistics has not been unaffected.

In linguistics there are many names in the twenty-first century, but none that can be singled out as a galvanizing force and lightning rod across disciplines, such as Chomsky was in the later fifties and early sixties. Perhaps that is why the shift in thinking that has occurred in linguistics (and elsewhere) may not be so high-profile or so noticeable as Saussure's or Chomsky's ideologies. But a radical shift has been taking place since the eighties, slow at first, but now significant, from a theory of mind abstracted from context and time to a theory of mind that includes the social being behaving and interacting dynamically with others in time and space. Empirical evidence for abstract theory, and explicit attention to heterogeneity, whether in social or structural variations, are coming to be of central concern. So is micro-analysis within macro-theory.

Whatever the force of changes outside of linguistics, there was a very specific event in linguistics that helped change practices and ideologies: the advent of corpora (digitized data collections). This opened up access to vast quantities of text and spoken language, and encouraged work on language as use and on frequency (in other words, on parole, and performance). Many of these were corpora of English. There was the *Brown Corpus*, a corpus of written American English developed in the mid-twentieth century (Kucera and Francis). Then came the *Helsinki Corpus* of the History of English developed by Rissanen and his colleagues, which allows us to retrieve examples in context, and from a balanced series of texts meant to represent the development of standard British English.[3] We find trials, education manuals, manuals for veterinarians, and scientific works, as well as Chaucer and Shakespeare. A large number of other corpora were developed. Some are literary and historical (e.g., LION). Many are synchronic, using both written and spoken data (BNC, COBUILD, LOB and many others), with greater and lesser attention to normalization (of size of text, so that percentages might mean something), and to genre, speaker, and other register issues. A further contributing factor was the advent of computerized dictionaries (e.g., DARE, DOE, MED, OED). Suddenly usage studies came to be in, as did investigations of frequency effects (e.g., Bybee and Hopper, and Bybee on *Frequency*, 2007). Invaluable as they are, corpora nevertheless have their problems, since they are dependent on editions and choices of compilers; and, of course, much depends on what one searches for, especially what one considers equivalent (for discussion see Kytö and Romaine, Lindquist and Mair, and Meyer).

At about the same time, in the 1980's, various alternative forms of linguistic theory arose, with focus on meaning as well as form. Especially in the work of people associated with cognitive linguistics (e.g., Lakoff, Langacker), construction grammar (e.g., Fillmore and Kay, and Goldberg), and of typologists working on grammaticalization (e.g., Bybee, Perkins and Pagliuca, and Croft), there has been a return to form-meaning pairings, and to the centrality of metaphor and metonymy (e.g., Barcelona, Ortony, Panther and Radden). Some of the implications for literary studies of this change in perspective are reflected in works by Lakoff and Turner, Stockwell, and Turner, among others.

While linguists who work in these frameworks are often called "functionalists," and thought not to be concerned with formalisms, some want to "generate" (or predict) all and only the possible sentences of the language, much as Chomsky originally proposed (e.g., Goldberg *Constructions*, 1995, 7), and can be quite formal in orientation, either with respect to grammars (e.g., Michaelis) or to variation (e.g., Bybee 2006). The diagram in Figure 3 shows a formal representa-

---

[3]   There is also a dialect corpus. The Brown, Helsinki, and several other corpora are available at ICAME.

tion of *much snow* in one variety of construction grammar. Note how rich with information, both syntactic and semantic, this diagram is compared to Cinque's minimalist syntactic one in Figure 2:

Figure 3. A construction grammar diagram (Fried and Östman 34)

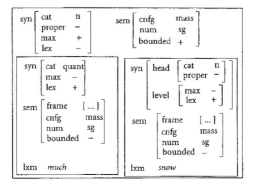

But if there has been a return to form-meaning pairings, they are quite different from Saussure's sign. For one, they are often conceptualized within a theory of language use. For another, they are chunks. In an effort to get away from the universal minimal structure XP, and claims that distinct XPs are innate, attention has been paid to such locutions as *let alone, the more the better, give X to Y,* as fixed expressions. In his paper "Mental packing" and elsewhere, Turner has used the metaphor of language-users walking around with a suitcase of linguistic units of various shapes and sizes that they unpack and use as needed, in different combinations, rather than picking uniformly paired branches off trees. Far from being innate, the chunks are language-specific. What is innate, and universal, if anything, is cognitive ways of experiencing and categorizing the world visually, aurally, etc. It is hypothesized that these ways of experiencing and categorizing the world underlie the dynamic processes by which we put stories together, projecting and blending conceptual meanings, to interpret our world, not language-specific abilities, and certainly not purely syntactic ones.

Erman and Warren proposed that most texts are made up of "prefabs" or "combinations of words" (see also Skandera on formulaic language). A prefab is defined as a combination of words (e.g., *a waste of time, I've got to run*) that is conventionalized, and therefore can be memorized (32). Prefabs "can be assumed to constitute single multi-word retrievals from our mental store of words" (48), with restricted interchangeability. *Good friends* is a prefab not interchangeable with *nice friends* since reciprocity is lost, *I can't see a thing* is not equivalent to *I can't see an object,* nor is *not bad* ('good') equivalent to *not lousy.* Among prefabs are "text monitors" of various types such as *and then, well you know, I mean*, which signal how the relationship between prior and subsequent text is to be understood, and "social monitors" of various types such as *wouldn't it, I see, do sit down*, which signal that attention is being paid to the hearer.

3.1. Some ways in which the object of linguistics has changed for many practitioners

Over the last few decades the object of linguistics has, in other words, changed for many practitioners, as have the evidence for it and the methodologies considered appropriate. Of course no one person does all the things I mention in this section, or regards all of them as equally important, and some people have not made the transition at all; but I think we can see a general pattern of change in the field of linguistics, and hence of English language studies as whole. Below I point to a few of the ways in which this has happened. It is very important to understand that "From X to Y" does NOT mean that X has been abandoned: rather it has been incorporated within the new way of thinking about language (and sometimes has undergone a change as a result).

I must admit a bias toward a constructional and diachronic view of grammar in the ideological shifts I identify here. Since construction grammar grew out of cognitive linguistics, there is a certain bias in that direction too. I have not included work on evolution, genetics, contact languages such as creoles, second language acquisition, translation studies, the materiality of the text, seeking evidence with experimental techniques, etc. Instead my comments are mainly directed toward the language and linguistics sections in the 2007 IAUPE program, where there were sections on lexical semantics, figurative language, discourse linguistics, corpus linguistics, English in the world, and the history of English. Also, I have greatly restricted the number of references in view of length limitations. For aspects of the converging trends mentioned here, see Marmaridou, Nikiforidou, and Antonopoulou; Taylor with focus on work from a cognitive linguistic perspective; and Fischer with focus on change. It is also instructive to look at the two Handbooks on English Linguistics that Blackwell published in 2006 (Aarts and McMahon, and Kemenade and Los) and the two multi-articled Histories of English that also came out in 2006 (Hogg and Denison, and most especially Mugglestone).

   a)   What was marginal in the 1970's has come to be of central interest, above all pragmatics. The Greeks and Romans had no useful terms for expressions like *I mean, I think, well, you know*, and these used to be thought to be a) meaningless, b) if meaningful, not "core." "Why do you study what we edit out?" asked a colleague many years ago, as did my book publisher, until the publication of Schiffrin's *Discourse Markers* revealed their interactional and structural importance. "Core" grammar (semantics, syntax, morphology, phonology) is no longer privileged; everything is of equal importance (Croft 2001, and Goldberg), including pragmatics and phonetics, and idiosyncratic constructions.

b) From homogeneity to heterogeneity. Variation through space, social group and time, multidisciplinarity, and multiculturalism have all come to play center stage (an early work is Weinreich, Labov and Herzog). The talking heads are now more like the couple in Figure 4 than the couple in Figure 1, though they should probably also be multitasking with a TV, computer or other such medium.

Figure 4. Asymmetric, partial communication.

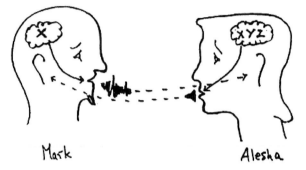

Mark   Alesha

c) From strictly synchronic to dynamic and diachronic. Change is once again considered important, at least as variation through time (Hopper and Traugott); Bloomfield's idea that language change in progress cannot be analyzed has long been exploded by Labov.

d) From cognitive functions alone to cognitive and communicative/interactional functions (e.g., in very different ways, Birner and Ward, Croft in *Explaining Language Change, 2000*, and Givón; see also discussion in Penke and Rosenbach).

e) From competence alone to use as well. It is now almost a truism that virtually no speaker has just one homogeneous system; there are different knowledge structures in different domains (work, family, religion), and no domain proves a complete range of communicative power. In connection with this shift toward language use, Bybee's title "From usage to grammar: The mind's response to repetition" is telling[4]—note "usage," "mind," and the implication that grammar does not preexist use, but arises out of use. Relatedly, there has been a shift of interest in work on language change

---

[4]   This is the written version of her presidential address to the Linguistic Society of America.

from individuals to members of social groups (Nevalainen and Raumolin-Brunberg) and of networks (Fitzmaurice).

f) From introspective data (this is often very close to written language, and restricted to what can occur at the beginning of a discourse) to data of all kinds. For contemporary language, this includes urban speech as well as rural dialects, blogs as well as the *London Times*, letters from death-row inmates as well as from presidents, and also introspection. In historical work texts include Salem witch trials, Old Bailey Proceedings (BAILEY), and recipes, as well as Shakespeare's dramas (Kryk-Kastovsky, Fitzmaurice and Taavitsainen). Grice's assumption of polite, cooperative interaction has given way to a view of interaction that allows for discussion of machiavellian, aggressive interaction.

g) From sentences out of context to clauses in context (the Chomskyan "sentence" is regarded by many, e.g., Thompson and Hopper, as a unit of writing, not of speech). Context may be linguistic (prior and upcoming discourse) or social (sex, social status of speakers, genre), even cultural. Some intriguing work is being done on correlations between meanings and cultural scripts by Wierzbicka and many others. This is a very far cry from the last sentence of Saussure's *Course* that I cited earlier: "the only true object of study in linguistics is the language, considered in itself and for its own sake."

h) Relatedly, from decontextualized product to interactional process and rhetoric. Rhetoric used to be a bad word, associated with political manipulation and brainwashing (Hayakawa), and, from another perspective, Chomsky's comment in 1991: "the best rhetoric is the least rhetoric"—a clearly rhetorical statement! It has, however, become the basis of much discourse analysis (e.g., Mann and Thompson).

i) From discrete to gradient, even hybrid categories (e.g., Denison, Malouf, and Ross). As Fillmore pointed out in a lecture some fifteen years ago, *home* is a "less good/prototypical noun" than *house* (consider *go home*, vs. *go to the house*). Hybrids include complex predicates with gerunds, such as *give a kicking, give a roasting*, which are iterative/durative and perhaps lexical (Trousdale), in contrast to *give a kick/shrug*, which are arguably completive and grammatical (Brinton).

j) From focus on the mind as a computer with little interest in metaphor, metonymy, emotions, or meaning in general to a focus on these (e.g., Barcelona, Panther and Radden). For example, Kövecses discusses how conceptual metaphors such as ANGER/LOVE/CONFLICT/ENTHU-SIASM IS FIRE underlie such idioms as *Smoke was coming out of his ears* (anger), *She carries a torch for him* (love), *The killing sparked off the riot* (conflict), and *He was burning with excitement* (enthusiasm). This kind of thinking motivated two titles in the late eighties: *More than Cool Reason* by Lakoff and Turner, and, taking a line from Wallace Stevens, *Death is the Mother of Beauty* by Turner.

Discussing metonymy, Radden and Kövecses (47-48) show how idiomatic expressions are attributable to perceptual selectivity: MORE OVER LESS (*How tall are you?*; here the upper rather than lower end of scale is chosen; *?How short are you?*); NON-BOUNDED OVER BOUNDED (*We had chicken today*; bounded entity construed as mass substance; *?We had a piece of chicken today*).

    k)   From objectivity to subjectivity and subjectification (Traugott 2003, Athanasiadou, Canakis, and Cornillie, and Cuyckens, Davidse, and Vandelanotte). In *All he said was I want to go home*, *all* does not mean "everything"; the speaker subjectively evaluates his *I want to go home* as inadequate to the situation. *Give a kicking/roasting* are also negative evaluations.

    l)   From child language acquisition to life-long acquisition (Bergs, Milroy).

Of course, the big challenge, as in any field that deals with micro-systems and micro-changes, is how to interpret their relationship to the larger categories that we intuitively and scientifically posit.

4. Two examples

To suggest the flavor of the kind of work done from the new perspectives, I give two very brief examples, one synchronic and the other diachronic.

4.1. Example I (Use of the –s-genitive)

In a recent number of *English Language and Linguistics*, Rosenbach wrote on a subject typical of the twentieth century: -*s*-genitives, but from a not-so-twentieth-century perspective. She looks at "non-proto-typical *s*-genitives" in an electronic corpus of women's magazines, teasing apart different types of meaning.

    Rosenbach takes as relevant a number of well-known factors, such as the animacy and referentiality of the dependent (the nominal marked by –*s*) and also its function: does it restrict a token and denote an individual (this function is usually thought of as a determiner), or does it express a type, is it descriptive, metaphorical, etc. (this function is usually thought of as a modifier)? Consider:

(1)   a.   *John's book* (the dependent is referential, and animate. It restricts the token *book*; this is a determiner construction)

         b.   *women's magazines* (the dependent is non-referential, and animate; this is a construction that is descriptive of a kind)

Rosenbach points out that it has been said (e.g., by Lyons) that it is a peculiarity of English that "the possessor in a determiner genitive renders the whole possessive NP definite, even if the possessor is itself indefinite" (80).

(2)   a teacher's book = the book of a teacher

But it can also express an indefinite relation, as in *a book of a teacher*. The latter may be somewhat hard to interpret (though one can construe "a book for teachers" on a par with "women's magazines"), but with other possessors an ambiguity is easily understood, as in (3).[5]

(3)   I went to a solicitor's office
       a. but he wasn't in (specific, referential reading)
       b. but they are always so overcrowded (non-specific, non-referential reading)

Constructed examples like (3) are often said to be resolvable as in (4a) and (4b).[6] However, in actual use the ambiguity about whether there is a specific referent or not is often not resolved; cf.:

(4)   a. that by ... volunteering as a *physical therapist's assistant* at Children's Hospital, she succeeded in working through her grief ... (J. Franzen, *The Corrections*, 349 [Rosenbach, 104])
       b. 'I'm so starving,' she said. It was *a thin woman's apology* for being corporeal (J. Franzen, *The Corrections*, 241 [98])

Neither the specific nor the non-specific interpretation contradicts the other, even though one may be more likely in context. Therefore speakers and addressees may have different interpretations without miscommunication. It is a "bridging example" (Enfield 318). This is just the sort of thing we look for in historical work as a possible entry-point for a change (of course, ambiguity does not go away with change; it simply enables it if one of the meanings has not been around before).

Among Rosenbach's several conclusions is that there is a mismatch between

---

[5]   This kind of ambiguity is not limited to possessive constructions, but is typical of indefinites—an old example is:
       (i)   John wants to marry a Finn.
              a. J knows a particular Finn and he wants to marry her (specific).
              b. John likes Finns and wants to marry one, but he hasn't met her yet (non-specific).
[6]   Rosenbach 203 cites Lyons section 4.3.

syntax and semantics here, and that the key to understanding what is going on is the semantics, not the syntax. A look at the historical development confirms this approach, since Old English did not have an article, yet the distinction between specific (determiner) and type (descriptive) possessives can already be found there. She also concludes that the difference between constructions is gradient, and that descriptive possessives are much more frequent, at least in the genre she investigated, than is usually assumed in work using constructed data.

4.2. Example 2 (Aspects of the development of WH-pseudo-clefts)

There are various types of "cleft" sentences in English: IT-clefts introducing noun phrases and prepositional phrases, for example, *It was Jane that I talked to*, *It was a peach that Susan ate*,[7] and "pseudo-clefts" starting with *what, all, the thing*, etc., which introduce clauses as well as noun phrases and prepositional phrases, for example, *What Jack said was that he'd leave*, *What Susan ate was a peach*. I will report on one small aspect of research I have been conducting on the development of WH- and ALL-pseudo-clefts: investigation into the contexts in which the WH-cleft construction might have come into being.

According to what I have crudely called the twentieth century account, one starts with the syntactic string of the kind in (5):

(5)   WH NP V BE X

and constructs a number of examples out of context and tries to determine what pragmatic and semantic structures are associated with them. One typically thinks of them as answers to questions, such as:

(6)   What did Susan eat?

Pseudo-clefts are said to express uniqueness and contrastiveness, and to give an exhaustive listing (Susan ate the peach, not the plum, banana, etc.). The literature is vast; here I just refer to three early works by Collins, Higgins, and Prince. Pseudo-clefts are said to start with a "given" part (that Susan ate something has been mentioned, or is recoverable from context), and serve to highlight the X (this is called the "focus") in a split-focus construction, specifying the unknown (the "something") in the given part:

---

[7]   *Peach* is stressed in the *it*-construction.

(7)   WH NP V   BE X
       ⎵⎵⎵⎵⎵⎵⎵   ⎵⎵⎵⎵
         GIVEN   FOCUS

They are functionally different from similar strings in which the relationship between WHAT NP V BE X is simply descriptive, as in (8):

(8)   What she did is a shame (non-referential nominal, cf. What she did is shameful)

If one takes what I am crudely calling a twenty-first century approach, one starts not with the syntax, but with the meaning-form pairing, as do Lambrecht and Patten, who use a construction-grammar perspective that privileges meaning and function. The perspectives from syntax and from semantics are not fundamentally different as long as constructed examples are used. However, Kim and Hopper investigate the use of WH-clefts in interactional conversation and suggest that WH-clefts have rather different characteristics from those usually identified. Kim argues that in conversation, WH-clefts often do not refer to information retrievable from prior context and are used primarily to express a counteractive stance, specifically disagreement with the addressee or topic-shift. He also argues that they are closely related in function to left-dislocations (these have "resumptive pronouns," as in *Well, Mister Henry, he came up*). Using part of the COBUILD corpus, Hopper determined that WH-clefts play a significant role in turn-taking in Present Day English conversation: "to *delay* an assertion for any of a number of pragmatic reasons" (111, italics original). He argues that since most examples are not "complete" (do not have fully developed focus), they are not primarily motivated by a desire to highlight the focus-constituent, as assumed by most linguists working with constructed examples. Instead, WH-clefts are used to:

> "impress[ ] the listener with the 'social' significance of something about to be said, and mak[e] the listener aware that what follows is part of a considered argument worthy of attention and not a casual comment" (124).

Hopper says that the ideal locus for using the WH-cleft construction is the turn, where the listener's attention must be held, or shortly after, where keeping the floor is important.[8]

There has been a lot of interest in using contemporary conversation as evi-

---

8   Similar observations have been made about French pseudo-clefts by Jullien and Müller and about Brazilian Portuguese by Lilian Ferrari (p.c.).

dence for determining possible reasons for change. Since turn-taking has been suggested by Detges and Waltereit and Detges as a possible trigger for certain kinds of changes, such as the development of discourse markers, or of obligatory subject-markers in languages like French, I was interested in seeing whether it was possible to find evidence that the kind of turn-delay that Hopper identifies for contemporary use could have been a trigger for the development of WH-clefts. One difficulty, of course, is that our earlier historical data are written. Nevertheless, representation of dialogue in records of trials, dramas, and conversations in novels can give us some insight into how changes came about.

Investigation of historical data bases for English from Middle English on shows that WH-clefts arose c. 1680. Prior to that time, strings with the structure WH NP V BE X are descriptive (9a) or purposive (9b):

(9) a. and then **what** he said, was little, cold, and ambiguous (1645 Buchanan, *Passages of Things* [LION: EEBO])

b. Nay, conceive ("understand") me, conceive me, sweet coz. **What I do is to** pleasure ("please") you, coz. Can you love the maid? (?1597 Shakespeare, *Merry Wives of Windsor* I.i.250 [LION: Shakespeare])

There are also some left-dislocations with WH-objects:[9]

(10) a. Duke of *Guise*. Why, I am no traitor to the crown of *France*.
What I have done, 'tis for the Gospel's sake.
(c. 1593 Marlow, *Massacre at Paris*, scene 17 [LION: English Prose Drama])

b. For **what** he spake, for you he spake it, Dame,
And **what** he did, he did himself to saue. (1596 Spenser, *Faerie Queene*, VI,2.13.5-6)

(11) is an early example of a WH-cleft:

(11) his Fame will live for ever, in his own works. **What I have done, is only to pay a grateful respect to his Ashes,** as he was my friend. (1670 ICAME: Lampeter: mscb.sgm])

What I have done is given/accessible information (an encomium is being given

---

9   Thanks to Carol Kaske for drawing my attention to the potential importance of left-dislocations in the history of the WH-clefts, and for example (10b).

by the speaker), but seems to have little to do with turn-taking, and especially a question (although one could imagine the speaker supposing that someone might be asking "what are you doing?"). The focus *is only to pay a grateful respect…* appears to highlight as salient the speaker's view of his own actions, and his desire to humble himself. Interestingly, the exclusivity is expressed overtly by *only*.

While WH-clefts could be used at turns, there are very few examples, and none is incomplete. For example, the Old Bailey trials 1678-1743 have many examples of *What did you/he say/do?*, *What did you mean by it?*; but WH-clefts do not appear in response. A plain, non-clefted response is preferred:

(12)   here I met Trevor, and seeing a Bundle of Goods, I ask'd him, what it was? 'Tis a Bundle, says he, that I brought in just now. (Dec. 1951, Trial of William Trevor and Robert Knowland [BAILEY: s17311208-428173112080001]; not *What it is is a bundle*)

WH-clefts are found turn-initially in only one trial within the period, the deposition in (13) by a silver-smith with a lisp[10]:

(13)   ***What I have to tha ith thith, I lotht a thilver Dith belonging to Brigadier Churchill, out of my Grate in Compton-Thtreet, the Corner of Greek-Thtreet, but I can't tell when, becauth it ish impothible.*** (June 1733, Trial of Alexander Watson and William Howard [BAILEY: s17330628-441173306280001])

This appears directly after the recorder's statement of who is accused and what for; the question that the judge presumably asked is not recorded, only presupposed. In another three examples in the period (all first-person), the WH-cleft appears only after the speaker states his or her credentials with respect to the trial, e.g., in (14) only after the witness' denial that he can contribute much information:

(14)   - French. I keep an Alehouse in Cross-Lane. P– has been at my House in Company with the Prisoners.
        - Pain. I could have but a short Acquaintance with I–, for I am but just come from Sea. ***What I know of him is, that he is a Cooper by Trade, and that when he was taken up, he deny'd that he knew any thing of the Watch.*** (Dec 1731, Trial of Samuel Cole and Edward Paine of St. Sepulchres [BAILEY: s17311208-428173112080001])

---

10   This shows that the recorder was aware of language issues and did not normalize in ways we now expect from a court recorder.

In conclusion, there is no evidence that turn-taking or questioning was a reason or even a context for the development of WH-clefts. But WH-clefts do seem to be used largely for introducing what the speaker regards as salient in the situation. In the trials, WH-clefts function primarily to identify what the speaker considers crucial parts of the narrative of events in his or her deposition. There is therefore partial similarity to Hopper's findings regarding the use of WH-clefts in contemporary conversation.

More generally, although it is often tempting to assume that contemporary conversational or even constructed data give us insight into exactly how a change originated, we cannot project present findings on the past because without investigation, we cannot know whether present variation reflects earlier stages of a construction or only later ones, after other significant changes have emerged. The best the contemporary data can do for us is suggest what might have been possible entry-points or reasons for using the construction, but even then we must not restrict ourselves to this guidance. We must be open-minded and ready to see what the textual evidence shows us.

What is "twenty-first century" about this? No doubt Lightfoot, who is a "hardcore" generative historical syntactician, would call it "nineteenth century historicism," because I am taking "E-language" (usage) very seriously, and am not asking questions about how a child could have acquired the new WH-structure. But I think it is very much twenty-first century linguistics, because it is micro-analysis that investigates corpora, non-traditional data (trials), usage contexts, and rhetorical strategizing, among other things. At the same time, in the larger study of which the examples above were just a glimpse, I ask questions about information structure, the mental grammars that must be assumed to have changed when the new pseudo-cleft came into being, and ultimately about how grammatical structure comes into being.[11] One way of thinking about this work is that it is the "New Philology"—the study of linguistic (textual) discourse contexts for change, within the larger context of far-reaching theoretical frameworks.

5. How does all this impact language arts?

The effects of the changes I have described are, to my knowledge, somewhat minimal to date in the language arts, especially the more technical aspects of the research. But there is an increased sense of the urgency to get language back in the curriculum.

---

[11] The development of pseudo-clefts is a case of grammaticalization, but not the type one thinks of that is associated with Meillet: lexical item > grammatical item. Rather, it is "grammaticalization without lexical input" (Lehmann). It is also grammaticalization of a construction (Trousdale).

In the UK there is discussion of an A-level (last years of high school) examination in Linguistics and Area Studies (LLAS). The LLAS website includes an article on good practices in teaching pidgin and creole languages, and the *English&MediaCentre* emagazine (EMAGS) provides on-line clips on why a person might care about language.

I am not aware of an equivalent attempt to impact high school programs in the US. But Old Dominion University in Virginia has a new English PhD program that "integrates writing, rhetoric, discourse, technology, and textual studies … Our focus is on how the creation and reception of texts and media are affected by the form, purpose, technology of composition, audience, cultural location, and communities of discourse."[12] And the Modern Language Association in the US (MLA) issued a call to action in 2007 which arose in the context of the growing diversity of populations, including language diversity, and in the context of globalization. "Globalization" might suggest some faceless homogenization. But recently it has been theorized in two ways that fit the twenty-first century ideologies I have outlined well, one concerning English as a world language, the other concerning awareness of the global village.

With respect to English as world language, first of all, there is no one World English. There are many Englishes developing locally (Kortmann and Schneider). Some are native, as in South Africa or Australia, some are near-native, as in Singapore, and are likely candidates for co-existence with Standard English or other languages. There are also different uses of English in different domains in various parts of the world, e.g., airline English. In "Into the Twenty-first Century," Crystal estimates that about a quarter of the world's population (six billion in 1999) has some command of English (425). He argues that as long as the UK and the US are conceived to be important forces politically, militarily, technologically, and economically, English will be used by others around the world. In "English world-wide" he stresses the vital role media play in the spread of English: advertising, broadcasting, movies, international travel operations, and the internet. Crystal's major interest is in arguing that the global spread of English is a "fresh testing-ground for sociolinguistic hypotheses which previously had only regional validity" (2006a, 422). Social validity should be added, but the point is well taken. He emphasizes that English has always been in contact, and has always had a "lexical mosaic" (435) based on several languages. However, although there have been lingua francas in the past, e.g., Latin and French, we have no knowledge of how a language that has emerged so rapidly as a global force will change. In a companion piece, McArthur discusses the shift from British to American English as the "target." Particularly challenging is his suggestion that,

---

[12] <http://al.odu.edu/english/academics/phd.shtml>.

given the hold it now has all over the world, English in its many varieties could survive even if it were no longer spoken in the UK or US. This is because it has become "the primary language of a psycho-cultural *West*" (381, italics original), including modernization (390).

There is a parallel, though less well developed, view that globalization also means becoming aware of the global village through learning other languages. Especially, there is a feeling that there is also a geopolitical imperative for native English speakers to learn other languages, and this is where the MLA statement comes in:

> "In the context of globalization and in the post-9/11 environment, then, the usefulness of studying languages other than English is no longer contested. The goals and means of language study, however, continue to be hotly debated…. At one end, language is considered to be principally instrumental, a skill to use for communicating thought and information. At the opposite end, language is understood as an essential element of a human being's thought processes, perceptions, and self-expressions; and as such it is considered to be at the core of translingual and transcultural competence… Language is a complex multifunctional phenomenon that links an individual to other individuals, to communities, and to national cultures."

6. Conclusion

Looking to the future, I trust that the recent changes in linguistics that I have mentioned, most especially grounding in empirical evidence and in meaning, may lead to greater connectivity with important social issues, and that we can show that precisely because language is a complex multifunctional phenomenon, it should be considered a crucial, not just contingent, link to a better understanding of the many fields to which the octopus's tentacles are reaching out. Let us turn around and seek to influence that future that lurks behind us, by making English Language and Linguistic Studies more relevant to society at large than it may have been in the not too distant past.

Works cited

Aarts, Bas and April McMahon, eds. *The Handbook of English Linguistics.* Malden, MA: Blackwell, 2006.

Athanasiadou, Angeliki, Costas Canakis, and Bert Cornillie, eds. *Subjectification: Various Paths to Subjectivity.* Berlin: Mouton de Gruyter, 2006.

BAILEY. *The Proceedings of the Old Bailey, London 1674 to 1834.* Feb. – Aug. 2007. <www.oldbaileyonline.org>.

Barcelona, Antonio, ed. *Metaphor and Metonymy at the Crossroads: A Cognitive Perspective.* Berlin: Mouton de Gruyter, 2000.

Bergs, Alexander. *Social Networks and Historical Sociolinguistics: Studies in Morphosyntactic Variation in the Paston Letters (1421-1503).* Berlin: Mouton de Gruyter, 2005.

Birner, Betty J. and Gregory Ward. *Information Status and Noncanonical Word Order in English.* Amsterdam: John Benjamins, 1998.

Bloomfield, Leonard. *Language.* New York: Holt, 1933.

BNC. *British National Corpus.* <http://www.natcorp.ox.ac.uk/>.

Brinton, Laurel J. " 'Where Grammar and Lexis Meet': Composite Predicates in English." *New Reflections on Grammaticalization 3.* Eds. Maria José López-Couso and Elena Seonane-Posse. Amsterdam: John Benjamins (forthcoming).

Bybee, Joan. "From Usage to Grammar: The Mind's Response to Repetition." *Language* 82 (2006): 711- 733.

Bybee, Joan. *Frequency of Use and Organization of Language.* Oxford: Oxford UP, 2007.

Bybee, Joan and Paul Hopper, eds. *Frequency and the Emergence of Linguistic Structure.* Amsterdam: John Benjamins, 2001.

Bybee, Joan L., Revere Perkins and William Pagliuca. *The Evolution of Grammar: Tense, Aspect, and Modality in the Languages of the World.* Chicago: U of Chicago P, 1994.

Carter, Ronald, ed. *Language and Literature: An Introductory Reader in Stylistics.* London: Allen & Unwin, 1982.

Chomsky, Noam. *Syntactic Structures.* The Hague: Mouton, 1957.

Chomsky, Noam. *Aspects of the Theory of Syntax.* Cambridge, MA: The MIT Press, 1965.

Chomsky, Noam. "Language, Politics, and Composition: A Conversation with Noam Chomsky." *(Inter)views: Cross-disciplinary Perspectives on Rhetoric and Literacy.* Eds. Gary A. Olson and Irene Gale. Carbondale: Southern Illinois UP, 1991. 61-95.

Cinque, Guglielmo. *Restructuring and Functional Heads: The Cartography of Syntactic Structures,* Vol. 4. Oxford: Oxford UP, 2006.

COBUILD. *Collins Birmingham University International Language Database.* <http://www.collins.co.uk/Corpus/CorpusSearch.aspx>.

Collins, Peter C. *Cleft and Pseudo-cleft Constructions in English.* London: Routledge, 1991.

Croft, William. *Explaining Language Change: An Evolutionary Approach.* Harlow, Essex: Longman, Pearson Education, 2000.

Croft, William. *Radical Construction Grammar: Syntactic Theory in Typological Perspective.* Oxford: Oxford UP, 2001.

Crystal, David. "Into the Twenty-first Century." *The Oxford History of English.* Ed. Lynda Mugglestone. Oxford: Oxford UP, 2006a. 394-413.

Crystal, David. "English World-wide." *A History of the English Language.* Eds. Richard Hogg and David Denison. Cambridge: Cambridge UP, 2006b. 420-439.

Curzan, Anne and Michael Adams. *How English Works: A Linguistic Introduction.* New York: Longman, Pearson, 2006.

Cuyckens, Hubert, Kristin Davidse, and Lieven Vandelanotte, eds. *Subjectification, Intersubjectification and Grammaticalization.* Berlin: Mouton de Gruyter, forthcoming.

DARE. *Dictionary of American Regional English.* <http://polyglot.lss.wisc.edu/dare/dare.html>.

Denison, David. "Gradience and Linguistic Change." *Historical Linguistics 1999: Selected Papers from the 14th International Conference on Historical Linguistics, Vancouver, 9-13 August 1999.* Ed. Laurel J. Brinton. Amsterdam: John Benjamins, 2001. 119-144.

Detges, Ulrich. "From Speaker to Subject. The Obligatorization of the Old French Subject Pronouns." *La Linguistique au Coeur. Valence verbale, grammaticalisation et corpus. Mélanges offerts à Lene Schøsler à l'occasion de son 60e anniversaire.* Eds. Hanne Leth Andersen, Merete Birkelund and Maj-Britt Mosegaard Hansen. *University of Southern Denmark Studies in Literature* 48 (2006): 75-103.

DOE. *Dictionary of Old English Corpus.* <http://ets.umdl.umich.edu/o/oec/>.

EMAGS. *English & Media Centre*, emagazine. 19 July 2007. 7 Sept. 2007. <http://www.englishandmedia.co.uk/engine/emag/base/emag_emagclips_base.html>.

Enfield, Nicholas J. "Micro- and Macro-dimensions in Linguistic Systems." *Reviewing Linguistic Thought: Converging Trends for the 21st Century.* Eds. Sophia Marmaridou, Kiki Nikiforidou, and Eleni Antonopoulou, with the assistance of Angeliki Salamoura. Berlin: Mouton de Gruyter, 2005. 313-325.

Erman, Britt and Beatrice Warren. "The Idiom Principle and the Open Choice Principle." *Text* 20 (2000): 29-62.

Fillmore, Charles and Paul Kay. *Berkeley Construction Grammar*. Berkeley: U of California at Berkeley, 1997. <http://www.icsi.berkeley.edu/~kay/bcg/ConGram.html>.

Fischer, Olga. *Morphosyntactic Change: Functional and Formal Perspectives*. Oxford: Oxford UP, 2007.

Fitzmaurice, Susan M. *The Familiar Letter in Early Modern English: A Pragmatic Approach*. Berlin: Mouton de Gruyter, 2002.

Fitzmaurice, Susan and Irma Taavitsainen, eds. *Methods in Historical Pragmatics*. Berlin: Mouton de Gruyter, 2007.

Freedman, Donald C., ed. *Essays in Modern Stylistics*. London: Methuen, 1981.

Fried, Mirjam and Jan-Ola Östman. "Construction Grammar: A Thumbnail Sketch." *Construction Grammar in a Cross-Language Perspective*. Eds. Mirjam Fried and Jan-Ola Östman. Amsterdam: John Benjamins, 2004. 11-86.

Givón, T. *Mind, Code, and Context: Essays in Pragmatics*. Hillsdale, NJ: Erlbaum, 1989.

Goldberg, Adele E. *Constructions: A Construction Grammar Approach to Argument Structure*. Chicago: U of Chicago P, 1995.

Goldberg, Adele E. "Constructions: A New Theoretical Approach to Language." *Trends in Cognitive Sciences* 7 (2003): 219-224.

Goldberg, Adele E. *Constructions at Work: The Nature of Generalization in Language*. Oxford: Oxford UP, 2006.

Harris, Roy. "Translator's Introduction." *Course in General Linguistics*. Ferdinand de Saussure. Trans. by Roy Harris. Chicago: Open Court, 1983. ix-xvi.

Hayakawa, S. I. *Language in Thought and Action*, with Alan R. Hayakawa. San Diego, CA: Harcourt, Brace, Jovanovich, 1990. 5th ed.

Higgins, Francis Roger. *The Pseudo-cleft Construction in English*. New York: Garland, 1979.

Hogg, Richard, and David Denison, eds. *A History of the English Language*. Cambridge: Cambridge UP, 2006.

Hopper, Paul J. "Grammatical Constructions and their Discourse Origins: Prototype or Family Resemblance?" *Applied Cognitive Linguistics I: Theory and Language Acquisition*. Eds. Martin Pütz, Susanne Niemeier, and René Dirven. Berlin: Mouton de Gruyter, 2001. 109-129.

Hopper, Paul J. and Elizabeth Closs Traugott. *Grammaticalization*. Cambridge: Cambridge UP, 2003. 2nd revised ed.

Huber, Magnus. "*The Old Bailey Proceedings, 1674-1834*; Introducing a Corpus of 18th Century Spoken English." *eVARIENG* 1, forthcoming.

ICAME. *ICAME Corpus Collection*. <http://nora.hd.uib.no/corpora.html>.

Jullien, Stéphane and Gabriele M. Müller. "French Pseudo-cleft and Presentational Cleft in French Conversation: Two Grammatical Resources for Maintaining the Floor." Paper presented at the Tenth International Pragmatics Conference (IPra), Gothenburg, July 2007.

Keller, Rudi. 1994. *On Language Change: The Invisible Hand in Language.* Trans. Brigitte Nerlich. London: Routledge, 1994.

Kemenade, Ans van and Bettelou Los, eds. *The Handbook of the History of English.* Malden, MA: Blackwell, 2006.

Kim, Kyu-hyun. "WH-clefts and Left-dislocation in English Conversation: Cases of Topicalization." *Word Order in Discourse.* Eds. Pamela Downing and Michael Noonan. Amsterdam: John Benjamins, 1995. 247-296.

Kortmann, Bernd and Edgar Schneider, eds. *A Handbook of Varieties of English: A Multimedia Reference Tool,* 2 Vols. Berlin: Mouton de Gruyter, 2004.

Kövecses, Zoltán. *Metaphor and Emotion: Language, Culture, and Body in Human Feeling.* Cambridge: Cambridge UP, 2000.

Kövecses, Zoltán. *Metaphor: A Practical Introduction.* Oxford: Oxford, 2002.

Kryk-Kastovsky, Barbara, ed. *Historical Courtroom Discourse.* Special issue, *Journal of Historical Pragmatics* 7, 2 (2006).

Kucera, Henry and Nelson Francis. *The Standard Corpus of Present-Day American English.* Brown U, 1979. Revised ed. (see ICAME).

Kytö, Merja and Suzanne Romaine. *Grammaticalization in English: The Life Cycle of Constructions.* Cambridge: Cambridge UP, forthcoming.

Labov, William. *Sociolinguistic Patterns.* Philadelphia: U of Pennsylvania P, 1972. Chapter I.

Lakoff, George. *Women, Fire, and Dangerous Things: What Categories Reveal about the Mind.* Chicago: U of Chicago P, 1987.

Lakoff, George and Mark Turner. *More than Cool Reason: A Field Guide to Poetic Metaphor.* Chicago: U of Chicago P, 1989.

Lambrecht, Knud. "A Framework for the Analysis of Cleft-constructions." *Linguistics* 39 (2001): 463-516.

Langacker, Ronald W. *Cognitive Linguistics,* 2 Vols. Stanford, CA: Stanford UP, 1987, 1991.

Lehmann, Christian. "Information Structure and Grammaticalization." *New Reflections on Grammaticalization 3.* Eds. Maria José López-Couso and Elena Seonane-Posse. Amsterdam: John Benjamins, forthcoming.

Lightfoot, David. *The Development of Language: Acquisition, Change, and Evolution.* Malden, MA: Blackwell, 1999.

Lightfoot, David W. "Cuing a New Grammar." *Handbook of the History of English.* Eds. Ans van Kemenade and Bettelou Los. Oxford: Blackwell, 2006. 22-44.

LION. Chadwyck Healey website. Jan.-Aug. 2007. <http://lion.chadwyck. com>.

Lindquist, Hans and Christian Mair, eds. *Corpus Approaches to Grammaticalization in English.* Amsterdam: John Benjamins, 2004.

LLAS. *Subject Centre for Languages, Linguistics, and Area Studies.* July 23 2007. <http://www.llas.ac.uk/index.aspx>.

LOB. *Lancaster-Oslo-Bergen Corpus.* <http://khnt.hit.uib.no/icame/manuals/ lob/INDEX.HTM>.

Lyons, Christopher. "The Syntax of English Genitive Constructions." *Journal of Linguistics* 22 (1986): 123-143.

Lyons, Christopher. *Definiteness.* Cambridge: Cambridge UP, 1999.

Malouf, Robert. *Mixed Categories in the Hierarchical Lexicon.* Stanford, CA: CSLI Publications, 2000.

Mann, William A. and Sandra A. Thompson. "Rhetorical Structure Theory." *Text* 8 (1988): 243-281.

Marmaridou, Sophia, Kiki Nikiforidou, and Eleni Antonopoulou, eds., with the assistance of Angeliki Salamoura. *Reviewing Linguistic Thought: Converging Trends for the 21st Century.* Berlin: Mouton de Gruyter, 2005.

McArthur, Tom. "English World-wide in the Twentieth Century." *The Oxford History of English.* Ed. Lynda Mugglestone. Oxford: Oxford UP, 2006. 360-393.

MED. *The Middle English Dictionary.* Ann Arbor: U of Michigan P. 1956-2001. Jan. – Aug. 2007. <http://www.hti.umich.edu/dict/med/>.

Meillet, Antoine. "L'évolution des formes grammaticales." *Linguistique historique et linguistique générale.* Antoine Meillet. Paris: Champion, 1958. 130-148. (Originally publ. in *Scientia* (*Rivista di Scienza*) XII (1912).)

Meyer, Charles F. *English Corpus Linguistics.* Cambridge: Cambridge UP, 2002.

Michaelis, Laura A. "Type Shifting in Construction Grammar: An Integrated Approach to Aspectual Coercion." *Cognitive Linguistics* 15 (2004): 1-67.

Milroy, James. "On the Role of the Speaker in Language Change." *Motives for Language Change.* Ed. Raymond Hickey. Cambridge: Cambridge UP, 2003. 143-157.

MLA. Report on Foreign Languages and Higher Education: New Structures for a Changed World, May, 2007.

Mugglestone, Lynda. *The Oxford History of English.* Oxford: Oxford UP, 2006.

Nevalainen, Terttu and Helena Raumolin-Brunberg. *Historical Sociolinguistics: Language Change in Tudor and Stuart England.* Harlow, Essex: Pearson Education, 2003.

Núñez, Rafael E. and Eve Sweetser. "With the Future Behind Them: Convergent Evidence from Aymara Language and Gesture in the Crosslinguistic Comparison of Spatial Construals of Time." *Cognitive Science* 30 (2006): 1-49.

OED. *Oxford English Dictionary.* 3rd ed. <http://dictionary.oed.com/>.

Ortony, Andrew. Ed. *Metaphor and Thought.* Cambridge: Cambridge UP, 1993. 2nd revised ed.

Panther, Klaus-Uwe and Günter Radden, eds. *Metonymy in Language and Thought.* Amsterdam: John Benjamins, 1999.

Patten, Amanda. "How Specificational are Cleft Sentences?" Paper presented at the Second International Conference on the Linguistics of Contemporary English (ICLCE), Toulouse, July 2007.

Penke, Martina and Anette Rosenbach, eds. *What Counts as Evidence in Linguistics: The Case of Innateness.* Special issue, *Studies in Language* 28, 3 (2004).

Prince, Ellen F. "A Comparison of WH-clefts and *It*-clefts in Discourse." *Language* 54 (1978): 883-906.

Radden, Günter and Zoltán Kövecses. "Towards a theory of metonymy." *Metonymy in Language and Thought.* Eds. Klaus-Uwe Panther and Günter Radden. Amsterdam: John Benjamins, 1999. 17-59.

Rissanen, Matti. *The Helsinki Corpus of English Texts.* Helsinki: U of Helsinki, 1989.

Rissanen, Matti, Merja Kytö, and Kirsi Heikkonen, eds. *Grammaticalization at Work: Studies of Long-Term Developments in English.* Berlin: Mouton de Gruyter, 1997.

Roberts, Paul. *Modern Grammar.* New York: Harcourt, Brace & World, 1968.

Rosenbach, Anette. "Descriptive Genitives in English: A Case Study on Constructional Gradience." *English Language and Linguistics* 10 (2006): 77-118.

Ross, John Robert. "The Category Squish: Endstation Hauptwort." *Proceedings of the Eighth Meeting of the Chicago Linguistic Society.* Eds. Paul M. Peranteau, Judith N. Levi, and Gloria C. Phares. Department of Linguistics, U of Chicago, 1982. 316-328.

Saussure, Ferdinand de. *Course in General Linguistics.* Trans. Roy Harris. Chicago: Open Court, 1983. (Originally publ. as *Cours de Linguistique Générale,* 1916.)

Schiffrin, Deborah. *Discourse Markers.* Cambridge: Cambridge UP, 1987.

Skandera, Paul. Ed. *Phraseology and Culture in English.* Berlin: Mouton de Gruyter, 2007.

Stockwell, Peter. *Cognitive Poetics: An Introduction.* London: Routledge, 2002.

Taylor, John R. "Cognitive Semantics and Structural Semantics." *Historical Semantics and Cognition.* Eds. Andreas Blank and Peter Koch. Berlin: Mouton de Gruyter, 1999. 17-48.

Thompson, Sandra A. and Paul J. Hopper. "Transitivity, Clause Structure, and Argument Structure: Evidence from Conversation." *Frequency and the Emer-*

gence of Linguistic Structure. Eds. Joan Bybee and Paul Hopper. Amsterdam: John Benjamins, 2001. 27-60.

Traugott, Elizabeth Closs. "From Subjectification to Intersubjectification." *Motives for Language Change.* Ed. Raymond Hickey. Cambridge: Cambridge UP, 2003. 124-139.

Traugott, Elizabeth Closs. " 'All that he endeavoured to prove was …': On the emergence of grammatical constructions in dialogic contexts." *Language Change and Evolution.* Eds. Ruth Kempson and Robin Cooper, forthcoming.

Trousdale, Graeme. "Constructions and Grammaticalization and Lexicalization: Evidence from the History of a Composite Predicate Construction in English." *Constructional Explanations in Modern English Grammar.* Eds. Graeme Trousdale and Nikolas Gisborne. Berlin: Mouton de Gruyter, forthcoming.

Turner, Mark. *Death is the Mother of Beauty: Mind, Metaphor, Criticism.* Chicago: U of Chicago P, 1987.

Turner, Mark. *The Literary Mind: The Origins of Thought and Language.* Oxford: Oxford UP, 1996.

Turner, Mark. "Mental packing." Plenary address presented at the Eighth Conference on Conceptual Structure, Discourse, and Language (CSDL), U of California, San Diego. Nov. 2006.

Waltereit, Richard and Ulrich Detges. "Different Functions, Different Histories: Modal Particles and Discourse Markers from a Diachronic Point of View." Ed. Maria Josep Cuenca. Special issue on discourse markers, *Journal of Catalan Linguistics,* 2007.

Weinreich, Uriel, William Labov and Marvin I. Herzog. "Empirical Foundations for a Theory of Language Change." *Directions for Historical Linguistics.* Eds. W. P. Lehmann and Yakov Malkiel. Austin: U of Texas P, 1968. 95-189.

Werry, Chris. "Reflections on Language: Chomsky, Linguistic Discourse and the Value of Rhetorical Self-consciousness." *Language Sciences* 29 (2007): 66-87.

Wierzbicka, Anna. *English: Meaning and Culture.* Oxford: Oxford UP, 2006.

20

Minoji Akimoto

On Rivalry in the History of English

1. Introduction

Problems of rivalry are of particular interest in the history of English. Rynell (1948) is a typical study which describes in detail the process of replacing *nimen*, a verb of native origin, by *taken*, an Old Norse loan word. Samuels (1972: 77-79) refers to the competition between *cast* and *throw*. Another example of competition is between *kill* and *slay*. These examples are cases where one ousts the other (i.e. *throw* ousts *cast* and *kill* ousts *slay*), and those ousted are limited to a narrow range of use in terms of registers. Decline and replacement, and consequent narrowing of meaning, are often associated with the semantic field advocated by Trier (1931: 1-26), where emphasis is placed on the organization and interrelation of words in the semantic field, although we cannot discuss this problem owing to space limitation. His well-known examples are given in Ullmann (1964: 248-249).

A parallel phenomenon can be observed in the grammaticalization process. The development of the auxiliaries expressing future, such as *shall, will* and *be going to*, reveals rivalry among the auxiliaries. *Shall*, which was used most frequently in earlier English, has become less and less frequent in present-day English, and now *will* and *be going to* are frequent auxiliaries expressing future. *Be going to*, which is newer than *will*, is very frequent, particularly in present-day American English. *Shall* has become archaic, and now *will* and *be going to* are used differently depending on pragmatic contexts.

I will take up three cases of rivalry and discuss common properties underlying these cases, together with the implications produced by the rivalry or competition between the items. These cases are:

1. verbs of the 'wanting' type – *desire, hope, want* and *wish*
2. *put* vs. *set*
3. *pray* vs. *please* as courtesy markers

In studies of 1 and 2, rivalry takes place in the major category, verbs, and 3 is a case where rivalry takes place in the process of grammaticalization. A few words on the corpora are in order.

As regards the data for this investigation, I used the *Oxford English Dictionary* on CD-ROM, the electronic version of the *Middle English Dictionary*, the Helsinki Corpus, the Archer Corpus, and the FLOB corpus for present-day English. Regarding the rivalry between *put* and *set*, I used the text of the Sherlock Holmes stories and the electronic versions of Modern English Collection and Modern English Text Collection.

2. Verbs of the wanting type

The verbs of the wanting type, e.g. *desire, hope, want* and *wish*, have developed in competition with one another. *Hope* and *wish* were already in existence in the Old English period, and *desire* and *want* came in during the Middle English period – *desire* from Old French, *want* from Old Norse. It was around 1500 that these four verbs entered the phase of rivalry.

What follows only shows the results of my investigation, including some representative examples. Table 1 shows the frequency change of syntactic patterns of *desire* from ME to present-day English. Table 2 shows the frequency change of syntactic patterns of *hope*. Table 3 shows the frequency change of patterns of *want,* and Table 4 shows the frequency change of patterns of *wish*.

Table 1: Change of syntactic frequency of desire from ME to PDE

	ME				EModE			LModE				PDE
	I	II	III	IV	I	II	III	I	II	III	IV	
desire + NP	1	5	21	23	8	12	25	26	27	16	10	93
desire + to-inf	0	2	17	24	5	18	33	19	32	23	9	3
desire +NP + to-inf	0	0	0	0	8	4	9	27	50	9	0	0
desire + that-cl	0	0	1	2	1	4	3	2	10	3	1	0
desire +φ	0	0	0	1	2	1	9	3	22	0	0	0
be+desired+to-inf	0	1	8	5	5	3	12	5	14	10	5	5
other	0	0	6	4	4	1	3	3	11	4	1	0

(1) I *desire more acquaintance* of you.

          (d. folio 1623(1597) The Merry Wives of Windsor[HC])

(2) … in as moche as it lyveth naturely, that forletith the talent or appetyt of his beynge and *desireth to come* to deth … (… in as much as it lives naturally, it gives up the disposition and appetite of his being and desires to approach death)

          (?a1425 (c1380) Chaucer, Boethius[HC])

(3) She *desired me to excuse* her not writing to you ...

(1665 econ. x1[AC])

(4) ... þu hast wrowt in me, *desiyng þat* I schulde deyin in myschef & gret disease.
(... you have worked in me, desiring that I should die in mischief and great disease)

(a1438 The Book of Margery Kempe[HC])

(5) The Inhabitants *are desired to be* careful of their Doors, Windows ...

(1773nyol. n4[AC])

(6) I *desire of* God if it were his will hee would let me goe to Rochdale ...

(1661 newc. j1[AC])

Table 2: Frequency change of syntactic patterns of *hope* from ME to PDE

	ME				EModE			LModE				PDE
	I	II	III	IV	I	II	III	I	II	III	IV	
hope + NP	1	1	0	2	0	0	0	0	3	5	2	0
hope + to-inf	1	3	2	8	2	15	4	15	43	35	25	45
hope + that-cl	0	0	2	9	0	1	1	6	13	28	31	39
hope + φ	1	3	5	6	0	33	42	33	115	77	93	72
parenthetical use	0	0	0	0	1	9	8	8	30	12	12	2
hope + for	0	0	0	0	0	2	4	3	7	12	14	8
be+hoped+to-inf	0	0	0	0	0	0	2	4	4	9	4	0
other	0	24	3	8	1	7	4	5	19	14	12	4

(7) Ston he dude lede, þer he *hopede spede*. (He led the stone, there he hoped for speed)

(1300 (?1225) King Horn[HC])

(8) Sere, I *hope to be* her a-geyn þe next woke ... (Sir, I hope to be here again next week)

(a1438 The Book of Margery Kempe[HC])

(9) *I hope that* you find your selfe in a better condition as to your health than formerly.

(1653 finc. x1[AC])

(10) Ffor wha-swa wil it here or rede, *I hope* he sal be stirred þar-by. (For who-ever will hear or read it, I hope he shall be stirred.)

(a1425(a1400) The Prick of Conscience)

(11) But this cloud *I hope* will doe my soule good.

(1661 newc. j1[AC])

(12) Mayn't we *hope for* the Honour to see your Ladyship added to # our Society, Madam?

(1697 The Relapse[HC])

(13) … it is to *be hoped that* those who are responsible for the results will …

(1883 tim1. n6[AC])

Table 3: Frequency change of the syntactic patterns of *want* from ME to PDE

	ME				EModE			LModE				PDE
	I	II	III	IV	I	II	III	I	II	III	IV	
want + NP	1	2	8	2	1	24	19	5	16	21	39	155
want + to-inf	0	0	0	0	0	0	0	4	34	105	359	390
want +NP+to-inf	0	0	0	0	0	0	0	0	6	27	71	96
other	0	0	0	0	5	6	1	1	0	0	0	9

(14) And all-þogh þai in helle *want* light … (And although they lack light in hell …)

(a1425 (a1400) The Prick of Conscience[HC])

(15) I chiefly *want to prosecute* this design.

(1671 cary. d1[AC])

(16) I *want you to observe* closely, Jeeves, and …

(1923 wode. f8a[AC])

Table 4: Frequency change of the syntactic patterns of *wish* from ME to PDE

	ME				EModE			LModE				PDE
	I	II	III	IV	I	II	III	I	II	III	IV	
wish + NP	9	4	4	4	2	2	5	4	11	12	2	0
wish + to-inf	1	1	0	0	1	1	1	3	48	73	50	64
wish+NP+to-inf	0	0	0	1	0	8	4	1	10	20	7	0
wish + that-cl	5	0	1	2	1	7	2	0	6	4	5	2
wish + φ	2	0	0	2	1	2	7	11	46	63	55	29
wish for	0	0	0	0	0	1	2	2	12	4	1	4
wish + o + o	0	0	0	0	1	1	1	8	22	0	3	0
other	11	3	0	0	1	4	5	6	21	8	5	0

(17) *Gretter worshypp* I cannot wysshe than for to sytte in the # kynges owne Benche. (I cannot wish greater worship than to sit in the king's bench)

(1497 In Die Innocencium[HC])

(18) For there is in our nature an inbred desire to ayme at the best, and to *wish to* equalize them in each commendable quality ...

(1627 Ludus Literarius or The Grammar Schole[HC])

(19) þe fyfte virtue or thewe es 'sleghte' or 'sleghenes,' þat *wysses vs to be-warre* with wathes of þe # werlde. (the fifth virtue is 'sleight', which urges us to be aware of the wrath of the world)

(c1440 Dan Jon Gaytryge's Sermon)

(20) & ec forr þatt te33 *wisstenn* wel *þat* Godd comm. Her to manne ... (and for that you wish well that God would hear her lament)

(?1200 Ormulum[HC])

(21) As Nero the Emperor wold to his mayster Seneca, the same *wysshe* I wold to my mayster I love soo well. (As Nero the Emperor went to his master Seneca, I desire that I would go to my master I love so well)

(1497 In Die Innocencium[HC])

(22) I do more than *wish for* her Safety, for ev'ry wish I make I find immediately changed into a Prayer ...

(1714 pope. x2[AC])

(23) I *wish* you joy of your new honour …

(1688 crow. d1[AC])

From the Tables given before, we can point out some tendencies as follows.

Desire has been decreasing in frequency, after its peak during the late Modern English period. Its usage has almost been confined to the pattern 'desire + NP'. The other uses, such as 'desire + NP + to-inf' and 'desire + (that) clause', are not in use in present-day English.

Hope has spread its function of *that* or zero clauses particularly since the Late Modern English period, and this use is now major in present-day English. Next to this function is that of taking the *to*-infinitive, which has also increased since the Late Modern English period. *Hope* cannot take the direct object now, and instead has developed the 'hope + for' construction. The parenthetical use of *hope* is not so frequent in present-day English.[1] Its use was more frequent in Late Modern English.

Want began to be very frequent during the Late Modern English period, particularly the 'want + to' construction. The 'want + NP + to' construction has also been on the increase since 1800.

Wish has narrowed down its construction to 'wish + to' and 'wish + φ clause'. The 'wish + φ clause' construction expresses unrealized facts with the preterite verb forms in present-day English.

Taking into account these functional and semantic changes of the verbs from the Old English period to the present time, I can hypothesize that the following replacement and reshuffling took place in the history of English, with the proviso that other verbs, such as *demand, expect* and *require,* may have influenced the system. Before that, I show ratios of the syntactic and semantic areas of each verb from Middle English to present-day English in Figures 1 through 4. The shaded bars show other uses of each verb.

---

[1] I checked the parenthetical use of I *hope* in the BNC corpus, and found 34 examples.

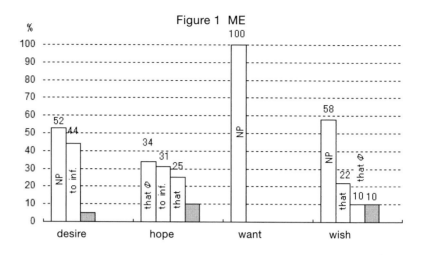

Figure 1 ME

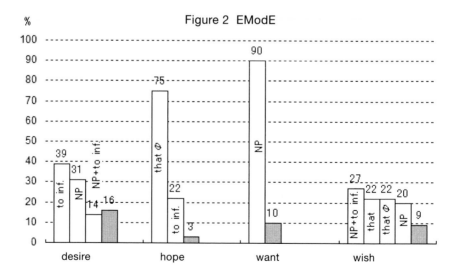

Figure 2 EModE

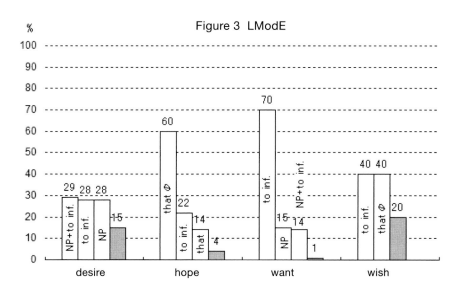

Figure 3 LModE

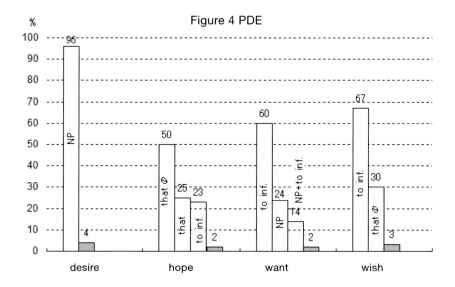

Figure 4 PDE

I. Reshuffling among the verbs

(a) desire + to
(b) desire + NP + to $\Big\}$ → want (+ NP) + to

(c) desire + that (indicative) ⟶ hope that (indicative)
(d) desire + φ (subjunctive/periphrastic) ⟶ wish + φ (mostly subjunctive)
(e) wish that (indicative/periphrastic) ⟶ hope that (indicative)
(f) wish + NP + to ⟶ want + NP + to

As a result of the reshuffling, the following constructions have remained in present-day English:

II. After the reshuffling

1. desire + NP
2. (a) hope + that/φ (indicative)
   (b) hope + to
   (c) parenthetical *I hope*
3. (a) want + to
   (b) want + NP + to
4. (a) wish + φ clause (subjunctive)
   (b) wish + to

3. Put vs. set

The first citation of *put* in the OED is c1050 *Rule of Chrodegang*, but in the classification of signification the first example is c1175 in the sense of 'To thrust, push, to shove; to knock'. No example of *put* in OE is found in the Helsinki Corpus. Pauwels (2000: 53) says 'The low frequency of *potian/pu-tian/pytan* in (written) OE is confirmed by the complete concordance of OE, Toronto-corpus (Healey and Venezky, 1980) which only contains five attestations.' See Figure 5 regarding the frequency change of *put* and *set* from OE to present-day English.

I will show the major patterns which *put* and *set* have developed in Tables below. Tables 5 and 6 show the *put* and *set* patterns from EModE to present-day English in comparison with Pauwels (2000: 92, 94, 192, 247), whose data are EModE and PDE. Note that my classification differs slightly from that of Pauwels (2000) in Tables 5 and 6. For instance, my phrasal verbs include

Pauwels's 2-place particle and 1-place particle. I cannot see the distinction between these two patterns, because the position of a particle is optional before
and after the noun object. Table 7 shows the breakdown of the prepositional
phrases after the object NP which constitute a great part of *put* and *set* patterns. Tables 8 and 9 show the frequent phrasal verbs of *put* and *set* based on
the Archer Corpus.

Figure 5

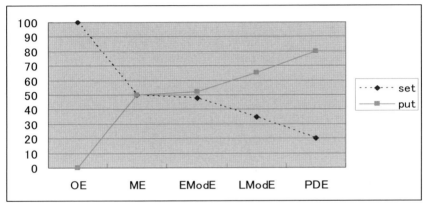

(based on Pauwels (2000) except LModE)

Table 5: *Put* patterns from EModE to PDE

EModE (Helsinki)	LModE (Archer)	Present-day (LOB)
1) 3-place	1) put + NP + PrepPh	1) 3-place
2) 2-place particle	2) phrasal verb	2) 2-place particle
3) 2-place	3) put + NP	3) 2-place + Adverb
4) 2-place + Adverb	4) put + NP + Adverb	4) 1-place particle
4) 2-place + to-inf	5) 2-place	5) 2-place + NP
4) 2-place PP		6) 2-place + Adjective
4) 1-place particle		7) 2-place PP
8) 2-place + NP		
8) 2-place + IO		

Table 6: *Set* patterns from EModE to PDE

EModE(Helsinki)	LModE(Archer)	Present-day(LOB)
1) 3-place	phrasal verb	2-place particle
2) 2-place particle	set + NP + Prepphrase	3-place
3) 2-place	set + NP	1-place particle
4) 2-place + Adverb	set + NP + Adjective	2-place
5) 1-place particle	set (vi)	2-place PP
6) 2-place + Adjective	set + NP + ing	1-place
7) 2-place + to-inf	set + NP + Adverb	2-place + Adjective
8) 2-place PP	set + NP + to-inf	2-place + ing
9) 1-place	set + NP + a-ing	2-place + Adverb
10) 2-place + ing		2-place + to-inf

Table 7: PrepPhrases in the *put* and *set* patterns (Archer)

	put	set
1)	in + NP (160)	on + NP (45)
2)	into + NP (154)	at + NP (25)
3)	to + NP (142)	to + NP (24)
4)	on + NP (120)	in + NP (21)
5)	out of + NP (13)	before + NP (3)
6)	under + NP (11)	by + NP (2)
7)	at + NP (10)	for + NP (1)
8)	(a)round + NP (9)	into + NP (1)
9)		within + NP (1)

(24) The plate being *put in rapid rotation,* no sensible effect was produced on the disk.

(1825 chri.s5b)

(25) They knew that the moment when the plans of the conspirators were to be *put into execution* was close at hand…

(1896 duff.j6b)

(26) … in the day of their visitation, by him whom they had injuriously treated, rejected, and *put to death.*

(1732 berk.h3b)

(27) Let us, my friends, support her all in our power, and set on foot an immediate association…

(1776 leac. D4a)

(28) My stammering tongue was *set at liberty* & the house seemed filled with the
glory of the Lord.

(1790 hill.j4a)

(29) General Pemberton *set to work* in reorganizing the army for the last desperate struggle.

(1863 anon.j6a)

Table 8. *Put* phrasal verbs (Archer)

	1650-1699	1700-1799	1800-1899	1900~	total
1) put on	8	28	29	27	92
2) put in	6	15	10	21	52
3) put up	8	12	10	18	48
4) put down	1	6	14	18	39
5) put off	3	9	5	7	24
6) put out	5	3	8	8	24
7) put together	0	5	5	4	14
8) put up with	0	2	3	6	11
9) put aside	0	0	8	3	11
10) put away	0	1	3	6	10
11) put forward	0	0	1	8	9
12) put forth	2	1	1	2	6
13) put over	0	2	1	2	5
14) put through	0	1	0	3	4
15) put back	0	1	1	1	3
16) put before	0	1	0	2	3
17) put about	0	0	1	1	2
18) put by	0	1	1	0	2
19) put past	0	0	0	2	2
20) put across	0	0	0	1	1

(30) That his coming Home so long before the Divertisements were ended, and un-
dressing himself, had given him the Unhappy Curiosity, *put on* his Habit …

(1692 cong. f2b 13)

(31) A herd of antelope has just passed us, but no Baffalo have as yet *put in* an appearance.

(1872 hart. j6b 14)

(32) He *put up* at an inn, walked forth as if to visit some one in the town ...

(1832 bulw. f5b 9)

(33) But Sir Peter is such an enemy to scandal, I believe he would have it *put down* by parliament.

(1777 sher. d4b 90)

(34) I wrote to Edward yesterday to *put off* our nephews till Friday.

(1815 aust. x5b 73)

(35) ... at length he *put out* his tongue and made towards it as tho he would lap ...

(1683 list. m2b 44)

Table 9: Set phrasal verbs (Archer)

	1650-1699	1700-1799	1800-1899	1900-	total
1) set out	6	85	14	14	119
2) set up	10	21	9	24	64
3) set in	0	18	16	15	49
4) set down	14	16	2	3	35
5) set before	6	5	3	3	17
6) set forth	4	2	6	2	14
7) set aside	0	1	3	4	8
8) set forward	2	3	1	0	6
9) set off	0	1	4	1	6
10) set about	0	1	0	4	5
11) set on	2	3	0	0	5
12) other	1	5	0	3	9

(36) We *set out* for the frontier with our caravan.

(1880 haml. j6b 49)

(37) Towards the evening, the seamen took possession of another small fort, and *set up* the English colours.

(1704 poco. j3b 29)

(38) Thus, in the month of July, rainy weather *set in* on the fifth, and …

(1775 hors. s4b 78)

(39) … wherein I had *set down* at large the principal of the Experiments I had tried …

(1676 newt. s2b 70)

(40) She enabled her to view her own condition in its true light, and *set before* her the indispensable advantages of marriage …

(1799 brow. f4a 2)

(41) … and after this we *set forth* to go a stage with Belgrave on his journey.

(1827 marc. j5b 11)

Since there is no complete synonymity in terms of syntax and semantics, two items, unless one falls out of use, continue to be used in parallel in their respective habitat.

In the case of *put* and *set*, they have the following common properties:

a. Both verbs constitute the pattern of 'V + NP + PrepPhrase'.
b. Both verbs constitute a variety of phrasal verbs.

However, when we look into the breakdown of these patterns, we can see great differences between the behaviours of *put* and *set* in these combinations. From Table 7, we can see the following similar, but at the same time different, combinations:

a. 'Set + NP + at + NP' is very frequent, but that of *put* is low.
b. 'Out of + NP' and 'under + NP' phrases are often combined with *put,* but none with *set.*
c. Also, 'into + NP' is uniquely combined with *put.*

In this connection, the OED (*s.v. put* v.25, 26; *s.v. set* v.25) gives a list of this phrasal pattern. Regarding the 'put + NP + PrepPhrase' combinations, *to* is by far the most frequent, *in/into* patterns come next, and then *on* patterns follow. Regarding the 'set + NP + PrepPhrase' combinations, *at* is most frequent, followed by *in* patterns.[2]

---

[2] I have had no space to discuss another rival verb, *bring*. The OED (*s.v. bring* 8.*fig.*) gives over fifty examples of prepositional phrases, such as *bring ~ to death, bring ~ to shame; bring ~ in doubt, bring ~ in fear; bring ~ into action, bring ~ into harmony.*

Further research is needed to integrate these relationships.

In the case of phrasal verb patterns, see Tables 8 and 9.

More variety is found in the phrasal verbs containing *put* than in those containing *set*. What is of particular interest regarding the development of phrasal verbs by *set* is that the verb has developed its aspectual function in due course. The OED describes some of these functions as follows:

a. set out (s.v. *set* 149. intr. x) (b) const. *inf.* To begin one's career or start off with the object of doing something …

b. set on (s.v. *set.* 148. c.) (b) To instigate, incite, urge on (a person) *to do* something

c. set about (s. v. set. 127. a.) (a) To begin working at, take in hand, begin upon.

(b) const. *inf.*

(c) const. *gerund*

Another pattern which *set* has developed but *put* has not is to take the complementizer of such variety. The figures in parentheses show frequency in the Archer corpus:

a. set + NP + adjective (20)

+ ing (8)

+ to-inf (7)

In this way, *put* and *set* have their separate fields; that is, *put* has developed the pattern of 'put + NP + PrepPhrase' and phrasal verbs, while *set* has developed its aspectual functions in the form of some phrasal verbs and taking *ing* or *to*-inf complementizers. Set can be said to be developing into a semi-auxiliary in some functions. [3]

4. Pray vs. please

It was in the 19th century that *pray* was replaced by *please* (see Akimoto 2000), and therefore I will focus on this period in the process of *pray* and *please* replacement. The following figure shows a rough chronological order of the variants of *please*:

---

[3] Bolinger (1980: 297) says: "The moment a verb is given an infinitive complement, that verb starts down the road of auxiliariness."

Figure 6

```
a.   if it please you  -------->  Φ
b.   if you please ( 15ᵗʰ ~16ᵗʰ )----------------------------------- 20ᵗʰ
c.   please to                            ------------        20ᵗʰ
                                     19ᵗʰ
d.   please                               -------------------- 20ᵗʰ
```

The following Tables show frequency changes of *pray* and *please* in the Late Modern English period. Table 10 is the result based on the Archer corpus. Table 11 is the result of Modern English Text Collection and Modern English Collection. Table 12 shows the result of frequency of *pray* and *please* based on Conan Doyle's Sherlock Holmes stories. His stories cover the Late Modern and the early 20ᵗʰ century periods.

Table 10: Frequency change of pray and please (Archer)

	1600-1699	1700-1799	1800-1899	1900
pray	38	99	32	4
please	0	1	23	90

(42) Mr. Sparkish, *pray* come hither, your Friend here is very troublesome, and
        very loving.

(1675 wych. d2b 67)

(43) *Please* put the enclosed scraps in the drawer and I will scrapbook them.

(1879 twn-. x6a 92)

Table 11: Frequency change of pray and please in Modern English Text Collection and Modern English Collection:

	P&P (1813)	WH (1847)	TTC (1859)	WW (1860)	CYFH (1864-5)	MM (1871-2)	RN (1878)
pray	26	8	16	35	28	47	2
please	0	0	0*	14	1	11**	21

    * please to V (4 times)
    ** please to V (7 times)
P&P = Pride and Prejudice
WH = Wuthering Heights
TTC = A Tale of Two Cities
WW = The Woman in White
CYFH = Can You Forgive Her?
MM = Middlemarch
RN = The Return of the Native

Table 12: Pray and please in the Sherlock Holmes stories

	Scarlet (1887)	Sign (1890)	Adventures (1892)	Memoirs (1894)	Baskervilles (1902)	Return (1905)	Fear (1915)	Last Bow (1917)	Casebook (1927)
pray	0	3	26	12	1	4	0	3	6
please	1	1	3	0	5	2	3	1	1

(44) '*Pray* take a seat,' said Holmes.

(A Scandal in Bohemia: 244)

(45) 'Holmes!' I cried – 'Holmes!' 'Come out,' said he, 'and *please* be careful with the revolver.'

(The Hound of the Baskervilles: 116)

I will not discuss the development of *please*, except to say that *please* seems to have developed out of the phrase *if you please* (cf. Brinton 2006); but *please to* also appeared frequently. In the Archer Corpus, *please to* occurred 6 times between 1600 and 1699, 19 times between 1700 and 1799, 3 times between 1800 and 1899, and not at all after 1900. Eliot uses *please to* 7 times and Dickens 4 times. It seems that *please* is a stylistic phenomenon, limited to certain authors.

5. Some discussion on the subjunctive forms in subordinate clauses

We have seen syntactic and functional changes in the verbs of the wanting type, as well as competition between *put* and *set*, and between *pray* and *please*. The following points are noteworthy:

The balance of co-existence of items collapses, and replacement and reshuffling affect the system as a whole. In the case of *desire*, which took the indicative and subjunctive in *that*-clauses, and accusative with infinitive, it transfers its functions to *hope* in the indicative form, to *wish* in the subjunctive form, and to *want* in the accusative with infinitive form respectively. The decline of *desire* spreads such effects to its fellow verbs.

Further repercussions can be observed in the choice of tense and mood. Let us take *desire*, for instance. Table 13 shows frequency of the change of mood forms in subordinate clauses after *desire*.

Table 13: Indicative, subjunctive and periphrastic forms in subordinate clauses after *desire* in LModE, based on the Helsinki corpus and the Archer corpus

	ME				EModE			LModE			
	I	II	III	IV	I	II	III	I	II	III	IV
desire + that											
(a) indicative	0	0	1	0	0	1	1	0	1	0	0
(b) subjunctive	0	0	0	1	0	0	0	0	0	1	1
(c) periphrastic	0	0	0	2	1	2	2	2	9	1	0
desire + φ											
(a) indicative	0	0	0	0	0	0	4	1	4	0	0
(b) subjunctive	0	0	0	0	0	0	0	1	0	0	0
(c) periphrastic	0	0	0	0	1	1	5	1	18	0	0

(46) An impoundment order was in accordance with standard practice and the lawyer involved *desired that* confidentiality *be* maintained.

(1988 atto.10[AC])

(47) … if that you doe *desire that* I *should* then come unto you …

(1570 – 1640 Private Letters[HC])

(48) … as he came to Paris to send to *desire that* he *might* waite upon my Lord Stair …

(1715 sara.x2[AC])

(49) His Honour *desires* you'*ll* be so kind …

(1697 Relapse[HC])

(50) he *desires* noght that it *be*. Bot he says as it sall be …
(a1500 (c1340) The Psalter or Psalms of David[HC])

(51) I *desire* he *may* be made to explain himself.

(1778 reev. F3[AC])

Generally speaking, the subjunctive form has been expressed in the form of peri-phrastic auxiliaries.[4] But in connection with rivalry, I would like to touch on another development of the subjunctive. In American English, the non-inflected subjunctive (Övergaard 1995) is predominant over the periphrastic subjunctive, particularly with *should*. In the history of English, with the decline of the inflec-tional subjunctive, the periphrastic subjunctive with *shall*, *should*, *may* and *must* has developed. The choice of these auxiliaries is determined by the verbs and the intensity of volition which the speaker expresses. As we have observed (see Figure 7), competition has appeared between inflectional and periphrastic sub-junctives, and a third type of subjunctive has appeared – non-inflected subjunc-tive in American English. Within the framework of grammaticalization, what is this subjunctive? Is this a case of exaptation? I shall leave this problem for future research.[5]

Figure 7

inflected	inflected periphrastic	inflected periphrastic non-inflected	periphrastic non-inflected
OE	ME	EModE	ModE

rivalry

---

[4] Poutsma (1926: 177) includes *shall*, *should*, *may* and *must* in the periphrastic auxiliaries.
[5] For some discussion of exaptation and related notions, see Hopper and Traugott (2003: 135-7).

6. Conclusion

Rivalry has rarely been discussed fully in the history of English, despite its frequent occurrence. This concept, as stated before, involves various factors leading to decline in and reshuffling of verb syntax and meanings, and the replacement of *pray* and *please* as courtesy markers.

In this paper, firstly, we have considered the interplay of verbs of the wanting type, *desire, hope, want* and *wish*, on the basis of various corpora. The verbs have changed their functions drastically in the history of English. *Desire* was very frequent in Middle English, but became infrequent in present-day English. *Hope* and *wish* have been used since Old English, separating their 'habitats' – indicative and subjunctive respectively. *Want*, which was borrowed from Old Norse about the Middle English period, has become very frequent since 1800 in the construction of 'want + (NP) + to', encroaching on the functions of the other verbs. Consequently, these changes in the verbs have brought about the reshuffling of their system.

Another example of rivalry between verbs is the competition between *put* and *set*. *Put*, which rarely appeared in OE, has increased dramatically since the Late Modern English period. In present-day English, *put* has developed its unique pattern of requiring 'object NP + prepositional phrase'. *Set* has developed its similar pattern, but at the same time has developed its aspectual and modal functions in the patterns of 'set about -ing', and 'set + NP + to-inf/ing'.

The replacement of *pray* by *please* took place in the 19th century. There are various reasons for this replacement. Firstly, a new form is dynamic, new to the ear, and more expressive. Secondly, *pray*, because of its religious connotations, may have been narrowed down in its context of use; and finally, a long vowel in *please* may have been more affective in the sense of 'earnest appeal'.

In the process of replacement, both *pray* and *please* are used in the Sherlock Holmes stories, where Holmes's use of *pray* when urging his client to go on telling his/her story shows stylistic markedness with the use of *please* becoming more predominant during that time.

The factors that promote the predominance of an item over others vary, including expressiveness, frequency and productiveness. Another important factor to be taken into account is 'constructional analogy'. Once a construction has been in line with the directionality of the development of language, items tend to be attracted to the current of language change. When we look into rival forms in a language, we must always pay attention to internal changes in the category, such as grammatical ones, as well as to external changes, such as socio-cultural ones.

Text

Sherlock Holmes. *The Complete Novels and Stories*, Vols. I, II. 2003. With an Introduction by Loren D. Estleman. New York: Bantam Dell.

Corpora

AC = Archer Corpus (A Representative Corpus of Historical English Registers).

BNC = British National Corpus (100 million words) distributed by Shogakkan Company.

FLOB = The Freiburg update of the Lancaster/Oslo/Bergen Corpus. A Corpus containing about 1 million words of British English in 1991. (Included in ICAME.)

HC = *Helsinki Corpus of English Texts, Diachronic Part*, ed. by Matti Rissanen, Merja Kytö, and Palander-Collins. (Included in ICAME.)

MED = *The Middle English Dictionary*. 1952 – 2001. Kurath, Hans, Kuhn Sherman M. and Lewis Roberts (eds.). Ann Arbor, MI: University of Michigan Press. http://ets.umdl.umich.edu/m/mec/.

Modern English Collection. University of Virginia Text Center. http://etext.lib.virginia.edu/modeng/modengO. browse.html.

Modern English Text Collection. http://www.hti.umich.edu/cgilp/pd-modeng-idx.

OED = *The Oxford English Dictionary* on CD-ROM. 1989 [2nd ed.]. Simpson, John A. and Weiner, Edmund S. C. (eds.). Oxford: Oxford University Press.

References

Akimoto, Minoji. 2000. 'The grammaticalization of the verb *pray*,' in Olga Fischer, Anette Rosenbach and Dieter Stein (eds.), *Pathways of Change: Grammaticalization in English*. Amsterdam/Philadelphia: John Benjamins: 67-84.

Bolinger, Dwight L. 1980. 'Wanna and the gradience of auxiliaries,' in G. Brett-schneider and C. Lehmann (eds.), *Wege zur Universalienforschung: Sprach-wissenschaftliche Beiträge zum 60. Geburtstag von Hansjakob Seiler*. Tübingen Beiträge zur Linguistik 145. Tübingen: Gunter Narr: 292-297.

Brinton, Laurel J. 2006. 'Pathways in the development of pragmatic markers in English,' in Ans van Kemenade and Bettelou Los (eds.), *The Handbook of the History of English*. Oxford: Blackwell: 307-334.

Hopper, Paul J. and Elizabeth C. Traugott. 2003 [1993]. *Grammaticalization*. Second Edition. Cambridge: Cambridge University Press.

Övergaard, Gerd. 1995. *The Mandative Subjunctive in American and British English in the 20th Century*. Uppsala: Almqvist & Wiksell International.

Pauwels, Paul. 2000. *Put, Set, Lay and Place: A Cognitive Linguistic Approach to Verbal Meaning.* Munich: Lincom Europa.

Poutsma, Hendrik. 1926. *A Grammar of Late Modern English.* II.II. Groningen: P. Noordhoff.

Rynell, Alarik. 1948. *The Rivalry of Scandinavian and Native Synonyms in Middle English, especially taken and nimen.* Lund: C.W.K. Gleerup. Lund Studies in English 13.

Samuels, M. L. 1972. *Linguistic Evolution.* Cambridge: Cambridge University Press.

Trier, Jost. 1931. *Der deutsche Wortschatz im Sinnbezirke des Verstandes. Die Geschichte eines sprachlichen Feldes.* Band I. Von den Anfängen bis zum Beginn des 13. Jahrhunderts. Heidelberg: Carl Winter.

Ullmann, Stephen. 1964. *Semantics: An Introduction to Meaning.* Oxford: Basil Blackwell.

21

Andrea Sand

Morphosyntactic Parallels in Englishes Around the World

1. Introduction

The spread of English around the world has resulted in a large number of new varieties, which are the result of language contact between English and one or – in most cases – several indigenous languages. Academic interest in the so-called 'New Englishes' has soared since the 1960s (cf. Viereck, Schneider and Görlach 1984, Glauser, Schneider and Görlach 1993), and recent advances in the compilation of computer-readable language corpora have broadened the scope of analysis in the study of English as a World Language. When work on the *International Corpus of English* (ICE) was under way, Sidney Greenbaum's (1996:10) vision of its potential uses ran as follows:

> As the parallel corpora become available, new possibilities open up for rigorous comparative and contrastive studies. I envisage the search for typologies of national varieties of English: first-language versus second-language, British-type versus American-type English, African versus Asian English, East African versus West African English. Researchers might explore what is common to English in all countries where it is used for internal communication, demonstrating how far it is legitimate to speak of a common core for English or of an international written standard.

The present study aims at contributing to the fascinating picture painted by Sidney Greenbaum by exploring the dichotomy between contact varieties and non-contact varieties in order to identify features which are the result of language contact, regardless of the languages involved. This includes 'New Englishes' (cf. Platt et al., 1984), such as Indian English or Kenyan English, as well as 'old' varieties such as Irish or Welsh English. Typically, research investigating contact varieties has mainly been concerned with describing their specific features (e.g. McArthur 2002), comparing these features to British or American English (e.g. Sharma 2001) or tracing individual features across a large number of varieties (e.g. Schneider 2000 on negation). The few studies in which common features of contact varieties are discussed (e.g. Platt et al. 1984, Simo Bobda 1998 and Kortmann/Szmrecsanyi 2004) all lack a solid comparable database, as they are based on anecdotal evidence or typological questionnaires. Nevertheless, they have identified a sizeable list of features. The present study provides a contribution to closing the gap between previous claims and corpus evidence with regard to two features, namely subject-verb concord and *wh*-questions.

2. Database

The analysis presented below is largely based on various subcorpora of ICE, which consist of 1,000,000 words of a controlled sample of several spoken and written text types ranging from spontaneous conversations to academic prose.[1] While the corpora from Great Britain (ICE-GB) and New Zealand (ICE-NZ) are used as linguistic benchmarks, the contact varieties under analysis are Jamaican English (ICE-JAM), which coexist with an English-lexifier Creole within a continuum spanning basilectal and mesolectal Jamaican Creole as well as various varieties of English (cf. Sand 1999:68-75); Indian English (ICE-IND), which coexists with a large number of indigenous languages, most of them Indo-Aryan (e.g. Hindi, Punjabi), some Dravidian languages (e.g. Tamil, Kannada) in the South and some Tibeto-Burman languages (cf. Kachru 1994:497-509); Kenyan English (ICE-EA(K)), which coexists with numerous indigenous languages, mostly from the Bantu family (e.g. the regional lingua franca Swahili or Kikuyo) and the Nilo-Saharan family (e.g. Luo) (cf. Skandera 2003:16-24); Singapore English (ICE-SIN), which coexists with the other official languages Malay, Mandarin and Tamil as well as a number of other varieties of Chinese and Bazaar Malay (cf. Görlach 2002:107-110); and finally Irish English, which coexists with Irish Gaelic (cf. Kallen 1997). Irish English, an 'old' variety which is mainly spoken as L1, was added to the list to determine whether it is language contact rather than L2 status that leads to shared morpho-syntactic features. Unfortunately, ICE-Ireland was not yet available at the time of writing, so two smaller corpora were used instead. The *Northern Ireland Transcribed Corpus of Speech* (NITCS) was shortened to correspond to the 200,000 words of the conversations (S1A) in the ICE corpora. In addition to this, the *Potsdam Corpus of Northern Irish English* (PNIE), a smaller corpus of about 50,000 words consisting of discussions and published prose, was used to provide more ICE-compatible text types. This proved to be

---

[1]   For more information on the ICE-Corpora see Greenbaum (1996).

sufficient for a number of features (cf. Sand 2004); but in the case of the two features presented here, the Irish data remains largely inconclusive, so that the discussion below will concentrate on the ICE-corpora and include Irish data only when feasible.

3. Subject-Verb Concord

Standard English grammar requires the subject and the predicate of a finite indicative clause to agree in number and person. Owing to the reduced inflectional system of English, this agreement or concord is not marked systematically across all persons and numbers, but plural subjects are marked and 3rd person singular predicates are marked in the present tense, as in *she comes* vs. *they come*. Only the verb *be* shows a few more distinctions, as 1st person *I am* vs. 2nd person *you are* vs. 3rd person *he/she/it is* or past tense 1st and 3rd person singular *I/he/she/it was* vs. past tense 2nd person singular and 1st to 3rd person plural *you/we/they were*. Finite and non-finite clauses, as well as prepositional phrases and adverbs used as subjects, take singular predicates. Quirk at al. (1985: 756, fn. [a]) thus formulate the general rule that "a subject which is not clearly semantically plural requires a singular verb." There are a few exceptions to this rule of thumb (cf. Biber et al. 1999: 180-188; Quirk et al. 1985: 756-758), for example with nouns which are plural in meaning but singular in form, so-called collective nouns, such as *audience, police, family* and *government*, which may take singular or plural predicates. With regard to these nouns, usage is sometimes divided between British and American standard English, as in example (1):

(1)   a. *England have won the Cup.*
      b. *America has won the Cup.*

Grammarians speak of 'notional concord' when the verb form takes the plural to agree with the plural meaning of the subject. Quirk et al. (1985: 758) point out that this usage is more common in speech than in writing and advise those who wish to adhere to the British standard to use a singular verb form when in doubt. There is a wealth of previous research on concord with collective nouns in British, American or New Zealand English, e.g. Bauer (1994:61-66), Hundt (1998:80-89), Levin (2001) and Depraetere (2003).

The regular pattern of grammatical concord may be disturbed by proximity, i.e. the tendency of speakers or writers to let the verb agree with the noun closest to it although it is not the head of the noun phrase (Biber et al. 1999:189; Quirk et al. 1985:757), as in example (2):

(2)   a. *One of the girls have got bronchitis.*
     b. *No one except his own supporters agree with him.*

Quirk et al. (1985:756) note that proximity concord more often leads to a change from singular to plural than vice versa. They (Quirk et al. 1985: 757) also note that it mainly occurs in unplanned discourse, since it is deemed ungrammatical and will be edited out of written texts. Biber et al. (1999:190) add that the principles of proximity and notional concord may reinforce each other, as in (3):

(3)   *It remains to be seen what precise form of words are agreed by the 12 heads of government.*

They also report that a number of non-standard forms of concord can be found in conversations, especially *I says* to report the speaker's own speech and *he don't*, which appear in 40 – 50% of all occurrences in informal conversations. Biber et al. (1999:190f.) conclude that these forms are due to speech processing in chunks rather than to changes in the concord rule as such. As stated before, the concord rule shows a certain degree of variability in standard English usage, regionally (British vs. American) as well as stylistically (informal conversation vs. formal writing), which makes it especially susceptible to change in language-contact situations. And indeed, non-observance of the concord rule is reported for the New Englishes in general (cf. Platt et al. 1984:46, 67; Simo Bobda 1998:9), as well as for African English (e.g. Schmied 1991:65-70), Singapore English (e.g. Wee 2004:1059), Jamaican English (e.g. Sand 1999:133-140) and Indian English (e.g. Sridhar 1996:61-63). The reasons provided for the non-application of the concord rule range from substrate influence to a tendency to reduce word-final consonant clusters.

As the ICE subcorpora – with the exception of ICE-GB – are not POS-tagged, smaller subcorpora were manually tagged for the analysis of subject-verb concord. A total of 20,000 words from the categories of direct conversations (S1A), student essays (W1A) and private letters (W1B) were used for each variety, and non-observance of the concord rule was categorized according to the categories listed above. The results are given in Figure 1.

Two main points are immediately noticeable in Figure 1: Concord exceptions are far more frequent in contact varieties (see dark bar on the right), and the few exceptions found in ICE-NZ are all in line with the possible exceptions discussed above. In the contact varieties, narrative *says*, which occurs once in ICE-NZ, does not occur at all, and invariant existential *there's* and *how's* are very rare. Proximity concord is more frequent in the contact varieties, especially in written texts when the head of a complex noun phrase is not placed in the immediate vicinity of the verb. This is illustrated in the following examples:

Figure 1

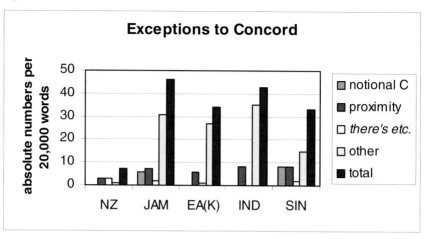

(4) *Still for some, the sacrifices made to acquire a university education motivates them to aspire for excellence.* (ICE-JAM W1A-003)

(5) *The major decline under primary products were recorded in tea.* (ICE-IND W1A-007)

(6) *But despite this, his attempts to bring order into the meeting is initially frustrated by his colleagues [...]* (ICE-EA(K) W1A-004K)

(7) *And yes, when it's a full moon the karmic particles that form an invisible bridge does help us to remember you better.* (ICE-SIN W1B-008)

The differences between ICE-NZ and the other subcorpora are more of degree than of type because proximity concord is a typical feature of unedited writing.

The occurrence of notional concord varies greatly between the corpora under analysis. Only in the small corpora from Jamaica and Singapore do we find any examples of this type, as in:

(8) *And the fees paid by the students is a means of paying for this level of professional help [...]* (ICE-JAM W1A-003)

(9) *Is 13 billion dollars adequate funding for primary and secondary level education?* (ICE-JAM W1A-003)

(10) *The United Nations has emerged as a strengthened organization.* (ICE-SIN W1A-009)

(11) Since the SAF [=Singapore Armed Forces, A.S.] *is small [...]* (ICE-SIN W1A-009).

In each of these examples, the noun phrase is grammatically a plural, but can be viewed as one semantic unit, such as a sum of money or an organizational body. In fact, the author of the essay ICE-SIN W1A-009 (11) alternates freely between singular and plural verb forms when referring to the *SAF*. In those three cases in which he uses singular predicates, he is presumably thinking of 'army' rather than 'armed forces'. As many of the examples of notional concord given in Quirk et al. (1985:758f.) and Biber et al. (1999:187f.), as well as those found in the corpus data, refer to institutions or groups of people, I checked the concord patterns for a number of collective nouns denoting groups of people in the widest sense in all the corpora under analysis. In those cases where no finite present tense verb form occurred, pronominal reference was also taken into account.

According to Biber et al. (1999:188), their corpus data revealed that *audience, board, committee, government* and *public* prefer singular concord in over 80% of all occurrences, while *staff* prefers plural concord in over 80% of all occurrences and *family* commonly occurs with both singular and plural. In Levin's (2001:120) corpus of British, Australian and American newspapers and the spoken component of the BNC, *couple, staff, public* and *crew* are most likely to be followed by plural verbs and pronouns across varieties. In the case of American English, it is only *couple* that frequently takes plural concord, while other nouns like *crew* or *family* may occasionally appear with plural concord but mostly with plural pronouns, and this only in less than 20% of all occurrences. Hundt (1998:82) confirms Biber et al.'s findings and also reports that *police* takes plural concord in almost 100% of all occurrences in her corpus of British, American and New Zealand newspapers. In Hundt's (1998:82-89) analysis, the American newspapers showed a definite preference for singular concord, while the British newspapers still had a higher percentage of plural concord and the New Zealand newspapers patterned neatly between the two other varieties. In addition, she (Hundt 1998: 88) noted that text type also plays a role in the concord patterns of certain nouns, but a diachronic comparison revealed that the general trend is leading towards singular noun concord. Levin (2001:78-86) also reports on genre-specific variation, showing that there is less variation between the different sections of newspapers in American and Australian English than in British English. The highest frequency of plural concord in the spoken data from the BNC occurred in the informal conversations. The ICE corpora contain a larger number of text types, both spoken and written; but the absolute frequencies of the individual nouns did not allow for a text-type-specific analysis. Nevertheless, an overall trend could be identified. Interestingly, ICE-NZ contains more instances of plural concord than ICE-GB, which is contrary to Hundt's (1998) analysis of the newspaper texts. However, the general trends reported by Biber et al. (1999), Hundt (1998),

Levin (2001) and Depraetere (2003) with regard to British and New Zealand English still hold. *Staff* and *police* prefer plural concord, while the case of *family* is divided and the other nouns prefer singular concord. For the contact varieties, two main points can be stated: The overall trend towards singular concord even affects *family* and *staff*, as illustrated in the following examples:

(12) *Yeah the family insists on but it is illusion* (ICE-IND S1A-034)

(13) *The Mallon family has called for a full public enquiry into the situation* [...] (PNIE news1)

(14) *We'd a, all the family was home, you know* (NITCS belfl17)

(15) *The family has since returned with wonderful memories* [...] (ICE-SIN W1B-017)

(16) *Njogu's family, for instance, is living with his mother-in-law in another part of the district.* (ICE-EA(K) rep-fe1)

(17) *Subcentres are not functioning staff is not there* (ICE-IND S1B-028)

(18) *I'm at the parish library <,> staff is here books* (ICE-JAM S1B-043)

(19) *But he disclosed that the hospital's health staff has been put on the alert.* (ICE-EA(K) popular social sciences1)

(20) *[...] then the staff usually hasn't any difficulty* (PNIE discussion1)

In the case of *police*, usage in the contact varieties is divided: While the Northern Irish and the Kenyan corpus do not contain any cases of singular concord, ICE-JAM and ICE-SIN at least contain a certain number of singular forms, and in ICE-IND they are more frequent than the plural forms.

(21) *The police has detained a security guard in connection with the murder.* [...] (ICE-JAM W2C-002)

(22) *Police says search operations will continue till Saturday* [...] (ICE-SIN S2B-014)

(23) *The police has made elaborate bandobast at all booths.* (ICE-IND W2C-006)

In the following example, the headline of a newspaper article contains a plural verb, while the opening sentence immediately following it has singular verbal and pronominal concord:

(24) *J&K Police call off stir. The Jammu and Kashmir Police, which threatened to go on an indefinite strike from today, has called off its stir after the authorities reached an agreement with the ad hoc committee of the state police.* (ICE-IND W2C-005)

This example illustrates that even within one single newspaper article, concord patterns are by no means stable. The two cases of singular concord with *police* are in line with the findings of Depraetere (2003: 111, fn. 158), who points out that the singular forms only occur as part of proper names, such as *Metropolitan Police*, in the spoken component of her corpus. This is also the case in the majority of examples of singular concord with *police* in the BNC, as in (25):

(25) *The recession has exacerbated this problem to such an extent that the Metropolitan Police has a Fraud Squad division detailed to look at the issue.* (BNC AHT 557)

There may also be a historical dimension to the concord patterns of this lexeme, since the *Oxford English Dictionary Online* shows a small number of citations of *police* + singular verb in the period before 1850, but later examples are 'colonial' in the widest sense, e.g. from Montserrat, Australia, South Africa and India. This could mean that we might be dealing with a case of superstrate retention of 19th century British usage, but a more detailed study of historical data would be necessary to prove this point.

In the case of *government,* which was the most frequently occurring collective noun under analysis, the numbers also allowed for text-type-specific analysis. According to Hundt (1998:88), plural concord is more likely in 'officialese', that is government documents and related text types, while singular concord tends to be used in newspaper texts. In the corpora used in this study the overall trend towards singular concord could be confirmed, as the two smaller corpora from Kenya and Northern Ireland did not contain any instances of plural concord. However, the remaining plural forms tended to occur in the spoken texts, mainly in S1B (public dialogue), S1A (conversations) and S2B (public monologues). In ICE-JAM, there are also two instances of plural concord in student essays (W1A). Only in ICE-GB do we also find a single occurrence in a newspaper text (W2C). Compare the following examples:

(26) *I can't tell you exactly what how much the government give.* (ICE-GB S1A-003)

(27) *They should do what the government want.* (ICE-NZ S1B-035)

(28) *In addition, the government have implemented a fairly new examination* [...] (ICE-JAM W1A-013)

(29) *And if government charge us 10 70 dollars 40 dollars they don't subsidise us much* [...] (ICE-SIN S2A-022)

(30) *Government have to bring all the people to the mainstream.* (ICE-IND S1A-025)

The analysis reveals that the instances of notional concord discussed above are not related to a tendency to use notional concord with collective nouns. On the contrary, the use of singular verb forms with NPs with overt plural marking, such as in the case of *United Nations* in the example above, are manifestations of a tendency towards uniform singular concord in these varieties. Even lexemes such as *police*, which is generally used with plural verbs in British English, are shifted into the singular concord pattern. This means that notional concord in the contact varieties does not mean plural verbs with singular noun forms, but rather singular verbs with plural nouns – whether in form or meaning.

The most striking difference between the data from ICE-NZ and the other corpora is the large number of cases labelled 'other' in Figure 1, consisting of those exceptions to the concord-rule that are specific to the contact varieties. These can be subdivided into three groups, the largest of which is made up of cases with unmarked verbs. Typical examples are shown in (31) – (34) below:

(31) *After he get married he want everything to be spick and span.* (ICE-SIN S1A-020)
(32) *It really don't sound healthy to me.* (ICE-JAM S1A-099)
(33) *It contain morphine,* [...] (ICE-IND S1A-003)
(34) *Thirdly, cliteridectomy expose women to chronic vaginal diseases.* (ICE-EA(K) W1A-009)

A special case in this group is the verb *seem* (cf. examples 35-38), which is found lacking 3rd person singular -s in all varieties under analysis. Schmied (1991:6) suggests that this may be due to its semantic affinity to modal *may* which is also not inflected. Evidence from the BNC (cf. example 39) suggests a development in British English resulting in the formulaic expression *it seem to me*, which is also found in the Jamaican example (35):

(35) *And it seem to me* [...] (ICE-JAM S1A-092)
(36) *Seem like a joke to be laughed off* [...] (ICE-EA(K) W1B-001)
(37) *This is almost* <,> *seem the Simla pattern of Orissan.* (ICE-IND S1A-047)
(38) [...] *but Keith seem to be quite okay.* (ICE-SIN S1A-067)
(39) *I mean, it seem to me it would be an ideal one.* (BNC KE6)

The data are so far insufficient to determine the exact status of *seem* in the contact varieties, and more research is definitely needed.

About the same number of non-observances labelled 'other' in Figure 1 is due to verbs with 3rd person singular marking not required by their subjects, as illustrated in examples 40-43:

(40) *Narcotics relieves pain & induces pain.* (ICE-IND W1A-003)

(41) *Most of the people who are uhm works in the lab* [...] (ICE-JAM S1A-005)

(42) *The end of the Cold War has created conditions that has given cause for some optimism.* (ICE-SIN W1A-009)

(43) [...] *so I still wait after the weekend which we was going to Nakaru.* (ICE-EA(K) W1B-001)

In studies of the New Englishes, such forms tend to be categorized as hypercorrect (e.g. Schmied 1991:66 on African Englishes or Sand 1999:140 on Jamaican English), implying that speakers are aware of the need to mark 3rd person singular in standard English and therefore sometimes overdo it for the sake of formality. However, such cases must also be seen against the backdrop of an inherent variability in the marking of 3rd person singular –s, as illustrated by examples (44)-(46), in which marked and unmarked verb forms occur in the same sentence:

(44) *You know the court works out what you say your contribution is and on that basis make a ruling as to what your interest in that property is.* (ICE-JAM S1A-099)

(45) *Then she remains out of work normally for whole day & keep busy in her routine work.* (ICE-IND W1A-001)

(46) *Sometimes it play a negative role & undermines the stability.* (ICE-IND W1A-005)

In this context, the situation in Irish English merits consideration. Filppula (2004:88-90) points out that subject-verb concord is highly variable, as a number of – sometimes contradictory – influences have shaped the variety: Northern Middle English and Scots contributed the so-called Northern Subject rule, according to which pronominal subjects do not take 3rd person singular marking. There are several and at times competing factors involved in the development of concord patterns in Irish English: Southern English dialects favouring –s for all plural verbs, as well as some dialects of Irish Gaelic without overt concord after plural subjects, and a general trend in English to ignore subject-verb concord, especially in existential constructions, as illustrated in Figure 1 above. This mixture of influences leads to a high degree of variability, but only in a small percentage of all finite clauses, very similar to what we find in the ICE-corpora of the contact varieties. Compare the following examples (47)-(48) from the NITCS:

(47) *If they pass it, well the girls goes to the convent, [...]* (NITCS belfl22)

(48) *And they go, the teachers is from around here that goes to Creggan School, and they take some of the children with them.* (NITCS belfl 17)

It is therefore very likely that the variability of subject-verb concord in the New Englishes is also due to a range of sometimes contradictory factors, of which the substrate languages only play a minor role because the languages involved range from highly inflecting, such as Hindi, to completely analytic languages without verb inflection, such as Mandarin Chinese or Jamaican Creole. More relevant factors are a tendency to regularize the irregular verb inflections of Modern English by either using the unmarked verb or the marked verb for all persons or numbers, a tendency to use prestigious standard forms more often or also not paying attention to 3rd person singular –s as it is redundant in terms of information processing. These findings are also in line with language-acquisition research which reveals a certain degree of variability with regard to the marking of 3rd person singular –s, and occurrence in some contexts and speakers may be as low as 0% (Long 2003:499-501). Typological factors, such as the development of English from a synthetic to an analytic language and the marked character of 3rd person singular –s, also contribute to variation and change with regard to this feature, which is not entirely random, as the shared patterns across different varieties show.

4. Interrogatives

When a speaker requires information and wishes to invite a reply from an open range of possible answers, a *Wh*-question is used. *Wh*-questions are formed by placing an interrogative pronoun, such as *who, what* or *why*, in clause initial position, as in (49) – (51):

(49) *Who's calling?*

(50) *What are they doing?*

(51) *Why did you buy that?*

If the interrogative pronoun is the subject of the clause, as in example (49), the word order of the clause remains the same. If the interrogative pronoun fulfils another function in the clause, the word order of subject and the finite element of the predicate is exchanged, as in example (50). Grammarians call this movement subject-verb inversion. In clauses in which there is only a finite lexical verb rather than an auxiliary, the auxiliary *do* is introduced to form the question, as in example (51) (Biber et al. 1999:204-206; Quirk et al. 1985:817-823). If questions are formulated indirectly, an embedded *Wh*-clause is used. In this case, inversion and DO-periphrasis are not required (Biber et al. 1999:690), as in (52):

(52)   *He wants to know who will attend the conference.*

According to Platt, Weber and Ho (1984:127f.) and Kortmann and Szmrecsanyi (2004:1200), lacking DO-periphrasis and/or lacking auxiliary inversion in direct questions, but also inversion in indirect questions, are widespread in L2-varieties of English, such as Indian English (cf. Kachru 1994:520), Jamaican English (cf. Sand 1999:141-143), African Englishes (Schmied 1991: 74) and Singapore English (Wee 2004:1063f.). In most cases, these deviations from the standard English interrogative construction are explained with reference to the substrate languages involved.

In order to test these claims, all direct *Wh*-questions in the conversations (S1A-001 – S1A-100) were analysed,[2] which yielded several hundred tokens per variety. When we compare the percentage of non-standard interrogative constructions across the corpora (cf. Figure 2), the difference between ICE-GB and ICE-NZ on the one hand and the contact varieties on the other is striking.

The comparatively low frequencies in ICE-EA(K) may be due to the fact that S1A was supplemented with material from S1B to make up for missing material, and this included parliamentary debates and court proceedings in their published rather than transcribed form. Regardless of the varying frequencies, the questions that do not comply with the rules of international standard English generally fall into three categories which are well-attested across all contact varieties.

The first type consists of questions with a fronted *Wh*-pronoun which maintain the usual SVO-word order of English declaratives and do not display inversion of the subject and the auxiliary or main verb BE, as in examples (53)-(56):

(53)   *What this is* (ICE-EA(K) broadcast discussion)
(54)   *What you're talking about* (ICE-JAM S1A-092)
(55)   *Hey what you're doing there* (ICE-SIN S1A-007)
(56)   *What kind of job you are seeking* (ICE-IND S1A-070)

As can be seen in the examples, the use of a contracted form of BE favours this type of question construction; but is not a prerequisite, as the examples Kenya (53), Jamaica (54) and India (56) show. This type of non-standard question is the

---

2   In the case of ICE-JAM and ICE-EA(K), which did not contain the full 200,000 words in S1A, the more formal public dialogues (S1B) were included in the analysis. In the case of ICE-EA(K), these also contain printed versions of parliamentary debates and court proceedings instead of transcriptions.

Figure 2

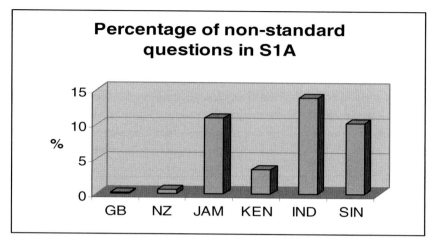

second most frequent in ICE-IND, but the least frequent type in the other ICE corpora of contact varieties.

The second category is the one which also (rarely) occurs in the benchmark corpora from Great Britain and New Zealand. In these cases, there is no inversion because the necessary form of BE or DO is not used. In the L1-varieties, this is probably due to processes in casual allegro speech in which clitic *d'*, *'s or 're* are completely elided, as in the only example from ICE-GB (57):

(57)　*So what you know* (ICE-GB S1A-075)
(58)　*What job you doing* (ICE-NZ S1A-073)

The examples from the contact varieties are more numerous and may also contain a tensed verb form, which shows that we are not dealing with an elided form of *'d*, but with a complete lack of DO support. Compare examples (59) – (62):

(59)　*So what you did* (ICE-JAM S1B-064)
(60)　*What we do* (ICE-EA(K) broadcast interview)
(61)　*What he died of ah* (ICE-SIN S1A-082)
(62)　*What she does* (ICE-IND S1A-038)

This kind of question without DO support is the most frequent type of non-standard question in ICE-IND and ICE-JAM, as well as the second most frequent in ICE-EA(K) and ICE-SIN.

In the third type of non-standard question, the *Wh*-element remains in situ instead of being fronted to clause initial position. Constructions of this type may occur in international standard English, but only in very restricted contexts. On the one hand, Quirk et al. (1985:817, fn. [f]) mention the occasional use of questions with declarative word order and the *Wh*-element in situ in the context of interrogations and interviews, as in example (63):

(63)   *A: So you boarded the train where? B: At Los Angeles.*

On the other hand, the *Wh*-element is not fronted in so-called echo questions, in which at least part of the previous utterance is repeated and the speaker wishes to seek confirmation of the aforesaid or express incredulity or irony, as in (64):

(64)   *A: I'll pay for that. B: You'll what?*

Quirk et al. (1985:835f.) consider this type of question familiar or even impolite, unless it is accompanied by an apology. There is one example (65) of an echo question in the conversations in ICE-NZ (in 494 direct *what*-questions) and none in ICE-GB:

(65)   *A: She looked a bit struck*
        B: She was what
        A: She looked a bit struck (ICE-NZ S1A-087)

In the contact varieties under analysis, this type of question is much more frequent and also occurs instead of a neutral *Wh*-question in a variety of contexts in everyday conversations, as shown in the following examples (66) – (69):

(66)   *We are going to do what* (ICE-JAM S1B-007)
(67)   *Now discuss what* (ICE-EA(K) conversation)
(68)   *Do you know what* (ICE-IND S1A-048)
(69)   *You get diploma in what in what* (ICE-SIN S1A-052)

This is the most frequent type of non-standard interrogative construction in ICE-SIN and ICE-EA(K), and the second most frequent type in ICE-JAM. The corpus analysis revealed that contact varieties indeed display not only more non-standard *Wh*-questions, but also different types of constructions when compared to ICE-GB and ICE-NZ. While their individual frequencies may vary, all types are attested in all varieties under analysis, regardless of the substrate languages involved.

With regard to embedded questions, I looked at those indirect *what*-questions which showed inversion of subject and auxiliary, and systematically checked embedded clauses following the reporting verbs *ask* and *wonder*. In many cases, it was very difficult to decide in the transcriptions whether an utterance was intended as a direct or an indirect question. Generally, I counted those as definite direct questions in which the question is preceded by a pause, displays operator inversion and is transcribed as a new utterance, as in the following example from ICE-IND (70):

(70) *And in fact people ask me <,> How do you compare a champion of a <,> nineteen twenties or thirties* (ICE-IND S1B-047)

In this example, the transcription, the syntax and the choice of pronouns (*me* vs. *you*) all confirm that the question is a direct quote. Unfortunately, however, things are often much less clear-cut. To be on the safe side, I relied on the transcriptions and counted all instances without a pause or a new utterance between reporting verb and interrogative as embedded. Interestingly, similar cases also occur in ICE-NZ and ICE-GB, but with lower frequencies than in the contact varieties. The difference is one of degree rather than of absolutes, as is illustrated by the figures in Table 1.

One could argue on the basis of these percentages that speakers of contact varieties more often blend direct and indirect questions than speakers of British or New Zealand English. This might be related to the degree of formality as well, since the more formal *wonder* is followed by considerably lower percentages of inverted embedded interrogatives than the neutral or less formal *ask*. Besides, all occurrences after *wonder* could be analysed as direct questions as well since they occur in spoken texts, do not contain the subordinators *whether* or *if* and display subject–auxiliary inversion; in addition, the pronouns are not changed according to speaker perspective. Compare the following example (71):

(71) *I wonder do they really live like that* (ICE-NZ S1A-081)

The situation is different with *ask*. Here, we find a larger number of clearly embedded clauses – based on the verb form and the pronouns – in the contact varieties which do not follow the rules of international standard English:

(72) *And I asked him had he a spare Saturday Night, you know, the sportspaper.* (NITCS belfl 14)

(73) *I ask her whether will they be advertising.* (ICE-SIN S1A-023)

Table 1: Embedded interrogative clauses after *ask* and *wonder*

	*ask** + embedded interrogative		*wonder** + emb. interrogative	
	Total	% inversion	total	% inversion
ICE-GB	100	13%	91	1.1%
ICE-NZ	144	7.6%	111	3.6%
ICE-EA(K)	144	14.6%	113	5.9%
ICE-JAM	50	32%	64	9.4%
ICE-IND	75	28%	46	10.9%
ICE-SIN	170	27.6%	88	9.1%
NITCS/PNIE	19	47.4%	14	0%

(74)   [...] and *I was asking his wife how does she feels now* [...] (ICE-IND S1B-035)

(75)   *The gunmen asked him where was the money from the sale of irish [sic] potatoes.* (ICE-JAM W2C-012)

(76)   *Ask him was he in the office on the day of 17ᵗʰ Feb.* (ICE-EA(K) business letter)

Example (73) from Singapore, which combines the subordinator *whether* with the syntax of a direct question, is an exception, but it serves well to illustrate that these questions really are meant to be embedded questions. As the examples show, they may also appear in written texts in some of the corpora, namely in ICE-JAM and ICE-EA(K). The use of inverted syntax affects both *Wh*-questions and *yes/no*-questions. The examples from ICE-GB and ICE-NZ, on the other hand, are restricted to spoken texts and could generally also be interpreted as direct questions, as in the examples for *wonder* above. These examples demonstrate that contact varieties indeed display a blend of strategies in the case of embedded questions which go beyond the possibilities of international standard English usage.

As inverted *Wh*-questions are cross-linguistically rare, the tendencies in the contact varieties are in line with general typological trends (Whaley 1997:239-242). Uninverted *Wh*-questions are also attested in SLA research in the initial stages of acquisition, and DO-periphrasis is generally acquired after inversion, regardless of the learner's L1. Similarly, embedded questions with inversion tend to occur in the second stage of acquisition, when the inversion rule for direct questions is acquired and overgeneralized with embedded questions (Braidi 1999:28-32). As in the case of subject-verb concord, a small degree of variability in international standard English and strong cross-linguistic and acquisitional trends overrule the possible influence of the substrate languages.

5. Conclusions

The two features discussed in the present paper are only two of a larger number I originally investigated which all support the view that it is the phenomenon of language contact in itself that is responsible for many differences between contact and non-contact varieties of English. The evidence presented weakens previous claims in favour of substrate influence as the resulting forms and constructions are very similar, regardless of the substrates involved. In a few cases, superstrate retention from non-standard varieties of English spoken by the English speakers present during the formative stages of a variety may also have played a role, as in the case of the possible dialectal influence on the observance or non-observance of the subject-verb concord rule discussed above. As has been shown, typology and SLA-research present more promising candidates for explanatory factors for these parallel features. In some cases, all four factors – substrate, superstrate, typology and SLA – may reinforce one another. The contribution of each is thus difficult to determine. It appears to me that language contact generally magnifies the 'problem areas' or 'weak spots' in the grammatical system of English, and intensifies a development to overcome these, despite the normative influence of grammar books and school-teaching. It remains important to note, however, that all the forms and constructions presented are not the preferred ones in the speech and writing of educated speakers as represented in the ICE corpora. They are a stylistic option rather than a cut-and-dried rule and more likely to occur in informal and spoken language than in formal and written language. This is easily shown in corpora consisting of various text types.

The two features presented here only provide a glimpse of the whole picture, but they nevertheless show the usefulness of a corpus-based comparative approach to variation in English. More research along these lines is needed in order to arrive at a clearer picture of what happens in the morphosyntax as English is adapted by more and more L2-speakers around the world.

References

Bauer, Laurie. 1994. *Watching English Change.* London: Longman.

Biber, Douglas, Stig Johansson, Geoffrey Leech, Susan Conrad and Edward Finegan. 1999. *Longman Grammar of Spoken and Written English.* Harlow: Longman.

Braidi, Susan M. 1999. *The Acquisition of Second-Language Syntax.* London: Arnold.

Depraetere, Ilse. 2003. "On verbal concord with collective nouns". *English Language and Linguistics* 7(1): 85-127.

Filppula, Markku. 2004. "Irish English: morphology and syntax". In *A Handbook of Varieties of English*, Bernd Kortmann, Kate Burridge, Rajend Meshtrie, Edgar Schneider and Clive Upton (eds), vol. II, 73-101. Berlin: Mouton deGruyter.

Glauser, Beat, Edgar W. Schneider and Manfred Görlach. 1993. *A New Bibliography of Writings on Varieties of English 1984-1993*. Amsterdam: Benjamins.

Görlach, Manfred. 2002. "English in Singapore, Malaysia, Hong Kong, Indonesia, the Philippines...A second or a foreign language?" In *Still More Englishes*, 99-117. Amsterdam and Philadelphia: John Benjamins.

Greenbaum, Sidney (ed.). 1996. *Comparing English Worldwide: The International Corpus of English*. Oxford: Clarendon.

Hundt, Marianne. 1998. *New Zealand English Grammar: Fact or Fiction?* Amsterdam and Philadelphia: John Benjamins.

Kachru, Braj B. 1994. "English in South Asia". In *The Cambridge History of the English Language: English in Britain and Overseas: Origins and Development*, (Robert Burchfield ed.), vol. v, 497-553. Cambridge: CUP.

Kallen, Jeffrey L. (ed.). 1997. *Focus on Ireland*. Amsterdam and Philadelphia: John Benjamins.

Kortmann, Bernd and Benedikt Szmrecsanyi. 2004. "Global synopsis". In *A Handbook of Varieties of English*, Bernd Kortmann, Kate Burridge, Rajend Meshtrie, Edgar Schneider and Clive Upton (eds), vol. II, 1142-1202. Berlin: Mouton deGruyter.

Levin, Magnus. 2001. *Agreement with Collective Nouns*. Lund: Lund University Press. Lund Studies in English 103.

Long, Michael H. 2003. "Stabilization and fossilization in interlanguage development". In *Handbook of Second Language Acquisition*, Michael H. Long and Catherine Doughty (eds), 487-535. London: Blackwell.

McArthur, Tom. 2002. *Oxford Guide to World English*. Oxford: OUP.

Platt, John T., Heidi Weber and Mian Lian Ho. 1984. *The New Englishes*. London: Routledge.

Quirk, Randolph, Sidney Greenbaum, Geoffrey Leech and Jan Svartvik. 1985. *A Comprehensive Grammar of the English Language*. London: Longman.

Sand, Andrea. 1999. *Linguistic Variation in Jamaica: A Corpus-based Study of Radio and Newspaper Usage*. Tübingen: Narr.

Sand, Andrea. 2004. "Shared Morpho-Syntactic Features of Contact Varieties: Article Use". *World Englishes* 23(2): 281-298.

Schmied, Josef. 1991. *English in Africa: An Introduction*. London: Longman.

Schneider, Edgar. 2000. "Feature diffusion versus contact effects in the evolution of New Englishes: A typological case study of negation patterns". *English Worldwide* 21: 201-232.

Sharma, Devyani. 2001. "The pluperfect in native and non-native varieties of English: A comparative corpus analysis". *Language Variation and Change* 13: 343-73.

Simo Bobda, Augustin. 1998. *The Indigenization of English in Cameroon and New Englishisms.* Essen: LAUD.

Skandera, Paul. 2003. *Drawing a Map of Africa: Idiom in Kenyan English.* Tübingen: Narr.

Sridhar, S.N. 1996. "Toward a syntax of South Asian English". In *South Asian English: Structure, Use and Users,* Robert J. Baumgardner (ed.), 55-69. Urbana, IL: University of Illinois Press.

Viereck, Wolfgang, Edgar W. Schneider and Manfred Görlach. 1984. *A Bibliography of Writings on Varieties of English 1965-1984.* Amsterdam: Benjamins.

Wee, Lionel. 2004. "Singapore English: morphology and syntax". In *A Handbook of Varieties of English*, Bernd Kortmann, Kate Burridge, Rajend Meshtrie, Edgar Schneider and Clive Upton (eds), vol. II, 1058-1072. Berlin: Mouton deGruyter.

Whaley, Lindsay. 1997. *Introduction to Typology: The Unity and Diversity of Language.* Thousand Oaks: Sage.

22

Yoshihiko Ikegami

'Subjective Construal' and 'Objective Construal' in Grammar and Lexicon: Typological Considerations

I start by discussing a pair of contrasting notions, 'subjective construal' and 'objective construal', which occur as technical terms in cognitive linguistics. I then proceed to argue that the speakers of different languages may differ in the extent to which they prefer one type of construal to the other, that speakers of Japanese tend to indulge in subjective construal more readily than speakers of English (and of western languages in general, for that matter) and that subjective construal, for Japanese speakers, can in fact be regarded as underlying what Benjamin Lee Whorf once called 'fashions of speaking', while for speakers of English (and again also of western languages in general) objective construal is the most natural stance to take in linguistically encoding a situation. I conclude by referring to several characteristic semantic features in the grammar and lexicon of English as compared with those of Japanese which presumably derive from the language speaker's preferential choice of one type of construal over the other.

1. An Illustration

Rather than engaging in a theoretical discussion of the contrast between subjective and objective construal, let me start by discussing a concrete example illustrating the contrast. The example in question concerns the initial sentence of the novel *Snow Country* by Yasunari Kawabata (1899-1972), the winner of the 1968 Nobel Prize for literature, and its four translations:

(0) 国境　　の　長い　トンネル　　　を　　　　抜ける　　　　と
　　 boundary　's　long　tunnel　'path' marker　pass through　and/when

　　 雪国　　　　　　　で　　　　　あった。
　　 snow country　'location' marker　was
(literally, something like '[I] PASSED THROUGH [THE] LONG BOUNDARY-TUNNEL, AND [I] WAS IN / [THERE] WAS [THE] SNOW COUNTRY.')

(1) The train came out of the long tunnel into the snow country. (E. Seiden-sticker)

(2) Als der Zug aus dem langen Grenztunnel herauskroch, lag das Schneeland vor ihm weit ausgebreitet. (O. Benl)

(3) Jenseits des langen Tunnels erschien das Schneeland. (T. Cheung)

(4) Un long tunnel entre les deux régions et voici qu'on était dans le pays de neige. (B. Fujimori)

The scene to be linguistically encoded here is the following: 'The train, on which the hero of the novel is travelling, passes through the long tunnel which lies at the county-boundary and comes out to the snow-covered land.'

Although the four translations are supposed to linguistically encode one and the same scene, they diverge rather drastically from one another in the ways they construe it and linguistically encode it. The most notable difference is that translations (1) and (2) encode the train, while translations (3) and (4) do not. (Incidentally, the original sentence in Japanese does not mention the train.) Why is it that the English and the first German translation, but not the second German and the French translation (or, for that matter, the original Japanese sentence), mention the train?

The hero of the novel is on the train, watching the changing scenes outside as the train goes through and comes out of the long tunnel into the snow-covered open areas. Imagine yourself on the train, looking out of the window and watching the successive scenes as they fly past you. And imagine yourself reporting what you see – what is directly perceived by you. Since you are on the train and are moving with the train, the train is part of your expanded self, so to speak. You don't have to, and actually can't, see the train (that is, in its entirety, to be more precise). The train is not an object of your perception. Hence the train doesn't have to be encoded. This, in fact, is the subjective construal. The speaker is embedded in the environment, and he sees his environment but not himself; hence he is encoded as zero (Ikegami 2007). The translators of (3) and (4) were fully aware of the subjective way of construal in which the original Japanese sentence was encoded and obviously tried to reproduce the feature in their translations. The translators of (1) and (2) behaved differently. They let the hero of the novel in the train undergo a self-split, one part of him stepping out of the train and perceiving from outside the train carrying his other counterpart. This is the objective construal. (Cf. Kawabata (2004[1924]), whose poetically rendered version contrasts the two types of construal in terms of 'Am I within the lily?' versus 'Do the lily and I exist independently of each other?')

2. The Definition of the Two Types of Construal

In terms of cognitive linguistics, the two types of construal we are concerned with can now be defined as follows:

Subjective construal: the speaker is on the very scene he is to construe and construes the scene as it is perceivable to him. Even if the speaker is not on the scene he is to construe, he may mentally project himself onto the scene he is to construe and construes it as it would be perceived by him. His stance is egocentric, and consequently he may encode himself as zero.

Objective construal: the speaker is outside the scene he is to construe and construes it as it is perceivable to him. Even if the speaker is on the scene he is to construe, he may mentally displace himself outside the scene he is to construe and construes it as it would be perceived by him. As part of the object of conceptualization, he will encode himself in explicit terms as he does others.

Here is a triplet of example sentences discussed by Langacker:

Cf.   (5) Vanessa is sitting across the table from Veronica.
      (6) Vanessa is sitting across the table from me.
      (7) Vanessa is sitting across the table.   (Langacker 1991: 326, 328)

Sentence (5) will be uttered by a speaker who locates himself outside the scene in which Vanessa and Veronica are seated at the table. The speaker who watches the scene and the scene being watched and spoken about by the speaker are fully distinct. Hence we have objective construal here.

Skipping sentence (6) for the moment, we turn to sentence (7) first, because sentence (7) is most clearly contrasted with sentence (5). Sentence (7) refers to a situation in which the speaker is sitting across the table from Vanessa and describing the scene as it is perceivable to him. The speaker is fully involved in the very scene he is describing; moreover, he is located at the origin of his perceptual field. Hence he does not see himself and does not have to encode himself. Here, the speaker as perceiving subject is fully merged with the object of his perceptual world. Hence we have subjective construal here. Notice the zero-encoding of the speaker.

What happens with sentence (6), then? Sentence (6) will most appropriately be uttered when the speaker is looking at a picture which shows the speaker and Vanessa sitting facing each other across a table. Since the speaker is looking at himself as shown in the picture, the perceiving subject is fully distinct from the object of his perception. Hence what we have here is objective construal. Notice also that sentence (6) could be uttered in the same situation to which sentence (7) is applicable, namely when the speaker is on the very scene he is describing. What happens then, however, is that the speaker mentally undergoes a self-split, steps out of the scene he is describing and from his new vantage point observes his counterpart left on the scene.

Interestingly enough, the reverse process is also conceivable. Thus sentence (7) could be uttered in the same situation to which sentence (6) is applicable, namely when the speaker is looking at a picture which shows him sitting across the table from Vanessa. Thus the speaker empathizes with his image in the picture and imagines his experience at the moment the picture was taken (cf. Langacker 1991: 365). The speaker mentally projects himself into his image in the picture and imagines himself describing the scene in which he himself is involved. Thus the contrast between the perceiving subject and the object of his perception is neutralized. The speaker is located at his vantage point and hence does not have to encode himself.

3. Preferential Choice between the Two Types of Construal as 'Fashions of Speaking'

Shifting our focus onto the speaker, we can characterize the two types as follows:

> The maximally subjectively oriented speaker will prefer to conceptualize the situation to be encoded as if he were on the scene and were experiencing it himself, irrespective of whether he is actually there or not. His stance is egocentric, and consequently he may encode himself as zero.
>
> The maximally objectively oriented speaker, by contrast, will prefer to take a detached outlook on the situation to be encoded; even if he is involved in the situation, he tends to conceptualize himself as he does others. As part of the object of conceptualization, he will encode himself in explicit terms as he does others.

Speakers of different languages may differ in their preferential choice between subjective and objective construal. For the Japanese speaker, linguistic encoding in terms of subjective construal is apparently a 'fashion of speaking' (Whorf 1956), while the English speaker (or, for that matter, speakers of western languages in general) prefers encoding in terms of objective construal.

Consider the following examples:

(8) [asking the way in a strange place]
   a) Where am I?
   b) Koko wa doko desu ka? (word-for-word: 'HERE TOPIC WHERE IS QUESTION'; literally, 'WHERE IS HERE?' or 'WHAT PLACE IS THIS PLACE?')

The objectivity of the English sentence is marked by the explicit use of the first-person pronoun referring to the speaker. The Japanese sentence is based on sub-jective construal, with the speaker being unencoded.

(9) [a piece of the speaker's monologue in an empty room]
    a) Dare mo inai. (word-for-word: 'ANYBODY TOPIC/EMPHATIC NON-EXIST-ENT'; literally, 'NOBODY IS (HERE)')
    b) Es ist niemand da (außer mir). (Nobody is here (except me).)

The Japanese speaker doesn't encode her-/himself. The German speaker could construe objectively her-/himself looking at her-/himself.

(10) [in a telephone conversation]
    a) 'May I speak to Mr. Jones?' 'This is he.'
    b) 'Jones-san to ohanashi dekimasuka?' 'Watakushi desu.' (word-for-word: 'JONES-MR.WITH SPEAK(honorific) CAN(honorific)' 'I AM'; literally, 'MAY (I) SPEAK WITH MR. JONES?' 'I AM' or '(IT) IS ME')

The English speaker readily objectifies her-/himself. A sentence encoded in the same way would sound extremely bizarre in Japanese.

(11) [Little Red Riding Hood knocks on the door and then the following conversation ensues between her and her grandmother]
    a) 'Wer ist draussen?' 'Rotkäppchen, das bringt Kuchen und Wein.' ('Who's there?' 'Little Red Riding Hood, who brings you cake and wine.')
    b) 'Dare desuka?' 'Akazukinyo. Keki to wain o motte kita wa'. (word-for-word: 'WHO-IS(honorific)' 'RED-HOOD CONFIRMATORY PARTICLE. CAKE AND WINE OBJECT-MARKER HAVING CAME-FEMALE CONFIRMATORY PARTICLE'; literally, 'WHO IS (IT)?' '(IT'S) LITTLE RED RIDING HOOD. (I) HAVE BROUGHT CAKE AND WINE.')

In the German sentence the speaker objectifies herself in relation to the ad-dressee. In the Japanese sentence, the speaker adheres to the egocentric slant, herself being encoded as zero.

4. Further Indices of Subjective Construal

4.1 Discourse and Syntax
The difference in the preferential choice between one type of construal over the

other leaves certain marks in various aspects of the languages of the respective speakers. At the level of discourse, we thus find that frequent alternations of past and present tense characterize the narrative of a past event in Japanese, where over seventy per cent of the predicates can be found encoded in present rather than past tense forms (Ikegami 1986), showing how readily the narrator projects him-/herself into the situations being talked about. On the other hand, the zero subject to be interpreted as first person in the Japanese original text is often found to be rendered explicitly as third-person subject in the English translation (e.g. '[WE] WENT OVER SEKIYAMA AND ARE (NOW) ON THE BEACH OF OTSU' (Japanese original) rendered as 'They passed on through Sekiyama and came to the Beach of Otsu' (English translation)).

4.2 Lexicon

Subjective construal, as we have seen, is characterized by the speaker's direct involvement with the situation he is to construe and encode. This particular stance on the part of the speaker may have certain effects on the way the meaning of a lexical item is conceived. Being subjectively conceived, the lexical meaning will be conceived either physically, in terms of the way in which the speaker interacts with the referent in question, rather than in terms of the distinctive features attributed to the referent in question or psychologically, in terms of the private mental state of the speaker rather than in terms of the outwardly manifested behaviour of the speaker.

4.2.1 Nouns

The meaning of a noun referring to a place where a certain human activity takes place can be interpreted either as 'a locus of activity' (i.e. subjectively, or in terms of the way in which the speaker interacts with the place in question) or as 'an entity located on the spot in question' (i.e. objectively, or in terms of the building in which the activity is performed). Definitions given in English and Japanese dictionaries offer a clear contrast in this respect:

> *crematorium* = 'a building in which the bodies of dead people are burned at a funeral ceremony' (*LDOCE*4)
> *kasojo* = 'a place where cremation takes place'
> *stadium* = 'a building for public events, esp. sports and large rock music concerts, consisting of a playing field surrounded by rows of seats' (*LDOCE* 4)
> *kyogijo* = 'a place where games are played'

4.2.2 Adjectives

The meaning of the adjective *tall* is generally defined in the dictionary as 'of a greater height than normal'. This is an objective definition, referring to the object with which the speaker interacts. Evaluation of the collocations of the adjective *tall* in terms of the seven scales (Dirven and Taylor 1988) offers the following ratings: 'tall person' (1.05), 'tall poplar' (1.71), 'tall reeds' (1.97), 'tall lamppost' (2.02), 'tall telegraph pole' (2.53) … 'tall pyramid' (3.97), 'tall mountain' (4.86), 'tall cloud' (6.40) …

On the basis of these ratings, it will be possible to define the prototypical sense of *tall* as 'applied to something long and slender, typically in an upright position and growing or having grown upwards.' This, however, is still an objective definition. Can't we propose a subjective definition here, namely 'applied to something with which the speaker interacts in such a way that he is obliged to bend back when he approaches it and tries to look at its top'?

Cf. also the semantic shift of the adjective *wide*, which originally meant 'having great extent (esp. horizontally)', as in 'wide sea' and 'wide world', of which the subjective impression one has is 'no boundary being visible'. However, it now means 'having great extent from side to side', generally being 'restricted to applications in which actual mensuration from point to point is possible or contemplated' (OED *wide*).

Mightn't it be worthwhile to assume that the meanings of such adjectives as *heavy* and *beautiful* were also initially conceived of subjectively (i.e. giving certain impressions to the speaker in interaction, either physically or psychologically) rather than objectively (i.e. having certain attributes which give certain impressions to the speaker)? Can we talk of the 'evolution' of lexical meaning here – with regard not only to the chronological development of language, but also to the developmental process of language acquisition?

The English adjective *kind* is defined as 'saying and doing things that show that you care about other people and want to help them or make them happy' (*LDOCE* 4). Its meaning is defined, objectively (i.e. referring to a certain type of outwardly manifested and publicly perceivable behaviour). The semantically corresponding Japanese adjective *shinsetsu-na* tends to refer to the private psychological states motivating a certain type of outwardly manifested behaviour. Note that *kind* can be used in the imperative (i.e. *Be kind!*), and that its nominalized form *kindness* can readily be used as a count noun (i.e. *a kindness, kindnesses*).

The language note on the adjective *kind* and the adjective *kindly* in *LDOCE* 3 says that the latter 'describes a person's general character', while the former 'often describes someone's behaviour at one particular moment'. Cf. also a contrastive pair of English and Japanese adjectives like *polite* (defined as 'behaving or speaking in a way that is correct for the social situations you are in, and showing that you are careful to consider other people's needs and feelings' (*LDOCE* 4)) and *teinei-na* (which could be defined as 'being careful to consider other people's needs and feelings').

4.2.3 Verbs

There are verbs of action which imply the achievement of the goal intended by the action (e.g. the English verb *kill* and the semantically corresponding Japanese verb *korosu*) and verbs of action which do not necessarily imply any such achievement (e.g. the English verb *invite* and the semantically corresponding Japanese verb *shotaisuru*):

> 'I killed him, and he died / *but he didn't die.'
> 'I invited him to come to the party, and he came / but he didn't come.'

There are, however, cases in which English verbs of action imply the achievement of the intended goal, but the semantically corresponding Japanese verbs of action do not necessarily do so:

> 'I woke Daddy, and he woke up / * but he was fast asleep.'
> 'I helped John (to) pass the exam, and he passed / *but he didn't pass.'
> (The corresponding Japanese verbs of action can be used in either way.)

There are no cases in which semantically corresponding English and Japanese verbs of action behave in opposite ways (i.e. the English verbs do not necessarily imply the achievement of the intended goal, whereas the Japanese counterparts do). Cf. Ikegami (1981).

Now the question is: why do Japanese verbs of action tend to behave unmarkedly as to the implication of the successful achievement of the goal? The answer will probably be: the Japanese speaker, oriented towards subjective construal, tends to conceive himself as being in the process of action, at which moment he is not certain whether he is going to achieve his goal or not.

5. Concluding Remarks

In subjective construal, the speaker fully involves himself in the situation he is going to construe and encode. The speaker describes the situation as it is perceivable to him and as it is directly experienced ('erlebt') by him. He verbalizes on the basis of his private experience through his own body. One may well speculate that this represents the earliest stage of the use of language – the stage at which the language used by the speaker is closely associated with, and is not yet alienated from, his own body. At this stage, the use of language is characteristically egocentric and monologic, its dominant function being 'expressive' (or ego-oriented). A step out of this highly 'subjective' stage is made possible through the awareness on the part of individual speakers that they, as fellow humans, perceive and experience things largely in the same way. This leads certain utterances of theirs to attain 'intersubjective' status. And it will be only a few steps from here to the further stages in which language is seized upon and used as the means of conveying information to other fellow humans – in short, as the means of communication. Here language is turned into an 'objective' entity, quite alienated from the body. Whether or not an evolutionary scenario like this can really be verified is of course still an open question.

References

Dirven, Rene and John R. Taylor (1988) 'The Conceptualisation of Vertical Space in English: The Case of *Tall*', in Brygida Rudzka-Ostyn, ed.: *Topics in Cognitive Linguistics*, Amsterdam: John Benjamins.

Ikegami, Yoshihiko (1981) *SURU to NARU no Gengogaku: Gengo to Bunka no Taiporoji eno Shiron* (Linguistics of DOING and BECOMING: An Essay towards a Typology of Language and Culture), Tokyo: Taishukan. (In German: *Sprachwissenschaft des Tuns und des Werdens: Ein Essay über die Typologie von Sprache und Kultur*, Berlin: LIT Verlag, 2007.)

Ikegami, Yoshihiko (1985) '"Activity" – "Accomplishment" – "Achievement": A Language That Can't Say "I burned it, but it didn't burn" and One That Can', in Adam Makkai and Alan K. Melby, eds.: *Linguistics and Philosophy: Essays in Honor of Rulon S. Wells*, Amsterdam: John Benjamins.

Ikegami, Yoshihiko (1991) 'Transitivity and Tense Variation in Narrative Text', in *Proceedings of the Fourteenth International Congress of Linguistics*, Berlin: Akademischer Verlag.

Ikegami, Yoshihiko (2005) 'Indices of a Subjectivity-Prominent Language: Between Cognitive Linguistics and Linguistic Typology', *Annual Review of Cognitive Linguistics* 3. (Originally, a plenary talk at the Seventh International Cognitive Linguistics Conference in Santa Barbara, July 2001.)

Ikegami, Yoshihiko (2007) 'Subjectivity, Ego-Orientation and Subject-Object Merger: A Cognitive Account of the Zero-Encoding of the Grammatical Subject in Japanese', in Viktoria Eschbach-Szabo et al., eds.: *Selected Papers on Semantic and Cognitive Japanese Linguistics*, Tokyo: Kuroshio.

Ikegami, Yoshihiko (in press) 'Subjective Construal as a "Fashion of Speaking" in Japanese', in María de los Ángeles Gómez González et al., eds.: *Current Trends in Contrastive Linguistics: Functional and Cognitive Perspectives*, Amsterdam: John Benjamins.

Kawabata, Yasunari (2004 [1924]) 'Shin-Shin-Sakka no Shin-Keiko' (Some New Trends in Newly Emerging Authors), translated by T. Cheung, in *Schneeland*.

Langacker, Ronald W. (1991) *Concept, Image, and Symbol,* Berlin: Mouton de Gruyter.

LDOCE = Longman Dictionary of Contemporary English (1995, 3ʳᵈ ed.; 2004, 4ᵗʰ ed.)

Whorf, Benjamin L. (1956 [1939]) 'The Relation of Habitual Thought and Behavior to Language', in Benjamin L. Whorf: *Language, Thought and Reality,* Cambridge, MA: MIT Press.

23

Dieter Kastovsky and Barbara Kryk-Kastovsky

Crimes and misdemeanours: legal terminology versus lexical semantics and the role of pragmatics

1. Introduction[1]

1.1.

Both lexical semantics and terminology deal with the content and function of lexical items (lexemes) as designations for some extralinguistic referent(s), or, more precisely, referent classes. But they do so in different ways, as may be illustrated with reference to the "semiotic triangle" proposed by Ogden and Richards (1923 [1946]: 11); the terms in parentheses are those usually employed today:

(1)

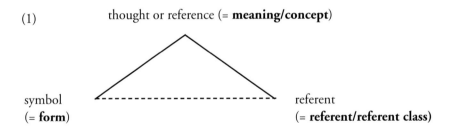

thought or reference (= **meaning/concept**)

symbol
(= **form**)

referent
(= **referent/referent class**)

Lexical semantics typically starts out from lexemes as designations of referents or referent classes and investigates their content in terms of concepts by means of which they can refer/designate: meaning is interpreted as conceptual, i.e. as different from a pure description of the referent or referent class. Whether these concepts are described in terms of semantic features or prototypes (two apparently rivalling approaches) will not be discussed in the following, since we will assume that

---

[1]   We are grateful to Corinna Weiss, Vienna, for her help with the data, especially the *MED* references.

these are not necessarily contradictory but rather complementary (cf., e.g., Lipka 1987). Both approaches abstract from individual properties of the referent classes for which the lexical items in question can serve as designations. Especially in the structural semantics approach, closely linked to the notion of lexical fields (cf., e.g., Coseriu 1973), the meaning of lexical items is described in terms of minimal oppositions within a group of semantically related lexical items sharing a common semantic basis (an archilexeme or archisememe). This approach can be classified as "semasiological", i.e. it starts out from a semantic analysis of the lexeme in question and defines its content in terms of its referential potential, usually in contrast to other semantically related signs. In this respect, modern lexical semantics differs significantly from an approach current in the late 19th and early 20th century, known under the label "Wörter und Sachen", which started out from a referent – or rather set of referents – and asked how these are referred to in different dialects or languages. This approach is also known as "onomasiological".

We would like to claim that this latter approach underlies any typical terminology or nomenclature. This starts out from an exact definition of the potential referent or referent class and assigns it a designation, whose content is basically equivalent to an exact description – scientific or otherwise – of the referent (cf., e.g., Arntz and Picht 1989: 59ff. ; Gerzymisch-Arbogast 1996). In terms of (1), "concept" here coincides with a description of the referent or referent class in question. Such an approach can therefore indeed be classified as "onomasiological". This is most obvious in the natural sciences, e.g. chemistry, where the meaning of a term can be equated with a formula describing the chemical constituency of the substance to which it refers, e.g. H_2O, $NaCl$, $HCOH$. Put differently, we provide a chemical analysis for a specific referent (substance) and then assign it a designation that represents this analysis. This is frequently a technical term restricted to this domain, i.e. it is just part of this particular terminology and only exceptionally makes it into the general vocabulary, as, e.g., *formaldehyde* for *HCOH* or *alcohol* for C_2H_5OH (technically = *ethanol*). Sometimes, however, a lexeme that forms part of the general vocabulary also comes to be used in a terminological function, i.e. it is terminologized and thus becomes polysemous; cf. *water* and *salt* as technical designations for H_2O, $NaCl$ and their normal everyday use, in which they are usually not associated with these chemical formulas. In strictly scientific or technical terminology, there is usually no problem, because the terminological use is easily kept apart from its non-technical use on the basis of the context. But in other domains, the demarcation of non-technical and technical-terminological usage is far more difficult, especially when the majority of the technical terms are taken over from everyday language or when there is a constant interplay of terminological and non-terminological usage. A typical example of this situation is the language of the law and its terminology, where terms such as *murder, kill, lie, deceive, slander, steal, theft,* and many others are part of our everyday language, but are at the same time used for the designation of criminal offences each of which is associated with a particular punishment – i.e., they serve as technical legal terms. This has certain consequences for the status of legal terminology, as the Hon. Justice Kirby from the High Court of Australia aptly puts it in his introduction to Cao (2007: vii):

> Like most judges and lawyers, I spend my life puzzling over the meaning of words. The words may exist in a national or sub-national constitution. They may appear in local legislation. Or they may emerge from judicial reasons, written over centuries, in the exposition of common law.

It is this problem – the conflict between a semasiological understanding of lexemes and their onomasiological definition for technical purposes – that will be dealt with in the following. We will first look at the pragmatic requirements for legal language and the terminology involved. Then we will illustrate the difference between dictionary definitions and legal definitions with some examples taken from the *OED online* and two legal dictionaries (Jowell 1959; Saunders 1988). Finally, we will show how everyday usage and legal understanding may clash in the evaluation of a particular case, viz. Clinton's Lewinsky statements, or: why Clinton **did** and **did not** lie.

2. The (socio-)pragmatics of legal language

2.1

The most obvious and closest connection between the language of the law and pragmatics is the notion of the speech act. It was Searle (1975) who emphasized the crucial role that performatives (especially declarations) play in legal language, whereas Danet gives priority to directives, as "within the facultative-regulative functions of law they are the most prominent (performatives) in legislation that impose obligations" (Danet 1980: 458). Speech acts are among the pragmatic concepts that most frequently occur in legal language; or, as Hencher (1980: 254) puts it, "speech act theory and the law are made of much the same stuff".

According to Danet (1980: 458 ff.), legal discourse is permeated with performatives, which include the following:

a) **Representatives** commit the speaker to the truth of a proposition expressing a strong or weak commitment, e.g. actions of testifying or swearing vs. asserting or claiming, respectively.

b) **Directives** are future-oriented speech acts intended to change the current state of affairs by making someone perform some action, e.g. subpoenas, jury instructions, and appeals. Since law can be interpreted as a set of commands, they are even more important to the legal language than representatives.

c) **Commissives** commit the speaker to a future action which includes any kind of contract, whether a business contract, a marriage, or a will.

d) **Expressives** cover cases where the convicted persons are asked before the sentence is announced whether they have anything (personal) to say. This is when they have the last opportunity to apologize, excuse themselves, or deplore the crime, which might mitigate the punishment.

e) **Declarations** produce a fit between the words and the world, a change that comes about because of the speaker's utterance, as in the classic *I declare the meeting closed.*

When an illocutionary act, e.g. a promise, is performed, it always has a perlocutionary effect, which consists of the verbal or non-verbal consequences it brings about. The significance of these consequences in everyday discourse differs considerably from those in courtroom discourse, since an insincere promise or a lie when uttered in a private conversation only has moral consequences (people might be disappointed or offended), whereas a lie under oath in court is defined in legal language as perjury, and this terminological re-labelling has immediate legal consequences, i.e. the perpetrator of the respective act is subject to legal punishment. An interesting case in point is the Miranda Rights, which require informing the suspect of his/her constitutional rights, and which has multiple perlocutionary effects: thus the suspect has the right to remain silent, and he need not answer any questions; if he does answer questions, his answers can be used as evidence against him; finally, he has the right to consult with a lawyer, cf. Shuy (1998: 52). Now if the suspect can show that he had not been so informed, any testimony he gave may be deemed invalid. Thus one speech act ("informing") has an effect on the legal status of other speech acts.

What is most important here, and what will be illustrated below, is that all perlocutionary effects of courtroom discourse follow from the definitions of the crimes at issue and the activities involved in them.

2.2.

Let us now turn to the structure of courtroom discourse. Intuitively, one of the major characteristics of courtroom discourse might be seen in its effectiveness with regard to the achieving of discoursal goals. From this point of view, it might at first glance look similar to everyday conversation, where the participants might have similar goals. But Atkinson and Drew (1979: 68) rightly warn non-initiates against hasty generalizations:

1. If we consider the structural characteristics of conversation as outlined by Sacks *et al.* (1974) in terms of turns, TPS, repairs, etc., everyday conversation is much more loosely organized than courtroom discourse.

2. While the distribution of power relations is obvious in the courtroom context, in everyday conversation these are not demonstrated overtly.

3. Courtroom discourse consists predominantly of Question/Answer exchanges, which are not the norm in everyday conversation.

4. In courtroom discourse, turn order is fixed, and so is the type of turn taken by each participant (interrogators ask questions and the interrogated provide answers, but not vice versa).

5. A unique property that differentiates courtroom discourse from everyday conversation are "legal metacomments" (interrogators' comments on whatever is going on in court). They refer anaphorically to a portion of the previous discourse, as in (2), or exophorically to a situation outside the actual discourse situation, as in (3):

(2) So you say you actually ran away on Friday night? (Johnson 2004:105).

(3) Q: All right. Now the car the man was driving, was it a brown, a brown 1972 Chevrolet Nova?
OPPOSITION LAWYER: Objection.
JUDGE: Sustained, leading the witness. (O'Barr 1982: 142).

The primary goal of such exchanges is to establish facts as the basis for determining whether any crime – or which type of crime – is involved, and this in turn determines the establishment of guilt and the corresponding punishment. The basis of all this is therefore made up of definitions of crimes, which should be as precise as possible; but, as has been indicated above, this is not as simple as it seems, especially in a legal system which is based on case law, as the Anglo-Saxon system is. Here, individual judgements of cases may change the definition of the term in question, i.e. definitions are to a certain extent a matter of agreement between the side of the plaintiff, the side of the defendant and the judge: they are negotiable, at least to a certain degree.

3. Legal terminology vs. lexical semantics

3.1.

This brings us to the central problem of this paper, the relationship between legal terminology and everyday usage, which has to be seen in an historical context –

especially in the domain of case law, much less so in the case of civil law. In civil law, crimes are defined in terms of abstract concepts with a relatively strong theoretical legal-philosophical background ultimately going back to Roman law (cf. Cao 2007). In common law – the Anglo-Saxon legal tradition – there is of course also a basic classification of crimes, often in terms of so-called "statutes", i.e. by Acts of Parliament; but this is supported – and modified – by reference to individual instances, i.e. cases, and how they have been handled. Moreover, everyday lexemes can become terminologized, but specifically legal terms can become determinologized as well. And here the history of the Anglo-Saxon legal system and its terminology is of particular importance, because part of it is Anglo-Saxon, i.e. Germanic, like *murder, manslaughter, theft*, whereas many other terms are Norman French or Latin, like *crime, felony, misdemeanour, homicide, perjury*. With the native terms, we often observe the phenomenon of terminologization, i.e. the legal discourse tries to provide them with strict definitions to make them distinct from everyday usage. The noun *murder* is a case in point. *Murder* is defined by the *OED* as follows:[2]

(4)   *OED*, s.v. **murder**
        1. The action or an act of killing.
        a. The deliberate and unlawful killing of a human being, esp. **in a premeditated manner; (*Law*) criminal homicide with malice aforethought** (occas. more fully ***wilful murder***); an instance of this.
        In Old English the word could be applied to any homicide that was strongly reprobated. It is therefore sometimes difficult, esp. in early use, to distinguish clearly between this sense and sense 1c. More strictly, however, it denoted *secret* murder, which in Germanic antiquity was alone regarded as a crime (in the modern sense), open homicide being considered a private wrong calling for blood-revenge or compensation. [...] **The 'malice aforethought' which enters into the legal definition of murder, does not (as now interpreted) admit of any summary definition. Until the Homicide Act of 1957, a person might even be guilty of 'wilful murder' without intending the death of the victim, as when death resulted from an unlawful act which the doer knew to be likely to cause the death of someone [...]. By this act, 'murder' was extended to include death resulting from an intention to cause grievous bodily harm. It is essential to the legal definition of murder that the perpetrator be of sound mind, and (in England, though not in Scotland) that death should**

---

[2]   The most important passages are in bold type.

ensue within a year and a day after the act presumed to have caused it. In British law no degrees of guilt are recognized in murder; U.S. law distinguishes 'murder in the first degree' (or in the course of a crime, and without mitigating circumstances) and 'murder in the second degree' (intentional but unpremeditated) [...].

✝**b.** Terrible slaughter, massacre, loss of life; an instance of this. *Obs.*

c. The action of killing or causing destruction of life, regarded as wicked and morally reprehensible irrespective of its legality (e.g. in relation to war, death sentences passed down by tribunals, and other socially sanctioned acts of killing); an instance of this.

Thus, the dictionary clearly makes a definitional distinction between everyday and legal usage, the latter apparently deriving from the former by terminologization in connection with the development and codification of the legal system. This explains the extensive explanatory definition including the historical development (narrowing of meaning) for the legal use and highlights the features 'malice aforethought' and 'possible mental make-up of the suspect', which seem to be relatively irrelevant in the everyday understanding of *murder*.

3.2.

With the non-native terms, we observe both developments, i.e. terminologization and determinologization. Since we are dealing with loans, we would also need an investigation as to whether independent borrowing or native development is involved in these processes, an investigation which was not possible in this connection. As examples will serve the terms included in the title of our paper, viz. *crime* and *misdemeanour*, to which a third, viz. *felony*, has to be added. All three are of French origin.

Crime according to the *MED* (but not the *OED*; cf. below) was first used in a religious context in the sense of 'sinfulness, wickedness', i.e. not as a strictly legal term; cf.:

(4) **crīme, n.** s.v. *MED*
    2.   Sinfulness, wickedness
        1250 *Louerd asse þu ard* (Trin-C B.14.39) 80: Þe smec was iwonken of ure heuene kinke, þat of þutte [read: of þucte] cryme.

The first quotation in a legal sense in the *MED* is from the Wyclif Bible 1384, but the *OED* has an earlier Wyclif quotation from 1382; cf.:

(5) **crime, n.** s. v. *OED Online*

1. **a.** An act punishable by law, as being forbidden by statute
   or injurious to the public welfare. (Properly including all
   offences punishable by law, but commonly used only of
   grave offences.)
   1382 WYCLIF *Acts* xxxiii. 29 Hauynge no cryme worthi the
   deeth, or bondis
   b. *collective sing.* Action of such kind viewed collectively or ab-
   stractly; violation of law.
   1485 CAXTON *St. Wenefr.* 3 Hast slayn by cryme as an homy-
   cyde this noble vyrgyn.
2. **a.** More generally: An evil or injurious act; an offence, a
   sin; *esp.* of a grave character.
   1514 BARCLAY *Cyt. & Uplondyshm.* (Percy Soc.) 11 Longe after
   this began this cursed cryme
   b. *collective sing.* Wrong-doing, sin.
   *c***1440** *Gesta Rom.* xxii. 74 (Harl. MS.) For no man may lyve
   withoute cryme.

It would thus seem that the religious sense was fairly soon replaced by the legal
one, although the former lingered on. Whether the religious sense can also be
regarded as terminological would require a separate investigation as to its place in
religious terminology, but neither the religious nor the somewhat later legal use
seems originally to have been part of everyday, non-technical language. Eventually,
crime came to be regarded as the most general term for any punishable act. This explains the following remark in Saunders' *Words and phrases legally defined* (1988):

> There is no satisfactory definition of crime which will embrace the many acts and
> omissions which are criminal, and which will at the same time exclude all those acts
> and omissions which are not. Ordinarily a crime is a wrong which affects the security
> or well-being of the public generally so that the public has an interest in its suppres-
> sion. […]
>
> A crime, or misdemesnor, is an act committed, or omitted, in violation of a pub-
> lic law, either forbidding or commanding it. **This general definition comprehends
> both crimes and misdemesnors; which, properly speaking, are mere synonymous
> terms: though, in common usage, the word, 'crimes', is made to denote such
> offences as are of a deeper and more atrocious dye: while smaller faults, and
> omissions of less consequence, are comprised under the gentler name of 'misde-
> mesnors' only.** (Emphasis added, D.K., B.K.K., Saunders 1988, s.v. *crime*).

Felony has entered the language both as a general lexeme and a legal term more or less at the same time around the end of the 13th century, according to both the *MED* and the *OE*, but its general meaning soon became obsolete; cf. the *OED* definitions 1. – 3. below. As a legal term it survived as a subcategory of *crime* together with its co-hyponym *misdemeanour* till 1967, when a Criminal Law Act did away with the distinction between the two. But then this division had already been seriously weakened by the loss of some essential features of *felony*: its punishment by the forfeiture of land, which was abolished in 1870, or by penal servitude, which was abolished in 1948 (clearly a change in the description of the referent involved, i.e. its onomasiological status); cf.:

(6) **felony** s.v. *OED Online*
    †**1.a.** Villany, wickedness, baseness. *Obs.*
        *c***1290** *S. Eng. Leg.* I. 31/75 Ake ȝut for al is felonie, ne bi-lefde ore louerd nouȝt þat [etc.].
    † **b.** Anger, wrath. *Obs.* After OF. in which it is very common.
        *c***1290** *S. Eng. Leg.* I. 62/299 For ore louerd euenede himsulf to a tomb..And for it is with-oute felonie, and milde ase ihesu crist.
    †**2.** Guile, deceit, treachery, perfidy. *Obs.*
        1297 R. GLOUC. (Rolls) 1446 He biþoȝte him of felonie.
    †**3.** A crime, misdeed, sin. *Obs.*
        *a***1300** *Cursor M.* 16852 (Gött.) Ioseph..of arimathie, Ne grantted neuer wid will ne werk, to þaire gret felune.
    4. *Law.*
        a. (Feudal Law.) An act on the part of a vassal which involved the forfeiture of his fee.
        [**1292** BRITTON I. vi. §3 Volums, que lour terres alienez puis lour felonies fetes soint eschetes as seignurages des feez.] *c***1330** R. BRUNNE *Chron.* (1810) 207 Somond haf þei Jon, to Philip courte him dede, To tak his Jugement of þat felonie [MS. *felonse*; rime-word *Bretaynie*].
        b. (Common and Statute Law.) Formerly the general name for a class of crimes which may loosely be said to be regarded by the law as of a graver character than those called misdemeanours. No longer differentiated from misdemeanour (see quot. 1967). The class comprises those offences the penalty of which formerly included forfeiture of lands and goods, and corruption of blood, together with others that have been added to the list by statute. […]
        [**1292** BRITTON I. ii. §10 Si la felonie eyt esté fete hors de me-soun.] **1303** R. BRUNNE *Handl. Synne* 1310 Sle no man wyþ

þyn honde Wyþoutyn iustyce, for felonye.. **1967** *Act Eliz. II* c. 58 Criminal Law Act. An Act to amend the law of England and Wales by abolishing the division of crimes into felonies and misdemeanours.

Finally, *misdemeanour* is first quoted as a purely legal term in 1504, and then also in a more general sense as 'bad behaviour, misconduct' only a few years later.

(7)   **misdemeanour,** s.v. *OED Online*

> **1.** *Law.* An offence not involving forfeiture of property and thus regarded as less serious than a felony. Now chiefly *U.S.* (*hist.* in British use). […]. In the United Kingdom forfeiture was abolished in 1870, and all distinctions between a felony and a misdemeanour were abolished by the Criminal Law Act of 1967.
>
> **1504** *Act 19 Hen. VII,* c. 14 §8 in *Statutes of Realm* (1816) II. 659 This Acte to take his effect and begynnyng for such reteynours and offences and other Mysdemeanours as shalbe doon..contrary to the forme of this acte.
>
> **2.** *gen.*
>
> **a.** Bad behaviour, misconduct.
>
> **1516** R. FABYAN *New Chron. Eng.* (1811) II. clvii. 146 For the whiche mysse demeanure of this woman, that she had innaturally slayne hir lorde and husbonde [etc.].
>
> **b.** An instance of this; a wrongdoing, misdeed, transgression, now *esp.* a minor one.
>
> **1516** R. FABYAN *New Chron. Eng.* (1811) VI. ccvi. 218 Some mysdemeanures and rules that were occupyed and exercysed in his absence. **1592**

Misdemeanour seems to have been mainly used in this latter sense in everyday speech, whereas all punishable offences technically falling under this rubric are commonly called crimes, i.e. the legal distinction between crimes and misdemeanours does not seem to be systematically made in everyday language.

Thus, *felony* and *misdemeanour* had originally been introduced as hyponyms of *crime*; the delimitation was based on a list of specific offences which counted as *felonies*, such as treason, piracy, murder, manslaughter, rape, larceny, robbery, burglary, arson, some kinds of assault and certain acts resembling treason. *Misdemeanour,* on the other hand, was defined negatively as those offences that were not listed as felonies; cf. also:

Misdemeanour, any indictable offence less than felony, as perjury, obtaining money by false pretences, endeavouring to conceal a birth, and fraudulently obtaining property on credit and not having paid for it within four months of bankruptcy, which are misdemeanours by statute; and any attempt to commit a felony or misdemeanour, whether the crime attempted be so by statute or common law; any disobedience to a statute; any incitement of another to commit a felony where no such felony is actually committed; sale of provisions unfit for food; public nuisances; and very many other offences, which are misdemeanours at common law. Every indictable offence which is neither treason nor felony is a misdemeanour.

Similarly to statutory misdemeanours to which no express punishment is attached, common law misdemeanours are punishable by fine or imprisonment or both (Jowell 1959, s.v. *misdemeanour*).

Thus, the Sergeant of the Police in Gilbert and Sullivan's *The Pirates of Penzance* could still speak of "felonious little plans" with reference to "enterprising burglars" and be understood, whereas today the term has lost its legal background, having been eliminated from legal terminology.

As these examples have shown, there is a constant interplay between legal and non-legal definitions of legal terms, and as a consequence much legal work consists of semantic-pragmatic interpretation.

4. Did Clinton lie or not?

4.1.

Let us conclude this paper with an example of such an interpretation in action, viz. President Bill Clinton's handling of what came to be called his *zippergate* in 1998.[3]

The following quotations from the *Starr Report* summarizing the official investigation into Clinton's *crime/felony/misdemeanour* leading to his (unsuccessful) impeachment highlight the most important facts and will serve as the basis for our analysis.

In connection with the allegations made by Paula Jones that he had sexually harassed her, President Clinton had been asked whether he had also had an affair with his intern Monica Lewinsky, as had been intimated by Paula Jones. This is presented in the *Starr Report* as follows (the relevant passages are in bold type):

---

[3] The following is based on Oswald (1999), unpubl. M.A. thesis, Vienna University, supervised by D.K.

(8)   On January 17, 1998 Bill Clinton, when asked about his rela-
        tionship with Monica Lewinsky in the Jones deposition, "denied
        having had **a 'sexual affair', 'sexual relations' or 'a sexual re-
        lationship'** with Ms Lewinsky" (WWW.cnn.com/starr.report/
        7groundsa.htm):
        Q: Did you have an **extra-marital affair** with Monica Lewinsky?
        A: No.
        Q: If she told someone that she had a **sexual affair** with you beginning
        November of 1995 would that **be a lie**?
        A: It's certainly **not the truth**. It would **not be the truth**.

When questioned, Monica Lewinsky first denied but then admitted, both in
court and also publicly, to having had an affair with Clinton. As a follow-up,
Clinton made two public statements in a news conference and a public broadcast, relativizing his first statement somewhat:

(9)   January 26, 1998, White House Education News Conference state-
        ment:
        "I want to say one thing to the American people. I want you to listen
        to me. I'm going to say this again: I **did not have sexual relations** with
        that woman, Miss Lewinsky" (www.cnn.com/starr.report/7groundsa.
        htm).

(10)   August 17, 1998, public broadcast:
        "I did **have a relationship** with Miss Lewinsky that was **not appro-
        priate**. In fact, it was wrong. It constituted a critical lapse in judge-
        ment and a personal failure on my part. […] I know that **my public
        comments** and my silence about this matter gave a false impression. I
        misled people, including even my wife. I deeply regret that" (cited in
        Fineman 1998:16).

It must be emphasized in this connection that Clinton never actually confessed
to having lied under oath, or to having had sexual relations with Lewinsky, neither in court nor publicly. Clinton was impeached for perjury and obstruction
of justice. The trial ended on 23 February 1999 with his acquittal. How could
that happen?

Obviously, the question whether he had lied under oath (= perjury) and thereby obstructed justice was answered negatively by the court. Nevertheless, the majority of the American people believed that he had lied. So: had he or had he not
lied? The answer is simple: he had, and he had not – depending on the context.

In everyday parlance, the term *sexual relations* would clearly include having oral sex, and Clinton did not deny having had this kind of activity with Lewinsky, or, rather, her with him. But in a public broadcast he denied having had a *sexual relationship* with her – in everyday understanding a patent lie. But it was only a lie, not perjury, because he had not lied in court under oath. Thus he was only morally, but not legally, guilty, the reason being that there was a nice legal terminological escape hatch the lawyers had constructed previously in the Paula Jones case by mutual agreement – an escape hatch which only became known later and was not quite understood by the general public.

In the Paula Jones case, it had been agreed to accept the following legal definition of *sexual relations*, which is clearly much narrower than any everyday understanding of this expression:

(11) **sexual relation:**
[a] person engages in "sexual relations" when the person knowingly engages in or causes (1) contact with the genitalia, anus, groin, breast, inner thigh, or buttocks of any person with an intent to arouse or gratify the sexual desire of any person. "Contact" means intentional touching, either directly or through clothing (www.thomas.loc.gov.).

As long as Clinton could persuade the court that Lewinsky had been the active party and it was she who touched him, but not he who touched her, the activity they had engaged in did not fulfil the criteria set out in (11). The President thus correctly "maintained that there can be no sexual relationship without sexual intercourse, regardless of what other sexual activities may transpire" (www.thomas.loc.gov.). In other words, he did not indeed have a sexual relationship with Lewinsky, and legally he was not guilty of perjury denying it. Pragmatically and morally, he was of course guilty, but only of lying to the public, and this is not punishable, since politicians do it all the time: it is merely a matter of pragmatics and not the law.

5. Conclusion

We would like to conclude this paper with another practical application of this interplay of legal and non-legal understanding of legal terms as an aftermath of Clinton's *zippergate*, reported to us by our friend Steve Nagle, Coastal Carolina University:

Mother to daughter: "Is it true that you've had sex with Tom?"
Daughter to mother: "Not according to President Clinton's definition."

References

Arntz, Reiner – Picht, Heribert. 1989. *Einführung in die Terminologiearbeit.* Hildesheim: Olms.

Atkinson, J.M. – Drew, P. 1979. *Order in court.* London: Macmillan.

Cao, Deborah. 2007. *Translating law.* (Topics in Translation 33.) Clevedon, etc.: Multilingual Matters.

Coleman, Linda – Kay, Paul. 1981. "Prototype semantics: the English word *lie*". *Language* 57: 26-44.

Coseriu, Eugenio. 1973. *Probleme der strukturellen Semantik.* Ed. Dieter Kastovsky (Tübinger Beiträge zur Linguistik 40). Tübingen: Narr. [2nd ed. 1976].

Danet, Brenda. 1980. "Language in the legal process". *Law and Society Review* 14: 445-464.

Fineman, Howard. 1998. "Clinton in crisis". *Newsweek*, 31 August: 16-18.

Gerzymisch-Arbogast, Heidrun. 1996. *Termini im Kontext. Verfahren zur Erschließung und Übersetzung der textspezifischen Bedeutung von fachsprachlichen Ausdrücken.* (Forum für Fachsprachen-Forschung 31). Tübingen: Narr.

Hencher, M. 1980. "Speech acts and the law". In Shuy, Roger, and A. Shnukal (eds), *Language use and the uses of language.* Georgetown: Georgetown University Press, 245-256.

Johnson, A. 2004. "*So?* Pragmatic implications of *So*-prefaced questions in formal police interviews". In: Cotterill, J. (ed.), *Language in the legal process.* Basingstoke: Palgrave Macmillan, 91-110.

Jowell, Earl (ed.). 1959. *Dictionary of English law.* London: Sweet & Maxwell.

Kryk-Kastovsky, Barbara. 2002. *Synchronic and diachronic investigations in pragmatics.* Poznań: Motivex.

Kryk-Kastovsky, Barbara. 2006. "Legal pragmatics". In *Encylopedia of English language and linguistics* 2. Amsterdam: Elsevier, 13-20.

Lipka, Leonhard. 1987. "Prototype semantics or feature semantics: an alternative?", in: Lörscher, Wolfgang, and Rainer Schulze (eds) 1987: 282-298.

Lörscher, Wolfgang, and Rainer Schulze (eds). 1987. *Perspectives on language in performance. Studies in linguistics, literary criticism, language teaching and learning. To honour Werner Hüllen on the occasion of his sixtieth birthday* (Tübinger Beiträge zur Linguistik 317). Tübingen: Narr.

MED. 2001. *The Middle English Dictionary. Electronic Version.* Ann Arbor. University of Michigan.

O'Barr, W. E. 1982. *Linguistic evidence: Language, power, and strategy in the courtroom.* New York: Academic Press.

Ogden, C. K. – I. A. Richards. 1923. *The meaning of meaning. A study of the influence of language upon thought and of the science of symbolism.* [8th ed. 1946]. London: Routledge and Kegan Paul.

Oswald, Martina. 1999. "Pragmatics of lying: A case study on the basis of Clinton's statements." Unpubl. M.A. thesis. Vienna: Vienna University.

Oxford English Dictionary online. 2007. Oxford: Oxford University Press. [www.oed.com]

Sacks, H. – Schegloff, E. – Jefferson, G. 1974. "A simplest systematics for the organization of turn-taking in conversation". *Language* 50: 696-735.

Saunders, John B. (ed.). 1988. *Words and phrases legally defined.* 3rd ed. London: Butterworths.

Searle, John. 1975. "Indirect speech acts". In Cole, Peter, and Jerry Morgan (eds), *Syntax and semantics* 3. New York: Academic Press, 59-82.

Shuy, Roger W. 1998. *Language of confession, interrogation, and deception.* Thousand Oaks: Sage.

24

Anita Fetzer

Cognitive Verbs in Discourse: Subjectivity Meets Intersubjectivity

1. Introduction

An investigation of the semantics and pragmatics of cognitive verbs in discourse may not only account for their form and function but also for particular co-occurrence patterns, thus refining primarily quantity-based results with context-sensitive quality-based insights. The aim of this contribution is to examine the form and function of cognitive verbs in discourse, accounting for their distribution in the social context of political discourse and for collocation patterns reflected in their local linguistic contexts.

The paper is organized as follows. The following section examines the form and function of cognitive verbs in the research paradigm of functional grammar, comparing and contrasting cognitive verbs with speech-act verbs; particular attention is given to negation. Section 3 analyses the distribution and co-occurrence patterns of the parentheticals *I think* and *I believe* in spoken political discourse, giving particular attention to local linguistic contexts. Section 4, the conclusion, summarizes the results obtained.

2. Cognitive verbs

In contemporary English grammar and corpus linguistics, cognitive verbs are classified as *private verbs* (Biber 1988), *psychological verbs* and *psychological predicates* (Leech 1983). Prototypical representatives are, for instance *think, believe, assume, guess* and *suppose*. Cognitive verbs, as they are referred to in the following, have attracted a lot of attention in formal and functional linguistics (Barbiers et al. 2002, Brinton 2001, Givón 1993, Horn 1989) and in corpus linguistics (Kärkkäinen 2003, Thompson and Mulac 1991). This is particularly true of the cognitive-verb construction *I think*, which represents a polysemic construction par excellence (Aijmer 1997; Simon-Vandenbergen 1996, 2000).

The category of cognitive verbs is based on the semantics of its members focussing on the verb's internal, private domain of reference, that is the speaker's psychological disposition. It is concerned with epistemic modality and subjectification (Aijmer 1997, Traugott 1995). Cognitive verbs are frequently contrasted with public verbs of speaking, and consequently private (or subjective) domains of reference are contrasted with public (or external) domains of reference.

In discourse, cognitive verbs indicate that subjectively qualified information is made explicit, thus attributing an intersubjective dimension to the private domain. For instance, the qualification of the proposition "it's a question of that" with the private-domain reference "I think" realized in the matrix clause as "I think it's a question of that", and its qualification by a public-domain reference "I say" realized in the matrix clause as "I say it's a question of that", has different communicative outcomes. While the former restricts the validity of the proposition over which the cognitive verb has scope to the speaker's subjective domain, assigning it the status of a personal opinion, the latter extends the validity of the proposition to a public domain, making explicit that the speaker has uttered the proposition before and is uttering it again in order to re-assert her / his claim.

In line with Verhagen's argumentation about the intersubjective dimension of negation and of complementation (Verhagen 2005) to the function of cognitive verbs realized in the matrix clause, the *I think* construction, analogously to negation and complementation, is assigned the function of a construction of intersubjectivity operating "in the dimension of intersubjective coordination (…). It consists of instructions to perform inferential operations of a certain type, independently of the 'objective' content of the utterances. The accessibility of certain cultural models (topoi) to provide material for these inferential processes is presupposed, but nothing about their content is itself coded in the conventional meaning of the elements of the system" (Verhagen 2005:76).

From a semantic point of view, the two verb classes, that is cognitive verbs and speech-act verbs, are different; but from a functional perspective, they are closely related. Their connectedness and the connectedness between the acts of making private domains explicit by attributing them to public domains of reference has been pointed out by Givón (1993) in his classification of verbs into a single PCU-class, that is perception-cognition-utterance class, with its prototypical representatives *see, know* and *say*. In his contrastive-linguistics-anchored examination of the form and function of mental verbs and speech-act verbs accommodating both diachronic and synchronic perspectives, Shinzato (2004) demonstrates that the verbs *think* and *say* are closely connected from a semantic perspective. This is not only reflected in their distribution across different languages, but also in their co-occurrence patterns. The results make the author give the two verbs the status of "allolexemes" which occur in complementary distribution (Shinzato 2004:868).

2.1. Form

A necessary condition for a cognitive verb to form an appropriate construction is its connectedness with an intentional subject. To use Givón's own words, "[t]he subject of the verbs (…) either perceives or cognizes a state or event (…). That proposition is then coded in the complement clause. The complement clause thus functions, in a way, as the object of the mental (…) activity depicted in the main clause" (Givón 1993:133).

If the subject position is filled with a 3rd person subject, the matrix clause is used to describe the cognitive state of the subject (or mental process, to use Hallidayan terminology) and the proposition codes the content of that cognitive process. With 1st and 2nd person subjects, however, the meaning expressed through matrix clause and complement clause can be different. On the one hand, it can describe the subject's cognitive state and the proposition can code the content of the cognitive process. On the other hand, a construction composed of 1st or 2nd person subject and cognitive verb can be used parenthetically. Depending on its status as a grammaticalized and pragmaticalized construction, it can be assigned the function of a modal particle, as has been demonstrated by Aijmer (1997) for the construction *I think*, which has become very frequent in spoken discourse. Like a modal particle, *I think* shows syntactic detachability and mobility. That is, it can be used in the initial position of a sentence, communicative contribution or turn, in the final position of a sentence, communicative contribution or turn, and in the medial position.

In Hallidayan Systemic Functional Grammar (Halliday 1994, Simon-Vandenbergen 2000), *I think* has been classified as an *interpersonal metaphor* expressing the epistemic modality of probability.

2.2. Function

Cognitive verbs in discourse may describe the cognitive states of the intentional subjects to which they are attributed, and when used with a 1st and 2nd person subject may be assigned the status of a parenthetical construction expressing epistemic attitude. To be assigned that status, the construction must have undergone a process of grammaticalization and pragmaticalization (Traugott and Dasher 2002).

Cognitive verbs with 1st person subjects tend to express epistemic modality, thus intensifying the pragmatic force of the proposition. Jucker et al. (2003) assign a hedging function to them, Kärkkäinen (2003) classifies them as personalized stance markers, and Hooper (1975) categorizes them as weak assertives. The hedging and attitudinal force assigned to the 1st person parenthetical is due to the fact that its verb has a reduced semantic content in the matrix clause, and that is why its complement is only weakly asserted. This is also reflected in Traugott's

(1995) and Thompson and Mulac's (1991) grammaticalization-based examination of cognitive verbs. Both arrive at the conclusion that cognitive verbs with 1st person subjects realized in the matrix clause express subjectivity, and that that is why they contribute to the subjectification of discourse.

Nuyts takes the argument one step further by examining the function of cognitive verbs in interaction. He claims that these verbs do not only signify subjectivity, but rather intersubjectivity, which he defines as follows: "Intersubjectivity means that the information (and the epistemic evaluation of it) is generally known, and hence is not new (or surprising) to the speaker and hearer(s)" (Nuyts 2001:396). In his work on constructions of intersubjectivity, Verhagen (2005) examines the connectedness between cognitive verbs and finite complements with respect to the coordination of communicative action. He comes to the conclusion that in "a complementation sentence the addressee is invited to adopt the perspective of the onstage conceptualizer. When this is a third person the utterance exhibits the same argumentative orientation as when it is a first person" (Verhagen 2005:106). That is to say, by using the *I think* or the *I believe* parenthetical the speaker invites the hearer to adopt her / his perspective, and that is why a 1st person-cognitive-verb parenthetical is assigned the status of a construction of intersubjectivity.

The claim does not only entail Kärkkäinen's classification of cognitive verbs as stance markers but also their hedging function postulated by Jucker et al. (2003). Moreover, it corroborates Aijmer's classification of the parenthetical construction *I think* as a pragmatic marker. All of those force-anchored functions are only possible if the validity of the speaker's information qualified by the cognitive verb is presupposed. This presupposition is also reflected in Shinzato's classification of cognitive verbs and speech-act verbs as allolexemes (Shinzato 2004).

Cognitive verbs are also of great importance to the investigation of *evidentiality* (e.g., Aikhenvald 2004, Chafe 1996, Mushin 2001), which examines the qualification of knowledge and information regarding (1) source, (2) attitude and qualification, (3) degree of reliability, (4) specification added to a factual claim, and (5) epistemological stance. Of particular interest is the expression of belief, which is anchored to 1st person pronouns and cognitive verbs, for instance *think, guess* and *suppose*. If the examination of the expression of evidentiality is adapted to an interaction-based frame of reference, a speaker does not only need to make explicit her / his personal stance or epistemic attitude; she / he also – in line with the ethnomethodological principle of accountability of social action – needs to be able to provide evidence should her / his communicative contribution be queried or challenged (Fetzer 2004, Garfinkel 1994). This adds further support to the assignation of an intersubjective function to 1st person-cognitive-verb parentheticals.

2.3 Negation

The examination of negation is a very interesting phenomenon as such (Fetzer 1994, Horn 1989, Tottie 1991, Verhagen 2005), but the investigation of negated cognitive verbs is even more intriguing. In Leech and Svartvik's *Communicative Grammar of English*, the negation of 1st person cognitive-verb constructions used parenthetically is called transferred negation (Leech and Svartvik 1994:310), as is the case in the following example:

(1) *I don't think it's a question of that at all*

The function of the negated cognitive-verb construction is not to express the negation of the speaker's cognitive process or state, but rather to attenuate the pragmatic force of the rejection. Horn refers to the above construction as NEG-raising (Horn 1989:323). He restricts Leech and Svartvik's claim that cognitive verbs classify for transferred negation to particular verbs from the classes of opinion, perception, probability, intention / volition, judgement and weak obligation. Moreover, he claims that a certain degree of conventionalization and grammaticalization is a further necessary requirement, thus corroborating Aijmer's argument for pragmaticalization (Aijmer 1997). In spite of the different theoretical groundings, both Leech and Svartvik and Horn agree upon the function of the negated 1st person cognitive-verb parentheticals, that is attenuation.

3. Cognitive verbs – in particular *I think* and *I believe* – in discourse

The semantic class of cognitive verbs has become very important in discourse-analytic approaches to present-day English. This is due to the fact that a number of cognitive verbs, in particular *I think* and *I believe*, have undergone a process of grammaticalization and pragmaticalization, which has not been the case – at least not to that extent – with their German, Dutch or Swedish counterparts (Aijmer 1997).

3.1 Distribution and co-occurrence

In previous corpus-based investigations of *I think,* a number of different functions have been identified for the parenthetical construction, and that is the reason why it has been classified as multifunctional as well as polysemic. Furthermore, its distribution and function have been found to be context-dependent with respect to genre and mode of transmission (Aijmer 1997, Biber 1988, Jucker 1986, Kärkkäinen 2003).

3.1.1. Frequency of I *think* across modes and genres

In her investigation of the function of *I think* in political discourse based on the British National Corpus (BNC), Simon-Vandenbergen (2000) found 22 tokens per 10,000 words in spoken discourse and only 2 tokens per 10,000 words in written discourse. In spoken discourse, the frequency was 24 tokens per 10,000 words in dialogue and 14 tokens per 10,000 words in monologue. In written discourse, the frequency was 4 tokens per 10,000 words in fiction occurring mainly in fictive dialogues, and 0.6 tokens per 10,000 words in scientific writing. These results are somewhat different from Aijmer's (1997) analysis of *I think* in the London-Lund corpus, with 51 tokens per 10,000 words.

3.1.2. Cognitive verbs in televised political interviews

The data on which this examination of the form, function and distribution of cognitive verbs in political discourse is based comprise 20 full-length pre-election interviews recorded between 1997 and 2003 from the BBC and ITV[1] as well as 9 full-length interviews recorded from the programme 'On the Record' (BBC) in 1990.

In the dialogic data, which have 182,792 words, there are 660 tokens of the parenthetical constructions *I (don't) think* and *we (don't) think*[2], which is roughly equivalent to 37 tokens per 10,000 words. The result is again different from Simon-Vandenbergen's examination of radio interviews, in which she found 68 tokens per 10,000 words. The difference may be due to the media-specific auditory and audio-visual formats, and to the length of the interviews under investigation. The construction *I (don't) believe* and *we (don't) believe* occurs 135 times, which is roughly equivalent to 7 tokens per 10,000 words. The cognitive verb *suspect* occurred 8 times and only with 1st person singular self-reference. The construction *I suppose* occurs 6 times, followed by five tokens of *I feel*, two tokens of *I guess* and one token of *I assume*.

A comparison between the distribution of the *I / we (don't) think* and *I / we (don't) believe* constructions in the full-length interviews collected in 1990 and in the interviews produced roughly 10 years later indicates that the frequency of both constructions has increased. The frequency of the *I / we think* construction has increased from 33 tokens per 10,000 words with 14 % transferred negation in the 1990 data to 40 tokens per 10,000 words with 11 % transferred negation in the pre-election interviews. The frequency of the *I / we believe* construction has increased from 5 tokens per 10,000 words with 20 % transferred negation to

---

[1] I wish to thank Peter Bull (University of York, UK) for sharing some of his data with me.
[2] Because of the particularized contextual constraints and requirements of political discourse, in which speakers speak on behalf of themselves and on behalf of their party, 1st person singular and 1st person plural references count as self-references. For this reason, both forms are included in the analysis.

8 tokens per 10,000 words with 24 % transferred negation. The results indicate that both constructions have become more conventionalized and more grammaticalized, and that transferred negation has become more conventionalized with the *I / we believe* construction.

In the data[3] analysed, the *I / we think* construction occurs initially, as in (4). It co-occurs with the discourse markers *well* and *but* and with the address term *Jonathan* sharing the initial position, as in (2) and (3), and it occurs medially as in (5) and (6):

(2)   # ***well I think*** all the party from the prime minister downwards ...

(3)   # ***but Jonathan I think*** that is the case in any dispute

(4)   # ***I think*** that's an absurd charge and ...

(5)   it's moving in the right direction ***and I think*** that we ...

(6)   at any time during the last 20 years ***so I think*** that ...

The *I / we believe* construction has a similar distribution, but has not been found in the turn-initial position. Its preferred realization is turn-medially as in (7), and it co-occurs with the discourse markers *and* and *now*, as in (8) and (9):

(7)   erm erm Mr Kennedy you you you have forty six seats ***I believe*** you said in parliament

(8)   ... ***and I believe*** that although we've got a lot more to do for pensioners no one can say that we haven't done anything for pensioners

(9)   ... ***now I believe*** that we can make a real start on education in this country and let me tell you ...

The cognitive verbs *suspect, suppose* and *feel* occur both turn-initially and medially, as in (10), (11), (12) and (14). In (12) *suppose* shares the initial position with the discourse marker *well*. The cognitive verbs *suppose, guess* and *assume* occur in the medial position only, as in (15) and (16), where *believe* co-occurs with the discourse marker *and*. In (14) *guess* co-occurs with the discourse marker *and*:

(10)   ... we've known that for many years ***I suspect*** they were trying to cause the mapsimu maximum disruption ...

(11)   ***I suspect*** they will probably go for the other route ...

(12)   ***well I suppose*** we could have artificially restricted your salary ...

(13)   ***I I feel*** you speak for the erm ***I feel*** that you speak for the majority of the people ...

---

3   To facilitate readability, the transcription mode employed follows orthographic norms. Stress is only marked when it is of relevance to the argumentation. '#' denotes the turn-initial position.

(14)   *... that is precisely what we are trying to do **and I guess** you know the only honest answer to say to you is ...*

(15)   *... and if you just trust me **I guess** you find I'll be able to explain a thing or two...*

(16)   *yes I accept we have to do better **and I believe** we will do better **I assume** that the Tories are going to improve on their position in London*

Transferred negation occurs with the cognitive verbs *think, believe* and *feel,* as in (17), (18), (19) and (20). Its preferred position is medial; but it also occurs turn-initially, sharing the initial position with the cohesive device *no,* as in (21), the hesitation marker *erm,* as in (22), and the discourse marker *but,* as in (23):

(17)   *... but what **I don't believe** is right is to have a position ... **I don't think** ...*

(18)   *... **I don't believe** they should have to pay taxes ...*

(19)   *... **we don't believe** the nursery voucher scheme is right ...*

(20)   *... **I don't believe** that is sensible either that money would better go ...*

(21)   *#**no I don't think well I don't believe** that's the way the public look at it but ...*

(22)   *#**erm I don't believe** so for two reasons ...*

(23)   *I have a huge respect for Nelson Mandela **but I don't feel erm** that I'm doing the wrong thing ...*

Cognitive verbs tend to co-occur with markers of epistemic modality, discourse markers, further cohesive devices and further cognitive verbs, as is the case with a number of examples, for instance (2), (3), (8), (9), (11), (12), (15), (16) and (21) analysed above, and with (24):

(24)   *... because I I could obviously see my father in tremendous distress **I I think** that that **erm I mean I I sort of believe** that in part people's lives are shaped by struggle ...*

Cognitive verbs are not only very interesting with respect to their distribution across turns and genres but also with respect to co-occurrence patterns, as is discussed in the following.

3.1.3. Collocation and co-occurrence

In the data analysed, the *I / we think* - *I / we believe* construction realized turn-initially with and without the complementizer *that* plus complement collocates with the following lexemes, as is systematized in table 1:

Table 1. Collocations of initial *I / we think* and *I / we believe*

#[I/ we think] [[+/-that] [complement]]	NEG	#[I/ we believe] [[+/-that] [complement]]	NEG
I think	I don't think	I believe	I don't believe
I *really* think	I *really* don't think		
We think	We don't think	We believe	We don't believe
We *do* think		We *do* believe	
I *am just* think*ing*		I *do* believe	
I *can't* think			
I *should* think			
		I *truly* believe	
		I *honestly* believe	

Transferred negation occurs with both 1st person singular and 1st person plural *think / believe* parentheticals, *emphatic do* occurs with 1st person singular and plural *believe* parentheticals, but only with 1st person singular *think*. While the parenthetical *I think* is qualified with modal verbs, the parenthetical *I believe* is qualified with the adverbs *truly* and *honestly* boosting the pragmatic force of the proposition.

The *I think / believe* construction can also share the initial position with a discourse marker, as is systematized in table 2:

Table 2: Collocations of initial *I think* and *I believe* with discourse marker

#Discourse marker [I think] [[+/-that] [complement]]	#Discourse marker [I believe] [[+/-that] [complement]]
And I think	And I believe
And I always think	
And so I think	
Also I think	
Because I think	
Of course I think	
Then I think	
Yeah I think	
Well I think	
Oh well I think	
But I think	But I believe
So I think	
No I think	
Now I think	Now I believe

While *I think* collocates with a wide variety of discourse markers, *I believe* only collocates with *and, but* and *now*. What is also of relevance is that discourse markers neither collocate with *we think* nor with *we believe* in the data investigated.

Turn-medially, the parentheticals *I think* and *I believe* co-occur with the relative pronouns *which, what, that* and with the conjunction *when*. Again, there are co-occurrence restrictions with *I believe*, which only collocates with *when* and *what*, as is systematized in table 3:

Table 3: Collocations of medial *I / we think* and *I / we believe*

... [I/ we think] [[+/-that] [complement]]	... [I/ we believe] [[+/-that] [complement]]
When I think	When I believe
When we think	
Which I think	
What I think	
	What I do believe
That I think	
That we think	

Turn-medially, the cognitive verb *believe* only occurs with 1st person singular subjects, while *think* occurs with 1st person singular and plural subjects.

In the following, the function of the parenthetical constructions *I think / believe* is examined more closely with respect to the expression of the speaker's commitment in discourse.

3.2 Function

The parenthetical construction *I think / believe* has been assigned the function of expressing the speaker's commitment to truth-value of the proposition (Aijmer 1997, Simon-Vandenbergen 1996, 2000). Depending on its position, phonological realization and co-occurrence with other pragmatic markers, it can boost the force of the speech act, thus expressing a higher degree of speaker commitment. Alternatively, it can attenuate the force of the speech act, thus expressing a lower degree of speaker commitment.

In the following, the function of initial *I think / believe*, medial *I think / believe* and final *I think / believe* is examined in its linguistic contexts. Initial, medial and final does not refer to the initial or final positions of a turn, but rather to the initial and final positions of utterances within turns.

3.2.1. Initial

In the data investigated, the parenthetical *I think* tends to co-occur with other attitudinal markers, such as the cognitive verb *mean* used parenthetically and the modal adverb *perhaps,* as in (25), the modal adverbs *certainly* and the marker of subjectivity *my view,* as in (26):

> (25) **I think** *this is* **I mean perhaps** *too erm too tough a view of the world but I often think ... with my own kids well it's important that they have to struggle a bit if they don't struggle they don't realise ...*
>
> (26) *It is* **certainly my view** *I* **think** *it would be perfectly absurd ...*

The function of the parenthetical *I think* in (25) is to attenuate the pragmatic force of the speech act. This is supported by the linguistic context, which is made indeterminate by the epistemic modality of possibility realized by the modal adverb *perhaps*. In (26), the linguistic context of *I think* is made more determinate by the modal adverb *certainly* expressing the epistemic modality of certainty, which boosts the subjectivizing device *my view*. Realized directly after these boosting devices, the parenthetical *I think* can only be assigned the function of booster, expressing a higher degree of speaker commitment.

In (27) and (28), the parenthetical *I (don't) believe* co-occurs with the modal adverbs *certainly* and *obviously*, which contribute to making the proposition more determinate:

> (27) **No I don't believe** *that's necessary but* **certainly** *we'll have to slow the economy down*
>
> (28) *Erm* **I don't believe** *so for two reasons. First of all we're we're* **obviously** *...*

Realized in the initial position, the parenthetical *I think* can attenuate and boost the proposition over which it has scope, which is not the case with the *I believe* parenthetical, which only functions as a booster.

The communicative function of the parenthetical *I think* depends strongly on local linguistic context and phonological stress. Co-occurring with markers of epistemic modality expressing probability and possibility, *I think* has an attenuating function, and with markers expressing certainty and necessity it has a boosting function.

3.2.2 Medial

In the data investigated there are only very few instances of *I think* and *I believe* realized in the medial position of an utterance, and often the medial realization of *I believe* is a borderline case allowing for a medial as well as initial classification.

The local linguistic contexts of the medially realized *I think* and *I believe* parentheticals contain further cognitive verbs, that is *mean* and *know* in (29); markers of personal stance, that is *personally* and *my personal view* in (30); and markers of epistemic modality, that is the modal verb *should* in (30):

(29) *Well **I mean I n- I- I know** the situation in Glasgow only too well I've lived in that city for five years myself and I'm a regular visitor and **I know** the problems in certain parts of Glasgow <u>what you're referring to</u> **I think** is part of a much wider social problem to do with poverty to do with lack of opportunity to do deal w to do with erm insufficient investment in…*

(30) *Well let us wait and see … but **I personally my personal view** is that if people have seen to have seriously misbehaved then the House of Commons should take a severe view of it but **I believe** we **should** have the report we **should** have the report we **should** have the examination we **should** have the representations …*

Analogously to the function of the parentheticals *I think* / *I believe* realized in the initial position, *I think* can boost and attenuate the pragmatic force, which is not the case with *I believe*. In (29), *I think* is used as a postmodifier attenuating the validity of the underlined proposition *what you're referring to*. In spite of the fact that the linguistic context contains cognitive verbs underlining the validity of the argument, the function of *I think* is to weaken the pragmatic force. This is primarily due to its local status as a postmodifier. In (30), the argument is introduced as a *personal view*. Nevertheless, the co-occurrence of *I believe* with the modal verb *should* boosts the force of the argument.

3.2.3. Final

In the data there are only very few instances of *I think* and *I believe* realized in the final position of an utterance, and analogously to the results of the previous section, the *I believe* cases are ambiguous. The linguistic contexts of the two parentheticals do not contain other cognitive verbs or markers of epistemic modality. Instead, there are numerous realizations of the hesitation device *erm*:

(31) *<u>I'll put you down as a doubtful</u> **I think** erm but **erm erm** but first of all but first of all …*

(32) *<u>**Erm erm** Mr. Kennedy you you you have forty six seats</u> **I believe** you said in parliament*

In both extracts, the parentheticals are assigned the status of local postmodifiers. While *I think* attenuates the pragmatic force of the underlined proposition, *I believe* boosts it.

In the following, the function of the parentheticals *I think* and *I believe* is examined from a sequentiality-based perspective.

3.2.4 *I think / I believe* in sequences

All of the excerpts[4] below contain *I think* and *I believe*. The local contexts of *I think* contain markers of indeterminacy, for instance the modal adverb *probably* in (33) and the universal quantifier *all* in (34). This is not the case with *I believe* in (35):

(33) IR₁ *Do you regret that, in retrospect?*
      IE₁ **Well I think** *I said in my conference speech last year that **probably** it wasn't in retrospect a sensible thing for a government to try and run a visitor attraction I only/*
      IR₂ *No, no, do you regret the money being spent*
      IE₂ *Well I was about to come to the money ...*

In response to a direct yes/no-question (IR₁), the initial position neither contains 'yes' nor 'no', but rather the negative discourse marker *well* (Fetzer 1994, Schiffrin 1987) and the *I think* parenthetical. In that particular setting, the interviewee indicates that she / he does not intend to answer the question with a simple 'yes' or 'no'. The interviewer does not accept the vague answer (IE₁) but rather initiates the follow-up move IR₂. Only then does the interviewee comply with the partial reply IE₂.

In (34), the interviewer also asks a yes/no-question which the interviewee does not respond to in a direct manner. Again, the initial position is occupied by *I think* and an extended reference from 'you' to 'all', signifying that the answer does not provide the information requested:

(34) IR *One more question just before the Labour landslide last time round John Major said "we keep on playing until the final whistle" you share that outlook*
      IE **I think all** *politicians share that outlook elections are not decided until the votes have been cast and the votes have been counted and I always think it's very arrogant of pundits and commentators and*

---

4 IR denotes interviewer, IE denotes interviewee and AM denotes a member of the audience who acts as an interviewer.

some politicians to say "oh this is all a foregone conclusion your votes don't matter you don't have any say in it"

(35) AM$_1$ *When does Blair the politician put the interests of the country before his own naked ambition or Blair the the prime minister put honesty of presentation to the electorate before his government's re-election or are you just simply desperate to win at all costs*

IR$_1$ *What's your central charge inside that where's he being dishonest with you*

AM$_2$ **I believe** *that he's dishonest in presentation. There's too much spin, du-double accounting erm*

IR$_2$ *ok*

AM$_3$ **Erm and generally speaking,** *his whole government erm lacks trust*

IE$_1$ **Right so I think** *I'll-*

While the realization of *I think* in the initial position signifies a non-compliance in the communicative genre of a political interview, the realization of *I believe* in the initial position has a different function. In (35), the parenthetical *I believe* introduces the reformulated utterance AM$_2$, which boils down to a single accusation blaming the interviewee for being dishonest. This is picked up in the follow-up move, and the accusation is extended to the whole government in AM$_3$. What is of relevance to our argument is that the interviewee acknowledges the accusation with *right so* and then introduces her / his argument with *I think*, signifying that it is not going to be in full accordance with the information requested by the member of the audience.

4. Conclusions

In this contribution, the form, function and distribution of cognitive verbs are examined. Particular attention is given to the parentheticals *I think* and *I believe*, and to the linguistic contexts in which they are realized. It is shown that their generalized function is that of an epistemic quantifier whose communicative meaning depends strongly on other epistemic expressions and markers of subjectivity with which they co-occur. If the context is coloured by markers of indeterminacy, the parenthetical attenuates the pragmatic force of the argument; if the context is coloured by markers of certainty and necessity, it boosts the force of the argument. While *I believe* tends to boost the force of the argument only, *I think* can fulfil both an attenuating and a boosting function.

If *I think* and *I believe* are used initially with wide-scope interpretation in a linguistic context coloured by epistemic certainty and necessity, they signify the speaker's plus-commitment to the truth-value of the proposition (cf. Simon-Vandenbergen 1996). If they are used finally with wide-scope interpretation in a similar context, they signify the speaker's minus-commitment to the truth-value of the proposition. If *I think* is used medially with narrow-scope interpretation, it signifies the speaker's minus-commitment to the appropriateness of the constituent over which it has scope.

The particularized function of the parentheticals *I think* and *I believe* depends on the linguistic and social contexts in which they are realized. If the context is characterized by redundancy with respect to explicit epistemic qualifiers, discourse markers fulfilling a similar function and other subjectivizing devices, they signify the speaker's non-compliance with one or more of the Gricean maxims of quality, quantity and manner (Grice 1975). They indicate that the speaker intends to get in a conversational implicature, which needs to be inferred by the addressee.

References

Aijmer, K. (1997): I think – an English modal particle. In: T. Swan, O. Jansen (eds.): *Modality in Germanic Languages. Historical and Comparative Perspectives*. Berlin: de Gruyter, 1-47.

Aikhenvald, A. (2004): *Evidentiality*. Oxford: Oxford University Press.

Barbiers, S., Beukema, F., van der Wurff, W. (eds.) (2002): *Modality and Its Interaction with the Verbal System*. Amsterdam: Benjamins.

Biber, D. (1988): *Variation Across Speech and Writing*. Cambridge: Cambridge University Press.

Brinton, L. J. (2001): From matrix clause to pragmatic marker. *Journal of Historical Pragmatics* 2(2): 177-199.

Chafe, W. (1996): Evidentiality in English conversation and academic writing. In: W. Chafe, J. Nichols (eds.): *Evidentiality: The Linguistic Coding of Epistemology*. Norwood: Ablex, 261-272.

Fetzer, A. (1994): *Negative Interaktionen: kommunikative Interaktionen im britischen Englisch und interkulturelle Inferenzen*. Frankfurt: Peter Lang.

Fetzer, A. (2004): *Recontextualizing Context: Grammaticality meets Appropriateness*. Amsterdam: Benjamins.

Garfinkel, H. (1994): *Studies in Ethnomethodology*. Polity: Cambridge.

Givón, T. (1993): *English Grammar: A Function-Based Introduction*. Amsterdam: Benjamins.

Grice, H.P. (1975): Logic and conversation. In: M. Cole, J.L. Morgan (eds.): *Syntax and Semantics. Vol. III*, New York: Academic Press, 41-58.

Halliday, M.A.K. (1994): *Introduction to English Functional Grammar*. London: Arnold.

Hooper, J.B. (1975): On assertive predicates. In: J.P. Kimball (ed.): *Syntax and Semantics Vol. 4*. New York: Academic Press, 91-124.

Horn, L. (1989): *A Natural History of Negation*. Chicago: Chicago University Press.

Jucker, A. (1986): *News Interviews: a Pragmalinguistic Analysis*. Amsterdam: Benjamins.

Jucker, A., Smith, S., Lüdge, T. (2003): Interactive aspects of vagueness in conversation. *Journal of Pragmatics* 35: 1737-1769.

Kärkkäinen, E. (2003): *Epistemic Stance in English Conversation. A Description of Its Interactional Functions, with a Focus on 'I think'*. Amsterdam: Benjamins.

Leech, G. (1983): *Principles of Pragmatics*. London: Longman.

Leech, G., Svartvik, J. (1994): *A Communicative Grammar of English*. London: Longman.

Mushin, I. (2001): *Evidentiality and Epistemological Stance*. Amsterdam: Benjamins.

Nuyts, J. (2001): Subjectivity as an evidential dimension in epistemic modal expressions. *Journal of Pragmatics* 33: 383-400.

Schiffrin, D. (1987): *Discourse Markers*. Cambridge: Cambridge University Press.

Shinzato, R. (2004): Some observations concerning mental verbs and speech act verbs. *Journal of Pragmatics* 36: 861-882.

Simon-Vandenbergen, A.M. (1996): Image-building through modality: the case of political interviews. *Discourse & Society* 7: 389-415.

Simon-Vandenbergen, A.M. (2000): The functions of *I think* in political discourse. *International Journal of Applied Linguistics* 10(1): 41-63

Thompson, S., Mulac, A. (1991): A quantitative perspective on the grammaticalization of epistemic parentheticals in English. In: E. Traugott, B. Heine (eds.): *Approaches to Grammaticalization*. Amsterdam: Benjamins, 313-348.

Tottie, G. (1991): *Negation in English Speech and Writing*. London: Blackwell.

Traugott, E. (1995): Subjectification in grammaticalization. In: D. Stein, S. Wright (eds.): *Subjectivity and Subjectivisation*. Amsterdam: Benjamins, 31-54.

Traugott, E., Dasher, R. (2002): *Regularity in Semantic Change*. Cambridge: Cambridge University Press.

Verhagen, A. (2005): *Constructions of Intersubjectivity*. Oxford: Oxford University Press.

25

Aleksander Szwedek

Objectification: a new theory of metaphor

In 1980, Lakoff and Johnson proposed a typology of metaphors into structural, orientational and ontological. That division is inconsistent with common sense and our everyday experience in that structure and orientation are aspects of ontology. Structure and orientation are always "structure of" and "orientation of", and they require an entity of which they are structure and orientation.

The present paper is organized in 7 sections:
1. Introduction
2. Lakoff and Johnson's description of metaphors
3. The nature of the physical and metaphysical worlds
4. *Objectification*: proposal of a new hypothesis
5. Mapping in *objectification*
6. Iconicity
7. Conclusions

1. Introduction

In consonance with the nature of the language sign, there are two aspects of metaphors that are subject to analysis: structure and function. Structure has commonly been described as consisting of source domain, target domain and mapping from source to target. Function was long regarded as a matter of style only. In recent decades, however, that approach has given way to the view that the function of metaphors is of a fundamentally cognitive nature, in all aspects.

The overwhelming majority of works on metaphors have so far concentrated on the description of target domains in terms of source domains (ARGUMENT IS WAR, LOVE IS A JOURNEY, etc.), with almost no regard to the question of the specific nature of source domains, a nature that has been only described in very general terms of bodily experience. However, an answer to the question about the nature of the source domain is absolutely crucial for the typology of metaphors and for understanding the mechanisms of mapping. The nature of the source domain is the main concern of the present study, whose main aim is to show that such general terms cannot constitute the foundation of a description of source domains, nor for any typology based on such a description.

2. Lakoff and Johnson on metaphors

Lakoff and Johnson's (1980) typology of metaphors, according to which metaphors are either structural, orientational or ontological, is based on our bodily, that is physical, experience of structure, orientation and mode of existence. Those categories are categories of the material world. The impression we get from Lakoff and Johnson's discussion of the three types of metaphors is that they are of equal status, though structural metaphors seem to be given some priority. In 2003, in the second edition of their 1980 book, Lakoff and Johnson modified their typology, asserting that all metaphors are structural, all are ontological, and some are orientational; but that modification has not changed the foundations of the typology.

Lakoff and Johnson see the essence of metaphor in "understanding and experiencing one kind of thing in terms of another" (1980:5). Thus the MIND IS A MACHINE metaphor allows us to understand the mind in terms of a machine by mapping some aspects of a machine onto the concept of mind. In other words, some aspects of the target domain come from the source domain. To answer the question about mapping, we have to know where the features to be mapped come from. In the words of Lakoff and Johnson, in structural metaphors they come from structure, in orientational metaphors from orientation, and in ontological metaphors from various modes of existence, for example as human beings in the case of personification (1980: chapter 7).

A further problem is whether those three source domains are independent of one another, as Lakoff and Johnson seem to suggest, or somehow related. The present study addresses two fundamental questions: What is the essence of source domains? and Where do the source domains come from, with particular attention to the relations between object, structure and orientation? More specifically, this study examines the essence of the three types of source domains proposed by Lakoff and Johnson as well as their respective sources, with particular attention to the criterion or criteria on which their typology was based.

In their typology, Lakoff and Johnson assume that the fundamental criterion is the experience of *all* our worlds. In their view, the physical and non-physical worlds form a unity: "social, political, economic, and religious institutions and the human beings who function within them *are no less real* than trees, tables, or rocks" (1980: 181). However, Lakoff and Johnson do not address the question why we experience those different worlds as a unity.

As I mentioned above, there seems to be common agreement as to the primacy of the physical, bodily experience; but views on that issue have only been expressed in very general terms. For example, as early as the 13th century Thomas Aquinas (1225 – 1274) wrote that the divine (and thus abstract in nature) must be presented in terms of the corporeal, i.e. material, world. Clive Staple Lewis, among many others, wrote that "The truth is that when we are going to talk at all about things which we cannot perceive by the senses, we are forced to use language metaphorically. Books on psychology, economics, and politics are as continuously metaphorical as books of poetry and devotion." (1947: 76-77). The following section is devoted to a brief discussion of the nature of our material world, its composition and relations between its components.

3. The nature of the material world

As I have pointed out in a number of studies (Szwedek 2000, 2002a, 2002b, 2007), our physical world is the world of objects, including ourselves (see below for a brief discussion of Kotarbiński's 1929 philosophical position which he himself called *reism*). It is interesting to note that although we are surrounded by objects all the time, we are aware of them only as specific objects, not as objects as such. The general level of objects is absent from everyday communication. We never say: "Oh, it's an object, and moreover it's a pen", or "It's an object and more specifically it's a cow", etc. Those examples indicate that the general level of objects is also absent from our consciousness. Why we are not aware of that level was brilliantly articulated by Wittgenstein (1953): "The aspects of things that are most important for us are hidden because of their simplicity and familiarity. (One is unable to notice something – because it is always before one's eyes.)" (Wittgenstein 1953:30)

From the phylogenetic point of view, over time, evolving socially and psychologically, mankind developed mental and emotional worlds which became as important as – if not more important than – the physical world. Those abstract worlds are not accessible to our senses; we can only perceive physical symptoms accompanying mental and emotional states and processes. Despite that inaccessibility, people talk about thoughts and emotions without restraint.

It is reasonable to claim that in the development of mankind, our ancestors first limited their communication to physical objects. Then, in the process of developing abstract concepts, they naturally based those on what had been known to them earlier, i.e. the physical objects and their properties. It is interesting to note that such a process of development, apart from its naturalness and plausibility, finds support in the development of writing from the pictographic to the ideographic.

In view of the omnipresence of objects, it is surprising that the object schema has never been elaborated in detail in cognitive linguistics (with the exception of Krzeszowski 1991), while such object-derived schemas as "container", "path", "force", "link" and others have been given a lot of attention. Those concepts are object-derived because the "container" schema highlights the relation between containment and object, whereas "path", "force" and "link" designate various relations between objects.

All this shows that the objects which surround us are an integral part of our existence, to the extent that that level of the material world is absent from our consciousness and language. Wittgenstein's observation is brilliant from the philosophical point of view, but there is also fascinating neurological evidence that explains this depth of integration.

In the physical world of physical objects, the most fundamental property of objects is the density of matter, that density being the basis for distinctions as regards three-dimensionality, boundaries (surface), size, weight, shape, etc. The only sense that allows us to experience density, surface and weight is touch.

Touch is the most fundamental and primeval of all senses for the following reasons:

– touch, unlike other senses, is a whole body sense;
– touch is the only sense requiring contact with matter;
– touch develops in the 8th week of pregnancy – the time when the foetus is sensitive to stimulation of the skin – and is simultaneous with the formation of the neural system. There is clear evidence that the sense of touch is programmed earliest and at the deepest level of the neural system;
– hands and mouth play the most important role in the recognition of the object's density, form, size, weight, etc. A child's earliest activities are catching and holding by hands and mouth, e.g. holding objects in hands and putting almost everything into the mouth;
– those touching organs, hands and mouth, have the biggest neuronal representation in the brain structures, as the well-known sensory and motor models at the Natural History Museum in London (see Wikipedia under "Homunculus") show;
– one of the most important functions of touch is the development of self-

identification, the awareness of the "own body – other body (bodies)" distinction, first in respect of the mother's womb and later with regard to other objects. The body thus functions as a frame of reference for the physical experience, including spatial orientation.

The phylogenetic (development of mankind, here from concrete to abstract) and ontogenetic (individual development, here of the neural system of individuals) evidence clearly shows the neural depth of the embedding of the physical-object schema, its primeval character, and in consequence explains its absence from our consciousness.

4. *Objectification*

I wish to claim that those arguments indicate that ontological metaphors are primary, whereas structural and orientational metaphors are derivative, secondary. It is always a matter of the structure *and* orientation of objects, never *objects of structure or *objects of orientation. Before we can talk about structure and orientation, we have to have an object that has structure and orientation.

The metaphorization of all abstract concepts (including relations) in terms of physical objects I call *objectification*. In that theory the OBJECT refers to any material entity, including animate beings, plants and (inorganic) things.

Objectification can be illustrated by two examples of a very abstract nature, THOUGHT and FEAR, from different spheres of human nature.

Example 1: THOUGHT
THOUGHT is not only abstract, but also processual in nature. Thinking is not a sequence of individual thoughts, but a continuous process. We first have to somehow identify and isolate a fragment of that thinking, and conceptualize it as an entity, most naturally as a physical object. The following expressions illustrate the object-like nature of THOUGHT in our conceptual system.

- THOUGHTS ARE OBJECTS:

    We **have** thoughts, **take** thoughts, **give** thoughts, just as we have glasses, take books, or give flowers.

    Thoughts can be **scattered, gathered** or **collected,** and **suspended,** just as beads can be scattered, and then gathered or collected, and hooks can be suspended from the ceiling.

- THOUGHTS ARE BOOKS (and books are physical objects):

    that is why *we can read thoughts.*

- THOUGHTS ARE CONTAINERS:

    We *can be deep or lost **in thought**, Thoughts can be **deep***, just as we can be in study, and a vase can be deep.

- THOUGHTS ARE MOVING OBJECTS:

  *Thoughts can be **passing**, **moving** or **fleeting***, just as cars move and pass, and ships fleet.

- THOUGHTS HAVE PROPERTIES; for example, as individual objects they can be counted, can have weight, colour, etc.:

  *We can **have many** thoughts, a **first** thought, a **second** thought and a **last** thought* – again, just as we have many books, our first car, etc. Thoughts are, then, countable, individual objects.

  *Thoughts can have **weight**; they can be **weighty**. They can be **hard**, **dark**, **brilliant**, **clear** and **gloomy**.* All those properties are first of all properties of physical objects.

- THOUGHTS ARE ANIMATE OBJECTS:

  They *can be **dangerous**, **happy**, **sober**; they can be **born**. They can **cross** one's mind, and **strike**.* Those properties are mainly characteristic of people who, when born, can be dangerous, happy and sober.

- Like all physical objects, THOUGHTS HAVE SPATIAL ORIENTATION, as in *a **current** of thoughts, a **train** of thought, the **next** and **last** thought.*

- As objects, THOUGHTS CAN BE EVALUATED:

  *They can be **good** or **bad**, **evil**, **wicked**, **sinful**, **criminal** and **ugly**.*

Example 2: FEAR

FEAR is an emotional state, an emotional response to impending danger. As an emotional state, FEAR is abstract and not accessible to our senses. What is perceptible are the physical symptoms of fear. Lakoff and Johnson (1980) come close to describing states as objects when they write that "states are containers" (1980:30), but somehow they overlooked the next fundamental step in reasoning, namely that containers are objects. Again, we first identify FEAR as an entity and conceptualize it as a physical object. That allows us then to use 'physical' vocabulary to describe this abstract state.

- FEAR IS AN OBJECT:

  He has no fear, There is no fear in him, He put the fear of God into them, The old hopes have grown pale, the old fears dim.

- FEAR IS A SUBSTANCE:

  Rub the fear of God into people, He was filled with fear.

- FEAR IS A CONTAINER:

  He lived in fear, The Barbarians fell into feare and disorder, Delyuer me out of my feare.

- FEAR IS AN ANIMATE OBJECT:

  I wil mocke when your feare commeth, Fear is the parent of superstition, If

> *hopes were dupes, fears may be liars, Fear gripped him, Then fear steps in, and tells me…, The fears of a general crisis are passing away, No passion so effectually robs the mind of all its powers of acting and reasoning as fear.*

All the arguments and the examples provided so far are sufficient to show that *objectification* is the main process in metaphorization. Before we can refer to any abstract concept (entity or relation), we must first give it the status of an object. Structural and orientational metaphorizations are possible only with or after objectification.

Objectification, discussed above and illustrated by examples, finds support in Kotarbiński's (1929) philosophical stance called *reism* and in the cultural model of the *Great Chain of Being*. In his criticism of Aristotelian categories, Kotarbiński suggested "adopting a stance in which all categories are reduced to the category of things." He claims that "every 'name' which is not a name of a thing, we take to be an illusory name" (1929:71), arguing that such sentences as *The eruption of Vesuvius destroyed Pompeii and Herculaneum* are only externally about events. "In fact, we have here only substitute phrases of such expressions as: 'Vesuvius erupted so that it destroyed Pompeii and Herculaneum', and so on. All so-called names of events disappeared. […] Since, therefore, to say '*N* exists' is only to say 'A certain object is *N*' … we can express our view in the sentence: 'Events do not exist'. Thus evaporates the whole category of objects which would be events." (Kotarbiński 1929:70-71; trans. A.S.).

Kotarbiński goes on to maintain that "in consequence of that reduction it turns out that there are no other objects except things. In other words: every object is a thing; whatever is, is a thing." However, "*…by a thing we do not understand only an inanimate block. … there are things inanimate, as well as animate, soulless, and 'endowed with psychic life', things in the narrower sense of the word as well as people* … The position of such a reduction can be called r e i s m." (1929:75).

Kotarbiński's reism is in consonance with the Western model introduced to cognitive studies by Lakoff and Turner (1989) as the Great Chain of Being. The basic version of the model has 4 levels (with the fifth level of God in the extended version).

levels \ properties	material substance	life	instincts	Reason
Humans	+	+	+	+
Animals	+	+	+	-
Plants	+	+	-	-
Inorganic Things	+	-	-	-

All levels share one property only: material substance (cf. "things" in Kotarbiński's reism, and "objects" in my objectification). There is no room for abstract entities in that model; it is a model of physical objects only, in full consonance with reism. Thus, an analysis of examples like THOUGHT and FEAR, neural evidence in the development of touch, Kotarbiński's reism and the Great Chain of Being clearly show that the basis of all our understanding and experience is the world of physical objects.

In my view, all the above arguments give us grounds for distinguishing two basic types of metaphorization: CONCRETE TO CONCRETE and CONCRETE TO ABSTRACT. The first type may be exemplified by expressions like *She is my little rose, He is a pig, He became a mere jelly, She is an iceberg*, and the second by *My mind is rusty, He gave his opinion*. In those examples the target is concrete or abstract, whereas the source is concrete. It is necessary to add, however, that other combinations of concrete and abstract are also possible, though definitely less frequent.

I wish to emphasize once again that the examples and the earlier arguments (*reism*, the Great Chain of Being, neuroembryological evidence) show that the first, fundamental step in metaphorization is experiencing and understanding all concepts in terms of physical objects, i.e. objectification. The other types of metaphors, structural and orientational, as aspects of objecthood, are the consequence of objectification. In addition, I claim that orientation is only an aspect of structure. For the description of the structure of any object to be complete, it is not enough to list parts; it is also necessary to describe relations between them, and those relations are describable only in terms of orientation (cf. paradigmatic and syntagmatic description).

5. Mapping in *objectification*

Lakoff (1990) and Turner (1990) proposed the *Invariance Hypothesis* as a way of explaining feature mapping. The invariance hypothesis claims that in mapping from the source to the target domain, the cognitive topology of the target has to be preserved. That means that the target must preexist and have a topology which would be preserved in the process of mapping.

However, this condition cannot apply to abstract concepts like THOUGHT or FEAR, as, at least phylogenetically, THOUGHT and FEAR had *no* preexisting, independent structure of their own. The objecthood of THOUGHT and FEAR is *created* during objectification, and only then are structure and other properties transferred from the source. That kind of transfer I prefer to call *inheritance of properties*, since the properties are inherited together with objecthood during objectification. As in the case of the invariance hypothesis, the *Inheritance of Properties*

Hypothesis has yet to answer the question which properties are inherited and in what conditions (see the pilot study by Janowski 2007). However, I would like to point out that as far as the basic premises are concerned, the inheritance-of-properties hypothesis is not only consistent with objectification, but is also simpler and more natural than the invariance hypothesis.

If abstract concepts are conceptualized as objects in the process of objectification, and structure, orientation and other properties are inherited by the newly formed 'objects', then the latter are similar to the former, which might be regarded as a case of iconicity.

6. Iconicity

Iconicity involves two elements: one of them is the original and the other is the image, figure, or representation of the original. So far, iconicity has mainly been concerned with the relation between form and meaning.

Objectification indicates that this relation is much deeper, taking place at the fundamental interface of the physical and metaphysical worlds, and that it is a relation between physical objects (original) and abstract concepts (the image of objects). Other selected features are inherited along with, or after, objectification.

Hence, we iconically create the ontology and then the structure and orientation of our abstract worlds *in the image and after the likeness* of the only world we know (in the original sense of knowing – "knowing through senses"), the world of material objects.

7. Conclusions

1) Our earliest and most fundamental experience of objects is their density through touch.

2) That experience is programmed onto our neural system at the earliest point in time and at the deepest level, so that we unconsciously conceptualize everything as objects.

3) Structure, orientation and other properties are potentially *inheritable* along with objecthood.

4) The physical world of objects is mapped onto our abstract worlds – in that sense our abstract worlds must be iconic to the physical world of objects as we experience it.

5) Such a view of iconicity is much deeper and broader than has heretofore been described in literature – our abstract worlds are iconically created IN THE IMAGE OF THE WORLD OF PHYSICAL OBJECTS.

References

Aquinas, Thomas. 2006. *Summa Theologica* (*The Summa Theologica of St. Thomas* [1265-1274] *Aquinas* Second and Revised Edition, 1920. Literally translated by Fathers of the English Dominican Province. Online Edition Copyright © 2006 by Kevin Knight).

Janowski, Michał. 2007. "Inheritance of Features in Metaphoric Transfer in English". (Unpublished PhD dissertation, Adam Mickiewicz University, Poznań).

Kotarbiński, Tadeusz. 1990. [1929] *Elementy teorii poznania, logiki formalnej i metodologii nauk*. [Elements of the theory of cognition, formal logic and methodology of sciences] Wrocław: Zakład Narodowy im. Ossolińskich.

Krzeszowski, Tomasz. 1991. "Metaphor – metaphorization – cognition". *Biuletyn Polskiego Towarzystwa Językowego* XLIII-XLV, 83-95.

Lakoff, George, and Mark Johnson. 2003. [1980] *Metaphors We Live By*. Chicago: University of Chicago Press.

Lakoff, George and Mark Turner. 1989. *More Than Cool Reason: A Field Guide to Poetic Metaphor*. Chicago and London: University of Chicago Press.

Lakoff, George. 1990. "The Invariance Hypothesis: is abstract reason based on image-schemas?" *Cognitive Linguistics* 1-2, 39-74.

Lewis, C.S. 1947. *Miracles: A Preliminary Study*. London and Glasgow: Collins/ Fontana Books.

Szwedek, Aleksander. 2000. "The ontology of metaphors: the sense of touch in language formation". *Scripta Periodica* 4: 193-199.

Szwedek, Aleksander. 2002a. "Shared or inherited entailments among metaphors". In Oleksy, Wiesław (ed.), *Language, Function, Structure, and Change*. Frankfurt am Main: Peter Lang. 61-65.

Szwedek, Aleksander. 2002b. "Objectification: From Object Perception to Metaphor Creation". In Lewandowska-Tomaszczyk, Barbara and Kamila Turewicz (eds), *Cognitive Linguistics To-day*. Frankfurt am Main: Peter Lang. 159-175.

Szwedek, Aleksander. 2007. "An Alternative Theory of Metaphorization". In Fabiszak, Małgorzata (ed.) *Language and Meaning*. Frankfurt am Main: Peter Lang. 313-327.

Turner, Mark. 1990. "Aspects of the Invariance Hypothesis". *Cognitive Linguistics* 1- 2, 247-255.

Wittgenstein, Ludwig. 1953. *Philosophical Investigations* (translated by G.E.M. Anscombe). Oxford: Basil Blackwell.

26

Alexis Weedon

Textual production and dissemination in book history: A case study of cross-media production between the wars

In researching the history of a text's production and dissemination, literary scholars and editors may need to examine how book historians have used quantitative measures to increase our understanding of a book's origins and influence. These statistics add a further dimension to the history of the book, providing a context for the interpretation of other evidence from the correspondence and similar sources, and are a means of gaining a greater understanding of an author's status. Reconstructing the story of the trails and successes of author's life, or telling the tale of the entrepreneurs who started a publishing firm, is empirical work which can be supported with evidence of, for example, the authors' growing financial security or the growth of the firm's sales and their investment in copyrights. Similarly, an author's contemporary popularity and success can be measured in part by the number of books sold, the distribution of those sales nationally and internationally, the length of time the work was in print and the extent of coverage given to it in the media through reviews and advertising. Such quantitative measures can support qualitative contemporary judgements and subsequent literary evaluations.

Providing a context for the understanding and interpretation of literary production, I have researched the growth of British publishing in the Victorian period. The costs of book production were gathered from the archive and formed the basis for estimating the increase of the publishing industry between 1836 and 1916 by volume and value (Weedon 2003). From this study, I became interested in the methods that authors and publishers employed to reach and enlarge their readerships, and I am currently working on a project examining the cross-media practices of British authors from the end of the Victorian period until the Second World War. This involves quantifying the effect of rights-management practices in the staged dissemination of fiction, first through serialization in newspapers and then through book publication, second serial rights and subsequent editions. In this period, that sometimes entailed the inclusion of rights for adaptation for stage, radio or the movies, and I am researching authors' and publishers' practices in engaging with the movie releases. Some of this work will be discussed here.

Sources, publishing statistics and the reading experience

Quantitative book history has focused on extracting and analysing statistics in the historical record and compiling databases which allow this data to be subjected to descriptive statistical analysis.[1] This has not been an easy task; there is often little consistency between sources – the reasons why the information was collected are different from one to another, what was recorded varied considerably, and the methods of collection are often lost. However, where the data has survived it can offer insights we would otherwise not have. Key sources of this historical evidence are the records kept by those engaged in textual production and dissemination: the book trade, book buyers and the regulators of the trade. Such sources include business accounts, trade publications and the papers and publications of guilds, agents, associations and societies from the book and allied trades. More specifically, publishers' and printers' own archives have been the source of data on print runs, prices, intellectual property and readerships. In addition, data has been obtained from the records of those who governed and wanted to legislate for the book trade, needed to measure its size, output and value and kept this information. Similarly, librarians, scholars and bibliophiles kept hold of their catalogues, lists and descriptions.

Quantitative book-historical studies have measured how the increase in population in the nineteenth century combined with improvements in literacy to lead to a growth on the part of the reading public which outstripped the market (Eliot 1994, Weedon 2003). What this 'unknown public' read and how they obtained their reading material is the subject of further research by book historians (McAleer 1992, Rose 2001, St Clair 2004). One long-term collaborative project which aims to do this is the Reading Experience Database 1450 to 1945. Designed to investigate historical reading practice, it contains evidence of reading events drawn from a range of sources including autobiographies, diaries, letters, scrapbooks and annotations in books (RED 2007-). In a manner reminiscent of Mass Observation's survey of leisure use, which has been a source for researchers of twentieth-century reading and library use, RED is incorporating relevant parts of Mass Observation into its database.

---

[1] For a detailed introduction to the sources and statistical methods, see Weedon 2007a.

Spatial analysis of historical data

The Reading Experience Database also holds location information, so historians can ask not only when and how a text was read but also where. And while RED is currently a database, there have been interesting developments in book history in the spatial analysis of historical data. Early studies of book distribution in Canada by Harold Innis traced the westward-spread communication routes through the building of roads and railways and the rise of newsagent networks, and in the 1950s and 1960s Innis and Marshall McLuhan demonstrated the importance of geography for our conceptualization of the historical spread of print. Following in that tradition, three Canadians have pioneered the use of Geographical Information Systems (GIS) in book history (Black 1998; MacDonald 2000). Through international collaboration, Fiona Black, Bertrum MacDonald and J. Malcolm Black have sought to combine available information from Scottish customs records, shipping manifests, and other book trade and demographic databases for *The History of the Book in Canada*. Research on the nineteenth century for the series has allowed analysis and comparison, by region and by town, of the ethnicity and religion and specific occupation of book-trade members compared with the general population for the same region (Fleming, Gallichan and Lamonde 2004). A second ambitious project follows Robert Darnton's pioneering work in the archives of Société typographique de Neuchâtel (Darnton 1979). The French Book Trade in Enlightenment Europe project, led by Simon Burrows at the University of Leeds, is using modern techniques to locate the book dealers and other correspondents of the publishing house and map the distribution and sales of their publications.[2] Both are long-term projects; however, mapping techniques can also be used for more focussed projects, such as Ian Gregory's collaborative project locating Coleridge's poetic references to identifiable landscape features in the Lake District using Google Maps. (Gregory 2007)

The capacity of GIS to store, map and interrogate spatial data has led book historians to revise their data-collection techniques to include more location in-

---

[2] The French Book Trade in Enlightenment Europe (1769-1787), an AHRC project at the University of Leeds. Principal investigator, Simon Burrows, Professor of Modern European History at Leeds; Dr Mark Curran and Dr Sarah Kattau, Leeds electronic text centre, database design. This project uses the STN's own accounting records to create a database of the totality of the STN's trade with all of Europe. From these sources it is possible to know both from where every book came and to whom it was sold by the STN, as well as when each transaction occurred. This information will be recorded in the database along with information on the genre, function and content of each work sold. It will be searchable by a range of fields, including author, title, subject-matter keywords, genre, and time-period, in addition to the names and places of residence of individuals who supplied or ordered STN books. Thus, future researchers will be able to use the database to map whole sub-sections of the STN's trade, whether by author, title, genre, theme or subject matter, without needing to mine the totality of the original archive.

formation. This can be point data, such as in the Coleridge project, or area data, such as territorial copyrights. The task of collating and combining databases to ensure that they are in a suitable form for analysis can be a big one, particularly if the databases were originally constructed without reference to the needs of GIS software. However, more and more historical data sets are becoming available for use with GIS and can be included as variables within the analysis of print culture. These aid the correlation of spatial and temporal data and give insights into links between infrastructure, economy and demographics and textual production.

Baroness Orczy, AEW Mason and Elinor Glyn: three examples of cross-media production between the wars

The mapping of historical data has afforded particularly valuable insights for our current project into cross-media influences and practices.[3] The project uses quantitative and qualitative techniques commonly used in book history to investigate how ten British authors (only three are discussed here) worked with a new professional class in film, radio, the press and publishers to get their works to the public. It analyses the practices of adaptation for screen and radio which emerged at that time, as well as authors' differing attitudes to them, and the economic rewards for authors, editors and other professionals. In addition, it asks how the professionals – from literary agents to newspaper editors – saw the role of tie-in. Finally, it investigates how the conceptualization of that new audience influenced the decisions of the professionals involved.

To answer these questions, we have been looking for evidence of the common practices of authors in the dissemination of their fiction through serialization in a newspaper, followed by book release, scenario preparation, continuity writing, and realization in the studio. This encompasses the practices of publishers in following movie releases with new editions, as well as specific film tie-ins and strategies by studios to link their films with authors' works to emphasize nationalistic values, or to indicate authenticity or literary quality. This has led us to a closer examination of rights management and the sale of scripts and scenarios by authors or others acting as their agents. Following RED, we have also looked for evidence in personal diaries and marginalia for information on cross-media consumption, and we have been piloting a database for evidence of film viewing and reading.

Archival evidence for these practices has come from authors, literary agents,

---

[3]   The ideas and analysis described in this section have come from the work and discussions of team members on the collaborative project on 'Cross-media cooperation in Britain in the 1920s and 1930s'. Please see acknowledgements.

and publishing firms. [4] Agents' archives are useful sources for contracts, rights management and some financial information. The Society of Authors has provided insights into professional rates and writers' expectations. It defended authors' interests, sought clarification on points of law and also negotiated broadcast fee scales with BBC radio in its early years. Authors' own financial, contractual and legal correspondence contains quantitative data on adaptations, sales and audiences for plays and movies. Some of this is to be found in film companies' papers, trade magazines and advertisements. Vital information is held in the repositories of audio-visual companies,[5] such as the BBC written archive in Reading, UK, and the Academy of Motion Picture Arts and Sciences, Los Angeles, USA. There are also relevant records in national centres, such as the British Film Institute and the Library of Congress, and special collections within University libraries, such as the Harry Ransom Center, University of Texas, which has audio-visual material as well as correspondence, and the University of East Anglia's silent-cinema collection. Museums such as the Imperial War Museum in London also have specialist audio-visual collections. These archives have been used by film historians and cultural historians, but more rarely by literary historians. Yet they contain information on the changes to the profession of authorship brought about by the advent of radio and film (Napper 2007).

To investigate the correlation between book and film audiences in this period, we have plotted book sales and royalties against film releases. For example, the publication history and film adaptations of Baroness Orczy's 'The Scarlet Pimpernel' show the relationship between editions of the novel and movie realisations. The original 'Scarlet Pimpernel' was first performed in a stage adaptation in 1903, and a book edition published by Greening followed in 1905. Film adaptations were made in 1917 (Stanton USA) and 1934 (Young UK). There were numerous sequels, some of which were also turned into films, including *I will repay* (Greening 1908: *film* Kolker UK/USA 1923), *The Elusive Pimpernel* (Hutchinson 1908: *film* Elvey UK/USA 1919) and *The Triumph of the Scarlet Pimpernel* (Hodder & Stoughton 1922: *film* Hayes Hunter UK 1928), and a movie entitled 'The Return of the Scarlet Pimpernel' (Schwarz UK) was released in 1937. The graph of sales of the original work published in the cheaper shilling and two-shilling editions shows a clear correlation between sales of the volume and the two film adaptations (figure 1). Leslie Howard, star of the popular 1934 film, was featured on the front cover of the two-shilling yellowback edition, and this common marketing device is almost certainly the reason for the increase in

---

[4] See http://www.nationalarchives.gov.uk/documentsonline/ (accessed December 2007).
[5] A good list of Public Moving Image Archives and Research Centres is at http://www.loc.gov/film/arch. html#ca (accessed January 2008).

Figure 1. Baroness Orczy, The Scarlet Pimpernel, Hodder & Stoughton 1/- and 2/- edition*

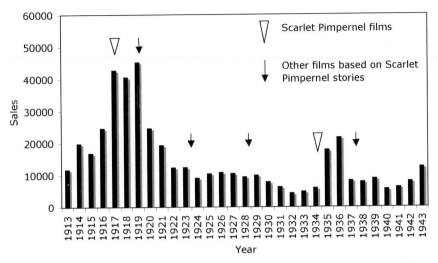

* My thanks to Dr Vincent L. Barnett for gathering the data on 'The Scarlet Pimpernel' from the Hodder & Stoughton ledgers and for the suggestion that these should be plotted against the film releases.

sales in 1935 and 1936. The sales peak in 1919 may be attributable to the Stoll Productions film of 'The Elusive Pimpernel' and their much publicized Eminent British Authors series. Otherwise movie adaptations of stories featuring the Scarlet Pimpernel do not appear to have had a significant effect on the sales of the work.[6]

AEW Mason's *At the Villa Rose* shows a more complicated relationship between book sales and movies made of other work by the author. The thriller's publication and movie history neatly marks the first four decades of the century. Originally issued in 1910 by Hodder & Stoughton in Britain, the book was published in editions from Scribner in the USA, McLoed in Toronto and Tauchnitz in continental Europe. These were followed the next year by translations into Swedish and French, and *At the Villa Rose* continued in print throughout the interwar period. The first film adaptation was released by Stoll Productions in 1920. In 1930 Julius Hagan Productions released a synchronized sound version, and a decade later a talkie was made by the Associated British Picture Corporation.

---

6   Data discussed here has been collected by the project members, and I am indebted to Dr Vince Barnett, Rebecca Delaney and Steven Conway.

Table 1. Sales of AEW Mason's *At the Villa Rose* (Hodder & Stoughton)

Year	Sales 9d	2/-	3/6 lib	4/-	3/6 (cloth)	5/- (leather)	5/- play	Royalty in £
1920		5868						42.78
1921		14112						89.07
1922		7090						45.56
1923		2912						18.20
1924		3416						21.35
1925		2562						16.01
1926		2657			611	65		66.61
1927		5564			686	26		39.26
1928		3650	3172		724	21		81.71
1929		2974	1539		264	11	406	66.57
1930		3392	1089		209	12	95	53.69
1931		3740	1245		211	14	13	51.83
1932		1732	1019		136	85	14	31.95
1933		1243	747		110	46	37	24.45
1934		1496	781		90	37	12	24.87
1935		1878	875		57	24	13	28.98
1936		3504	683		48	26	26	35.42
1937		1067	558		44	9	31	8.39
1938	13873	768	589	34	19	2		38.11
1939		652		299	24	1	16	27.74
1940		1647		398	14	0	8	10.63

Looking at the sales figures from Hodder & Stoughton's ledgers it is clear that the book sold steadily, but there is no evidence that the publisher timed new editions to follow the film releases nor that there were tie-in covers (table 1). The 3/6 and 5/- edition was issued in 1926, a library edition in 1928 and a ninepenny edition of 25000 in 1938. The sales of these editions do not show peaks which could be attributed to release dates. However, the royalties tell a different story: instead of a steady diminution and long tail, Mason's annual royalties between 1926 and 1931 were over £50, twice his average income, in the preceding four years. The issuing of a 5/- play edition in 1929 stimulated sales, and the cheaper 2/- yellowback edition of the novel shows a revival of interest around the time of the film releases. Three of Mason's other novels were adapted into films and released within two years of 'At the Villa Rose': 'The Four Feathers' (Cooper, Meddes and Schoedsack, USA 1929), 'The House of Arrow' (Hiscott UK/France 1930), 'The Flirting Widow' (Seiter USA 1930). There was a radio adaptation of *At the Villa Rose* broadcast in May 1930.[7] From our pilot database of evidence of film viewing, it is clear that two of the film adaptations of Mason's novels were shown in cinemas within months of each other – 'Mrs Wilton'[8] records seeing 'The Four Feathers' in May and 'At the Villa Rose' in September 1930. Therefore, the lack of a direct correlation between sales and the film release of 'At the Villa Rose' could be due to an interference from other adaptations of Mason's fiction.

Mason's work suggests that we should be looking for broader correlations between an author's books and film adaptations. To do this, I have been looking at a spatial analysis of the quantitative data found in the record. The archive of Elinor Glyn holds a considerable amount of information on her book sales, theatrical performances, film adaptations and agreements, though none of it is complete. Glyn was one of the top five international bestselling authors of her time and the originator of the term 'It' defining sexual attractiveness (Glyn 1955, Hardwick 1994). She wrote fiction, serials, letters and articles as well as scenarios for Hollywood studios. Her international profile and the extent of her archive make her a particularly good case study for using GIS to aid our understanding of cross-media influences. We have begun to use spatial analysis to overlay a map of the author's disposal of book rights across countries with film, serial, play, translation and other rights. This enables us to begin to build a picture of how the author creates and builds an audience for her work (figure 2). We have done this through plotting the information from the Glyn archive on the location, duration and income from play performances, sales of serial and translations rights and agreements made between Glyn's company and publishers, studios, newspapers and magazine companies.

Glyn's book and play agreements contain an assumption that theatrical performance and book-buying created an audience for the movie, and as we might expect the publicity for the plays and the movies link across media. This belief is also encoded in clauses for options on the film rights, which assigned a percentage of the income to the theatres and publishers who created the audiences. We want to use spatial analysis to investigate the extent to which the author and the agent acted upon this and established practices which capitalized on cross-media audiences.

---

[7] For which his agent AP Watts received £21 for the broadcast.

[8] 'Mrs Wilton' is the unknown author of a series of manuscript film diaries from 1925 to 1941. She lived in Liverpool and recorded viewing films in cinemas in Llandudno, London and her home town. Thanks are due to Samantha Lay for allowing us to use this source.

Massies, Glyn's agents though whom much of this business was transacted, had come to specialize in media rights, generally dividing and selling off subsidiary rights separately. In the 1920s and 1930s, technical development in film created nested rights. Performing rights which were originally defined for theatrical performances also came to include the performance element of the movie. And when the technology for sound was invented, copyright holders had to differentiate between silent- and talkie-movie rights. This was awkward and created a need for legal clarification both in the UK and the USA. It was a problem for authors, and some were caught out by the law. Famously, Baroness Orczy made an agreement with the Terrys for a play version of 'The Scarlet Pimpernel' when she failed to find a publisher for the novel. The movie rights resided in the play edition, and this led to years of legal wrangling for Orczy. Glyn too made a blunder over the disposal of her play rights. She mistakenly sold the stock rights to a play adaptation of her most famous novel *Three Weeks* (1907) to a friend in New York, unaware that the territory covered under the agreement prevented performances as far away as St Louis (Weedon 2006). She was strongly advised to use an agent after this incident, so when Roy Horniman wanted to adapt her book for a play to tour in the British Empire, Massies arranged the contract.

Mapping the territorial rights of her books, plays and serials on to a map, as in figure 2, gives us an understanding of the internationalization of rights in this period and Glyn's profile in particular. From the beginning, Glyn's book agreements were made with Duckworth and covered Great Britain and dependencies and English publications in Europe, but excluded Canada. In 1907, following the British publication of *Three Weeks*, an agreement was made with Duffield for an American edition, though this was transferred to Macaulay who printed the photoplay editions of the novel (Glyn 1907). The usual practice was for Canada to be included in the American rights for her books. This East-West publication route ended in 1919, when Glyn signed a contract with William Randolph Hearst's America-based International Magazine Company for serial rights in the English language for three new novels. Glyn herself crossed the Atlantic in 1920 to take up Famous-Players Lasky's invitation to work on film scenarios for their studios, and Hearst later capitalized on Glyn's move by contracting a regular series of articles for his Kings Features Syndicate. In this period her audience for translations in Europe grew; there are receipts for Swedish, Finnish, Danish and Norwegian book rights and serial rights in Dutch in 1923, and translation rights in Spanish, Italian and Czech from 1924. We do not know how widely the MGM silent movie of 'Three Weeks' was shown outside America, or whether it was released in Europe. However, we do know that MGM sought permission to release their film version in the UK.

Figure 2. Diagram of datasets to be used for a spatial analysis of an author's publications and adaptations

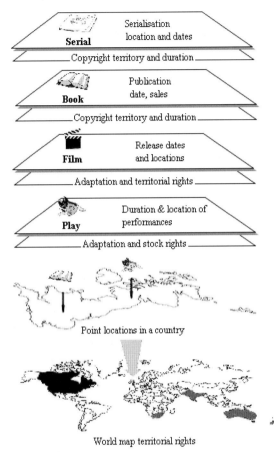

The British Board of Film Censorship had reservations, eventually conceding it could go out under a different name to disassociate it from the book[9] – a decision that was ridiculed in the press and gained the book additional publicity, which is reflected in its sales (table 2).

A comparison of the territorial areas covered by her publishing agreements

---

[9] A complaint was made to the BBFC concerning Elinor Glyn's novel about an adulterous affair, *Three Weeks*, that 'the film and the book were advertising each other, and now the play will' add to the 'mass of suggestiveness' of the book. BL Lord Chamberlain July 1917/1018. The movie was shown in the New Oxford Theatre Goldwyn-Cosmopolitan film season in March 1926 (*Times*, 26 March 1924, p. 12 issue 43610 col. c).

Table 2: Duckworth's sales of *Three Weeks* after Horniman's play adaptation agreement in 1917, showing the effect of the MGM film in 1924.

Date	6/-	Col	3/6	2/6	2/-	1/-	total	Royalty income (s)
Jun-17	18	27			1099		1144	370.42
Dec-20	10	6			1968	23834	25818	2229.08
Jun-23	8	7			1046		1061	133.75
Dec-23	1	5			1273		1279	161.92
Jun-24	4			309	6408		6721	845.33
Jun-25				69	2535		2604	314.92
Dec-25				50	1793		1843	223.33
Jun-26				131	1550		1681	221.25
Jun-29			132		538		670	104.83
Dec-29			72		477		549	78.42
Dec-30			74		462		536	77.33
Jun-31			5		152		157	21.25
Dec-31			54		116		170	30.92
Jun-32			56		110		166	30.83
Jun-36				241			241	37.00

Note: There are missing years 1918, 1919, 1927, 1933-5

in 1907 and 1927 show the extent of Glyn's international reach, from the time of the publication of her best-selling novel *Three Weeks* to her highest-grossing film 'It' starring Clara Bow (figure 3). The data plotted on this map is derived from 56 publishing contracts and 57 agents' receipts. Tables containing this data, which includes sales figures and royalty income, are embedded within the map. Zoom in on the UK, and location data on the place and duration of her play performances is viewable (a further 61 royalty receipts – Glyn received 5% on gross takings in Britain which averaged £14 14s 11d per year – a tiny amount compared with her book sales). The play toured British theatres annually until 1933, and its territorial coverage was extended to include Japan, China and Hong Kong.

The project is ongoing: Rebecca Delaney and Steven Conway have gathered and entered much of the data from the Glyn archive into spreadsheet forms which can be transferred to the spatial-analysis software, and more of this remains to be done. We need to add areas covered by territorial rights of her film contracts, location data on the release and exhibition of her films etc. In time it may also be possible to add in information from other databases, such as the reading experiences from RED and evidence of book ownership in Russia and South America from surviving editions. Some results are emerging from the wider project, however. Vincent L. Barnett has analysed Glyn's contractual negotiations with Irving Thalberg (Barnett 2007), and I have examined Glyn's system of writing for novel serialization and photoplays (Weedon 2006). Both reveal Glyn's

Figure 3. Territorial coverage of Elinor Glyn's book, serial and play copyrights.

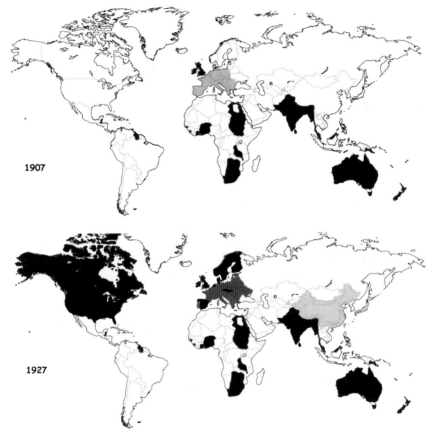

Note: Black areas show book and serial rights. Dark grey in 1907 shows Duckworth's rights to English editions in Europe which he sold on to Tauchnitz at a commission. Light grey shows rights to perform Horniman's play adaptation from 1917.[10]

---

[10] The shaded areas reflect the national boundaries and the extent of the British Empire in 1920. However, the country outlines are from a modern map.

enthusiastic adoption of film as a medium of communication and her commitment to making films of her books. Her willingness to engage with the industry and with the professionals, like Hearst, who worked across the publishing and film businesses in promoting her films meant that she was the only British author in the cohort invited by Lasky to stay in Hollywood. She continued to write to keep herself 'in front of her public', as her daughter put it, and to make films on her return to Britain in the 1930s.

Quantitative book history continues to be relevant to scholars of literary history. Its expansion into spatial analysis will only increase our understanding of textual production and dissemination. Web-based projects and the social analysis of reading, book clubs and print circulation have already taken book historians beyond the confines of a strictly historical methodology of the book. I believe we now need a bolder vision of textual history, one which encompasses the multiple versions of the text and the socio-economic factors which affect its production. We can only do this by embracing new methods of analysis which, while they build upon the work of bibliographers in the systematic gathering of archival sources, reach beyond historical inquiry to incorporate some of the more adventurous techniques currently being developed in historical geography, communication theory and media analysis.

Acknowledgements

The 'Cross-media cooperation in Britain in the 1920s and 1930s' is a collaborative project funded by the AHRC, grant number AR112216. My thanks to Vincent L. Barnett, Steven Conway and Rebecca Delaney, and to my co-investigator Simon Eliot, whose ideas and research are represented here in addition to my own.

References

Barnett, Vincent L. (2007). 'Picturization Partners: Elinor Glyn and the Thalberg contract affair'. *Film History*. 19(3): 319-329.

Black, F. M., Macdonald, B. and Black, J. M. (1998). 'A New Research Method for Book History: Geographical Information Systems.' *Book History* 1: 11-31.

Darnton, R. (1979). *The Business of Enlightenment: A Publishing History of the Encyclopédie, 1775-1800*. Cambridge Mass., Belknap Press.

Eliot, S. (1994). *Some Patterns and Trends in British Publishing 1800-1919*. London, The Bibliographical Society.

Fleming, P.L., Gallichan, G. and Lamonde, Y. (2004). *The History of the Book in Canada Vol. 1 Beginnings to 1840*. Toronto: University of Toronto Press.

Glyn, A. (1955). *Elinor Glyn : a biography*. London, Hutchinson.

Glyn, E. (1907). *Three Weeks*. New York, Duffield & Company.

Gregory, I. N. (2007). 'Getting to Grips with GIS'. *GIS in Historical Research workshop*. King's College, London, 24 October.

Hardwick, J. (1994). *Addicted to romance : the life and adventures of Elinor Glyn*. London, Deutsch.

MacDonald, B. H., and Black, Fiona (2000). 'Using GIS for Spatial and Temporal Analyses in Print Culture Studies: Some Opportunities and Challenges.' *Social Science History* 24(3): 505-536.

McAleer, J. (1992). *Popular Reading and Publishing in Britain 1914-1950*. Oxford, Oxford Historical Monographs.

Napper, L. (2008). *British Cinema and the Middlebrow in the interwar years*. Exeter, University of Exeter.

RED. (2007-). 'Reading Experience Database.' Retrieved 30 November, 2007, from http://www.open.ac.uk/Arts/RED.

Rose, J. (2001). *Intellectual Life of the British Working Classes*. New Haven and London, Yale University Press.

St Clair, W. (2004). *The Reading Nation in the Romantic Period*. Cambridge, Cambridge University Press.

Weedon, A. (2003). *Victorian Publishing: The Economics of Book Production for the Mass Market 1836-1916*. Aldershot, Ashgate.

Weedon, A. (2006). 'Elinor Glyn's System of Writing'. *Publishing History* 60: 31-50.

Weedon, A. (2007a). 'The Uses of Quantification' in *A Companion to the History of the Book*. Eds S. Eliot, J. Rose. Oxford, Blackwell Publishing: 33-49.

Weedon, A. (2007b). 'Keeping in front of the public: Elinor Glyn and the adaptation of *Three Weeks*'. IAMCR conference Paris, 23-25 July.

Notes on Contributors

Minoji Akimoto is Professor in the Department of English, Aoyama University (Tokyo). His books include *A Study of Verbo-Nominal Structures in English* (Shinozaki Shorin, Tokyo, 1989) and *Collocational and Idiomatic Aspects of Composite Predicates in the History of English* (with Laurel Brinton, John Benjamins, 1999).

Rosamund Allen has taught Middle English in London University since 1965. She has published on Richard Rolle and the English Mystics, Malory, *The Awntyrs off Arthure*, Gower and Lawman, and has edited a volume on travel in the Middle Ages. She has co-organised conferences on Lawman.

Donald Anderson teaches creative writing at the United States Air Force Academy. Editor of *War, Literature & the Arts: An International Journal of the Humanities*, Donald Anderson is also editor of *aftermath: an anthology of post-vietnam fiction*, *When War Becomes Personal*, and *Andre Dubus: Tributes*. His collection *Fire Road* won the John Simmons Short Fiction Award.

Michael Bell is Professor of English, and Director of the Centre for Research in Philosophy, Literature and the Arts, at the University of Warwick. His publications cover topics from the Enlightenment to the present, his latest book being *Open Secrets: Literature, Education and Authority from J-J Rousseau to J. M. Coetzee* (Oxford University Press, 2007).

Birgitta Berglund is a Senior Lecturer in English at Lund University. Her *Woman's Whole Existence: The House as an Image in the Novels of Ann Radcliffe, Mary Wollstonecraft and Jane Austen* (1993) is No. 84 in the Lund Studies in English. The author of articles on detective fiction and Charlotte Brontë, she is currently working on Austen and children.

Dinah Birch is Professor of English Literature at Liverpool University. Her books include *Ruskin's Myths* (Clarendon Press, 1988), *Ruskin on Turner* (Cassell,

1990) and *Our Victorian Education* (Blackwell, 2007). She reviews regularly for the *Times Literary Supplement* and the *London Review of Books*, and is currently preparing a new edition of the *Oxford Companion to English Literature*.

William Blissett, Emeritus Professor, University of Toronto, is a participating member of societies devoted to Richard Wagner, William Morris, G. K. Chesterton, and T. S. Eliot, as well as Hon. President of the David Jones Society and co-editor of *The Spenser Encyclopedia*. He is currently assembling essays under the working title 'Shakespeare and Ben Jonson not Compar'd and not Contrasted'.

Lawrence Buell is Powell M. Cabot Professor of American Literature at Harvard. His books include *Literary Transcendentalism* (1973), *New England Literary Culture* (1986), *The Environmental Imagination: Thoreau, Nature Writing, and the Formation of American Culture* (1995) and *Emerson* (2003). He was the 2007 recipient of the Modern Language Association's Jay Hubbell Award for lifetime contributions to American literature studies.

Anita Fetzer is a Professor of English Linguistics at Lueneburg University in Germany. She received her PhD from Stuttgart in 1993 and her post-doctoral degree (*Habilitation*) in 2003, and is currently engaged in research projects on the strategic use of pronouns and attitudinal markers. Her research interests focus on spoken English, functional grammar, contrastive analysis, discourse markers and context.

Paul Giles is Professor of American Literature at the University of Oxford, UK. His most recent book is *Atlantic Republic: The American Tradition in English Literature* (Oxford University Press, 2006). He is currently completing a book for Princeton University Press, to be entitled 'The Global Remapping of American Literature'.

Simon Haines is Reader in English and Director of the International Centre for Human Values at the Australian National University. His two principal monograph publications are *Shelley's Poetry: The Divided Self* (Macmillan, 1997) and *Poetry and Philosophy from Homer to Rousseau: Romantic Souls, Realist Lives* (Palgrave, 2005).

Ihab Hassan is Emeritus Vilas Research Professor at the University of Wisconsin in Milwaukee, and the recipient of honorary doctorates from Uppsala and Giessen. He is the author of thirteen books, including *Radical Innocence* (1961), *The Postmodern Turn* (1987), and *Selves at Risk* (1990), two memoirs, *Out of Egypt*

(1986) and *Between the Eagle and the Sun* (1996), and short fiction published in various literary magazines.

Yoshihiko Ikegami was educated at Tokyo University (B.A., M.A. in English) and Yale University (M.Phil., Ph.D. in linguistics). Professor Emeritus at Tokyo University, he is currently a professor at Showa Women's University and President of the Japanese Association for Cognitive Linguistics. He has had guest professorships at, i.a., Indiana University, Universität München and Freie Universität Berlin. Major fields of study: cognitive semantics, semiotics and poetics.

Elisabeth Jay is Professor of English, Director of the Institute for Historical and Cultural Research, and Associate Dean of Arts and Humanities at Oxford Brookes University. Her publications include a literary biography of Margaret Oliphant as well as editions of autobiographies, biographies and fiction by Victorian women writers, together with a range of work on nineteenth-century literature and theology.

Dieter Kastovsky studied English, Romance, German and General Linguistics (Dr. phil. in 1967, Tübingen). He was Research Assistant in Tübingen 1967-1973 and Professor of English Linguistics in Wuppertal 1973-1981. Since 1981 he has been Professor of English Linguistics at the University of Vienna. Research interests: English morphology and word-formation (synchronic and diachronic), semantics, language typology, and the history of linguistics.

Ian Kirby recently retired from the Chair of Medieval English at the University of Lausanne, Switzerland. His principal publications relate to the Bible in medieval Scandinavia, but he has also published widely on medieval English, as well as on Shakespeare and runic inscriptions. He was President of IAUPE from 1986 to 1989 and has been Secretary-General and Treasurer since 1995.

Barbara Kryk-Kastovsky studied English Philology at Adam Mickiewicz University, Poznan, Poland, where she was Professor of English Linguistics till 2007, and since then Professor Emerita. She currently teaches at the English Department of the University of Vienna. Research interests: synchronic and diachronic pragmatics, discourse analysis (with a current project on historical courtroom discourse), and inter-cultural communication.

Susan McCabe is a professor in poetry and poetics at the University of Southern California, Los Angeles. Her academic writings include *Elizabeth Bishop: Her Poetics of Loss* (Penn State Press, 1994) and *Cinematic Modernism: Modern Poetry* *and Film* (Cambridge UP, 2005). She is working on a biography of Bryher, 'The Female Husband of Modernism'. She has also written two books of poetry, *Swirl* (2003) and *Descartes' Nightmare* (2008).

Nicholas von Maltzahn (University of Ottawa) is the author of *An Andrew Marvell Chronology* (Palgrave, 2005) and a monograph on Milton's *History of Britain* (Oxford, 1991). His editorial work includes Marvell's *Account of the Growth of Popery* for the Yale *Prose Works of Andrew Marvell* (2003) and now Milton's tracts on religious liberty for the Oxford *Complete Works of John Milton*.

Andrea Sand is a Professor of English Linguistics at the University of Trier in Germany. She received her PhD and post-doctoral degree from the University of Freiburg and has taught at several universities in Germany and abroad. Her main research interests include corpus linguistics, language contact, and varieties of English.

Jürgen Schlaeger has held the Chair for British Literature and Culture at the Humboldt University in Berlin, where he is also Director of the Interdisciplinary Centre for British Studies, since 1995. His main fields of interest are Classicism and Romanticism, the history of life-writing, literary representations of emotions, and structures of cultural transformations.

Aleksander Szwedek is Head of the Cognitive Linguistics Department at Poznan University, Poland. He is the author of *Word Order, Sentence Stress and Reference in English and Polish* (1976) and *A Linguistic Analysis of Sentence Stress* (1986), and he was a co-editor of *Towards a History of Linguistics in Poland* (2001). Several recent publications deal with his new 'objectification' theory of metaphor.

Marianne Thormählen is Professor of English Literature at Lund University. She has written books about T. S. Eliot, John Wilmot Earl of Rochester, and the Brontës (most recently *The Brontës and Education*, Cambridge University Press, 2007), and edited *Rethinking Modernism* (Palgrave, 2003). She was President of IAUPE from 2004 to 2007.

Elizabeth Closs Traugott (PhD, University of California, Berkeley, 1964) is Professor Emerita of Linguistics and English, Stanford University. Her current research is on the pragmatic correlates of morphosyntactic change, and on developing a construction grammar approach to diachronic grammaticalisation. Publications include *A History of English Syntax* (1972), *Linguistics for Students of Literature* (with Mary L. Pratt, 1980), *On Conditionals* (1986; co-edited), *Gram-*

maticalization (with Paul Hopper, 1993, 2nd much revised ed. 2003), *Regularity in Semantic Change* (with Richard B. Dasher, 2002), and *Lexicalization and Language Change* (with Laurel J. Brinton, 2005). She holds an honorary doctorate from Uppsala University.

Elaine Treharne, University of Leicester, is Co-Director of the AHRC-funded project 'English Manuscripts, 1060 to 1220' and the author of eighteen books and edited volumes in English medieval studies. She is a Trustee of the English Association, Editor for Review of English Studies and Literature Compass, and General Editor of the new Oxford Textual Perspectives series.

Helen Vendler is the A. Kingsley Porter University Professor at Harvard. She is a frequent reviewer of contemporary poetry and has written books on Yeats, Stevens, Keats, Herbert, Shakespeare, and Heaney. Her essays have been published in three volumes: *Part of Nature, Part of Us: Modern American Poets* (Harvard UP, 1980); *The Music of What Happens: Poems, Poets, Critics* (Harvard UP, 1988); and *Soul Says: On Recent Poetry* (Harvard/Belknap, 1995). Her second book on Yeats, *Our Secret Discipline: Yeats and Lyric Form*, recently appeared from the Harvard University Press, and her 2007 Mellon Lectures will be published by Princeton University Press under the title *Last Looks, Last Books: Stevens, Plath, Lowell, Bishop, and Merrill.*

Alexis Weedon is Professor of Publishing Studies at the University of Bedfordshire in the UK. She is a specialist in quantitative book history and cross-media publishing, and her publications include *Victorian Publishing: The economics of book production for the mass market* (2003). She is co-editor of *Convergence: The journal of research into new media technologies.*

Index

Italicised pages refer to the authors of contributions in this volume. Where a person has been indexed in the running text, any additional reference in a footnote on the same page has been omitted. Literary and other texts whose sole function is to provide excerpts illustrating linguistic phenomena have not been indexed. Nor have entries in 'Works Cited' lists; the relevant author reference is indexed as it occurs in the running text.

Z

LUND STUDIES IN ENGLISH
Founded by Eilert Ekwall. Editor: Marianne Thormählen.

001 BERTIL WEMAN. 1933. Old English Semantic Analysis and Theory. With Special Reference to Verbs Denoting Locomotion. 187 pp.

002 HILDING BÄCK. 1934. The Synonyms for *child, boy, girl* in Old English. An Etymological-Semasiological Investigation. xvi + 273 pp.

003 GUSTAV FRANSSON. 1935. Middle English Surnames of Occupation. With an Excursus on Toponymical Surnames. 217 pp.

004 GUSTAV HOFSTRAND. 1936. *The Seege of Troye*. A Study in the Intertextual Relations of the Middle English Romance *The Seege or Batayle of Troye*. xv + 205 pp.

005 URBAN OHLANDER. 1936. Studies on Coordinate Expressions in Middle English. 213 pp.

006 VIKTOR ENGBLOM. 1938. On the Origin and Early Development of the Auxiliary *Do*. 169 pp.

007 IVAR DAHL. 1938. Substantival Inflexion in Early Old English. Vocalic Stems. xvi + 206 pp.

008 HILMER STRÖM. 1939. Old English Personal Names in Bede's History. An Etymological-Phonological Investigation. xliii + 180 pp.

009 UNO PHILIPSON. 1941. Political Slang 1759-1850. xvi + 314 pp.

010 ARTHUR H. KING. 1941. The Language of Satirized Characters in *Poëtaster*. A Socio-Stylistic Analysis 1579-1602. xxxiv + 258 pp.

011 MATTIAS T. LÖFVENBERG. 1942. Studies on Middle English Local Surnames. xlv + 225 pp.

012 JOHANNES HEDBERG. 1945. The Syncope of the Old English Present Endings. A Dialect Criterion. 310 pp.

013 ALARIK RYNELL. 1948. The Rivalry of Scandinavian and Native Synonyms in Middle English, especially *taken* and *nimen*. With an Excursus on *nema* and *taka* in Old Scandinavian. 431 pp.

014 HENNING HALLQVIST. 1948. Studies in Old English Fractured *ea*. 167 pp.

015 GÖSTA FORSSTRÖM. 1948. The Verb *to be* in Middle English. A Survey of the Forms. 236 pp.

016 BERTIL WIDÉN. 1949. Studies on the Dorset Dialect. 179 pp.

017 CLAES SCHAAR. 1949. Critical Studies in the Cynewulf Group. 337 pp.

018 BERTIL SUNDBY. 1950. The Dialect and Provenance of the Middle English Poem *The Owl and the Nightingale*. A Linguistic Study. 218 pp.

019 BERTIL THURESSON. 1950. Middle English Occupational Terms. 285 pp.

020 KARL-GUNNAR LINDKVIST. 1950. Studies on the Local Sense of the Prepositions *in*, *at*, *on*, and *to*, in Modern English. 429 pp.

021 SVEN RUBIN. 1951. The Phonology of the Middle English Dialect of Sussex. 235 pp.

022 BERTIL SUNDBY. 1953. Christopher Cooper's English Teacher (1687). cxvi + 10* + 123 pp.

023 BJÖRN WALLNER. 1954. An Exposition of *Qui Habitat* and *Bonum Est* in English. lxxi + 122 pp.

024 RUDOLF MAGNUSSON. 1954. Studies in the Theory of the Parts of Speech. viii + 120 pp.

025 CLAES SCHAAR. 1954. Some Types of Narrative in Chaucer's Poetry. 293 pp.

026 BÖRJE HOLMBERG. 1956. James Douglas on English Pronunciation c. 1740. 354 pp.

027 EILERT EKWALL. 1959. Etymological Notes on English Place-Names. 108 pp.

028 CLAES SCHAAR. 1960. An Elizabethan Sonnet Problem. Shakespeare's Sonnets, Daniel's *Delia*, and Their Literary Background. 190 pp.

029 ELIS FRIDNER. 1961. An English Fourteenth Century Apocalypse Version with a Prose Commentary. Edited from MS Harley 874 and Ten Other MSS. lviii + 290 pp.

030 The Published Writings of Eilert Ekwall. A Bibliography Compiled by Olof von Feilitzen. 1961. 52 pp.

031 ULF JACOBSSON. 1962. Phonological Dialect Constituents in the Vocabulary of Standard English. 335 pp.

032 CLAES SCHAAR. 1962. Elizabethan Sonnet Themes and the Dating of Shakespeare's Sonnets. 200 pp.

033 EILERT EKWALL. 1963. Selected Papers. 172 pp.

034 ARNE ZETTERSTEN. 1965. Studies in the Dialect and Vocabulary of the *Ancrene Riwle*. 331 pp.

035 GILLIS KRISTENSSON. 1967. A Survey of Middle English Dialects 1290-1350. The Six Northern Counties and Lincolnshire. xxii + 299 pp.

036 OLOF ARNGART. 1968. The Middle English *Genesis* and *Exodus*. Re-edited from MS. C.C.C.C. 444 with Introduction, Notes and Glossary. 277 pp.

037 ARNE ZETTERSTEN. 1969. The English of Tristan da Cunha. 180 pp.

038 ELLEN ALWALL. 1970. The Religious Trend in Secular Scottish School-Books 1858-1861 and 1873-1882. With a Survey of the Debate on Education in Scotland in the Middle and Late 19th Century. 177 pp.

039 CLAES SCHAAR. 1971. Marino and Crashaw. *Sospetto d'Herode*. A Commentary. 300 pp.

040 SVEN BÄCKMAN. 1971. This Singular Tale. A Study of *The Vicar of Wakefield* and Its Literary Background. 281 pp.

041 CHRISTER PÅHLSSON. 1972. The Northumbrian Burr. A Sociolinguistic Study. 309 pp.

042 KARL-GUSTAV EK. 1972. The Development of OE $\breve{y}$ and $\bar{eo}$ in South-Eastern Middle English. 133 pp.

043 BO SELTÉN. 1972. The Anglo-Saxon Heritage in Middle English Personal Names. East Anglia 1100-1399. 187 pp.

044 KERSTIN ASSARSSON-RIZZI. 1972. *Friar Bacon and Friar Bungay*. A Structural and Thematic Analysis of Robert Greene's Play. 164 pp.

045 ARNE ZETTERSTEN. 1974. A Critical Facsimile Edition of Thomas Batchelor, *An Orthoëpical Analysis of the English Language* and *An Orthoëpical Analysis of the Dialect of Bedfordshire* (1809). Part I. 260 pp.

046 ERIK INGVAR THURIN. 1974. The Universal Autobiography of Ralph Waldo Emerson. xii + 288 pp.

047 HARRIET BJÖRK. 1974. The Language of Truth. Charlotte Brontë, the Woman Question, and the Novel. 152 pp.

048 ANDERS DALLBY. 1974. The Anatomy of Evil. A Study of John Webster's *The White Devil*. 236 pp.

049 GILLIS KRISTENSSON. 1974. John Mirk's *Instructions for Parish Priests*. Edited from MS Cotton Claudius A II and Six Other Manuscripts with Introduction, Notes and Glossary. 287 pp.

050 STIG JOHANSSON. 1975. Papers in Contrastive Linguistics and Language Testing. 179 pp.

051 BENGT ELLENBERGER. 1977. The Latin Element in the Vocabulary of the Earlier Makars Henryson and Dunbar. 163 pp.

052 MARIANNE THORMÄHLEN. 1978. *The Waste Land*. A Fragmentary Wholeness. 248 pp.

053 LARS HERMERÉN. 1978. On Modality in English. A Study of the Semantics of the Modals. 195 pp.

054 SVEN BÄCKMAN. 1979. Tradition Transformed. Studies in the Poetry of Wilfred Owen. 206 pp.

055 JAN JÖNSJÖ. 1979. Studies on Middle English Nicknames. I: Compounds. 227 pp.

056 JAN SVARTVIK & RANDOLPH QUIRK (eds). 1980. A Corpus of English Conversation. 893 pp.

057 LARS-HÅKAN SVENSSON. 1980. Silent Art. Rhetorical and Thematic Patterns in Samuel Daniel's *Delia*. 392 pp.

058 INGRID MÅRDH. 1980. Headlinese. On the Grammar of English Front Page Headlines. 200 pp.

059 STIG JOHANSSON. 1980. Plural Attributive Nouns in Present-Day English. x + 136 pp.

060 CLAES SCHAAR. 1982. The Full Voic'd Quire Below. Vertical Context Systems in *Paradise Lost*. 354 pp.

061 GUNILLA FLORBY. 1982. The Painful Passage to Virtue. A Study of George Chapman's *The Tragedy of Bussy D'Ambois* and *The Revenge of Bussy D'Ambois*. 266 pp.

062 BENGT ALTENBERG. 1982. The Genitive *v.* the *of*-Construction. A Study of Syntactic Variation in 17th Century English. 320 pp.

063 JAN SVARTVIK, MATS EEG-OLOFSSON, OSCAR FORSHEDEN, BENGT ORESTRÖM & CECILIA THAVENIUS. 1982. Survey of Spoken English. Report on Research 1975-81. 112 pp.

064 CECILIA THAVENIUS. 1983. Referential Pronouns in English Conversation. 194 pp.

065 NILS WRANDER. 1983. English Place-Names in the Dative Plural. 172 pp.

066 BENGT ORESTRÖM. 1983. Turn-Taking in English Conversation. 195 pp.

067 EVA JARRING CORONES. 1983. The Portrayal of Women in the Fiction of Henry Handel Richardson. 183 pp.

068 ANNA-BRITA STENSTRÖM. 1984. Questions and Responses in English Conversation. x + 296 pp.

069 KARIN HANSSON. 1984. The Warped Universe. A Study of Imagery and Structure in Seven Novels by Patrick White. 271 pp.

070 MARIANNE THORMÄHLEN. 1984. Eliot's Animals. 197 pp.

071 EVERT ANDERSSON. 1985. On Verb Complementation in Written English. 293 pp.

072 WIVECA SOTTO. 1985. The Rounded Rite. A Study of Wole Soyinka's Play *The Bacchae of Euripides*. 187 pp.

073 ULLA THAGG FISHER. 1985. The Sweet Sound of Concord. A Study of Swedish Learners' Concord Problems in English. xii + 212 pp.

074 MOIRA LINNARUD. 1986. Lexis in Composition. A Performance Analysis of Swedish Learners' Written English. x + 136 pp.

075 LARS WOLLIN & HANS LINDQUIST (eds). 1986. Translation Studies in Scandinavia. Proceedings from The Scandinavian Symposium on Translation Theory (SSOTT) II. 149 pp.

076 BENGT ALTENBERG. 1987. Prosodic Patterns in Spoken English. Studies in the Correlation between Prosody and Grammar for Text-to-Speech Conversion. 229 pp.

077 ÖRJAN SVENSSON. 1987. Saxon Place-Names in East Cornwall. xii + 192 pp.

078 JØRN CARLSEN & BENGT STREIJFFERT (eds). 1988. Canada and the Nordic Countries. 416 pp.

079 STIG CARLSSON. 1989. Studies on Middle English Local Bynames in East Anglia. 193 pp.

080 HANS LINDQUIST. 1989. English Adverbials in Translation. A Corpus Study of Swedish Renderings. 184 pp.

081 ERIK INGVAR THURIN. 1990. The Humanization of Willa Cather. Classicism in an American Classic. 406 pp.

082 JAN SVARTVIK (ed). 1990. The London-Lund Corpus of Spoken English. Description and Research. 350 pp.

083 KARIN HANSSON. 1991. Sheer Edge. Aspects of Identity in David Malouf's Writing. 170 pp.

084 BIRGITTA BERGLUND. 1993. Woman's Whole Existence. The House as an Image in the Novels of Ann Radcliffe, Mary Wollstonecraft and Jane Austen. 244 pp.

085 NANCY D. HARGROVE. 1994. The Journey Toward *Ariel*. Sylvia Plath's Poems of 1956-1959. 293 pp.

086 MARIANNE THORMÄHLEN (ed.). 1994. T. S. Eliot at the Turn of the Century. 244 pp.

087 KARIN HANSSON. 1996. The Unstable Manifold. Janet Frame's Challenge to Determinism. 149 pp.

088 KARIN AIJMER, BENGT ALTENBERG & MATS JOHANSSON (eds). 1996. Languages in Contrast. Papers from a Symposium on Text-based Cross-linguistic Studies. 200 pp.

089 CECILIA BJÖRKÉN. 1996. Into the Isle of Self. Nietzschean Patterns and Contrasts in D. H. Lawrence's *The Trespasser*. 247 pp.

090 MARJA PALMER. 1996. Men and Women in T. S. Eliot's Early Poetry. 243 pp.

091 KEITH COMER. 1996. Strange Meetings. Walt Whitman, Wilfred Owen and Poetry of War. 205 pp.

092 CARITA PARADIS. 1997. Degree Modifiers of Adjectives in Spoken British English. 189 pp.

093 GUNILLA FLORBY. 1997. The Margin Speaks. A Study of Margaret Laurence and Robert Kroetsch from a Post-Colonial Point of View. 252 pp.

094 JEAN HUDSON. 1998. Perspectives on fixedness: applied and theoretical. 177 pp.

095 MARIE KÄLLKVIST. 1998. Form-Class and Task-Type Effects in Learner English: A Study of Advanced Swedish Learners. xii + 226 pp.

096 AGNETA LINDGREN. 1999. The Fallen World in Coleridge's Poetry. 264 pp.

097 BJÖRN SUNDMARK. 1999. Alice in the Oral-Literary Continuum. 224 pp.

098 STAFFAN KLINTBORG. 1999. The Transience of American Swedish. 171 pp.

099 LARS HERMERÉN. 1999. English for Sale. A Study of the Language of Advertising. 201 pp. + 53 reproductions.

100 CECILIA WADSÖ LECAROS. 2001. The Victorian Governess Novel. 308 pp. Ill.

101 JANE MATTISSON. 2002. Knowledge and Survival in the Novels of Thomas Hardy. 423 pp.

102 ROWENA JANSSON. 2001. Getting It Together. A genre analysis of the rhetorical structure of Open University television programmes in science and technology. 211 pp.

103 MAGNUS LEVIN. 2001. Agreement with Collective Nouns in English. 180 pp.

104 MONICA KARLSSON. 2002. Progression and Regression: Aspects of advanced Swedish students' competence in English grammar. 222 pp.

105 MARIA WIKTORSSON. 2003. Learning Idiomaticity. A corpus-based study of idiomatic expressions in learners' written production. viii + 182 pp.

106 LISBET KICKHAM. 2004. Protestant Women Novelists and Irish Society 1879-1922. 252 pp.

107 MATHILDA ADIE. 2004. Female Quest in Christina Stead's *For Love Alone*. 221 pp.

108 ANNIKA SYLÉN LAGERHOLM. 2004. *Pearl* and Contemplative Writing. 186 pp.

109 GUNILLA FLORBY. 2005. Echoing Texts: George Chapman's *Conspiracy and Tragedy of Charles Duke of Byron*. 181pp.

110 GUNILLA LINDGREN. 2005. Higher Education for Girls in North American College Fiction 1886-1912. 294 pp.

111 LENA AHLIN. 2006. The "New Negro" in the Old World: Culture and Performance in James Weldon Johnson, Jesse Fauset, and Nella Larsen. 205 pp.

112 MARIANNE THORMÄHLEN (ed.). 2008. English Now. Selected Papers from the 20th IAUPE Conference in Lund 2007. 384 pp.

113 ANNA WÄRNSBY. 2006. (De)coding Modality: The Case of *Must, May, Måste,* and *Can.* 244pp.